JONATHAN COBB

Logos and Liberation

The Path of Kenosis

Copyright © 2023 by Jonathan Cobb

Jonathan Cobb asserts the moral right to be identified as the author of this work.

Jonathan Cobb has no responsibility for the persistence or accuracy of URLs for external or third-party Internet Websites referred to in this publication and does not guarantee that any content on such Websites is, or will remain, accurate or appropriate.

First edition

Editing by Lilith Dorko

This book was professionally typeset on Reedsy. Find out more at reedsy.com

To my mother, Mari Cobb, whose courage taught me the power of surrender and kenosis. May your spirit live on in eternity.

Contents

Preface	ii
1 Genesis	1
2 Mythos	38
3 Logos	76
4 Institutions	119
5 Power	155
6 Markets	197
7 Capital	232
8 Technics	268
9 Cities	305
10 Empire	345
11 Ecology	381
12 Thriving	418
13 Eschaton	462
Bibliography	502
Index	510
About the Author	523

Preface

I vividly remember one September night in 2011. I was at an outdoor party along the river front, the city lights reflecting off the water. On the other side of the country, people in New York were occupying Zuccotti Park. Their movement, known as Occupy Wall Street, was soon to spread throughout the country, including my own city of Portland, Oregon, and I wasn't going to miss it for the world. Though I had a keen interest in politics, having studied many heterodox economic theories, I was not yet a radical. Nonetheless, I sensed something palpable in the air, a visceral feeling that the world was about to change. On October 6, we marched through the streets and occupied the plaza blocks of Chapman and Lownsdale Square in front of City Hall. We stood around one of the statues and did a "mic check" where someone would speak and others would repeat their words to amplify them. It was an ecstatic experience of communal participation.

My work schedule prevented me from staying at the encampment, but I visited every chance I got. They served free food to the crowd, had marches almost daily, and had teach-ins and skill shares where people spread their knowledge and wisdom to others. I signed up to give one such talk, hoping to spread the word about Georgism and the panacea of land value taxation. When I looked around, however, I couldn't escape the feeling that something much bigger was going on, and that I was the one who had more to learn from others. Here was a self-organized community modeling a different kind of society based on direct democracy and mutual aid. To be sure, it had its limitations. It relied on outside support, the consensus process could be pretty clunky, and of course if we're trying to create a new society, we need to think bigger than tents. Nonetheless, it became apparent to me that I had to expand my horizons beyond such technical fixes as tax and monetary reform. A new type of society was needed.

At the same time that this radicalization process was occurring for me, my mother was dying of cancer. She died well, making sure to leave nothing unsaid, to let go of it all and surrender to what was. This process of letting go, of *kenosis*, has stuck with me ever since. I came to realize over time how this principle of self-emptying would help me in my own life.

As I got swept up in this movement, I was sure we were going to change the world. Much to my disappointment, the energy eventually died down and the movement dissipated, as they always do. Yet I would see new upheavals over the years, including the Women's March, Idle No More, and Black Lives Matter. It became apparent that while each of these movements had its own focus and goals, they were all part of a single movement of movements. Any one movement may rise and fall, but they are all part of a greater trajectory toward liberation. In the summer of 2020, another mass movement erupted following the murder of George Floyd by Minneapolis police. By this point I was in my late thirties and had a long-term disability that limited my ability to march, so I wasn't able to participate to the extent I wanted. I was, however, inspired to write this book.

This book is the culmination of years of study, contemplation, reflection, and action. It comes from tirelessly devouring every book I could find to refine my analysis and outlook on the world. It comes from the passion for justice which has driven me to get involved in social justice movements. It comes from contemplation of the mysteries of the cosmos and the palpable sense of providential guidance I have felt throughout my life. It comes from a spiritual conviction I have that we are meant for so much more than this system has consigned us to.

I have never been very good at fitting into other people's boxes. I did not write this book intending it to make some minor contribution to an existing discourse. I freely draw from philosophy, theology, economics, sociology, anthropology, ecology, and several other fields. This book is an attempt to diagnose a fundamental flaw in the ethos of human civilization, and to suggest another path based on the principle of kenosis.

This principle, which had been such a profound lesson for me personally, has also been a guiding principle of my politics. I have come to see that our grasping at control and order blinded us to the organic order all around us. This original sin of grasping has led to all the systems of power and domination that have to come to control our lives, from patriarchy and white supremacy to capitalism, fascism, and technocracy. Only by a path of kenosis can we overcome these structures and see the Kingdom that is already spread out upon the Earth.

I trace this path through an exploration of myth, science, institutions, political economy, technics, philosophy, ecology, and spirituality. I find within all the great religious traditions some concept of the Logos. Indeed, whether consciously or not, one is always working with some Logos. The problem is that we have fallen into a false Logos. It is in fact this false Logos that the great Axial traditions rebelled against, and we too must find the courage to resist it in its current form. By recovering a sense of kenosis, we can build a new world within the shell of the old, in which we can truly thrive with one another in harmony with the natural world.

The trouble with kenosis is that it isn't reducible to some formula. It doesn't mean simple inaction. Indeed, it calls us to great struggle, sacrifice, and resistance. Yet there is a certain flow to it. It means aligning one's actions with the Logos, that transcendent order by which the cosmos operates. It calls us to reject the false Logos of power and domination by which the present world operates and seek instead the Logos of liberation.

I believe that we are not here by accident, but inhabit a world of meaning and purpose. I believe that this feeling I felt that one September night was more than just giddy anticipation. What I sensed back then, and have kept with me ever since, was nothing less than the heartbeat of creation, the birth pangs of a new world. It is the World to Come that beckons us, and whose call we must answer.

1

Genesis

In the beginning was creation. God called forth existence from nothing, form from the formless void. Then followed light and darkness, water and land, stars and living creatures, and finally humanity, carrying the image of its creator. So begins the creation story in Genesis. Everything was, and is, constructed in splendor for the greater glory of all.

This creation account differed from other creation stories in the Near East by virtue of its peacefulness. In the Babylonian creation myth, the world was created by a violent struggle between the god Marduk and chaos dragon Tiamat. In Marduk's slaying of Tiamat, order achieved victory over chaos. In contrast to this creation out of violence, Genesis speaks of creation by Word.

The Word is not the spoken word nor the written word, but the primordial self-expression of the divine mind. It is divine intellect manifest, divine intellect as substantive existence. It is God writing a story through history. This Word, also known as the *Logos*, is the grammar of existence; it is the logic by which all things live and move and have their

Being. Through the Word, creation partakes of the nature of its creator.

Blessed by divine inheritance, humanity finds itself immersed in a beautiful garden of plenty. In this paradise, humanity exists naked and innocent, living in communion with its creator. All of creation sings the praises of its divine origin. Creation is enchanted – a vibrant, ensouled landscape teeming with purpose and inner life.

But there is trouble in paradise. Humans are tempted by the forbidden fruit. We are taught that this fruit will make us "as God" by giving us knowledge of good and evil. The act of eating the fruit led us to see our own nakedness, to feel the vulnerability of our existence. We attained self-awareness, and thereby became responsible for our actions. No longer subject to sheer instinct, we became rational beings, cursed with the burden of knowing our own mortality and finitude.

We came to know not only our physical nudity but the vulnerability afforded by self-awareness. Humans seek to arm ourselves against this vulnerability, to become impenetrable and immovable. We seek to control our emotions to avoid the pain of self-knowledge. We seek to control others to avoid the pain of being hurt by them. We seek to abolish that which troubles us. We seek to grasp the sands of time only to watch it slip through our fingers, to make permanent that which is fleeting. We become slaves to this very desire for control.

Most of all, we seek to return to this primordial paradise that we remember in the depths of our soul. We seek to storm the gates of Eden, only to be fought off by the Cherub's flaming sword. There is a longing in our hearts to return to this sense of belonging. Yet in seeking after this state through our drive for control, we are creating and recreating the very fallen world from which we seek to escape.

Evolution

Modern science has its own creation story, one which famously contradicts any literal reading of Genesis, but if you squint at it just right, there is some overlap. We can say with a high degree of confidence that the Earth is not 6,000 years old and was not created in six 24-hour days. Yet the Biblical creation narrative does see creation unfold in stages, with certain lifeforms succeeding others, and if we understand the term "day" to mean some cosmic timeframe rather than what we would consider a day, we can find in the Genesis account a mythical understanding of what science tells us about the world.

The picture we get from the sciences goes something like this: About 13.8 billion years ago, a quantum singularity expanded to create all that is. This explosion was so hot that there was no matter itself as we know it, only energy, energy which eventually cooled and formed the first particles. These particles formed clusters which reached critical mass and created the first stars. These stars, made of hydrogen and helium, produced other elements, and over the life cycle of several stars exploding into supernovas, eventually the building blocks of life formed.

About 3.5 billion years ago, on a rock orbiting a star we call the sun, these building blocks of life formed organic compounds, and through a process still beyond our understanding, the first lifeforms emerged. Single-celled organisms developed with cellular systems that allow them to metabolize and reproduce. In the leading evolutionary theory known as symbiogenesis, the first eukaryotic cells were then formed through the incorporation of smaller bacteria into the organelles of larger cells. As cellular life covered the planet, organisms adapted to different environments and fed on different food sources. Some of them lived in extremely hostile environments, such as volcanic vents deep in the ocean. Some developed the ability to photosynthesize food out of sunlight and atmospheric carbon dioxide, giving off oxygen as a waste product. This oxygen was poisonous to many organisms at the time, but many of those that survived came to depend upon it. Over time, cellular lifeforms merged together into colonies, and these colonies could sometimes become differentiated into parts that perform specialized functions. These colonies would eventually become their own self-reproducing organisms, giving rise to multicellular lifeforms.

Life exploded onto the scene with a vast array of new forms during the Cambrian Period. Most modern phyla emerged from different lifeforms, each of which had taken a novel strategy of adaptation to its environment. These adaptation strategies are subject to natural selection, wherein those that adopt successful strategies live to pass on their genes to the next generation. This process has often been used to explain all change in organisms over time, but it is better understood as the process of weeding out unhelpful changes. Change is the norm. Life longs to express itself in as many ways as possible.

Life is made possible by certain principles that give it a kind of "order for free," in the words of complexity theorist Stuart Kauffman. Life is a type of self-organization characterized by negative feedback loops that help maintain homeostasis, low-level chaos that allows for adaptability, and metabolism that allows for reproduction. There seems to be some code to the universe that is inherently geared toward self-organized complexity, and once given a chance to take hold, it proliferates and becomes self-sustaining. In life, the whole generates the parts, which become wholes to other parts. Species emerge within ecosystems, and organisms emerge as members of a species. Life itself forms a kind of whole within which its entire evolutionary history is inscribed.

This wondrous and marvelous process eventually culminated in humans, that remarkable creature capable of conceptualizing its own existence and reflecting upon it. Equipped with an upright posture and opposable thumbs, we have the ability to manipulate our environment and shape it according to our imaginations. Vast empires, modern cities, and towering monuments emerged from the minds and hands of this new species.

We experience time not merely as mechanical, factual chronology, but as upheavals of meaning: We exist not only in time but in history. The mechanization of life brought about by modernity has obscured these factors of human life from us, but not completely. The spark of everyday life, of a life not just endured but fully lived, can construct a world other than the one we inhabit. In this spark lies human imagination, and we must liberate the imagination to realize what it truly is to be human.

No creature before had anything approaching this godlike ability to reshape the world according to its own designs. Therein lies the problem. All organisms construct their environment in some way, but they do so within environmental constraints that push back against them and keep them within a kind of ecological balance. Humans became so good at overcoming the challenges of the environment that we could run roughshod over it, creating our own environments and systems operating according to their own logic that runs counter to the balance of natural systems. We've created our own form of self-organizing complexity, but rather than the negative feedback loops that characterize life and allow it to adapt and maintain homeostasis, ours is a positive feedback loop like that of a hurricane, bringing destruction and chaos in its wake. We have distorted the Logos into an engine for infinite growth.

Imago Dei

Humans are beautifully and wonderfully made. We have minds that can process symbols, create abstract concepts, and contemplate our place in the cosmos. We have creative imaginations that can bring about new works of beauty that never existed before. We have rich inner lives in which we experience joy, sorrow, grief, purpose, and meaning. We experience the events of our lives not merely as discrete events, but as part of a larger narrative. The events of the past and present are woven together by patterns of meaning.

This narrative unity is constructed by our choices but by no means is it strictly our own creation. Our lives are woven together in a vast web of minds. Buddhists describe this as Indra's net, with each mind a jewel that reflects all others, each containing all others within its own nature—all parts contain the whole. Our own life story is nested within a vast ocean of other life stories that we interact and cross paths with along the way. It is in this intersection that meaning emerges for us. We understand who we are by interacting with others, learning their life story, comparing our own experiences to theirs, and finding models to follow in our own lives.

We are creatures of reason and creatures of habit, and as habitual creatures we take our cues from others in discerning how to behave. We find role models who embody values we seek to emulate. By the same token, we look at the bad behavior of others to learn what we can get away with. Through our actions we are tacitly giving others permission to act likewise. We are mimetic beings who can reason from the past into the present, and thereby become historical beings. Our memories extend beyond the horizons of our own lives and into shared cultural histories and grand narratives about history itself. We understand our current era within the grander context of world events.

We live lives intertwined with one another, engaged in a constant waltz of give and take with one another's worlds. Within this dance, we find friendship, love, admiration, respect, and interdependence. We also find ethics, values, and models of behavior. It is within the community that we come to understand values and acquire virtue. Values can be contested, even within the most insular of societies, yet they always arise within the social space itself. Our ability to interrogate these values is relative to our exposure to other sets of values. We develop our moral paradigm out of a continuous conversation with a broader community.

In this web of relations we find certain patterns repeating. We observe a certain order in how nature works. We attempt to systematize it with science, philosophy, theology, sociology, and all manner of intellectual disciplines. Yet whatever system we construct, its core meaning eludes us. As we grasp toward cosmic mystery with ever-finer tools, it continues to slip from our grasp, because it can never be contained within our constructs. Yet we know that by its light we can recognize its trace in all things.

The proper response toward this great mystery is worship. In this sense, worship does not mean adherence to specific doctrine, but rather maintaining a sense of childlike wonder. The great Logos can be found within as well as without. All of creation sings its praises, and our soul cries out for its source. This great mystery by which creation itself came to be is the same mystery that lives within us. It is our great inheritance, as well as the great height from which we have fallen. We have created our own idolatrous distortion of the Logos and must find our way back.

We come from nature. The principles of complexity that produced the vibrant ecological balance of the natural world have produced beings that threaten to destroy it. We have imprinted upon us the spark that created us, but we have used it to create systems of domination, exploitation, and oppression. We are nature's supreme creation — the image of God. Yet we have squandered this gift to create the conditions for our own destruction. What cruel fall has led us to create a prison out of paradise?

Temptation

The source of this fall lies deep within human nature. The

existence of human nature has been contested for several centuries: Georg Friedrich Wilhelm Hegel believed that our nature is always historically situated, while going back further Buddhists suggested that our very selfhood is an illusion, the product of an infinite web of causes and conditions. Yet if we understand that to adapt to different historical and material conditions as we do is itself an expression of a certain adaptable nature that could be otherwise, we see that the vast array of possibilities of creativity is itself deeply human.

In our drive for creativity, we seek some level of control over our environment. The environment presents itself to us as ready-to-hand, in Martin Heidegger's terms, available for us to manipulate to our purposes. In this drive for manipulating the environment, we seek to plan all facets, from the physical to the historical. The problem is, the more we plan, the less we listen. The drive to conquer territory, or to dictate the actions of increasing numbers of people, brought many a plotter and schemer to their doom. Yet they paved the way for the rise of hierarchy, nation-states, and even tyranny.

There is a drive within humanity to grasp, to seize, to flatten, to make the world in one's own image. It seeks to grasp the forbidden fruit, to own it. There is a need to assert oneself, to hold oneself over others, to maintain control. Traditionally this is known as the ego. It is our need to impose our own order over the world in order to maintain some control over one's own circumstances. To some degree, this is necessary: all species alter their environment to support their own survival, and humans are no different. But a difference of degree quickly becomes a difference of kind.

We seek not only to carve out a space for ourselves, but to conquer the space of others. There is a temptation to control others—through intimidation, force, or deception—to do our bidding. When we are forced to negotiate with others, we find ourselves having to compromise, to make sacrifices so that everyone is happy. Yet if one can get others under one's control, there is less self-sacrifice to be made, and the benefits can flow upward. This is the real forbidden fruit: to mold the world for oneself, to become a god unto oneself.

The Logos, I will argue, is characterized by a path of *kenosis*, or self-emptying. It is about holding onto one's own unique gifts while allowing others to shine. It means forsaking the urge to reduce others to mere means to our ends. We must learn to make space for the other, to seek that order to which we all belong, rather than that which we seek to impose on one another. We are corrupted when we feel that we must manipulate the world to our way of doing things. When we are aligned with the Logos, there is a kind of organic *unfolding* in which we make space for what is seeking to emerge. We are called to celebrate the diversity of gifts that each of us brings.

Our drive for self-assertion cannot simply be erased; it must find expression. Pursuits such as athletic prowess, music and art, and advancement in skills and knowledge all offer some goal to strive for. This drive for self-mastery, however, can give way to a drive for mastery over others, over one's environment, and most destructively over everything and everyone. When we seek to master ourselves, we become more adaptable to change, more attuned to the environment, more resilient against adversity. By seeking mastery over others, we seek to control the events around us, to flatten differences and bring everything within a scope of predictability and legibility to maintain control. We grasp onto some territory that we can control, and then seek to expand that territory and deepen that control.

This grasping is what Buddhism identifies as lying at the root of *dukkha*, or suffering. It is a kind of dissatisfaction that leads us to always seek out more. Jacques Lacan referred to this pursuit as *jouissance,* or "enjoyment." The problem with enjoyment in this sense is it's never truly enjoyable. It leaves an emptiness in us that cannot be filled. It's the itch that we continue to scratch, and in the process we exacerbate the wound.

This compulsive behavior lies at the heart of what is called original sin. It is the compulsion to seek what we know is wrong, a hurtful desire or concupiscence. We experience a yearning for passion, driving us to excess, a yearning to choose that which satisfies rather than what we know is right. Desires that are good in themselves are distorted through our tendency to cling to them, to reshape our world in accordance with them. We seek to control the world to satisfy passions that cannot be satisfied. We grasp at fleeting pleasures, striving to bring them under our control, and in the process we lose what made them sweet in the first place. Instead, we come to delight in this grasping itself, and seek out the heady high of asserting our control.

It is this seeking and grasping that has led to patriarchy, slavery, castes, states, empires, and all manner of oppression and despotism. The whole of history can be understood then as the story of this unfolding between the Logos and these distortions brought about by egoic drives. To bring about healing in these areas, it is first necessary to renounce this Luciferian drive within ourselves which seeks to subject others to our will and exploit them for our personal gain. Rather than impose our own order, we must remain attentive to the order around us and within us and seek to extend it into our own social relations. Let us remain in a state of openness and awareness of one another, to be attentive to the needs of our neighbor.

The path of the Logos does not preclude changing our environment. All organisms alter their environment in some manner that can be viewed as beneficial to them. Nor does it forbid the use of force. Self-defense, and by extension community defense, are crucial for the maintenance of thriving cultures and the protection of the vulnerable. Indeed, there is no desire or tendency of ours that is itself evil, save for our stubbornness in clinging to that which we must release.

We need control over our own lives. Exploitative systems throughout history have sought to restrict the autonomy of one class in favor of another. Evil emerges when our desire for control becomes an idol unto itself, toward which others must be sacrificed. Authentic autonomy aligned with the Logos seeks out collaboration with others as equals, to cooperate with the environment in a kind of conversation and not simply to impose upon it. The path of ego and sin is one that does not recognize limits. It makes an idol of the self or some ideology or object of desire and seeks it as an ultimate good at the expense of all else. This path ultimately results in ruin of the very thing we pursue, for the Logos alone is eternal, and all else is idolatry.

We can also fall into sin by example. As a mimetic species we take social cues from others and adjust our behavior accordingly. This helps us form the communities and cultures necessary for living together, but it also blinds us to our collective shortcomings. We look to what is socially acceptable to others in forming our own moral compass. The behavior of others teaches us what we can get away with, but more nefariously what prejudices are acceptable, which groups are acceptable targets, and whose lives matter. Any one of us will have our individual faults, but far more damning is our complacency within the social fabric. People who are viewed as pleasant, friendly, and generous can be monstrous in assenting to the evils of society. Redemption must likewise be realized socially.

The Fall

What does it mean to be fallen? Can we point to a moment and designate it as the Fall? In truth, there are several worthy of consideration. The rise of civilization could be viewed as one of them, as it introduced the subjugation of humanity to authoritarian rule. Some would say it was the rise of agriculture, in which we ceased to be wild and sought to control nature for our benefit. Going back further, one could argue it was the beginning of language, in which we broke out of our subconscious state and began to conceptualize our existence. Or it might go all the way back to the Big Bang, when the primordial atom split and became differentiated, and thus introduced duality into the world.

More recent events can also be conceptualized as falls. The rise of capitalism is a common culprit in left-wing discourse. Christians often see a fall from the early church into what faith has become. People in the Renaissance bemoaned the fall from antiquity. No matter what the age, there is always some sense of looking back to some lost golden era. In some sense, we are always falling. Perhaps the Fall can be best understood as the direction of time itself.

This view of a fallen world is hardly unique to Christianity. Hinduism teaches that there was once a time in the world age called the Satya Yuga, in which humanity was governed by the gods, virtue and altruism were abundant, and people reached enlightenment easily. This gave way to the Treta Yuga, then the Dvapara Yuga, and finally the Kali Yuga, in which we currently find ourselves. With each Yuga, humanity becomes more corrupt, ignorance spreads, the gods become more distant, and enlightenment becomes harder to reach. Time accelerates, with each Yuga being shorter than the previous one, and the human lifespan becoming shorter along with it. At the end of the Kali Yuga, the world will be cleansed of evil, and the cycle will start anew. Of course, this explanation of our world is no less a myth than the story of Genesis, but its essential meaning is a similar one: we have fallen from a great height, and the wisdom of our forebears has been lost to us. We live in a time of greater struggle and hardship; we have lost our way and must struggle against the ways of this world to find it once again.

This sentiment finds its way into Buddhism as well. The time in which the Buddha taught is seen as a golden age, but the teaching of the Dharma has been corrupted since then and must be sought after with greater effort. Buddhists teach that one day the Dharma will be entirely forgotten, until another Buddha named Maitreya will come and restore it. As time goes on and the world becomes more corrupt, it becomes increasingly difficult to reach enlightenment.

Sins such as avarice, lust, wrath, and greed will increase. Rulers will no longer care for the spiritual well-being of their subjects, but seek only power for themselves. Religion, spirituality, truth, tolerance, mercy, and kindness will all diminish. Life will become more and more about the increased pursuit of fleeting pleasure at the expense of inner cultivation.

Plato held an ontological view of the fall. For him, creation emanates from its purest spiritual source down to the eternal forms into different variations until we finally get brute matter. The material world of differentiation and flux has fallen from its spiritual source up above. For Plato, those who work with ideas—the philosophers—are closest to this spiritual source, while those engaged in manual labor are the most distant from it.

What are we to make of all this? Have we truly fallen from some great height? Can all the progress we've made only be viewed through this pessimistic frame? Surely, we have risen to great heights that surprise even the wildest dreams of our ancestors. We must be wary of nostalgia: selfish, power-hungry rulers are hardly new, and our ancestors committed any number of sins, including all kinds of interpersonal violence from which many of us in the developed world are mercifully shielded from today. Lynching was once commonplace here in the United States, and slavery was once a fact of life. Public executions were popular spectacles. People would bring their children to watch human sacrifices. The brutality of many past civilizations shocks us today. There are numerous ways in which we can credit ourselves with being more civilized than our ancestors.

Yet there is a sense in which our modern society has

regressed; our progress is history writ large but now offset by a shiny veneer. Modernity may have purchased for us a certain degree of cosmopolitanism, but the price is exploitation and bloodshed. Capitalism is the product of colonialism, a process which continues under new guises across the world. Settler colonialism reaches its zenith with fascism. Moreover, modernity has seen a continuous economization of life. The power of capital has transformed the world into one of quantity and utility. The logic of the market has overrun society. Intrinsic value is squeezed out and transformed into a utilitarian world that can be measured and assigned monetary worth. This process has continued apace since the dawn of the modern age. Going back further, we saw the rise of empires, and of tyrannical and coercive states.

Our great fall is defined by the unyielding reduction of the person into the machine. We are creative beings who seek value and meaning, yet consumerism teaches us to commodify and find our meaning in consumption. We rent ourselves out for 40 hours a week to maintain a power structure that keeps us from our true passions. We were meant for so much more than the cage of production and consumption that has come to rule our lives. There is so much more to the human experience than generating profit.

We live in a time when these promises of limitless growth are now revealed as the malicious lies they always were. The global recession of 2008 toppled world markets and undermined confidence more than any time since the Great Depression of the 1930s. The neoliberalism of the late 20th century sold the idea that globalization would lift all boats, that freeing up the flow of capital would help overcome the instability of the markets; instead it all came toppling down. Economists, once viewed as priestly oracles, had been exposed as false prophets. Yet rather than getting run out of town, the capitalist order simply went on without the facade.

Rather than hold up the high-minded ideal that we could grow our way to prosperity, the ruling class has resorted to naked plunder, seizing whatever they can from a world that is no longer growing, but shrinking before our very eyes. The "rising tide that lifts all boats" is rhetoric that no longer soothes our ailing world. As this scramble for the remains of a crumbling system progresses, is it any wonder that this new scarcity has filtered its way down and ignited animosities that had been just beneath the surface all this time? The myth of infinite growth held people's hostilities at bay for a time, all while continuing to siphon money and resources to the top, so that when the whole facade came crashing down, people were left more desperate than ever.

This is to say nothing of what all that growth entailed: the systematic looting of natural resources from the developing world; the overhauling of their economy to suit the needs of global capital under the coercive apparatus of debt peonage; intervening with foreign country elections; political assassinations; and a long list of other crimes, all to keep the expansion of capital going.

By directing our spiritual energies toward the false promises of Mammon, upon whose altar so many lives have been sacrificed, we have lost all sense of community, of higher purpose, and of the common good. That this descent into base materialism was perceived as already occurring centuries ago, long before the birth of capitalism, tells us how long the dangers of these tendencies have been known, and how foolishly we have failed to heed the warnings.

Matter

The cult of Mammon has done more than bring material oppression. It has harmed the very soul of the world. We have come to think of our existence in commodified, material terms. Before capitalization, before commodification, there is objectification—the reduction of creation to instrumental objects. We can see this in the story of the Garden of Eden: the plenitude offered in the garden was to be enjoyed as a gift. It was God's expression of love for humanity. Yet in taking the forbidden fruit for themselves, Adam and Eve treated it as an instrument for their own ends.

From the story of Adam and Eve, we can understand the first domination was that of woman by man. In some societies, family centered around the woman, with her siblings and extended family sharing in the obligations of child-rearing. Male visitors from other families might come for conjugal relations, but they did not have an active role in raising the children. They would instead help raise the children of their sister and other female relatives. Yet in other societies, patrimony became important, especially as it became attached to private property. Land would be passed down from one generation to another, with the eldest son generally granted the greater portion of inheritance, if a daughter was granted anything at all. Under such conditions, a woman's social life had to be limited to keep her under the watchful eye of her husband. His progeny was of ultimate concern, so she was confined to the domestic sphere with other women. From here sprang all other forms of social domination. The patriarchal household became the model for society.

Here in the fallen world, instrumental rationality and domination is altogether unavoidable. It was necessary to create the tools that helped our species reach the top of the food chain. These tools helped us assert power over our environment. We fashioned weapons to hunt living creatures, converting their meat into our energy. We bred plants and animals to serve as nourishment for our own benefit. We chopped down trees to build shelters in which to live. However much these things involved instrumentality, they were also mythologized, turned into sacred occasions. Hunters might thank the spirit of the animal for its sacrifice, or make some ritual offering for it. Fertility cults sprang up around agriculture, and the entire planting and harvesting cycle was memorialized in ritual and celebration. The life of the hunter-gatherer and Neolithic farmer alike was a network of relationships.

It was a different matter for the miner. As civilization emerged, the Stone Age gave way to the Bronze Age and then the Iron Age. The use of metals required digging them out of the rock, often going deep underground to do so. Mining was ugly business, and the ruling class wanted no part in it. As far back as antiquity, they commodified human bodies and sent them into the mines. Prisoners of war often faced this dismal fate. In the mines, the relational character of farming was replaced by an environment of brute matter. The metals mined were simply so many clumps of a certain kind of matter that could be commodified and manipulated into tools and weapons. The weapons borne of this process were used to conquer territories and subjugate others to the sovereign. This process continues today, with the mining class being one of the most exploited forms of labor.

The sovereign was the ultimate subject: they were the very embodiment of the people, and their will was a divine one. All others were servants to that will, instrumentalized to the ultimate glorification of the sovereign. Each social class was a subject relative to those below them and an object in relation to those above them. This chain of subjects and objects terminated with the sovereign at one end and nature at the other end. The domination of nature was a natural extension of the domination of humanity.

Markets furthered the materialization process. That which was objectified could then be commodified, bought and sold on the market for a price. Raw materials and finished goods alike circulated on the market, but most egregious among them was the commodified person: the slave. Auctioned off as livestock for the master to use, the slave was the ultimate person-as-object. Their life itself belonged to the master. Even so, many a household slave could come to be seen as a beloved family member. Particularly beloved slaves might even be granted their freedom by their masters. Yet it was still crucial that freedom was the master's prerogative to give or take.

Slavery as it existed in the antebellum South is sometimes mistakenly thought of as a kind of precapitalist holdover from feudalism. In fact, slavery had practically disappeared in Europe by the time of the Crusades, when even serfdom was declining. Slavery was revived with a vengeance in the post-Columbian era, when European powers embarked on a massive land grab on the newly discovered continents.

Europeans held in debt bondage were brought over as indentured servants, but had the ability to work off their debts and eventually become free. Indigenous peoples were kidnapped and enslaved to plow the fields and mine for precious metals, but since they knew the landscape better than Europeans, they tended to escape, and were difficult to recapture. Many more died off from diseases to which they had no immunity.

European powers then turned to Africa. The kingdoms of West Africa had slavery both for prisoners of war and as punishment for crimes. They were part of the already existing Arab slave trade. The European demand for slavery, however, caused a massive upheaval in that society. Wars with neighboring tribes escalated to capture new slaves, and slavery became a punishment for even minor crimes. People who had been secure in their place as citizens of the empire could find their freedom taken away at a moment's notice. Slaves were no longer simply the economic base of society: they became capital, brought onto the global market as a means for accumulation.

Wage labor, as we understand it in modern times, undoubtedly entails freedoms for the worker that the slave whose life belonged to the master could not enjoy. And yet, through wage labor, the person has been removed from the picture. It is not the person but their labor that is the commodity to be measured, bought and sold, and capitalized for profit. Wage labor did not begin with capitalism: the gospels contain references to field workers who were paid a day's wages harvesting the fields. Yet this can be deceiving, as what was called wage labor in the past often meant day labor or some service job such as a gardener or carpenter who we might today understand to be self-employed. Under capitalism, wage labor soared to an unprecedented level of commodification. Labor hours become budget items in corporate spreadsheets, and efforts are made to discipline labor for the maximization of profit— and ultimately the maintenance of power.

Over the last few centuries, the primary alternative to capitalism has been state socialism in both its parliamentary and authoritarian forms. Yet this alternative does not question the rationalization process that fueled capital's rise. Instead, this rationalization is baked into its foundation: it seeks the rational planning of the economy at large. This meant the same process of quantification, calculation, and even exploitation and growth, but directed them toward the state, which was then entrusted to distribute the gains of this accumulation process throughout society. It was a noble ideal, and real gains were made, but this ultra-modernist goal exacerbated the alienation intrinsic to modern capitalism. The machine of accumulation persisted with the state itself as the primary accumulator.

Not only labor, but debt, personal information, and ideas have all been capitalized, turned toward the engines of accumulation. We live in an era of base materialism and instrumentalism. Our consciousness has been colonized by markets. All of nature and society has been objectified into capital assets to be traded and speculated upon. We live in an era of spiritual destitution. Liberation requires not only the removal of oppressive social structures, but the spiritual healing of our collective consciousness. We must regain a relational sense of ourselves and our place in this world.

Materialism as we know it today is simply the ideological expression of a cosmos that has been thoroughly commodified. The animist world of ensouled nature gave way to a world sharply divided between spirit and matter and ultimately toward one that had dispensed with spirit altogether. The process of capitalization has reduced all things to commodity, and consumerism has in turn enchanted the commodity, even as our own lives are increasingly commodified. We live now as commodities pursuing commodities, our unique telos reduced to a set of consumer preferences. We have become objects not only to others, but unto ourselves. We have lost our sense of true personhood.

Lost Ways

The idea of a lost Golden Age captivated the minds of ancient civilizations. This often goes hand-in-hand with certain technological advances, as these advancements have a way of sending previous ways of life into upheaval. What was lost when language gave form to our ideas and brought us out of the immediate sensory world? What was lost when literacy retrained our senses yet again and separated the word from the speaker across time? What was lost when civilization arose, and people began to live in cities ruled by kings who demanded obedience? People may not be consciously aware of what exactly they are missing, but it finds its way into their dreams, especially those public dreams we call myth.

When innovations create major changes in society, they disrupt older ways of life, and in the process something is lost. This is the point so often missed by apologists for capitalism who post upward-pointing graphs proving how it has lifted people up out of poverty. The poverty they speak of is generally one of subsistence farming, living in tight-knit communities providing food for their own survival, sharing the burdens of work and the bounty of the harvest, and harnessing collective stories and memories. Under such conditions, they may have lacked television, internet, even electricity or a public sanitation grid, but they had community, family, and a sense of togetherness that is lacking in the breakneck, high-tech world we now inhabit.

While some may accuse me of romanticizing a difficult and strenuous life, it is a self-serving myth that this life was given up voluntarily. Such communities were uprooted, first by colonial European powers, then by their successors in international financial institutions. Colonizers plotted among themselves over how to solve the "laziness" of the colonized who preferred their traditional ways rather than working for interlopers at whatever wages they offered. Small communal farms were privatized and incorporated into large corporate farms growing cash crops for export, exposing themselves to international competition and shifts in global demand for their products. Under such circumstances, crops continue to be exported even in times of famine.

Where their land was once passed down from generation to generation, now they must pay a landlord for their right to the land, risking eviction if they can no longer pay the rent, which can be increased as the market demands. Now properly assimilated into the market economy, the capitalist congratulates themselves for lifting them out of "poverty" — a framework and definition foisted upon communities under capitalist structures. Is it any wonder that such "poverty" is deliberately sought by monastic orders of various faiths, or by Anabaptist groups such as the Amish or Hutterites?

Such upheavals did not begin with capitalism. Ancient empires subdued autonomous farming communities by military conquest. Following the conquest, they would demand tribute from the conquered colonies, as a kind of protection racket. According to anthropologist David Graeber, this may have been the origin of coinage. As empires began to find it a costly endeavor to continue sending soldiers out to the conquered territories to put down rebellions, they kept troops there as occupying armies. The places they were stationed would have operated on systems of mutual aid, but would be extremely hesitant to offer their goods and services to their conquerors. In response, empires began to mint coins, often with the image of the emperor, and used them to pay their soldiers. In turn, they would demand a certain amount of these coins back as tribute. This meant that farmers and artisans would have reason to exchange their goods and services for a certain amount of such coins. The coins would then circulate among the people, seeking to ensure that they had enough to pay the tribute expected from them, thus creating a market for them. In this way, markets and policing have always gone together.

Markets allowed for new ways of accumulating power. Traditionally, power required vast armies and the means to feed and pay them. One's power extended as far as one's army, which had to be able to defeat others' armies. However, with capitalism, one can build economic power that transcends national borders, and have it defended by the armed forces of others without having to raise one's own army. The spread of markets allowed things to be commodified, to be turned into property with an exchange value.

Commodification allows for capitalization. If capitalization can be understood as the process whereby a commodity's present value is discounted in expectation of future profit, then every commodity becomes a means of profit, which in turn provides the means to buy more commodities and generate more profit. Companies themselves can be seen as discreet commodities, subject to this process and leading to a system of mergers and acquisitions in which one firm devours another and increases total power without having to add any new production. This has allowed for a concentration of power that Genghis Khan and Alexander the Great could only dream of.

Under feudalism, a lord would command several serfs to raise enough crops and levy enough taxes to furnish knights to fight for him. The economy was built to enforce and expand the territorial claims of the nobles, who would use the territories they gained to expand their armies and thereby continue the process. However, this system took time to accumulate resources, and supply chains were essential to maintaining an offensive. In years of crop failure, their position would be considerably weakened. They might raise taxes to cover the costs, but this could lead to popular unrest. What many ended up doing was turning to the merchant class to borrow money. This gave them the resources to fight their wars more effectively. It also undermined the system on which their power was based. War and debt became paired, and over time the creditors gained power over the lords. The Hundred Years War was fought between England and France, but it was the emerging bourgeoisie that enriched themselves from it.

Capital accumulation became war by other means. Rather

than capital assisting the nobility in their military acquisition of territory, capital sought to enlist the military apparatus of the state to secure the means for its continued accumulation. Capital drove the formation of the modern nation-state and used it for its own expansion. The rule of law and the establishment of fixed borders provided the stability for capital to be secure in its market speculation. The creation and embedding of a national identity gave workers a sense of shared belonging with the capitalists they worked for. Capital could operate between nation-states through international trade, franchising, outsourcing, and international finance, while workers were restricted in their movements by border enforcement that required passports, work visas, and other papers. Capital brokered international trade agreements that standardized legal frameworks across different nation-states, allowing them to operate seamlessly across the globe. The world became, and continues to be, subsumed under the empire of capital.

Community

With each of these steps, we have become increasingly alienated from a primordial communion with nature and with one another. This is not to say these innovations have not brought with them advances that improved people's lives in measurable ways: infant mortality across the globe has plummeted, hunger and malnutrition are on the decline, and humans are living longer than ever before. Many would have us thank capitalism for these miracles of technology. They would have us believe that the human ingenuity behind such breakthroughs would not have been possible without the incentivized structure of self-interested, profit-seeking industry.

On the face of it, this is an insult. Capitalism did not create medical breakthroughs, people did. People dedicate their lives to such research because they feel called to it, not because they want to make the highest profit they can. Their research is built upon the research of countless others, and each discovery is ultimately a collective effort. This is how human creativity has always worked: we receive what has been passed down from others and find new ways to innovate with it.

Yet there is another sense in which these defenders of capital have a point: this level of interconnection would not be possible if capitalism had not transformed the world. It is largely because of capitalism that the world has become globalized to such a degree that people have such a massive pool of knowledge from which to draw. Yet this globalizing process began long before capitalism, and it is capitalism that brought it to its ultimate realization.

Trade has always been an integrative force. Traditional societies would often come together in seasonal festivals to trade with one another, often traveling great distances with none of the modern conveniences we enjoy afforded to their journeys. With the rise of civilization, it was merchants who tended to do the most traveling. Traveling merchants had a cosmopolitan character about them. From their travels, they would bring back not only goods and riches, but also tales of the strange lands from whence they came.

Trade can be a peace-making force. The classical economists were not wrong for thinking that trade could facilitate cooperation between nations. Capitalism at the time they were writing was essentially a mercantile capitalism, characterized by trading of surpluses. At the time, nations passed mercantile policies to gain an advantage over others by having a bigger trade surplus over others. The classical economists argued instead that free trade could benefit all parties. It so happened that a new era of free trade brought a long peace to Europe in the 19th century. But capital is ever evolving, finding new ways to bend this integrated world toward its own purposes.

At the end of the 18th century, a monumental shift occurred. Steam power unleashed the forces of production like never before. The previous era of merchant capitalism gave way to producer capitalism. Here the driving force of the economy was no longer that of merchants buying the products of producers in one country and selling them in another. It was capitalists buying the labor power of workers and selling the products at a profit. It was less a matter of one nation trading with another nation, but of capitalists selling the products produced by their workers to consumers, who were themselves workers and therefore needed to be paid enough to buy the products but low enough to exploit their labor power for profit. According to Marx, this created an imbalance in the system leading to periodic crises of overproduction.

Beginning around the 1970s, this producer capitalism gave way to financial capitalism. Finance had been an integral part of capitalism since its beginnings, but here it began to overtake production. The process of capitalization had reached new levels of abstraction. Under merchant capitalism, it was the commodity itself that was capitalized, transformed into an exchange value that could be used to buy more goods that could again be sold to accumulate more goods, and so on. Under industrial capitalism, the commodity was the productive powers of laborers themselves. The machines that were supposed to save labor became the means to control it. Laborers could not afford such machines themselves, and therefore could not compete as independent craftsmen. They had only their labor power to sell. With financial capitalism, companies became commodities to be traded for profit. This could be done wholesale through buyouts and mergers, or piecemeal through the selling of shares on the stock market. Financialization took this further and capitalized debt obligations, insurance claims, currency— anything that could be quantified and monetized.

Throughout this process, capital was able to transcend national borders. The defense of free trade by classical economists had rested on the idea of producers in one country selling their products in another country. Now, however, it was capital itself that crossed borders. A corporation could outsource its supply chains, setting up factories in other countries to produce products that would be consumed in their own country. Their business interests would dictate national policy in countries in which they operated, on the threat that if they were not pleased with the policies of one country, they could move their capital elsewhere and leave that country destitute. In this way, capital purchases loyalty. State policy is yet another commodity to be manipulated for profit.

In this globalized economy, people are both connected and isolated like never before. Supply chains seamlessly link factory workers in one country with retail workers in another country, yet each in their own way is alienated from the work they do. The community they enjoy is one mediated by production and consumption. So much has been gained materially, but so much has been lost socially and spiritually.

Here lies the paradox of our civilization. Human history is built upon a long lineage of increasingly sophisticated hegemonic power structures that have alienated us from communal and ecological life. Yet in so doing, these power structures have brought people together on a much larger scale and created what Pierre Teilhard de Chardin called a noosphere, a kind of collective mind from which our creative powers can draw at an unprecedented level. These power structures have eroded organic bonds while producing new synthetic ones. Exploitation and material abundance have expanded in tandem. We have never had so many resources at our disposal while facing such grim and horrifying prospects. Our very existence is at stake, and we must pool this vast expanse of knowledge into ensuring our survival.

To do this, we must rediscover community amid this strange new world while seeking liberation from the power structures that created this world in the first place. We must distinguish between liberatory innovation that increases conviviality, and authoritarian innovation that brings alienation. We must realize the ways in which our creativity has been stifled and captured by hegemonic power, and learn how to connect with creative powers that have become atrophied under a system that only cares about creativity that can be monetized and commodified. We must learn how to reinvent society itself.

Logos

The idolatry of this fallen world can only be corrected by worship in the most essential sense of the word. However, in an era of secularism and religious pluralism, we cannot insist upon any one religion as the North Star to guide society. Nor must we insist upon a theistic God whose existence we cannot empirically verify. Rather, I suggest, we should promote the Logos as an organizing principle of our lives and our institutions. All traditions have some form of Logos. In some, the Logos is identical with God, and therefore to worship the Logos is to worship God. In other traditions, the Logos is an order to which the gods belong. In others, it is simply the order of things, the foundation of the order seen in the world. This latter understanding is compatible with a secular viewpoint, and suggests a worshipful attitude that is due to the Logos, such as through the practice of science.

The Logos may be venerated in any number of ways, but if we do not show proper attention to this creative principle, we are liable to make an idol of its creations and thereby distort the Logos. We atomize nature, breaking it apart into components while ignoring the underlying creative unity that brought it forth. We have neglected Spinoza's *natura naturans* in favor of *natura naturata*, and thereby lost connection with our sacred source. Yet we have gone even further than *natura naturata* and worshiped social systems of our own creation. In the modern world, our worldviews are increasingly defined by economics. The ontological materialism of modernity stems from an economic materialism that has shaped our worldview. Nature is understood as competition, as trade-offs, as utility values, obscuring its cooperation, harmony, and intrinsic beauty.

The Logos offers us a common ground on which different traditions can communicate. Whether it is called Logos or Tao or Dharma, there is mutual recognition of something of profound significance, all the more profound because of how modernity has come to neglect it. I believe a genuine ecumenism can be founded upon the Logos, and this may guide us to a future of genuine dialog, and in turn secure a future for humanity.

The Logos hints at a paradigm by which we can make sense of both the sciences and humanities. This paradigm would suggest that values and meanings are as much a part of the cosmos as atoms and quarks. The Logos is the creative center by which all things come to be, and by which all knowledge is illuminated. In studying nature, in creating art, music, and poetry, in invention and discovery, in perfecting our skills, in practicing compassion to our fellow beings, in fighting for justice, we come to know some aspect of the Logos.

With this unifying understanding of the Logos, we can then observe patterns that show up repeatedly in different phenomena across different scales and forms. These patterns as identified in this book cannot be understood as physical laws in the same vein as gravity or electromagnetism. Some may have their basis in mathematical principles, though I am not a mathematician and will not seek proof in equations. Instead, I endeavor to show that there are principles of how the Logos operates both in nature and in social organization, or second nature, and by realigning second nature with first nature, we may achieve a harmonious society. If we understand Logos as the Word, constituting the language of reality, we can understand these principles as describing a syntax by which language is organized. We may thus call these principles syntactical.

This book covers ground that is metaphysical and social, spiritual and political, scientific and ethical. All of these phenomena are rooted in the Logos, and that is where I will direct our collective gaze. I hope to articulate the patterns by which the Logos unfolds and thereby help us in our own unfolding process as individuals and as communities. If you find these articulations wanting, or if you vehemently disagree with the syntactical principles I offer, I hope to at least ignite a discourse about the Logos as a guiding principle. Let others offer their interpretations of the Logos, bring their own pattern interpretations to bear. Such discourse is bound to be contested, sometimes violently so, but in recognizing their common source, we can ground such debates in a common framework that unites rather than separates. In such discourse, we might hope to overcome the fragmentation of modernity.

I propose a return to the Logos as a foundation for discourse across traditions. Recognizing this common foundation does not solve disagreements, but it can illuminate the ground from which they arise. We become more aware of our connections with one another, coming to identify with the ground from which these disagreements are borne. The Logos it that source from which all traditions arise and the truth toward which they all strive. It is the ground of all being and the light that beckons us toward our destiny. This common source, our deepest identity, the ground of all Being, shines through all contested ground to reveal its truth in the fullness of time.

Eschaton

We stand at a precipice. The forces of empire have enveloped the globe and threaten to destroy us all. Through a path of subjugation, exploitation, and oppression, we have been brought to the precipice of our own extinction. The horrors of history have been interwoven with our highest aspirations and noblest efforts to create the vast tapestry of time. Yet along this same path, we can create a world that we know in our hearts is possible.

The gates of Eden are guarded by the flaming swords of the Cherubim. There is no going back to such a paradise, but there is a way forward. The only way out is through. The expulsion from Eden is ultimately reconciled in the coming eschaton. The path from the one to the other is that of providence. What was lost is not gone forever, but can be regained in a higher form through the unfolding of history.

The descent into exploitation, oppression, materialism, and alienation has been a tragic one, but one through which we may once again find the treasure of what was lost and realize a higher unity with our spiritual source. The Fall implies the Eschaton, as the Eschaton implies the Fall. The end is in the beginning, as the beginning is in the end. The tragedy and injustices of history can only be answered and justified in the completion of creation — its ultimate fulfillment in things to come.

This World to Come must be understood as something that we can neither passively wait for nor bring into existence by sheer willpower. We are co-creators of the future: we can neither abandon our task in creating it nor can we immanentize the eschaton through sheer force of strength.

Indeed, power and force have brought us here in the first place.

Another force has been weaving itself through this story through the power of kenosis: it is what Taoists call *wei wu wei*, the path of action through non-action. It is found in the cry of the oppressed for justice, the solidarity among the poor, the compassion of those who look after their neighbor, the vision of those who seek a better world. It is the work of all who rise above the consciousness from which they are brought up to expand their horizons and see beyond the current circumstances.

We make history, but we are also made by history. We can only realize the possibilities that our own historical moment offers us. We cannot storm the gates of heaven, but neither can we wait passively for our collective redemption. We must always be prepared to rise to the moment when history calls upon us. To achieve our common liberation, we must heed the signs of the times and respond to the call.

We must act through redirection, using the system's weaknesses against it. We must rediscover the communal bonds we have lost, and build them up against the alienation of the system. We must deconstruct the barriers in which the system has ensnared us and seek the creative source from which all good in the world has always been born.

We must create a future in accordance with the deepest longings of our nature. The world that beckons us is inscribed upon the human heart. This future is our destiny because we cannot afford to do otherwise. To avoid failure, we must hold onto hope, which has always been a theological virtue. The hope for a better world is a gift of the Spirit. We must let it guide us, even if we cannot see the end towards which it leads. This is the hope of the World to Come, our New Eden.

2

Mythos

It is all too easy to look at history through the lens of what's left behind. In archaeological sites we find the tools people used, their burial pits and skeletal remains, and the structures they inhabited. From these, we infer things about what life was like for them, but in doing so we run the risk of thinking of those artifacts as the objects around which their lives revolved. Given how much our modern culture relies on technology, there is an immediate bias wherein we see tools and innovation as defining what it is to be human— but these things serve the rich and varied aspects of human experience, rather than define them. Innovation occurs first in the mind before it expresses itself in cultures and artifacts.

The spiritual and the symbolic are a vital part of what makes us human. They are not simply a set of beliefs, but the medium through which we experience the world. To understand where we come from, we must understand not only our physical history, but the history of the human psyche as well. By necessity this requires a good deal of speculation; the tapestry of humanity stretches far beyond the written word and ceramics of our ancestors. Nevertheless, there is enough evidence from anthropology, archaeology, psychology, religious studies, and various other convergent fields to make some educated guesses.

In the time before we had what we now call myth, we had dreams. We spend about a third of our lives sleeping, and with sleep also comes dreams. Any dog owner has, at some point, wondered if their pet was dreaming when watching their body movements while sleeping. Unlike the dog, however, we bring our dreams into our waking lives. Even in our waking hours, we spend time in escapist fantasies and daydreams. We devote at least as much mental activity to imagination as we do toward our sensory perception of the present.

There was a time before our ancestors had language. There may have been simple grunts and vocalizations that signaled friendly or hostile intent, or fostered cooperation among hunting parties, but nothing like the complex system of meanings we call language. Such a state of being is almost incomprehensible to our imagination today, which is thoroughly linguistic in its operation. People who've suffered brain damage or aphasia can only describe such a state once they have regained their syntactical and linguistic skills, and by then they are describing it from outside the experience.

We do know these ancestors had habit, and from habit came ritual. In minds haunted by imaginations that could conjure scenarios both pleasing and frightening, a sense of rhythm and order could be a comforting thing to calm the mind and redirect it. As mimetic creatures, copying these rhythmic movements and sounds from others helped create a kind of participation mystique.

These shared rituals eventually took on shared meanings, and these shared meanings became a system with their own semantics and grammar. As this new phenomenon of language developed, the pre-linguistic world would be a kind of unconscious dream from which we'd emerge, something incomprehensible to minds that had permanently been transformed by language. Yet we could experience some hint of it in the repetition of these rituals and the participation mystique they brought about. Narratives were built around these rituals: a ceremony might be performed to ensure a good hunt or safe passage on a long journey; systems of magic developed in an effort to bring that same control over external environments. Indeed, to control one's mind *was* to control one's environment. In focusing one's intentions, better outcomes could be assured, habitually if not infallibly.

Ritual

There is no single agreed upon definition of religion. We feel that we know it when we see it, but we are tempted to interpret it through the cultural frame we are most familiar with. In the modern era, the way we conceptualize religion is often shaped by a Protestant foundation that emphasizes the importance of belief. But religion is something that we *do*: the word is derived from the Latin *religio*, meaning "to bind fast." It is cultural practices that bind people to some shared past through bonds of meaning.

Rituals and practices become sources of meaning, and

belief has its origin in praxis. The recitation of sacred stories itself becomes a form of ritual. Images become stories, stories become myth, and myth becomes cosmology. This construction of meaning does not mean we are "making it all up," or inventing falsehoods. Rather, it is through this ritualized meaning-making that we can discover features of reality that are not otherwise apparent to us.

We construct our reality, but we construct it from a far greater numinous reality into which we are thrown. Our perception of the world is always already interpreted. We encounter a world of signs that connect to other signs in a continuous process of meaning-making. Our interpretation of signs is conditioned by prior interpretations. These interpretations define cultural understandings passed down as tradition. Culture is, if nothing else, a deposit of signs and interpretations.

Ritual is not unique to humans. Animals engage in all sorts of rituals for play, for mating, for displays of dominance or submission. What is unique to humans is symbolic thought communicated through language. Animal communication occurs through either icon (similarity to the object) or index (pointing to or indicating the object); symbolism, in which meaning is mediated through interpretive tradition, is uniquely human. This is found not only in language but in religious ritual. It is likely that religion emerged at the same time as language.

Religion is not easily disentangled from culture, but what we can tacitly say it deals in higher-order meaning. If I say the word "dog" means the animal referred to by that name, that is a low-level meaning — a simple semantic designation. If, however, we talk about the Eucharist referring to the Last

Supper and the sacrifice at Calvary, that is a deeper form of meaning beyond the literal sense. It speaks to a sense of ultimate meaning: the meaning of our existence.

Liturgical rituals enact an entire system of meaning. It is as true to say that the religion is in the ritual as it is to say the ritual is in the religion. The recursive quality of such rituals affirms the values and beliefs of their participants. Even if the participants don't live out those values, they reaffirm them through ritual. Ritual enacts the highest aspirations of a people. It represents their world to them not as it is but as they envision it.

Ritual manifests not only in personal actions such as prostration, prayer, or stories, but also in its shared practices, like art and architecture. Temples must be built according to specifications passed down throughout the ages, reflecting the structure of their cosmology. The temple is where heaven and earth meet, and rigorous standards for their creation are established to ensure that they convey this to the people. It does not merely represent heaven but in some way makes it present. Through the liturgical rites performed there, it *enacts* the mysteries of the faith.

Where art and architecture decorate space, ritual decorates time. It separates time between the sacred and profane, commemorates important events, marks natural as well as cultural cycles, and regulates the daily routine of adherents. Daily prayers can discipline the mind through repetition, while extraordinary liturgical observances can transport one outside of regular time into *kairos* or "higher time." Against the chronological flow of particularities, ritual offers the repetition of the eternal. Calendrical observance has always had a sacred character, from the seasonal observances of horticultural societies and the lunar cycles observed by hunters to the liturgical calendar of Christianity. Religion has always played a key role in shaping time, and even modern secular societies follow a calendar instituted by a pope and a week modeled on the seven days of creation.

Music and dance have a way of filling time with feeling and vitality. They offer a sense of transcendence from the mundane into kairotic time. Even in the present age, concerts, raves, and festivals can provide a feeling of communion rarely available in our otherwise secular society. It is not uncommon for people to report spiritual experiences from such events, with or without the assistance of intoxicating substances. Theater also serves spiritual purposes: since ancient times, myths have been acted out in public ceremonies, familiar to us today in Passion and Nativity plays. In some cases, one might play the role of a god and thereby become possessed by them. The line between play and invocation can be quite thin, and many a method actor has had an experience of "losing themselves" in a role.

Ritual envelops us within a universe of meaning. Every ritual, every commandment, every tradition is an articulation of the whole. This is the path of the Logos. We start with the whole, then new iterations are added that contribute to the greater whole. Each ritual enacts a new iteration of the faith, reaffirming it anew and preserving while transforming it. This is the meaning of tradition. It carries the past into the present, and with each iteration adds an element of novelty. A structure-preserving transformation occurs in the process of transmission. Inventing new rituals outright rarely goes well; instead, rituals are adapted or recovered as articulations of previous rituals.

Tradition preserves itself through transformation, and thus tradition encodes the Logos. A culture need not have an explicit concept of the Logos to follow it as a regulative principle, but a great many do. From the Egyptian *Ma'at* to the Zoroastrian *Asha* to Tao or Dharma, there is a persistent understanding of a transcendental truth that orders nature, social order, and the individual. Liturgy enacts this Logos by reiterating this timeless truth as it is understood within a tradition's system of meaning. Of course, different traditions understood this truth differently. While it is a mistake to understand religious traditions primarily in terms of beliefs, they nonetheless express what anthropologist Roy Rappaport calls "Ultimate Sacred Postulates": affirmations of what it is to belong to that tradition. Such postulates are unfalsifiable, non-material, and transcendental, yet such postulates become regulative principles by which all other thought is structured. In Christianity it is expressed as the Nicene Creed, in Judaism as the *Shema*, and in Islam as the *Shahada*. Liturgy reiterates these affirmations as one's uniquely understood Logos, in contradistinction to that of other traditions, and is used to understand these other traditions as approximating it to a greater or lesser degree. Truth and meaning articulated repeatedly across time through the power of liturgy, renewing itself in each generation. This can take on a conservative guise in which the existing social order is reified as the divinely sanctioned one. It can also have a revolutionary force and be used to accuse the existing order of having fallen away from it, as the Hebrew prophets did repeatedly. Indeed all cultural *logoi* must ultimately spring from the one true Logos, which no one may fully grasp, but from which all things are born and toward which all things are beckoned.

Tradition

Ritual and belief form the groundwork of tradition. Maurice Blondel defines tradition as mediating between doctrine and history—the temporal instantiation of the eternal. Rappaport's Ultimate Sacred Postulates are reconstituted in changing circumstances in which they are reinterpreted and reevaluated. A tradition is as much about disagreements as shared doctrines, and these postulates are expressed in prolific discourse. This discourse, in turn, forms the foundation from which new ways of understanding emerge.

Traditions are storehouses of the past, but they are only living traditions when they permeate the present. They offer a framework for interpreting and responding to changing circumstances. Tradition must evolve to remain itself. In this way, tradition acts as a generative field from which new understandings emerge that elaborate upon the Ultimate Sacred Postulates.

Tradition acts as a collective memory, but as observed by Charles Péguy, memory can be living or dead. Dead memory crystalizes the past as a kind of museum piece while living memory is generative. It brings the past into the present as a spark for new ideas, new questions, new developments, and discoveries. When tradition acts as living memory, it must not simply repeat the past as habit but reach back into its roots to begin anew. All that is old is made new again.

There is a concept called "ressourcement," a return to the sources, that was highly influential during the Second Vatican Council, when the Catholic Church sought to confront the crisis of modernity. Over the course of the 19th century, the church had entrenched itself in a reactionary, dogmatic Neo-Scholasticism that treated modernity as so many barbarians at the gate. A group of theologians sought instead to return to the writings of the Church Fathers for inspiration to renew the church and critically engage in modernity. They sought not to reproduce their historical thought, but to learn from what these foundational thinkers were trying to do and apply it to a modern context.

Constant return defines tradition. Reiterating what has come before and drawing from the deep well of our ancestors provides structure from which novelty can emerge. The ritual bond of tradition is the precondition of reason. It provides the foundation from which original thought can be born. The most productive thinking involves thinking-with. It is the community of, and in communion with, other thinkers that makes thought possible.

Magic

The human imagination was illuminated by fire. Stretching back before recorded history, stories have been told around the fire of times and events long past. Story fades into legend, legend into myth. Myth elaborates on ritual, and ritual elaborates on myth. Through this combination of myth and ritual, people could tap into a distant and often mysterious past, experiencing it anew in the present. Mythic time is of a different order: it brings about a sense of deep time, or *kairos*, in which time is marked by significance and purpose, as opposed to *chronos*, which is time as a sequence of events. Mythic time then marks the turning of a cycle, a rite of passage, an initiation into something new.

Myth and magic seem to be kindred at first. In the Paleolithic era, we see depictions of wild game in what appear to be temples for hunting rituals. These animal depictions may have served another purpose, one of memorial. It is common among hunters in various cultures to feel a sense of guilt for having to kill an animal and thus will seek to appease its spirit in some way. These cave paintings may therefore have served a paradoxical role in both achieving a successful hunt and memorializing its victims.

The famous Venus figurines from this same period depict what appear to be pregnant women, perhaps indicating an association with fertility. The fact that they tend to be miniature in size suggests that they may have served as charms to be carried on one's person, rather than cult objects to be venerated. Whatever myths may have been associated with these art forms are long lost to us, but they have the appearance of some sort of sympathetic magic.

Throughout the world we find elaborate graves in which people are buried with trinkets and tools that seem to indicate a belief in an afterlife, one in which the deceased could "take it with them." The practice of ancestor veneration can be traced across disparate cultures and may have been one of the earliest forms of proto-worship. While it's common among secular-minded people today to treat belief in an afterlife as a comforting illusion or wishful thinking to overcome one's fear of death, we have no reason to believe that these earlier people would even conceive of their own non-existence to begin with, let alone be frightened of it. In these instances it can be understood as less a fear of mortality than fear of reprisal by the ghosts of the dead if they are not properly appeased.

With veneration of ancestors we would also expect to find respect for elders. Without much in the way of a formal leadership structure, small bands of hunter-gatherers would have depended on the guiding wisdom of their elders. There would be a sense of reciprocity to this. The elders would no longer be in shape to go on hunts, and would have limited capacity for foraging, so instead they would mostly stay back and watch the young children, teaching them the ancestral ways and passing on the stories they were taught when they were children.

Care for the elderly and infirm is one of the first great advances we find in hominids. In ancient burials we find evidence of broken bones that have healed—injuries that in other animals would have been a death sentence. This is perhaps the greatest achievement in all human history, greater even than the pyramids or sanitation or agriculture or writing—the achievement of caring for those who cannot care for themselves. It is not in the battle of the strong against the weak, but in the strong defending the weak that human greatness lies.

Caring for one another led to the earliest forms of medicine, from which magic would have been inseparable. Herbal remedies were seen as having magical properties associated with the spirit of the plants. Throughout history, herbal medicine has long been associated with magic and witchcraft, and the process of mixing, grinding, boiling, and extracting medicines from herbs continues to be done in many traditional societies with a sense of intention, often reciting incantations and performing rituals to go along with the process.

The modern biomedical model has purged medicine of its magical and spiritual associations. For the ancients, medicine involved the search for patterns in both the human body and in the world around them; concepts like Galen's doctrine of signatures came from this search for order in nature. It is in medicine that we first find people exploring metaphysics, and this continues even to this day with the concept of the Medicine Wheel found among certain Native American tribes. Medicine is a matter of whole-making, rendering the body and mind whole in alignment with the cosmos.

Animals also formed a part of medicine, not simply by contributing ingredients to medicines in the form of chemical excretions, but as embodiments of magical principles—the lion is courage, the owl wisdom, the jackal cunning, and so on. Particular animals may be identified as a tribal ancestor, as we see today among tribes claiming descent from the jaguar, or the monkey. Gilles Deleuze and Félix Guattari spoke of a "becoming-animal," in which the animal becomes an attractor for shifting one's sense of identity.

Carvings of animals can be found throughout the site of Göbekli Tepe, believed to be one of the earliest temples and predating even humanity's oldest known civilizations. In this transitional site—just on the eve of the Neolithic, yet apparently pre-agricultural—we see society settle and organize around ritual. We have been conditioned by modern habits of mind to assume that material conditions precede and determine cultural components, and while this is true in the sense of verisimilitude, we often ignore the ways that culture organizes and develops material conditions.

Nature Deities

With the development of agriculture, the cycles of nature took on an increasing importance, as farmers relied on close study of the seasons to know when to sow and when to harvest. The importance of natural cycles would not have escaped the Paleolithic hunter-gatherer, as they would follow the migration of herds and may have taken notice of when various wild plants start fruiting, but it is when people sought to tame nature to provide a reliable source of food that such cycles took on central importance.

Where the Paleolithic Venus figurines speak to a concern for fertility, here the fertility of the soil becomes paramount. As people became more tied to the land, a new sense of domesticity arose, and we see the home take a new place of importance. The hearth, where food was cooked and prepared, became a center of worship as well.

There is an interesting paradox here: On the one hand, we see an increasing control over nature. Rather than simply rely on nature's fecundity, people seek to direct natural processes for their benefit. Yet in doing so, there is an increased attention to the cycles of nature. There is at once a movement of stepping above nature, but at the same time deepening our understanding of it. It is a mastery that is not fully a forceful assertion, but one of observing the unfolding of natural processes and adapting them to local use.

This knowledge of nature is one of cultivation. It is learning how nature works so that we may work with it to achieve something to promote human flourishing. This would have been a gradual process. As foraging people gathered wild plants for consumption, they would have learned how to ensure those plants grew back every season, and even to plant seeds to ensure it would grow back. Eventually they would have learned to set aside land where they lived to plant these seeds. They learned to bring nature's bounty into their domestic environment and become active participants in natural processes.

Natural processes become tied to rhythms of life. The changing seasons become times to commemorate with rituals and celebrations. Equinoxes and Solstices would be times of communal celebration as they experienced the vital energies of the climate. It was around this time that we see most of the great megalithic sites emerge, most notably Stonehenge with its famously accurate alignment with solar cycles.

For all the attunement to nature's cycles, there was a dark side. While warfare and interpersonal violence were extremely rare, there is evidence of human sacrifice in this era. Such practices would have made little sense for small bands of hunter-gatherers, for whom each human life is at a premium. In the Neolithic village, where life is tied to the land, a bountiful harvest is the most important thing, which means people were more vulnerable to drought, pests, and famine. Nature was a source of life but could also be frugal and withholds its favors. There arose a need to appease nature, and the spilling of blood—the essence of our own vitality—was the way to supplicate. Divine favor became the currency of life.

Stonehenge followed a pattern of circular enclosures found

throughout Europe during this time. Apart from their predictive function for agriculture, there is something mystical about this sense of enclosure itself. For Paleolithic hunter-gatherers, the campfire would radiate outward as a sphere of safety. Predators who feared the flames would keep their distance, but if someone wandered too far off, they risked being attacked. In the Neolithic village, the village itself functioned as an enclosure of safety.

The circle provides a kind of immunological barrier like that of a cell, determining what can come in and out of its boundaries. This enclosure takes on cosmological significance in the development of religion. Our sense of social enclosure expands into a cosmic enclosure, in which the universe itself is understood as a container, enveloping all things within a coherent order. The invention of pottery around this time mirrors this move toward a sense of the universe as a container. This container is initially a two-dimensional one, extending outward to the boundaries of the world, but eventually grows into three dimensions, from circle to sphere, with the heavens above forming the boundary of space and time, and the horizon of meaning expanding with it.

Sky Gods

With the rise of civilization, we find people moving their gaze upward, in more ways than one. The small Neolithic village, whose affairs could be run by its inhabitants, gave way to cities and empires run by a sovereign king, whose supreme will stands in for the will of the people. The king himself (here we are almost exclusively talking about a male sovereign) would claim some divine right to rule, whether as a god himself as in the case of Egyptian pharaohs, or as a descendant of the gods.

The gods themselves were descended from other gods before them, with multiple generations of gods starting from the first creation. There were often myths of one generation of gods rising up against their forebears, and a new victorious generation of gods would dominate the pantheon. We can see how this is subverted in the Christian myth of the War in Heaven, in which the angels who rise up are not victorious, but rather cast down to Hell. No wonder, then, that they should regard the pagan gods as demons.

While it's often remarked that people construct gods in the image of kings, in a profound sense the reverse is also true. Societies that we would consider stateless would not necessarily see themselves that way. While acknowledging no earthly ruler, they find themselves subject to a supernatural despotism. The appeasement of gods and spirits to maintain harmony with the environment is a pressing concern. In Ireland, the practice of leaving offerings to appease the faeries remained a common practice long after their conversion to Christianity.

In anthropology, there is a distinction between sacred kingship and divine kingship. In sacred kingship, there is a ceremonial priest-king who is a mediator with the divine. In divine kingship, the king himself takes on a divine role, mimicking the arbitrary authority of the gods and thus demonstrated through arbitrary use of force. It is this arbitrariness which sets them apart from society as divine beings. Their will was absolute, as befitting a living god. Yet tension existed between these two forms of kingship, and the more a king became surrounded by ritual and ceremony, the more their ability to wield absolute power was weakened. In some extreme circumstances, the king could almost become a kind of prisoner in their own palace. When the Portuguese first encountered the Kingdom of Kongo in the 15th century, their monarchy was not particularly ritualized compared to that of their own crown. However, as the kingdom collapsed under civil war, the sacredness of the monarchy became increasingly more pronounced, with ever-more elaborate rituals and the king confined to the throne room, until we find the king physically castrated upon ascending to the throne.[1] Thus, a power struggle would play out, where on the one hand kings themselves seek to make themselves divine kings with absolute authority, while the people could win power by foisting the ceremonial duties of a priest-king on his shoulders.

The gods gained a higher and more exalted place with the rise of civilization. The nature goddesses of the Neolithic maintained a place in their pantheon, but a new class of gods descended from the sky. Now it was not only the cycle of the seasons that occupied people's interests, but the planetary cycles in the heavens above. The planets became gods, and their movement foretold events here on Earth. Every sovereign had a court astrologer interpreting the will of the gods. They are the order of the planetary movements, and they sought to reflect this order in their kingdoms. The will of the sovereign determined the distribution of resources, a

---

[1] Discussed in *Fragments of an Anarchist Anthropology* by David Graeber and *On Kings* by David Graeber and Marshall Sahlins

kind of early authoritarian socialism.

The people were mobilized by their sovereign to move the Earth in accordance with their divine will. Pyramids, ziggurats, and other monumental buildings exist because of simple tools like ropes and sleds, but these structures came to be with a far greater tool, what historian Lewis Mumford calls the "megamachine." This machine has largely passed our notice because it was made of people. The strict regimentation of people required to create these wonders could only be carried out by a population serving their God-King in accordance with the divine order they sought to create on Earth.

The megamachine was first and foremost a war machine. It was through brute force that people were subjugated and made to serve their king. The might of the conquering king was all the proof needed of his divine right to rule. "Might makes right" was the rule of the day. The victory of the conqueror was proof of divine favor. So too were the wonders constructed by the megamachine. Through a combination of force and religious devotion, the people were organized into this vast machine to create homage to their gods, especially to the God-King himself.

This level of regimentation would not be equaled again for centuries, but it lives on to this day in the form of the war machine. Militaries have always been built on the strict discipline of soldiers taught to act as a cohesive unit, forsaking their individual wills for total submission to one's orders. This war machine would in turn be the means to subjugate others through conquest, and bring the conquered into the service of the sovereign, whether through tribute or slavery.

However much devotion they may have inspired, being a sovereign was risky business. Not only could foreign kings conquer your territory and have you publicly executed, but someone from your own royal court could outmaneuver you and seize the crown for themselves. Kings who got complacent in their power could find their heads on the chopping block, succeeded by those more cunning than themselves. The Akkadian empire was founded by one such usurper who came to be known as Sargon the Great. Since might was right, such a coup would itself be proof of the usurper's divine right to rule.

The harshness of this life for ordinary subjects was justified by the wonders it produced. The pyramids may have been built as vehicles for the pharaoh's immortality, but ordinary citizens could still be moved to awe at such a wonder, and take pride in the mark it left on their civilization. The megamachine enabled the construction of such wonders, but it also required them in order to justify itself. Those who built these wonders could feel a sense that they were working toward something greater than themselves. Through their work, they could in some way have a share in the king's immortality. They served the sovereign as they served the gods, for the two were one in the same.

It was this participation mystique that guided civilized life. The God-King was not simply one to be feared and worshiped, but also to be identified with. He was the manifestation of civilization itself, and one's own fortune was tied to his. Where the Paleolithic band sought to secure a successful hunt and the Neolithic village sought a successful harvest, here the might and glory of the city and empire was paramount, and the sovereign and his wonders were its earthly embodiment.

The megamachine in fact required the construction of such wonders. The people would not have endured this strict regulation of their daily life without something to show for it. Thus, the megamachine both allowed for their creation and necessitated it.

The regimentation of life was made manifest through the invention of writing. The earliest cuneiform tablets we have are inventories for tax records, documenting how many cattle or bushels of wheat were available for distribution across the kingdom. In some Egyptian wall carvings, certain despised figures have been carved out, as if to erase them from history. Yet this bureaucratic invention also made it possible to document the myths that had previously been passed on through oral tradition. The tales handed down from the elders to the next generation became etched in clay and stone, outliving the civilizations that told them. In this way, writing had a similar function to the monumental structures built during this time, a physical artifact that reached immortality. To be recorded is to have life.

Mammon

The enigma of debt has haunted the world for millennia, as David Graeber describes in his book *Debt: The First 5,000 Years*. Debt is peculiar in that it implies a relationship of equality that has been made unequal by some breach of contract. Debt is the lever by which equals are made unequal: that slavery and caste systems existed was less frightening to the ancients than the fact that through debt a free person might become a slave.

Debt presented a moral quandary: morality fundamentally assumed a logic of debt, as one's obligation to others; on the other hand, this debt caused horrific injustices. The rise of the state and its sky deities saw the rise of debt as a central issue. Stateless societies operated on a system of mutual aid, in which there were mutual debt obligations to all members of society. With the rise of state power, however, a divide grew between creditors and debtors. Previously, debt had been the moral fabric of society; it was simply what we owed to one another. Yet under this new stratification and subjugation, people found themselves owing debts they couldn't repay. People found themselves in debt peonage, or selling their wives and children into slavery to repay these debts.

This conflict extended to the very heart of religion. If people must pay their debts, what do we owe the gods? If our very existence is a gift beyond comprehension, one that has perplexed religion and philosophy for millennia, what could humanity possibly offer in return? Sacrifices, in the form of food offerings, animals, or even humans could be offered up to the gods as a kind of service on our primordial debt. The blood demanded by the gods was not unlike the earthly debts that justified creditors in slavery, rape, and murder.

It is no surprise, then, that the Axial Age religions spoke the language of debt, and each in their own way found a way to protest its hegemony. The Upanishads of the Hindu scripture raise this question and answer that one pays it forward. Your debt to your parents is paid by becoming a parent. Your debt to your teachers is paid by passing your knowledge on to others. Your debt to the cosmos, then, is to realize your cosmic nature. This effectively cancels out the debt, revealing its existence to be illusory in the first place. The Hebrew Bible describes the Jubilee as a sacred event in which debts are forgiven periodically. It is the forgiveness of debt rather than the debt itself that is truly divine. Christianity offers a powerful answer to the primordial debt, in which God Himself takes on the debts of mankind through his incarnation, suffering, death, and resurrection. The one to whom all is owed took on flesh and willingly suffered this debt for himself so that all may be forgiven.

The rise of markets came with conquest. Where credit systems were developed by local populations in peacetime, empires found it more convenient to pay soldiers in coin, which was transportable across great distances and could be demanded back from subjects in the form of tribute or taxation. Graeber suggests these traditions began as peace movements against the imperial systems of debt and conquest that arose with civilization. If markets are designated as places where profit and material gain are promoted, then religion and philosophy arise as spheres where charity and non-attachment are encouraged instead. In the ancient empires of Mesopotamia, the temples themselves were the primary lenders, and commerce flowed from them. In the Axial Age, by contrast, religion became a site of rebellion against the market.

Religion plays a crucial role in raising humanity from the values of commerce and accumulation to more enlightened values of charity and generosity. All too often, however, they fail to play this role: religions founded upon this rebellion against economic and political power align themselves with these same forces. The scriptures that condemn the corruption of the ancient temple systems are used to defend new forms of idolatry under different guises. Prosperity Gospel and the Law of Attraction are but a couple of the more egregious examples of these Mammon-friendly theologies.

Religion also plays a crucial role in dealing with excess. George Bataille spoke of an "accursed share" in the social surplus. In every society there is a superabundance of energy, which must be spent somehow. In some cases this takes on the form of sacrifice, up to and including human sacrifice. Yet it can also take the form of feasts such as the potlatch of the Pacific Northwest tribes. In some cases, it goes into non-productive but meaningful pursuits such as monasticism and mysticism. Sometimes it is simply spent on luxury for the wealthier classes.

Religion has always found ways to direct these energies. Beginning in the Middle Ages and culminating with the Protestant Reformation, there was a movement in the church to curtail the festivals that had been such a mainstay of peasant life, condemning them as displays of debauchery and idleness. There was a shift towards austere simplicity, and against elaborate altars, icons, and cathedrals. With Protestantism, monastic orders were abolished and their wealth seized. This led to a position where this surplus energy was recaptured but in need of a new outlet. This was found in growth. The Protestant work ethic praised production but shunned consumption. The one proper place to distribute one's profits was to reinvest it in more production. While this did not lead straightway to capitalism—many early Protestant communities practiced collective ownership and emphasized charity as a virtue—it planted the seed for the transformation of the economy from one in which the surplus energies were expended in communal participation to one in which they would be continuously reinvested into the economy.

The growth of the economy paved the way for materialism. It was not science that displaced religion; the church had long been the greatest patron of science. Nor was it the fight for democracy and human rights. There may have been opponents of the Enlightenment within the church, but it was only after the anti-clerical violence of the French Revolution that a deep entrenchment against modernity began. What truly toppled religion was the idol of economic growth. Without the religious festivals, glorious church architecture, sites of pilgrimage, or monastic paths of renunciation, the social surplus was instead increasingly directed toward the market. Economic growth would become the one universal god, displacing the God who hears the cry of the poor.

Mythopoesis

The symbolist approach of Carl Jung and Joseph Campbell sought to explain myth as a set of archetypes, with each part of the myth representing some part of the collective unconscious. The structural anthropologist Claude Levi-Strauss, on the other hand, looked at myth as more of a language, in which meaning is as much about the relations between the components as in the components themselves. Myth has a way of drawing out multiple meanings from the same source.

At some point there was a shift from a more goddess-centered pantheon to a newer pantheon of male gods associated with conquest and order. We see this in the slaying of Tiamat by Marduk. The goddesses seem to have some association both with the Neolithic culture of nature cycles and with the city as a center of culture, providing a subtle form of resistance to the megamachine and hearkening back a way of life that had been lost. The rise of the male pantheon seems to coincide with the rise of empire, and with it the rise of patriarchy. The goddess took a secondary position, but remained an important part of religion.

The gods of myth are far from perfect. In fact, they were often petty, selfish, and vengeful. Their relationships are primarily with one another, with humans as a kind of afterthought. In many mythic systems, humans were created by gods to do the work and drudgery they didn't want to do, as if a kind of extension of the God-King system. Such gods were worshiped not because they were good but because their favor was sought in some earthly matter.

Unlike the gods, heroes were meant to be identified with and emulated in their virtue. Indeed, the ancients understood better than philosophers today that virtue is best understood through narrative rather than rational argument. Their stories shed light on our own life stories, and their struggles teach us about our own struggles. Mythic heroes were not perfect—often they would have a "tragic flaw" of pride or hubris which would teach people about the importance of knowing one's place in the world.

A novel approach to mythology was proposed by René Girard, the founder of mimetic theory and whose analysis centered on what he deemed the sacrificial crisis. It starts with mimetic desire— the tendency for our desires to be led by the desires of others, which leads to rivalry over the object of our desires. This rivalry rises to the level of conflict in which the object of desire falls away and the conflict itself spreads as a contagion. Eventually, that mimetic rivalry zeroes in on a single individual or group that becomes the scapegoat for all collective grievances. The scapegoat is then sacrificed, restoring peace and order until the next sacrificial crisis. Since the sacrificial victim is both the scapegoat and the one who restores order, an ambiguous veneration of the act and actor is perceived. Girard hypothesized that the gods of various pantheons were once sacrificial victims themselves, who were then posthumously divinized and demanded further sacrifices for supplication. Girard, like Jung and Campbell, falls prey to the fallacy of the monomyth, treating all myth as saying one thing. But it is certainly true that many of the ancient gods were connected to the sacrificial crisis and its demand for victims.

Myths are not only an expression of a culture's values and beliefs, but the language by which they are able to examine and reflect upon them. Myths can be understood as not just the semantics of belief, but its syntax as well. It doesn't just express meaning: it's a grammar in which meaning is expressed. Thus, the fact that myths from the same culture often contradict each other should not surprise us any more than the fact that two people can express opposing viewpoints in the same language. The mythopoetic minds of the ancients were not so concerned with "canon" and could tolerate contradiction and ambiguity.

Jacques Derrida posited that language has the feature of multiple iterability. That is, the same word or sentence can be repeated, i.e. reiterated, in multiple contexts and take on multiple meanings. Context itself is constantly shifting, always incomplete. In this way, meaning is always deferred, leading to an ambiguity he called *différance*. If these things hold for language in general, it holds even more so for the cultural language of myth. Myth is not just a tale of what once was, but a template to be repeatedly applied to multiple circumstances.

This repetition is further played out in the rituals that enact these myths. The Eleusinian mysteries reenacted the myth of Demeter and Persephone, itself a myth about the changing of the seasons, eventually iterated into deeper myth about the initiate's descent into the underworld, and the transformation they experienced within. Myth reiterates ritual and ritual reiterates myth, and they do this in a way that allows for newer and deeper meanings to arise.

As ritual is the repetition of the eternal, and myth is retold through ritual, myth is not subject to the temporal constraints of history. This explains the tolerance for contradiction found in mythological narratives. A given culture might believe in several myths that contradict one another if taken as a rationally constructed system. Yet these myths are not set in a specific chronological period, but "once upon a time." Such contradictory myths can express different perspectives on similar phenomena. Rather than an overarching metaphysic that encompasses all perspectives under a single explanatory system, they express a family of perspectives that share common themes but do not claim to be definitive.

Myth and ritual express truth value in the way that poetry or music or theatrical performance express truth value. In his book *Personal Knowledge*, Michael Polanyi uses the example of a character killed onstage. We are gripped within the drama and in some way perceive it as real, but it is quite a different reality than if we thought the actual actor had been murdered before our eyes. The audience does not rush to call emergency services and run to the safety of their cars as they would with an actual murder, but they do become enraptured by the story and experience it as contextually true. Yet we understand a different truth as being conveyed than what we would look for in a news article or history book.

What makes myths difficult to understand, whether looking at other living cultures or long-dead ones, is that we aren't necessarily privy to their originating context. There is not a "real" world on one side and a mythic realm on the other. Myth interpenetrates lived experience in culturally specific ways that may be inaccessible to the outsider. One must develop the capacity to inhabit a mythos to unlock this mystery. If it seems strange that so many societies independently developed some idea of an afterlife, just remember that we inhabit different worlds constantly in our waking life, shifting our attention from one to the other without a moment's thought; it is not so difficult to imagine that beyond death would simply lie some other world.

The modern scientific worldview has its own mythos. The myth of the machine unconsciously guides entire research programs. Some might scoff at the idea that anyone *really* believed the Cartesian vision of the universe as a giant piece of clockwork, yet this myth seizes the imagination of many scientific endeavors even today. The reductionist approach to brains in terms of neurons, of cells composed of cellular machinery, of organisms as programmed by their DNA, all suggest a machine cosmos that is very much still powering the scientific imagination.

Occult

It's not just the stories and legends that people passed down: all of nature was infused with meaning. Augurs would read the flight patterns of birds, numerologists would find meaning in numbers, and astrologers would watch the heavens for signs. The whole world was infused with meaning and agency. There were magical "sympathies" between natural phenomena. Objects could be "signs" of other objects. The events of our lives had resonance throughout all of nature, and if one could interpret these signs, one could learn how to control one's destiny.

Such seers were first and foremost in service of the sovereign, as their will was the collective will, and their fate was the collective fate. Their prosperity was vital to the prosperity of all. They therefore sought signs and omens that would help them to maintain their power and govern their kingdom efficiently. Court seers remained fixtures of monarchies and empires well into modernity.

In some cultures, the shaman combined the role of seer and sovereign. It was precisely their connection to the spirits and ability to discern their messages that gave them the authority to lead their people. The rise of civilization saw the two roles become divided: a pharaoh may have been a living god unto himself, but he still required priests to consult him in the signs from above.

Of all the signs, it was the stars that had the most enduring fascination. There was an immaculate order to the heavens. The planets moved in discernible patterns across a bright background of fixed stars. They moved at steady and measurable speed along fixed pathways that allowed one to chart their course and predict where they would be days, months, or years into the future. Each planet had a particular energy to it, and its movement through the sky brought that energy into contact with the energies of other planets, while also traversing the twelve signs of the zodiac.

It is often mistakenly believed that the twelve signs are the same as the constellations they are named after. Yet even when the signs and their constellations lined up, the constellations took up different portions of the sky, while the signs divided the sky into twelve equal parts — sacred geometry laid out across an inky firmament. The twelvefold division of the sky was subdivided into four elements, and within each element, there were three modes: cardinal, fixed, and mutable. The fourfold division of elements represented the principle of balance. The threefold division of modes represented the principle of change.

Using this elegant framework, the order discerned in the heavens could be used to create order on earth. In applying this archetypal language to planning and ruling, the foundations of positivist science were laid. The kind of precise calculation used to chart the heavens could be used in the scientific management of society.

The invention of writing shepherded in a new era of divine authority and interpretation of the skies. Reading the skies and writing decrees were a continuous part of ruling. Statecraft was the art of simplifying society into measurable data that could be manipulated and managed. Writing could be applied to spells and incantations to manipulate the cosmos itself. Earlier magic was a way of drawing into oneself the forces of nature and becoming their vessel, but now it could be a matter of manipulating the elements to one's will. The heavens above ruled over mankind but the world below, whether human or natural, was subject to the will of the sovereign.

Herein lies the paradox of these magical practices: they form the landscape of an enchanted world that our modern world could only understand vaguely through tales passed down over the centuries, and yet with them lie the beginnings of the rationalization process that created modernity itself. As we will see, this rationalization process has been one of the primary means of securing power for the elite.

In a way, this rationalization process is its own form of magic. This becomes especially apparent in the form of currency. What is money but the manna with which to summon the objects of our desires? Ancient priests understood this when they left coin offerings for their deities. Under modern capitalism the situation has developed to the point that a sufficient level of financial capital will grant you considerable influence over world governments, who will sacrifice the welfare of their own citizens to placate your needs. Rationalized power is the magic by which the ambitious seek to become gods themselves.

Monotheism

Into this landscape stepped a wandering desert people known as the Israelites, who proclaimed one God over all others. The early Israelites were likely henotheists—that is, they acknowledged the existence of other gods, but deemed them unworthy of worship. While the city-dwelling peoples gave offerings to various gods to curry favor with them in a *quid pro quo* manner, the God of Israel was always with his chosen people. He was their constant guide—their shepherd—who led them out of the wilderness into the land of plenty.

Yet the Israelites were captured by the forces of empire. Egypt, Babylon, and Assyria all had their turns capturing and subjugating the Israelites. This would be devastating for them not just in material terms, but in an even more acutely felt spiritual sense. By the logic of the time, that meant that the gods of their conquerors were more powerful than their own God. One could easily be tempted in such a situation to abandon one's tribal God for the more powerful gods of their conquerors, and many did just that. But some took another path.

The various prophets that arose urged people to turn back to their one God and forsake the materialistic idols of the conquerors. Their God, proclaimed the prophets, was not merely a tribal god, but the one true God of all creation. Their captivity was not a matter of the enemy's gods being stronger, but a part of their own God's greater plan. Their God was not just a God of power, but of justice. This was not merely the swift, brutal justice of Hammurabi's Code, but the long-term arc of existence itself leading toward an ultimate reckoning. The idea of history, not as a mere chronology of events, but the mythologizing of time itself, begins with ancient Israel.

Girard sees the Abrahamic tradition as working against the sacrificial cycle, viewing the gods of the pagans as demons to be rejected. For Girard, myth obscures the sacrificial crisis by blaming the victim, while Abrahamic faith reveals the cycle in its pure form and declares the innocence of the victim. The various Jewish holidays are often summed up as, "They tried to kill us, we survived, let's eat." This is the arc of the Jews. They have never had a great empire. They have been conquered and subjugated by one empire after another. They have been hated and distrusted wherever they go. Yet they have survived and thrived throughout all this, as their conquerors have come and gone. No nation as small as theirs has had such an outsized effect on the world.

It is in this sense that they are the "chosen people." They are chosen, not to rule over all of humanity, but to transform it through their perseverance. Through the various conquests they have endured, they have been dispersed among the nations. Through their covenant with the one God, they have brought the monotheistic mythos with them wherever they go.

Monotheism does not mean simply reducing the number of gods to one. It also means positing a single, unifying order to the cosmos—not just a metaphysical order, but a moral one as well. Prior to monotheism, morality or justice was a religious matter only to the extent that obedience to the God-King was a moral and religious imperative. There was still a unified underlying order, but it was not a god so much as the *realm* of the gods. Codes of law were meant to guide the smooth administration of empire. From the Abrahamic perspective, however, the justice commanded by God does not belong to any sovereign ruler on earth. If anything, God's justice makes a greater demand upon rulers than upon their people.

The Abrahamic covenant spread in a new way when two religions were spawned that would far outnumber the Jewish people themselves. Christianity and then Islam had their own prophetic origins that brought the Abrahamic God beyond the people of Israel to become universal religions that welcomed people of all nations. As they grew, the whole world would come to know the God of Abraham.

Rulers would appeal to the Abrahamic God for legitimacy just as the God-Kings of the past had done, claiming "Divine Right of Kings" or that God is on their side. This is what is meant by "taking the Lord's name in vain": to appeal to the Lord in the name of power and self-aggrandizement. Yet this God was above all kings, and continued to be revealed not through the powerful, but through the example of those who humbled themselves and showed a different way. The path laid by the prophets continued through the path of the saints and martyrs. It is through their path, more than either the heads of state or the religious authorities that speak for their respective religions, that the covenant is renewed and relived again and again.

This is the path revealed through the God of Abraham — a path not of brute strength and power, but of steadfast commitment to a deeply held truth that sustains and strengthens through adversity. Justification is found not in who lives and who dies, or who triumphs over another in battle. It is a deeper spiritual truth that is to be revealed in the fullness of time. Martyrs have suffered horrendous deaths in the name of a truth they knew in their hearts to be far greater than the force of their torturers and oppressors.

According to this vision, there is a moral and spiritual truth that does not belong to any ruler or sovereign. Even the Catholic church, including the pope, is not centered upon its leadership so much as the "deposit of faith" that is passed along through the hierarchy. Priests are understood as ministers of the sacraments, however flawed they might be personally. Dante felt perfectly comfortable placing bishops and popes in Hell without in any way feeling his faith was compromised. Most important were the teachings of his tradition, which he sought faithfully to express in his epic poem. Authority is fleeting, but truth is everlasting. The good promised by the Abrahamic God would be realized in the fullness of time. The gods quibble amongst themselves and compete with one another for power, but the true God of justice reigns now and forever.

Meaning Making

Myth is the language of the soul. It is the grammar of our lives, our dreams, our fears and hopes. The mythopoetic sense perplexes us because we struggle to place it within our rationalist frameworks. The mythic is not literal, but neither is it pure metaphor. It is symbolic, yet its symbolism is multivalent and irreducible to a single meaning. Myths may overlap with history, and history can be mythologized. The legacy of a myth is not rooted in its factual content, but in the symbolic expression of values and meaning.

Joseph Campbell claimed that all myths are true. With this, he was attempting to express the idea that myths reveal a deeper truth beyond their literal meaning. It was a useful counterpoint to the association of myth with falsity. However, once we get past the need for literal interpretation, we can evaluate the truth of the values and ideals that myths express and still find them wanting. Indeed, just as myths can express deeper truths beyond their literal meaning, so too can they express deeper falsehoods.

Fascism, for example, has myths about "blood and soil" that are more profoundly false than any facts they may cite to support it. This is precisely why myth can be so dangerous: it cannot be refuted by mere facts. It requires a countervailing mythology. It is not that myth has nothing to do with facts. The function of myth is to give meaning to facts, to imbue them with value by weaving them into a larger narrative about our place within the cosmos. It is precisely because there are so many harmful myths out there that it is crucial to develop a positive and life-affirming mythos.

Mythology has always been a battleground. The same myth goes through multiple iterations of competing narratives and interpretations as different factions and ideologies compete for power. This plays out on a different dimension than rational debate. Indeed, a strong rational argument may convince one to adjust one's position on this or that topic, or to refine one's own argument, but to adopt a new worldview involves immersing oneself in a new mythos.

Families, tribes, nations, all have their own mythos. Even our own lives have a narrative with mythic dimensions. Our life narrative is something we tell ourselves, but it is not entirely of our own making. The story of who we are is interwoven with the perception of others and our web of relationships. Our identity is a myth by which we understand our place in society, in the world, and in the greater cosmos. Indeed, Buddhism centers around deconstructing this myth of the self. Yet if we understand myth not as falsehood but as a meaning-making narrative, we may then see the myth of oneself as, at least potentially, a true myth.

The struggle then becomes how this self-myth can grow in alignment with our greater good—with the attainment of *eudaimonia*. This self-myth is in turn developed by the broader mythology we adopt as our worldview. This is to say that we inhabit a world of myth within myth within myth: our understanding of ourselves shapes and is shaped by our understanding of the world around us. This vast fluid nexus of meaning shapes our understanding of the Good, the Beautiful, and the True.

Is our mythic understanding of these things then merely subjective? Is there only that which is good, beautiful, or true *for us*? Or is it that we can only ever perceive these things through the lens of mythos? There have been many secular attempts to codify and rationalize these things, but the rational and secular has its own mythos as well. A utilitarian, for example, may have a rational theory about what makes an action right or wrong (its potential to cause pleasure or pain), but such theory rests upon a particular mythos about what it is to be human or what a good life consists of. Perhaps the most insidious aspect of the modernist mythos is that it does not recognize itself as such.

Reason is crucial for discerning truth, but reason always operates within a wider mythos. Philosopher of science Thomas Kuhn seems to have some inkling of this with his concept of paradigms. For Kuhn, paradigms are research programs that determine what is observed, what kind of questions one can ask, how the questions are structured, what predictions can be made, how the data can be interpreted, and what counts as evidence. A paradigm then is a greater narrative within which scientific inquiry can be performed. Mythos operates in a similar manner. It does not give us the truth by itself, but structures our understanding of what truth looks like and how we relate to it.

How then can we measure how true our own mythos is? Only through a kind of comparative mythology can we understand what our own mythos looks like in the broader community of mythologies. We must look at the kinds of questions and meanings that are possible under other mythologies and expand our own mythos to incorporate them. It is in this dialogue that mythos comes to approximate Logos.

3

Logos

In the short span of a couple centuries we now define as the Axial Age, religious prophets across the globe proclaimed a vision of not simply a social and cosmic order, but a moral one. Prophets, philosophers, and reformers all proclaimed a new message of liberation. Until this point, religion had largely been a matter of maintaining a certain order by seeking blessings from the gods. A successful hunt, a bountiful harvest, even a safe pregnancy were all things for which people sought divine favor. These were the things needed to maintain the basic rhythm of life. With the rise of civilization, this order was centered on the sovereign. Using the order of the heavens to create order in their own kingdoms, the success of society was tied to the success of the sovereign; this sovereign will was the will of the gods. To defy them was to anger the gods, so absolute obedience was required.

With the Axial shift, we see an appeal to the transcendent as a means of critiquing the social order. The divine was now something other than the sovereign's will, and the sovereign himself must comply. Here the phrase "speak truth to power" begins to take meaning. In a previous age, such a statement would be absurd, as power *was* truth. People began to seek an order of how things *should* be, and to critique society as it was.

This shift involved a rejection of not only the hardships of civilization, but many of its purported benefits. These new movements stressed an attitude of renunciation. Wealth, sex, power, and all such worldly goods were to be forsaken in favor of a higher calling. There is more to life, these prophets decreed, than fleeting pleasures and the accumulation of possessions. Indeed, the unrestrained pursuit of such things is the path to ruin. This was a radical statement: the good life was to be measured by the development of the person. Quality, not quantity, truly mattered in life.

The Jewish prophetic tradition emerged around their captivity and liberation from Babylon. The first scriptures of the Torah emerged around this time. According to this prophetic tradition, it is God who liberates them — a God who is not tied to political power but transcends all the powers of this world. Through the Hebrew people a message of divine justice is brought to the world. The story of Exodus is one of liberation from an oppressive regime ruled by a God-King, and this pattern would repeat itself with the Babylonians, the Assyrians, and countless others.

During the Axial shift, we see the Hebrew prophets scolding their own people about their neglect of justice. In their neglect of the poor, the widowed, the orphaned, they had forsaken their God and incurred His wrath. The prophets call upon the Israelites to remember their covenant with YHWH and repent of their ways.

They warned the people that so long as they strayed from the path, their offerings and sacrifices meant nothing. This warning was antithetical to the logic of other religions at the time, wherein offerings and sacrifices were precisely the means by which people sought the favor of the gods. Gods could be enticed with gifts, and through them their cults sought their continued protection and blessings. Yet here we find a God who cares first and foremost about justice. Offerings and sacrifices are not to appease God, who needs nothing, but to remind the people of their covenant with Him.

Reason and Mysticism

The Axial Age was a turn toward reason. Philosophy emerged, not as something separate from religion, but as a new way of engaging in religious discourse through rational examination. In our present era, there is a tendency to suppose an opposition with reason and science on one side and faith and religion on the other. This historical emergence of reason was a realization of a deeper order of things. Mystics of all traditions have always encouraged this kind internal examination. Reason and mysticism developed together along similar lines. Plato saw reason as a path of access to the transcendent; the Buddha interrogated the nature of the self to find a path to liberation from suffering.

Reason does not just show us the logical consistency of propositions. The fact that it can come to a logical conclusion about something and consistently find that the real world bears out that result reveals that there is indeed a rational order to the world. When we use reason, we are reasoning with the world. There is a kind of reason to existence — a Logos — that transcends existence itself. This Logos can be personified as a supreme Being, or a kind of impersonal nature of reality such as Dharma or Tao, but is always understood as some sort of metaphysical ultimate. From its depths springs the Good, the Beautiful, and the True. Both mystical practice and cultivation of reason lead to realization because reason is itself something mystical.

What we find here is a refusal to take for granted the world as it presents itself to us. Behind the world of the senses is a transcendent order that can be accessed through reason and contemplation. Behind the social order of the day is an ethical order to which even the mightiest kings are obliged to submit. Behind the material order is an aesthetic order of proportion and form.

Mysticism starts where reason leaves off. It is transrational rather than prerational. The mystical conditions the rational, and in doing so grounds reason. Reason allows us to examine the world around us, but mysticism allows us to examine the examiner, and in the process see past the examiner to the ground of Being itself. The mystical is often called ineffable or indescribable, but mystical traditions have a vast language to describe their experience. It is only indescribable to those who have not experienced it. Those who have can communicate about it not only within their tradition but also across traditions. This is not to suggest that mysticism is the same across traditions, as Perennialism suggests, but the experience is similar enough that the frameworks surrounding the experiences are translatable.

Reason and mysticism are both phenomena of the transcendent breaking through into the particular. Both seek to grasp at that which is ultimately beyond our reach. Faith is not against reason: rather, it is an abiding trust in a reason beyond our understanding. The Logos orders the world according to its own designs. Through reason, mysticism, and science, we seek to approximate this order. The Logos is a beacon toward which we grasp in myriad ways, a beacon with which we hope to one day be reunited.

The Great Chain of Being

The cycles of nature memorialized in ancient rituals were shrouded in myth but reflected a deep understanding of nature. The Pre-Socratic Greek philosophers sought to understand nature in rational rather than mythic terms. Thales developed one of the first naturalistic theories, seeing all of nature originating in the material principle of water. Heraclitus saw flux as the fundamental principle of nature, whereas Parmenides saw Being as eternal and unchanging, and change as illusory. For Pythagoras, reality was fundamentally mathematical, composed of number and proportion.

Plato sought a synthesis of these ideas. In his system, there was an eternal, unchanging mathematical order beyond existence. From this emerged a world of unchanging ideal forms, giving way to variations on these forms, and finally culminating in the material world of flux and physicality. This system took seriously the world of matter but subordinated it to the mathematical world of form. For Plato, Parmenides was wrong to see change as an illusion, but it was still seen as a problem. Truth lay in that which was unchanging and eternal. The goal was to see past the ephemeral events of this world to the changeless forms above.

Where Plato built his system from above, Aristotle started from below. The forms that Plato saw as descending from on high were for him immanent within actual objects. He saw four types of causality at work in all things. There is material cause, the matter in which things have their physicality and particularity. There is efficient cause, in which one event brings about another event. There is formal cause, the particular form that objects take. Then there is final cause, the ends for which things act. We can say, relatively speaking, that matter and form are the causes of objects, while mechanism and telos are the cause of events. Of course, there is a sense in which objects are events and events are objects, and as such all things have all four types of causes.

Aristotle was a consummate taxonomist. Where Plato sought a higher realm from which all things sprang, Aristotle sought a natural hierarchy from the lowest to highest things. He was particularly interested in life and the soul. The soul for him was not some immaterial substance as it is often pictured today. Rather, it is the innate set of capacities in entities. He saw the soul emerging in layers. First, there is brute matter, whose soul was to be moved by external forces. Next was the vegetative soul one finds in plants, with the capacity for growth and reproduction. Then there was the sensitive soul, found in animals, with the capacity for sensation and movement. Finally, there was the rational soul, found in humans, with the capacity for thought and reflection.

Despite approaching from opposite directions, both Plato and Aristotle sought a great hierarchy of nature in which all things had their place. There was a plenitude to nature, from the lowest to the highest forms, with no gaps to be found. This principle continues to influence Western thought to this day. "No gaps in nature" is a scientific as well as metaphysical principle. It is not a scientifically testable hypothesis, but rather a necessary presupposition for scientific inquiry to occur at all. Along with it comes the principle of sufficient reason, which states that for something to exist, there must be a sufficient reason to exist. There are no "brute facts" whose existence is without cause.

The principle of plenitude led to a cosmic order known as the Great Chain of Being, and would become the blueprint for metaphysical systems throughout the ages. It was the lens through which the heavens and the natural world were understood as part of a single unified system. In the coming era, the Great Chain would spread to all corners of the known world.

Telos

It was understood that nature is more than brute fact. That is, nature is not only mechanical causality, but purpose and direction. Nature, in this view, is teleological. This telos does not mean purposes external to the entities of nature itself, as an Intelligent Design advocate would say. It simply means that all things in nature, from atoms to molecules to lifeforms of every sort, have some directedness toward something. When you get up to get something to eat, the movement of your muscles and joints are the efficient cause of your motion, but your hunger is the final cause — it is the "why" of your getting up. A plant similarly leans toward the sun in order to receive nutrients. This "in order to" form of causality is essential to all life, because life is purposive. It has ends that it seeks to fulfill. Note that such purposes do not imply conscious intention. The plant doesn't have to *think* about turning toward the sun. It does so because it has a natural function to fulfill. Thinking itself is the telos of the neural processes that carry out that function.

To understand the telos of something, we must understand what is essential to its nature. By "essential," I don't mean something that it necessarily *will* do. Barking is natural to a dog, and they do so for a variety of reasons, but some dogs may not bark, either because they have been trained not to or through some defect or accident they have lost the ability. What is essential to something is what it will tend to do under normal circumstances. A person may be born without arms or legs, or may lose them in an accident, but having two arms and two legs is still an essential property of being human. In logic, we are often accustomed to thinking in terms of "all" or "no" statements. "All men are mortal. Socrates is a man. Therefore Socrates is mortal." Yet suppose Socrates took some elixir that grants immortality. Would he still be a man? Yes, he would be an immortal man. But that would not change the fact that mortality is an essential facet of being human.

To understand how something can be essential without being universal, think about a game of cards. It is essential to a card game that people follow the rules and don't cheat. This does not stop some people from cheating. But if *everyone* cheated, then the game could not exist, because then the rules of the game would have no sense to them. Or take communication. Some people may be born without the ability to communicate, but if no one had the ability to communicate, we would lose all social behavior on which all human life depends, including those who lack that ability.

An exception to an essential tendency does not indicate any sort of failure or deficiency. Essential attributes are simply those that flow naturally from being a certain kind of entity. Being six feet tall with red hair is not essential to being human. These are traits that some people happen to have and others do not. These are called "accidental" properties. It is essential to a person to *have* a height, and having hair (even if not on their head) is also basic to humans, but the particulars of such features will be accidental.

From the essence of what it is to *be* human, we find those things that are essential to human life. These include food, shelter, rest, healthcare, family, friendship, community, education, art, music, leisure, and many other things that contribute to human flourishing. A person may live without many of these things, but these are essential components to living *well*. A person without a roof over their head, who must toil day and night with little sleep, who has no friends or community to turn to — such a person may *survive*, but they are not truly living what can be understood as a *fulfilling* life.

The human telos is one of flourishing – what Aristotle referred to as *eudaimonia*, or what Socrates referred to as "The Good Life." While there are resources that necessarily contribute to the good life, it is also a matter of how one lives one's life. The skills that contribute to flourishing are known as virtues. Virtue is taught mimetically: we learn by the example set by others. We become better people by having positive role models to look up to. We understand what a life lived well looks like by seeing others living a good life.

The danger here is that we can mistake "The Good Life" for an indulgent one. We look to people who have lots of wealth, power, sex, or prestige, and seek to mimic what they have. We can be led down a ruinous path of greed, lust, and ambition to acquire for ourselves what is possessed by others. After all, the ultimate aim of advertising is to sell us a lifestyle by selling us a product. We learn to be unhappy with what we have and seek to constantly acquire newer and better things. It also leads to a paradoxical disposition toward the wealthy: we become jealous of what they have, but also vicariously live through and identify with them because we wish to be them.

Virtue requires instruction not so much in how to act as what to value. Society inundates us with an onslaught of disordered values, showing us examples of "success" that have to do with the pursuit of fleeting pleasures and acquisition of material goods. Instruction in virtue and the provision of moral examples help us to understand what is truly worth wanting in life. This is not to say that material goods are not worth wanting. One who doesn't have enough to eat, who is exposed to the elements, who can't get the care they need, is likely to be miserable. Having one's basic needs met empowers one to pursue higher goods such as truth, justice, and beauty. In pursuing these higher goods, we also learn to pursue the common good: to provide for the good of others.

Hellenism

Aristotle's most famous student was not himself a philosopher, but a crown prince. Alexander of Macedon, whom he tutored until the age of 16, was the royal son of Philip of Macedon, a great conqueror in his own right until his death at the hands of an assassin. The young Alexander ascended to the throne at the age of 20, and by the time he died at 32, his empire encompassed Egypt, Persia, Babylon, and Central Asia all the way to the edge of India, thus uniting most of the great civilizations of the time. With his death the empire he built fell apart, but it would impact civilization as we know it down to our present age. Hellenistic civilization, as it's come to be known, was a bridge between civilizations. The Macedonians brought with them the great philosophical ideas of classical Greece, where they merged with the religions and cultures they encountered.

The blending of ideas influenced Buddhism, spreading along the Silk Road and contributing to what became known as the Mahayana school. The cult of the Greek Hero developed into the concept of the Bodhisattva. The Greek reverence for the human body led to some of the first depictions of the Buddha in statues as well as paintings. At the same time, Buddhist ideas were brought back to Greece. Pyrrho of Elis was among Alexander's army in India, and there he encountered Buddhist attitudes of inquiry into sense data and ideas that deconstructed them and relativized the human capacity for understanding. Pyrrho brought these ideas back with him and founded the school known as Skepticism, an idea that would emerge repeatedly under different guises in Western philosophy.

The West saw Greek philosophy, particularly Platonism, become a kind of infrastructure to its consciousness. This metaphysical framework had two poles, with an unchanging world of unifying spirit on one pole, beyond the world of the senses and accessible only to reason and contemplation, and on the other pole a world of matter and flux, in which things manifested a particularity and ephemerality. In the changing world of matter, we experience vulnerability, corruption, loss, and grief. But beyond this world is a world of perfect, timeless, changeless Being. The goal of philosophy was to rise above the corruption and vulnerability of matter to the transcendental realm of reason. Through reason, one could master one's senses and emotions to rise above the suffering of this world into the realization of higher mind.

If Hellenistic thought spread itself through conquest, Judaism saw its own spread through a kind of paradoxical anti-conquest. It was by repeatedly being conquered that the Jews were dispersed among the nations. The empires that conquered them, from Babylon and Assyria to the Greeks and Romans, measured themselves by their overpowering strength and might, but were shamed by Israelites in their faith and perseverance. These empires took their military victory over the Jews as proof of the greatness of their gods, but for the Jews, their God was the supreme author of history, and its events were the language in which He wrote.

Their suffering was their hope, their vulnerability, their strength, and their humility and wisdom. In submitting to a God who stood above all earthly power, they recognized a greater purpose to their subjugation and suffering and saw the promise of ultimate liberation. Where Greek thought saw a metaphysical fall into matter that could be overcome through reason, for the people of Israel there was a fall into exile that could only be overcome through time, patient perseverance, and trust in divine Providence. Where Hellenistic reason offered an escape from the trials of this world through rational control of one's faculties, Hebrew wisdom lay in its faithful service to an ultimate divine plan whose ultimate realization lay over the horizon in the age to come.

Christ

Into this world there arose a new movement, centered around arguably the most famous person in all of history: Jesus of Nazareth. Born inside a humble manger in the town of Bethlehem, raised in the backwater Galilean town of Nazareth, executed as an enemy of the state, he was the polar opposite of the imperial ideal. Yet in this very humility, he overcame the world. His crown was a crown of thorns, his throne a cross to which he was nailed. In his death, the power of empire seemed to assert itself, bringing him to a humiliating end.

Yet just when his followers seemed defeated and scattered, they found immense strength. According to them, the impossible had happened: their Lord had risen from the grave! They spread news of the wonders they had witnessed and followed in his footsteps. The path to liberation lay in "taking up one's cross" to follow him. This was a path of kenosis through which one could attain the glory of God through surrender of the self. This surrender manifested itself first and foremost in the blood of the martyrs. Just as Christ had entered through the gate of death to bring about eternal life, so too would his followers meet death with confident assurance of their own place in the hereafter. They would ultimately see their vindication in the coming of the Kingdom.

In Christ, there was reconciliation of all things: Heaven and Earth, God and man, beginning and end. Christ proclaimed the Kingdom of God, in which the order of this world — the rule of the strong, of domination and conquest — would be overturned. Christ was the ultimate exemplification of the ancient God-King, being fully human and fully divine. Yet he was also the ultimate inversion of this idea. His kingdom was not of this world. His throne was a cross and his crown was made of thorns. This kingdom is always here but always yet to come. Christ was a king who ruled through love rather than force. In this kingdom, it was the poor, the vulnerable, and the oppressed who would come first, and the rich and powerful who would be laid low.

As Christianity developed, there were several controversies over who exactly Christ was. Was he human? Divine? Half-human and half-divine? How did human and divine nature interact? Numerous councils were called to address these controversies, beginning with the Council of Nicaea, which established Christ as both fully human *and* fully divine. In working out what this meant, a new understanding developed of just what it meant to be human. The emotions, vulnerability, and human frailty that were shunned by the Stoics and Neoplatonists acquired a new dignity. Rather than needing to be strong and self-reliant, now there was an emphasis on our shared vulnerability and weakness. The Hellenistic ideal of self-mastery became hubris, ignorant of our utter reliance on God.

Nicaea also enshrined a mysterious doctrine called the Trinity, which dealt with the problem of Christ being both God and the Son of God. This paradox required a third term to resolve. There is Christ, the Logos, the eternal Word of God. Beyond that there is God the Father, the source of all things, the greater mystery of Being. And then there is the Holy Spirit, the love that moves between the two and unites them. This doctrine defies any attempt to fully rationalize because it points us beyond reason. Yet similar doctrines developed in Buddhism and Hinduism under the names of the Trikaya and satchitananda. The triune symbolism seems to embody a kind of consciousness that emerges around this time.

Christianity has a paradoxical relationship to the world. On the one hand, it stands in opposition to worldly things. "The World" was a fallen place, corrupted by sin, ruled by tyranny, oppression, and cruelty. Yet that same world is also the world of God's creation. It was created in divine glory, singing the praises of its creator. The world is both sacred and fallen, and moreover it was destined for redemption. The salvation promised by Christ is not merely a path to escape from worldly suffering, as various mystical traditions have taught. It promises the ultimate completion of creation.

God is the author of creation, of history, and the rational order of existence itself. The last of these is the Logos, the Word of God, which could be accessed through reason and mystical contemplation. The divine action in history was revealed first through sacred scripture, then through the subsequent history of the church, its saints, its rituals, and its coming to understand itself. The revelation of creation was revealed in the natural world through the principles by which it operated.

Islam

Scientific inquiry had its origins in the pre-Socratics and can be seen even further back with the dawn of civilization. It reached a peak with Aristotle, who established the dominant scientific paradigm for over a millennium. While some blamed Christianity for the decline of this classical knowledge in Western culture over the centuries, many of these texts had simply stopped being translated to Latin. Those that remained were meticulously copied and preserved in monasteries at a time when literacy was at a premium. Meanwhile, these texts continued to be circulated in Greek in the Eastern Empire. It was from here that they spread to the newly emerging Muslim caliphate.

Christianity had its origins at the margins of society, having to adapt to Roman conventions of governance when they arose to power. Islam, on the other hand, was itself born from a political leader. Yet Muhammed, unlike the pharaohs and God-Kings of old, did not seek worship of himself, but insisted that God alone be worshiped. He held Jesus to be a great prophet, affirmed the Virgin Birth and the Second Coming, but insisted that he was only a man, albeit one greatly favored by God. He emphasized God's ultimate transcendence, as one utterly unlike any other. Artistic conventions de-emphasized the depiction of people, or even creatures, lest they be taken as idols. Instead, geometric forms were emphasized, along with ornate calligraphy of Quranic verses.

It is common in the West to transpose the model of Christianity onto other religions. In the case of Islam, one might think of comparing The Qur'an to the Bible and Muhammed to Jesus. Yet a more apt comparison would be to compare the Qur'an to Jesus and Muhammed to Mary, the God-bearer. The Qur'an was the direct revelation of God, a gift unto His people. If Christianity teaches that the Word became Flesh, with Islam it comes back as Word. The Qur'an refers to itself as "the discernment," "the mother book," "the guide," "the wisdom," and "the revelation." It displays a unique literary style with a non-linear composition, using phonetic and thematic structures that assists in memorization. It is self-referential, instructing the reader in its own interpretation. Muslims assert that its style is inimitable, and point to these stylistic qualities as proof of its miraculous nature.

The Qur'an and its commentaries known as the Hadith laid repeated emphasis on education and knowledge. The study of these texts themselves was a sacred practice and led to widespread literacy. One of the distinguishing features of Islam was its political dimensions. Where Jesus was a humble carpenter's son turned wandering preacher, Muhammed led an army and created a political community. As such, Islam had its own legal code, called shariah, and the study of jurisprudence became a major pursuit tightly connected to the study of theology.

In taking the divine out of the particular and into the realm of the universal, Islam deepened the development of the rational. The Islamic Golden Age saw a flourishing of astronomy, philosophy, medicine, and mathematics. Contributing to this was the rich mixture of Jews and Christians who lived and prospered in this new environment, as well as trade routes with India and China, through which knowledge as well as goods passed.

This age saw the blending of knowledge from East and West, as well as cooperation between different faiths. Under Islamic rule, Christians and Jews were considered "People of the Book," and intellectuals from all three traditions prospered during this Golden Age. Philosophers like Ibn Sina and Ibn Rushd revived Aristotelian philosophy and made significant contributions to it. Ibn Sina, a Persian whose name was Latinized as "Avicenna," was one of the first philosophers to integrate Aristotelian philosophy with the Abrahamic tradition. Ibn Rushd, Latinized as "Averroes," was an Andalusian who sought to recover Aristotelianism even from what he saw as the Neoplatonic distortions of Ibn Sina. Both were hugely influential on the later Scholasticism of Europe. The use of paper instead of parchment made the transmission of writing much easier and allowed knowledge to be copied and spread like never before. Mathematics advanced by great leaps. The use of geometry grew to an art form in Muslim architecture, as intricate tiled patterns and elegant calligraphy became the preferred form of ornament. The empirical and rational investigation of the world reached new heights, and opened new horizons in human thought.

Scholasticism

With the Crusades, this treasure trove of knowledge was brought to Europe and inspired a new era of learning. Oxford, Cambridge, and Paris established universities in this period, with an emphasis on the development of the whole person.

The natural sciences flourished, particularly in the fields of medicine and optics. However, in contrast to the trend of modern universities, the natural sciences were subordinated to the humanities, with theology as the height of learning. The point of humanities was to form the person — to enrich their humanity. Education was about formation, and the skills attained in the process were meant to be directed toward that end.

In this holistic perspective, natural science was coextensive with natural philosophy. It is often said that "natural philosophy" is simply an older name for science. It is true that science was not yet understood as separate from philosophy, but that is also because it approached questions about nature in a philosophical manner. There was empirical observation, but there was also a great deal of abstract theorizing. It was a search to find the governing principles of nature, to understand the Logos by which God created.

This had implications not only for science but for ethics. Moral and physical law were from the same source, and both could be deduced from the operations of nature. Natural Law, as it came to be known, owed much to the virtue ethics of Aristotle, but was also grounded in the belief in a creator God who governed all of nature. It understood morality in terms of the *telos* of human life. That is, what is the end toward which the human life aimed? What is its purpose?

As previously mentioned, the answer for Aristotle was eudaimonia. This is often translated as "happiness," but in our age it is easy to misinterpret happiness in utilitarian terms of pleasure versus pain, or in acquiring what we desire based on our own personal preferences. Perhaps a better translation would be "thriving," though this verges on tautology if we understand thriving as life well-lived. Essentially, what is being said here is that the existence of human life implies the existence of a human life lived well. We can understand if scissors are tools that exist for a purpose, in this case cutting, then good scissors are scissors that cut well.

Living creatures do not have the same straightforward *extrinsic* teleology as the tools we use, but they do have an *intrinsic* teleology, determined by the conditions under which they thrive. It is a common misunderstanding today that all teleology is of the former kind, as a watchmaker's purpose in making a watch, but intrinsic telos of the kind one finds in creatures is simply what it means for the creature to live best according to its own nature. Where other creatures rely on instinct, humans are rational creatures, who must use reason to align themselves with their telos. We must seek to understand what thriving consists of, and what skills and habits are conducive toward it. These skills are known as virtues.

What virtue is to the individual, the common good is to society. As a virtuous person had the skills and habits directed toward human thriving, so too was a society directed toward the thriving of its people. It was society's responsibility to help make its members better, more fully realized people, and it was the people's responsibility to contribute to the harmonious functioning of society. Just as the engineer must build their constructions in accord with the laws of nature, so too was it necessary to construct society in harmony with certain natural laws.

This harmonious society was sought first through hospitals for the sick, orphanages for the orphaned, charity for the poor, churches for the faithful, and eventually grew to include guilds for the workers and guilds for the learned, that of the university. A proper society had institutions for upholding the dignity of the people. Dignity was understood according to one's social roles, and how one was best empowered to fulfill those roles.

Yet this emphasis on social roles had a constrictive quality as well. Feudal society had a rigid class hierarchy in which one's social position was determined by birth. The poor were to be taken care of, but not at the cost of the noble's privilege. The position of the noble was to be that of a generous protector, beholden to a *noblesse oblige* in their magnanimity toward the poor. The Great Chain of Being extended into the realm of human relations, with each person's social station forming a rung on the ladder, up to the divine hierarchy of angels and archangels. Human hierarchy reflected the divine hierarchy and was not to be trifled with.

Within this system, a new class emerged that upset this hierarchy. Guild craftsmen settled into self-governing cities called burghs, which were defended by their own citizens, without the need for knights or conscripted armies. The citizens of the burghs, known as burghers or bourgeoisie, did not directly challenge the feudal order, but essentially made a place for themselves outside of it. This merchant class created their own set of privileges for themselves like that of the nobility, and they would rise to prominence as princes and noblemen turned to them to finance their wars against one another, ultimately upsetting the agrarian economy upon which feudalism was based. The bourgeois class would bring unprecedented changes to the world as we knew it.

Enlightenment

While many distill the rise of the bourgeoisie into a simple paradigm of overthrowing the aristocratic class, history shows us a more nuanced view. Indeed, the aristocracy played a major role in developing the "putting out" system that displaced the guilds and paved the way for the industrial factory system. In fact, competition between the aristocracy and the bourgeoisie had a major effect on the social fabric of Europe. The bourgeoisie were transformative precisely because they forced the aristocracy to compete on their terms.

More than anything, the bourgeoisie affected new ways of thinking. In asserting their freedom from the established hierarchy, they developed new ideas about what freedom was. Instead of being a matter of fulfilling one's station in life with dignity, as the Scholastic approach would have it, freedom became understood in negative terms. Freedom was the absence of external force — the right to be left alone to one's own devices. This idea of freedom developed in many stages. Renaissance humanism gave a new importance to the individual over and above their class or social status. The emphasis on freedom of thought emerged at a time when classical works from ancient Greece and Rome were being rediscovered and published throughout Europe.

Then came the Reformation. Martin Luther, followed by Calvin and Zwingli, emphasized the private nature of faith and the authority of the individual in interpreting Scripture for themselves. In principle this could mean a dramatic democratization of the faith, yet in practice it meant that nobles and rulers could be heads of their own state churches.

It also meant the evaporation of the sacramental life that had been so central to Christianity throughout the Middle Ages, and an intellectualization of faith. Faith became less of a way of communion and living and became more a set of doctrines and creeds. The eucharist, long held to be the central ritual in all of Christianity, became a symbolic gesture stripped of its supernatural character. The Great Chain of Being became instead a duality, with heaven above and the secular world down below.

Parallel to this development in religious life, a revolution in science was taking place. Galileo's experiments in speed, velocity, gravity, and astronomy paved the way for a whole new conception of the cosmos. The principles of Copernicanism were not new: Copernicus himself was a Catholic priest who was in good standing with the church up to his death, and the Catholic church allowed his heliocentric theory to be taught. It was when Galileo published his *Dialogue Concerning the Two Chief World Systems*, which was perceived as an attack on the pope, that he alienated the pope and the Jesuits, who had up until then supported him.

The drama of his struggles with the church has since been mythologized as embodying a conflict between science and religion, yet the idea of this conflict did not really emerge until the 19th century. Even the Enlightenment philosophers who attacked the church did so not so much out of a sense that they opposed science but rather that they opposed freedom. Much of Galileo's opposition came not just from the church, but from other scientists. The Ptolemaic system was not just believed because of doctrine, but because it had been a productive research program for more than a millennium. New paradigms never have an easy birth. They are always opposed by those representing the old order. As Max Planck would later quip, "Science advances one funeral at a time."

Galileo's real innovation was not heliocentrism or physics experiments, but a new understanding of how the universe worked. The Aristotelian system was based on substances having different internal capacities. Physical objects fell to the earth because the earth was their natural home, while celestial objects remained in the sky because that was their natural place. The universe was characterized by interactions between objects with their own differential capacities. Galileo inaugurated a new understanding whereby objects were epiphenomena of fundamental forces of nature. A new kind of reductionism would lead to the search for these fundamental laws, a task taken up a generation later by Sir Isaac Newton.

Economism

The belief in a cosmos ordered by unchanging laws led to a religious view called Deism. The number of actual Deists was always small, and the people who most influenced it such as Newton and Locke were not themselves Deists, but it did become part of the cultural zeitgeist. Protestantism had separated the human and divine realms while the emerging scientific theories took substance and telos out of the created order. What was left was a material order created out of fundamental forces whose origin was left a mystery. In this cosmos, God became not an active agent interacting with creation through miracles and sacraments, but a distant watchmaker, creating an order by which the universe could operate on its own. Intrinsic teleology was dead. Only extrinsic teleology remained. Eventually people would seek to destroy this as well.

This order would be reflected in social theory. The Natural Law taught by the Scholastics was based on the Great Chain of Being, in which everything in the chain had its purpose. A new form of Natural Law emerged emphasizing natural rights. Life and liberty — the freedom to live one's life and pursue one's own interests — were considered essential.

Property was a matter of contention. Locke favored it as an extension of freedom from outside interference. It meant that one was sovereign over one's own land and possessions. Yet since property meant the right to exclude, it could be a barrier to freedom. Locke attempted to address this by adding the proviso that one can acquire property for oneself through labor but only if there is enough and some left for others. Whatever the merits of Locke's views, they certainly did not describe property as it existed in Europe: land was essential to the feudal economy. It was held by feudal lords and granted to their vassals. Landed property was central to the power of aristocracy. This power was extended through the enclosure movement, which saw common land that peasants had used for centuries divided up into private hands.

It was for this reason that the physiocrats and classical economists attacked landed privilege as a barrier to the economic freedom they espoused. *Laissez faire* did not mean freedom to buy and sell land at will and profit from it. They advocated free markets and free trade in goods and services, but this could only take place if the privileges of land ownership were stripped through taxation or otherwise.

Later economists conveniently ignored this. By the 19th century, feudal land privilege had given way to a private land market, and it was treated as a commodity like any other. In this way, the market that was praised as an engine of freedom became a means of commodifying every aspect of life. The rational agent idealized by Enlightenment thinkers became *homo economicus*, an isolated individual seeking to maximize their utility by fulfilling a fixed set of preferences via consumption.

In this way, the freedom sought by the great thinkers of the Enlightenment was reduced to the freedom to buy and sell. The variety of products available to consume became proof of the freedom people had under capitalism. The "freedom to choose" has been elevated above all others. Freedom in its teleological sense has long since been forgotten.

Rationalization

In this process, reason degraded from Logos into its now-deficient form of rationalization. The calculating instrumental reason of state and capital has penetrated the furthest depths of our culture. No longer a transcendent divine principle, reason has become synonymous with materialism and self-interest. The market has colonized our thought to the extent that our social relations are thought of in transactional terms. The measurement and quantification that were first developed for bureaucratic management have become the test of reality itself. Positivism and utilitarianism respectively form the epistemological and ethical foundations of the modern materialist mindset. They manifest today as scientism and economism. The former reduces the real to the measurable; the latter reduces the social to the instrumental.

The issue with ideas like essence, telos, or values is that they're not measurable. This is a problem for modernity, in which what is real is what can be studied, measured, and quantified. We live under what René Guénon called "The Reign of Quantity." The qualitative and intensive is, if not denied altogether, taken as epiphenomenal to the quantitative and extensive. The quantitative is taken to be explanatory of the qualitative. If something seems irreducibly qualitative, such as consciousness, many are willing to write it off as illusory.

This mechanistic view is associated with a kind of hard-headed materialism. Yet its origins are theological. The Scholastic views of medieval philosophers like Aquinas and Anselm emphasized the concepts of essence and telos. To some, however, this view was too limiting to a God who was supposed to be all-powerful and all-knowing. It posited powers, qualities, and purposes that were to be found in things themselves, whereas God was supposed to have all the power, and His purposes alone were supposed to be supreme. It was against this background that William of Ockham pursued the idea of nominalism, which held that there are no metaphysical universals, but only names of concepts that exist solely in the mind. He believed that the ways of God are beyond the grasp of reason, and that all we could know about the world was through empirical investigation.

This would prove highly influential in later developments

in science and philosophy. It was elaborated upon by the 17th century philosopher René Descartes, who posited a binary view of the world: *res cogitans* and *res extensa* – the worlds of consciousness and that of extension. On one side of this partition is a mental world that is subjective, intensive, and qualitative. On the other side is a physical world that is objective, extensive, and quantitative. Instead of being a composite of matter and form, as Scholastic philosophy had posited, he understood humans as a composite of mind and body. Mind was unique to humans and to the God in whose image they were made, while the physical universe, including the human body and all other living things, was made of matter. Matter had no final cause; it was merely a substance to be manipulated by thinking creatures.

This view of matter was influenced by the automatons he saw throughout Paris, life-like machines operated by a series of mechanical gears. This, he thought, must be how nature works. He thought that the genius of the tinkerers and inventors that made these machines must be similar to how God created the world. God was the supreme clockmaker, and the physical universe was a vast, divinely created machine. To some Deists, this also meant the physical universe was ordered and thus predictable. This clockwork universe could be investigated scientifically while the mind or soul would be the domain of religion and theology.

This framework had major consequences for science. The Scholastic view historically very much supported science, but its orientation toward hylomorphism and teleology lent itself toward a science of taxonomy. It studied different species of entities. There was a Great Chain of Being, going from mineral to plant to animal to human, then angels and finally

God Himself. Each link in the chain had its own principles by which they operated and had to be studied on its own terms.

The clockwork universe changed that: suddenly the universe was all one machine, operating by universal laws. The task of science became not so much to study the behavior of different kinds of entities, but to determine what laws govern the behavior of all entities. This task was later taken up by Isaac Newton. Newton's pursuit of universal laws of nature was a deeply religious quest. He saw space as God's sensorium. The universe for him was not a collection of entities with their own ends, but God's will expressing itself through universal laws.

This rationalization has spread to all corners of society. Religion itself was among the first to rationalize. Rationalization reached new heights with the rise of fundamentalism. Retreating from the ambiguities of symbolic and mystical interpretation that had once prevailed, fundamentalists met scientific modernity with the insistence on the literal facticity of their scriptures. The Church Fathers had all insisted on the mystical sense of scripture, and Augustine had argued forcefully against the literal interpretation of Genesis, but for the fundamentalist, the salvific promise of scripture could only be found in affirming their most literal and plain meaning as scientific truth.

Mysticism became an ugly word with the rise of modernity. Where historically mysticism had been the natural partner of reason, rising together during the Axial Age, now it was synonymous with the "irrational." Mysticism was associated with the kind of aesthetic practices that contradicted the logic of the market. In the Medieval era monasteries formed a vital part of the community, but now critics viewed monasticism as vulgar escapism, a withdrawal from the world and refusal to contribute to it. They became associated with the *ancien régime*, a holdover from a more superstitious era. "The world" was rapidly advancing economically, scientifically, and technologically, and those who would dare turn away from it were thought to be superstitious fools.

The modern political polarization between left and right has developed along the lines of this rationalized world. The Right still claims the mantle of religion but follows a thoroughly rationalized form of it. They claim to uphold traditional values, but by this they only mean prejudice, not authentic virtue and its concern for the common good. This is abundantly clear in their embrace of markets and capital: the market became synonymous with the common good. The rationality of the market is assumed to distribute goods and services precisely where they need to go, and to intervene in it is tantamount to playing God. In the name of "getting government off your back," they support the most vicious corporate tyrannies, with the state as capital's dutiful servant.

The left, meanwhile, has embraced the scientific management of society as its goal. Going as far back as Henri de Saint-Simon, socialists have sought to rationally plan all the workings of society, seeing the market not as hyper-rational, but far too irrational. To feed and clothe everyone and provide for the needs of all, the impersonal market would be replaced by bureaucratic planners who could coordinate the distribution of resources efficiently and equitably for the equal benefit of all. The Right held to the myth of market relations as organic rather than rationalized, and in this assessment, the socialists agreed. Their rational planning was precisely intended to develop society into a new scientific age, to create the new socialist human who would rise above their lower selfish drives and enter a new age of cooperation. The idea of a more organic society — one that had been repressed by capitalist modernity and was struggling to break free — is popular with another strain of the left: anarchism. Peter Kropotkin conducted a survey of findings in biology, history, and anthropology to uncover a principle of mutual aid at the heart of evolution. Without denying the reality of Darwinian struggle, he observed how it was cooperation that facilitated evolutionary fitness. Mutual aid has persisted from the dawn of humanity throughout all manner of historical change, and even as repressed as it is under capitalist modernity, this refusal to fully submit to our economization persists as a baseline of our social relations.

Organicism

This rationalization of the world was resisted with Romanticism. Yet where the mystics of old sought to turn away from the world, romantics sought to embrace it more deeply. They saw how rationality had hollowed the world and sought to reclaim the sense of enchantment that was once so much a part of people's lives. They sought a kind of poetic existence, choosing passion over reason — a choice that would shock the intellectuals of the ancient world as well as those of today. A similar shock spread with the explosion of psychedelics in the 1960s, with Timothy Leary teaching a generation to "Turn on, tune in, and drop out": an almost monastic message of simplicity with a Dionysian spirit of revelry.

In the Romantic flight from reason into the arms of passion, what has often been overlooked is the need to re-enchant reason itself — to reclaim the Logos in all its spiritual glory. What is most mysterious about our existence is precisely the gift of Being, and the rational order by which it organizes itself. Reason grasps at relations that transcend the phenomena they relate. The fact that the universe possesses the kind of order that allows for scientific and mathematical discovery of its own principles is a miracle of miracles.

There is a deep, transcendent ordering principle by which all order is possible. When we are out of balance with the Logos, we become deficient in one or more of these qualities. When we are centered in the Logos, science becomes an act of worship, mysticism a path of reason, and virtue a path to self-actualization. In a society aligned with the Logos, an organic order would emerge in which individualism and collectivism give way to a personalism that transcends both. The knowledge we have gained from the Scientific Revolution must be raised into wisdom. The colonized world of global capital must be transfigured into global solidarity networks. The disordered rationalism of scientism and economism must be exorcized into an enchantment of reason replenished with a sense of wonder. We must reject the false god of rationalism and return to the true Logos.

The descent into mechanism and rationalism has not been without its dissenters. A view emerged among some intellectuals beginning in the late 18th century who proposed that organism rather than mechanism should be the paradigm for understanding the cosmos. This view, known as "organicism," observed in living organisms a tendency toward self-organization, habit, memory, and creativity, and saw within it a richer way of understanding the cosmos than the reductive materialists who sought to explain everything in terms of mechanism. The mechanists sought to explain higher-level order in terms of the lower, terminating in the movement of atoms. Pierre-Simon Laplace believed that if he could tell the exact position and trajectory of every atom in the universe, he could predict all future events that would unfold from this. Against this view, organicists such as Johann Wolfgang Von Goethe saw higher-level organization influencing lower levels.

When an organism is developing in the womb, it is not built piece-by-piece with a head appearing, then a neck, then a torso, then limbs, etc. Rather, it begins with a single egg which then subdivides into differentiated wholes. Each sequence of its development is the iteration of a single whole. These structure-preserving transformations are achieved not so much through addition as division. It is the holistic process by which potentials are actualized. Wholes are differentiated into new wholes that themselves differentiate into new wholes, and so on. These new wholes are also created *within* a greater whole.

The greatest whole is, of course, the universe itself, which continually differentiates itself into new wholes through self-organization. Within the greater whole, these wholes then interact with one another, and create new wholes through a process called emergence. Emergence is often summed up as "the whole is greater than the sum of its parts," but what it is really saying is that the whole *organizes* the parts.

Neuroanthropologist Terrence Deacon offers a theory of complexity based on absences, where the whole is not *greater* than the sum of its parts, but *less than*. By this, he means that the organization of matter that comprises emergence consists of *closing off* possibilities. Only by doing so can the system "ratchet" up to improbable states and maintain them through dynamic equilibrium. This inverts Aristotelian substance theory in which matter is a kind of nothingness to which form is added. Instead, we can now see matter as pure activity and form as emptiness. In this way, we discover that, as Buddhism has long taught, the underlying substance of things is none other than emptiness. Form is a void in which matter is organized and differentiated. This organizing Logos is an absence by which all presence is known. It is that without substance that substantiates all things.

These principles of self-organization are notably absent in the technical achievements of humans. You cannot grow a house from a seed, and a car is not grown in a womb. These artifacts are the result of deliberate purposive actions by the people building them. The more complex the artifact, the more it requires an understanding of mechanics to create it. Descartes was particularly fascinated by the automatons that were popular in his day using interlocking systems of gears and screws that could simulate lifelike movement. For early mechanists like Descartes and Newton, the universe was a vast system of clockwork designed by an intelligent creator. God the transcendent clockmaker then gave way to the deistic God who set the initial conditions from which all else proceeded. Eventually the mechanistic view, once grounded in a theology of exalted divine omnipotence, abandoned God altogether.

Mechanistic science has led to all manner of discoveries.

In one field after another, material structures have been discovered underlying what were once thought to be inexplicable phenomena. The complex neural circuitry of the brain and the DNA inside nearly every cell of our bodies seem to offer material causes for such mysterious phenomena as mind and life. Yet *how* these things emerge remains mysterious. While such discoveries may threaten cruder forms of vitalism that treat such phenomena as purely immaterial or mystical, a more robust organicism would consider Aristotle's four causes. Mechanistic materialism considers only material and efficient causes, which deal with parts, but not formal and final causes, which are directed toward wholes. The search for the neural correlates of consciousness or the chemical building blocks of life will continue apace, but until they are also considered in terms of formal and final causes, such explanations will not be complete. The organism is a self-sustaining form that organizes the material components through mechanistic processes which emerge from the whole. The mind is a holistic process that organizes itself using neural pathways for encoding and retrieving information. The mechanics are subservient to the organism. The organism constitutes an organizing field that teleologically directs mechanical processes. Rather than a single divine clockmaker, the universe is composed of wholes that organize their own inner clockwork.

This self-organizing process happens within time, and this requires habit and creativity. Charles Sanders Peirce suggested that what we call "laws of nature" should instead be understood as habits of nature. Physical processes create precedent for other processes, which in turn influence future processes. Organisms grow and change while preserving their fundamental form. Their structure-preserving transformations exhibit a quality Aristotle referred to as *entelechy*, where a form works to maintain itself. Organisms undergo constant metabolic processes yet remain the same organism throughout. In the iterability of form, change is introduced through repetition. A repetition of form within the flux of changing circumstances allows for novelty within structure, leading organic forms to undergo mutation and evolution. This process finds its center in what Stuart Kauffman calls the "razor's edge" between order and chaos, in which true novelty emerges.

Unfolding

This repetition is the repetition of wholes. Each step of this whole-making process opens what Kauffman calls the "adjacent possible" in which new possibilities are born. Though our senses pick up diverse stimuli from the environment, we experience the moment as a unified whole. This is fundamental to the mysterious quality of mind. The holistic experience of qualia does not seem reducible to the quantitative data processed by our brains. Our thought has not only semiotic structure but semantic content. The scattered data of the senses are integrated into the whole through memory. Memory is mind extended across time. All of nature exhibits habit, and the interiority of habit is called memory. Memory is the form of the mind organizing the senses and concretizing itself into a unified experience that goes on to inform future experiences. The storehouse of past experiences creates an ever-growing field of information from which to inform new experiences. Experiences separated by time can be compared with one another to formulate opinions, render judgments, and make decisions. What we call "free will" is a function of time-freedom; it is the ability of the mind to move between past and present. A continuous circuit between past and present allows one to take in a larger whole beyond the present moment.

The holistic focus of organicism has managed to seep its way into mainstream science even as it sits uncomfortably with mechanistic science. Though modern biology is still often focused on such reductionistic sciences as organic chemistry, the holistic field of ecology has offered a vision of nature as self-organizing structures of mutual interaction. Systems theory, cybernetics, and complexity theory are among the fields that study interacting dynamic wholes. They offer us a mathematical understanding of self-organizing, whole-making processes. It seems that there is a kind of Logos to self-organization, and therefore life itself. It is characterized by a radical openness that Kauffman refers to as the "adjacent possible": self-organizing systems create an ever-growing field of possibilities that can never be exhausted.

So, what of mechanical artifacts that the mechanists take as their cosmic metaphor? Are there two types of order, one organic and one mechanistic? This theory was championed by Henri Bergson in his book *Creative Evolution*. He suggested that there is a geometric order that is perceived through reason, and a vital order that is perceived through intuition. Where reason abstracts the temporal flow of experience into a timeless extension of concepts, intuition places us within the flow of time and allows us to perceive the novelty and creativity in which life partakes. Yet emerging holistic sciences like complexity theory suggest that this novel and creative order itself has a geometric character — a single Logos that encompasses both mechanism and vitality. The difference between reason and intuition is not, as Bergson believed, a distinction between two distinct types of order, but rather between two forms of understanding the same order. Reason deconstructs phenomena into their component parts, seeking to understand how they all fit together. Intuition, on the other hand, perceives integrated wholes. It perceives harmony or disharmony, detects moods and vibrations, and tells us if something is off. When intuition leads, it reveals wholes that can then be analyzed by reason, but starting from reason, we cannot reach the intuitive whole. Reason can only truly serve its purpose in the service of intuition. It is by intuition that we can perceive the supreme reason known as Logos.

This intuition can guide us toward a deeper understanding of life in all things. Architect and design theorist Christopher Alexander developed a theory of architecture based on the degree of life that a built environment has. Buildings of course are not self-organizing in the way an organism is, but there are some that give a greater sense of life than others. Morphogenetic processes in nature operate by the differentiation and articulation of wholes and the creation of mutually supporting centers unfolding in a sequential process. Alexander suggests that architecture which possesses a greater degree of life displays this sense of holistic unfolding. It utilizes structure-preserving transformations not unlike organic metabolic processes. Traditional architecture unfolded according to these principles, but modern architecture emerged in rebellion against this organic order. Modern architecture exemplifies the triumph of mechanism: Le Corbusier believed that "a house is a machine for living in." Modern architecture has absorbed human life into the megamachine. But Alexander shows how architecture can once again be designed according to the system of organic unfolding. That is, the built artifacts of our environment can be brought into accordance with the Logos. He applies these principles not only to buildings but also to manufactured goods. There is a vitality to artisanal crafts that is missing from mass production because the craftsman is attentive to centers in the same way as a master builder.

As our manufactured environment has drifted further from this vitality, so has our conception of the cosmos. The divine watchmaker metaphor at least implied a sense of careful, artisanal craftsmanship in the creation of a mechanistic universe. It still had a sense that creation was beautifully and wonderfully made. Yet as the Industrial Revolution overtook the economy and replaced the artisan with the factory worker, the production process lost its sense of life. An artisan in their workshop can perceive the life in their product, and make adjustments to bring this life out more and more, just as the painter is able to perceive where their painting requires attention through continual interaction with the whole. The factory worker, on the other hand, repeats one task along an assembly line churning out identical products. This is the lifeless process of the capitalist megamachine. The megamachine that rules over our economic life has also colonized our very conception of the cosmos and our place within it. To transcend the megamachine, we must unlock our own creative abilities and become artisans of the social imaginary.

The megamachine works through mechanistic reduction and technocratic imposition. To move against it, we must rediscover the method of creating generative wholes. Planning must create a space in which vital processes can unfold. Our relationship with nature itself can be realigned with the Logos by understanding the principles of organicism. Instead of a dominating ethos that commands nature to do our bidding, we must learn to listen and respond. A familial relationship of mutuality with the natural world would realign second nature with first nature. It means learning to grow our food according to ecological principles, creating resilient local economies that sustainably use and replenish local resources, and overcoming the growth imperative of the capitalist megamachine. It means slowing down and listening to the rhythms of nature to understand its process of unfolding. Through kenosis we can loosen our grip upon the world and pay attention to where the Logos is directing us.

In this self-emptying, we begin to see a world not of extension and brute matter but of vibrant centers unfolding in relation with one another. This relational unfolding takes the form of dialogue. We are centers of life and creativity embedded in a vast network of other vital centers, forming a vast interconnected whole with all of creation. By encountering a world of wholes rather than parts, we can discover ways that we can contribute to greater wholeness.

We encounter these wholes as what psychologist J.J. Gibson calls "affordances." These are objects in the environment that offer possibilities for action. This action should not necessarily be understood in terms of manipulation. A landmark, for example, is an affordance we use to navigate, while leaving the object itself untouched. A healthy environment will have an ordered distribution of affordances. What these affordances offer is opportunity for interaction. A walkable neighborhood will connect people through the creation of positive space. A vibrant community will have a diversity of functions to allow for a multiplicity of interactions. A beautiful building or work of art will have a coherent distribution of affordances that connect the viewer to the whole. Nature, too, creates an ecosystem of affordances through its unfolding process: Gibson explicitly appealed to ecology to ground his concept in his book *The Ecological Approach to Visual Perception*. Nature's process of unfolding achieves complexity through simplicity, acquiring what Kauffman calls "order for free" through mathematical principles described by complexity theory.

Nature can be as much a subject of collaboration as an object of study. The scientific method tends to be framed in objectifying terms, where nature becomes the testing ground for one's hypothesis. Yet a hypothesis could just as well be seen as posing a question *to* nature in search of an answer. We can ask how nature goes about addressing a problem and discovering its underlying patterns. This was the method championed by Goethe, and this perspective continues to be explored in the integrative sciences of ecology, complexity theory, cybernetics, and systems theory. These fields do not replace the need for methodological reductionism but supplement it by giving it a broader context. We must start with the whole, and when we isolate some part to study it, we must then bring that perspective back into the whole.

Studying wholes also implies more interdisciplinary work so that connecting threads can become more visible, and the objects of study can become apparent to us in their multidimensionality.

Pedagogy too must become more discursive and cooperative. The Brazilian educator and philosopher Paulo Freire described the mainstream education system as relying on a "banking model." That is, the teacher is in possession of knowledge which must be "deposited" in the student's mind. It is a hierarchical unidirectional relationship between one who possesses knowledge and the other who receives it. By contrast, Freire envisions a facilitative role for the teacher. Their task is to draw knowledge from their students and help them to discover the answers for themselves. The students learn as much from each other as they do from the teacher. The most important thing they learn from the teacher is how to learn. Knowledge is collaborative by nature. A fully developed pedagogy would extend this collaboration beyond a small group of experts to a broader community of inquisitive minds.

By rediscovering the principles of organic unfolding, we can align our activities with the Logos. For our creations to unfold in this way, we must discover the enfolded order from which this unfolding takes place. The same creative principle that underlies the unfolding of life in the organism can guide the unfolding of life in human society. We must learn to overcome the megamachine and rediscover an organic creative order in which we can truly thrive. The creativity of the cosmos is also the creativity within us striving to burst forth. The macrocosm of the universe is imprinted in the microcosm of our minds. We are universal creativity seeking to express itself. Restoring ourselves to this creative Logos is the greatest quest of our existence.

4

Institutions

Margaret Thatcher claimed there is no such thing as society, expressing an extreme form of individualism wherein "society" is simply the aggregate of individual people within it. An opposing view holds "society" to be a whole to which all individuals belong. The individual is a social product, the sum of social influences upon their personality and the circumstances in which they find themselves. Both of these views assume a binary interpretation of the individual to some nebulous whole. Yet there is not some singular, amorphous collective, but numerous collectives with their own governing logic, intersecting with other collectives in ways that can range from friendly to hostile. The result is a dynamic balance known as "society," which can readily slip out of balance through crises and upheavals within this dynamism.

Institutions are collective habits. They are practices that people have done together over long periods of time that are ingrained into the fabric of society. An institution may be intentionally created by organizers or by an act of law, but most are simply developed by people following practices and procedures to the point that they become normative. What we formally call "institutions" in the sense of legal entities are special cases of this broader meaning of institutions. When a business, non-profit, or government "institution" is created, it is drawn from myriad other institutions embodied in law and social organization. This chapter focuses on institutions in this broader, primary sense.

Institutions are encountered in what Heidegger called *Das Man*. This is often translated as "the they," but Hubert Dreyfus considered a more accurate translation to be "the one." It is a preconscious source of habit in which we encounter the social. While "the they" implies the social as an other, for Dreyfus "the one" is a phenomenon in which we are all caught up. It is a matter of the things *one* must do, simply because that is the way things are done. *Das Man* is the anonymous public that conditions our thoughts and actions. On the one hand, its norms and practices constitute the very condition of our thinking about the world. On the other hand, it has a way of flattening our understanding of it, smoothing over distinctions to produce a false sense of objectivity. We can easily fall victim to *Das Man* when we take our social institutions for granted rather than critically examining them.

Institutions are the dynamic components that construct and reconstruct society. To analyze society as either a collection of individuals or as a cohesive whole is to ignore the complex networks, habits, and practices that form this collective. In some sense, Thatcher was right: society as such does not exist, but neither does the individual isolated from society. Society is not a thing unto itself but a process in which these associations are continually being made and remade. Society is community precisely in its institutional form.

The nodes in these networks are as important as the connective tissue. These "nodes" are not just people, but objects of all kinds. As Bruno Latour explained it, we don't analyze the military by having a bunch of naked soldiers in one column and their clothes, armor, weaponry, and supply lines in the other while positing "some dialectical relationship" between them. We are always already immersed in a world of objects, material and immaterial. There is no aspect of culture or society that is "merely" human: it is always an assemblage, and the connective tissue bringing it together constitutes a bricolage that is in constant flux.

Society may thus be conceived as an assemblage of institutions that organize human and non-human actors according to a set of norms, assumptions, and pathways. These institutions mutually interact, overlap, and shape one another. The transformation of society means the transformation of this institutional landscape. Transforming one institution will have a ripple effect on other institutions connected to it. The institutional ecosystem evolves in tandem.

Family

The first institution we encounter is family. Certainly, family has a biological component as a genetic pattern of inheritance, but it is also a social arrangement. Family is a kind of society within society; in some cases, family and society are one and the same.

Kinship systems vary widely among different cultures throughout the world. Foraging bands often tend to be composed of extended families who join up with other families for trade, religious festivals, sharing of stories and songs, and finding mates. Complex societies could come together in certain parts of the year and then dissolve during another. Mating can involve any number of arrangements. The woman from one band might join the man's family, or he could join a woman's family, or they could simply mate and go their separate ways, with the woman's family helping to raise the child. The idea of fatherhood or marriage is not universally found among cultures: often that analogous role is taken on by the mother's brothers.

Common practices among different clans set standards for such encounters and helped create a common cultural identity across familial bands. This shared culture defined the tribe. Tribal identity itself was rather porous, with new members joining from other tribes mainly through marriage, but also occasionally through adoption. But in marrying into another tribe, to some degree one was expected to adopt their culture.

Complex societies incorporate not only individuals but families into their social hierarchy. Caste systems developed in which one was expected to follow in the footsteps of one's parents. In traditional societies, people are judged much more by their family name than by their individual merits. Family came prior to the individual. It was in the context of family that private property developed. Property was precisely that which one passed on to one's descendants, allowing for the maintenance of inequality across generations.

National identity requires creating a higher order identity from that of family, tribe, or clan. It involves the creation of what anthropologist Benedict Anderson called "imagined communities." Historically this was often done through religion. Muhammed, for instance, attempted to unite people together under the *ummah*, the identity of all Muslims. Family bonds are one of the strongest barriers to creating new political orders, and many states and political institutions have fallen as a consequence of failing to overcome these bonds. Sometimes this means forbidding people from passing on property to their next of kin, as was done by China with its scholar officials, or by Pope Gregory VII when he mandated priestly celibacy.

Given that familial bonds are not so easily broken, what tends to emerge in constructing national identities is not an entity set apart from families, but a ranking of families by social status and perceived prestige. Monarchies and aristocracies form around these families, and family honor can become a regulative principle in society. Families trade in the currency of honor to attain status in society, and that status allows them to command greater loyalty from others. This currency of honor corresponds to property, but not always in a straightforward manner. In many societies, it is generosity that earns one high status. One exalts one's family honor by giving the most lavish gifts. Of course, having this honor also gives one the purchasing power to give such gifts. Those seeking to gain honor for themselves will seek to one-up them in such a gift-giving contest.

Patriarchy and patrilineality are related but not identical concepts. In a patrilineal culture, lineage is traced through the father, while in a matrilineal culture, it is traced through the mother. This in turn is often reflected in property relations and living arrangements. In a matrilineal society, property is often passed down through the mother's line. Either the husband will move in with his wife's family or he will stay with his own mother and come to visit. In patrilineal societies, the passage of property from father to son requires a way of ensuring patrimony. Because of this, women are often partitioned off from the rest of society, shut out from institutions in order to ensure that the only men they socialize with are their husbands and family. Patriarchy emerges as a means of ensuring patrimony.

A matrilineal society may be compatible with monogamy, but it is not as necessary for ensuring inheritance. A patrilineal society may practice polygamy, but it is a measure of power and social status for a man to have multiple wives. Such a polygamous society will have a few powerful men with multiple wives, many other men with one wife, and a remaining portion with no wives. The great kings, emperors, and sultans would have great harems of the most beautiful women in the land, sectioned off from the rest of society and guarded by eunuchs. Preserving their dynasty was of the utmost importance, so it was imperative that they have as many progenies as possible.

Patrilineal and matrilineal systems are both forms of unilineality, but other kinship systems exist. One alternative is a "house system" in which kinship is organized around corporately organized dwellings rather than descent or lineage. What connects all these systems is that they are not only forms of identity but also systems for distributing resources. It is precisely because of the fragility of "society" that family bonds can have such a strong influence on such matters.

Beginning in the 20th century, the concept of a nuclear family has overtaken the traditional extended family. People talk about getting married and "starting" a family, as if they do not already belong to one. At the same time, families of choice are an increasing phenomenon. This has long been an important matter for the LGBTQ+ community, in which many people have been ostracized from their blood relations. We also see with the emergence of polyamory the formations of new family bonds, in which a person's community of partners may share in the upbringing of children. Family is not a fixed institution, but a constantly evolving one, and re-imagining its contours is part of society's reinvention of itself.

Family models affect political models. Cognitive linguist George Lakoff outlined how human thought is modeled in frames based on our embodied experience. One of the most basic frames is that of family. Lakoff identifies a "strict father" frame and a "nurturant parent" frame. These frames exist within the same society. Even if we are raised in a nurturing environment, we all are at least able to understand the strict father frame. In the strict father frame, there is a clear chain of authority, a focus on obedience and self-reliance, negative reinforcement, and a sense of justice as retribution. In the nurturant parent frame, there is an emphasis on support and care, interdependence, and mutual respect taught by example. While Lakoff leaves a lot out by confining himself to these two frames, the political ramifications are easy to see.

The strict father frame goes by the familiar name of patriarchy, but reaches far beyond the subjugation of women.

It is the very model of tyranny. This patriarchal model spreads outward from the household to encompass the structure of society itself. Patriarchy is the model under which there is a strict hierarchy, with the male head of household at the top, followed by the mother, then the children at the bottom. It is a mentality of domination and subjugation as such. There is no mirror image that could properly be called "matriarchy." Societies referred to as "matriarchal" may have women in positions of power or high status, but the structures of domination that characterize patriarchy are noticeably lacking. The patriarchal logic of domination not only subjugates women under the rule of men but also subjects men to other men. Each patriarch is subservient to another patriarch until one finally arrives at the supreme patriarch, the tyrant.

Patriarchy can thus be understood as the father of all domination. It is the primordial distortion of the Logos from which myriad forms of oppression have sprung ever since. The Book of Genesis implies that patriarchy is a direct result of the Fall. To return to the Logos, we must deconstruct these forms of oppression and rediscover the feminine voice, not because the feminine is superior to the masculine, but because the feminine has been repressed and marginalized by the history of patriarchy, and once liberated it offers the opportunity for the emergence of a new masculinity liberated from its patriarchal trappings.

Taboo

Taboos define what behavior is prohibited in a given society, and are some of the first regulative principles for complex societies. Taboo underpins social hierarchies and governed relations between families, enforced by social sanction and a sense of limitation and transgression. Taboos are not necessarily moral directives except in the loosest sense of the term — they are simply things one does not do. Taboos can regulate what food one is allowed to eat and how it is prepared, how the dead are to be dealt with, who one can marry or have sex with, how one is to address different relatives or authority figures, and so on.

Taboos are often seen as descending from the gods. It would be anachronistic to describe them as "moral" laws. They are moral only in the sense that to violate them is to endanger the community by bringing upon them the wrath of the gods. The power of the chief was often surrounded by taboo. It may be taboo for a commoner to look the chief directly in the eye, or to stand before them, to eat before them at a meal, or to enter their house. The chief might be subject to taboos themselves, not permitted to leave their house or be seen by commoners, or not allowed to feed themselves, requiring servants to feed them instead. Such taboos meant to set a chief or royal apart from society can sometimes make them a prisoner in their own home, effectively shielding the people from their leader becoming too ambitious.[2]

Many of the prohibitions found in the Mosaic covenant would count as taboos. Rules about what renders a person unclean and how to purify oneself abound. Moses himself is commanded by God on Mt. Sinai to remove his sandals, for he is on holy ground. Rules about approaching the Tabernacle

---

[2] See Graeber, David, and Marshall Sahlins. *On Kings*. HAU Books, 2018.

are rife with taboos. The Mosaic laws blur the lines between taboo and moral law, as there are clearly moral precepts in, for example, the Ten Commandments. Yet there are also laws about ritual purity that are not directly concerned with morality. Nonetheless, they are meant to foster a sense of community and a connection to God who is Himself the source of morality, and therefore have a moral weight of their own.

Taboos delineate the sacred and the profane. The sacred must be kept pure, and the profane kept at a distance to prevent contamination. Taboos apply to social hierarchies, regulating how one is supposed to address or approach a superior while designating certain castes, classes, and professions as unclean or impure. One who violates a taboo may face social sanctions ranging from scolding for impropriety up to and including execution. There may be laws regulating such matters, such as with incest or cannibalism. Yet taboos are not themselves laws in any formal sense. They serve as a form of social regulation that is carried out by society's members without requiring some external power to enforce it.

Taboos are typically enforced by shunning. A person who transgresses will have to make some reparation if they wish to be welcomed back into society. In some societies this could manifest as banishment, which was as good as a death sentence. To be cut off from society was to be cut off from all means of support. We are social creatures by nature; humans and humanity have survived because of mutual aid. Our interdependence makes us strong, and maintaining those social bonds is a matter of survival.

Even today, social sanctions can have their effect. Boycotts and strikes are organized sanctions against businesses that transgress some demand of social justice. Deplatforming can have a significant effect on someone's ability to reach others. This is often treated as an infringement of free speech, even though it occurs on private platforms and not in the public sphere, and conflates morality with legality. Yet while such complaints tend to show an ignorance of constitutional law, they do in fact point to the social infrastructure on which we all depend in our daily lives.

Honor

The flip side of taboo is honor. Codes of honor form social regulating apparatuses without requiring external enforcement. In fact, the demands of honor can often go against the law. It is also not morality, or something private like one's conscience. Honor is a kind of social currency. It can apply to the individual, their family, or their culture itself. It is intrinsically public: a person's honor determines how they are seen by other members of society. If one is seen as dishonorable, then people will shun them or avoid dealing with them. This can be especially dangerous in cultures where bonds of mutual trust are central to the distribution of resources.

Cultures of honor tend to arise in places where laws are not easily enforced. The social currency of honor serves to limit things like theft or cheating in places where enforcing such rules through force is difficult. The word "honesty" has the same root as honor— to be honest in one's dealings with others is to acquire honor for oneself.

Honor also regulates violence. It does not stop violence but can determine the conditions of its use. In battle, one is supposed to fight with honor: this may involve such things as showing mercy to a defeated opponent or giving them a chance to face you head on rather than through a surprise attack. But honor can also demand violence in certain situations. Dueling, for example, was a traditional way to defend one's honor, and continued to be practiced in Europe and the United States long after it had been outlawed. The Catholic Church spoke out against the practice throughout the Middle Ages, yet it continued to be seen as necessary to defend one's honor.

Honor is about knowing one's place in society and fulfilling one's social role to the highest degree possible. What brings honor to one person may be dishonorable for another with a different social status. To be honorable is to live up to a social ideal. To be dishonorable is to fail to live up to that ideal. Another word for dishonor is shame. Shame, like honor, is a public status. Where guilt is a private feeling, in which one personally feels the graveness of one's offense, shame is something externally placed upon one. Shame is not merely a result of one's own actions, but of one's surroundings. The actions of one person can bring honor or shame upon an entire family, clan, or culture.

The demands of honor can often be cruel and manifestly unjust. A woman who is raped, we should all be inclined to think, is not at fault for what happened to her. An injustice was perpetrated against her, and it is the perpetrator who should bear the blame. Yet in an honor culture, she would be seen as having been contaminated, made impure, and had shame brought upon her and her family. In some cultures, this leads to the practice of "honor killing," in which a woman is killed, often by a family member, to restore that family's honor. Even if we find such practices barbaric in our own culture, we are not entirely immune to such ways of thinking. It is unfortunately common for some to assume that a woman who is raped was somehow "asking for it" and for a man to see her as "spoiled goods." The act is seen as defiling her, making her less pure.

Honor can also lead to feuds. If a murder takes place, rather than appealing to some legal system, the family of the murder victim is honor-bound to retaliate by killing one of the killer's family. That family, in turn, is honor-bound to reciprocate. In places where such practices still prevail, people can often become prisoners in their own houses, unable to step outside lest they be killed.

Cultural theorist Kwame Anthony Appiah argues that moral revolutions happen with honor codes not by turning away from honor, but by appealing to a higher sense of honor. Because honor is public, there is always a wider public to whose sense of honor one can appeal. What is honorable to one culture may be appalling to another, and by encountering such reactions, one can be moved to see one's own culture through alternate viewpoints. The once-common Chinese practice of foot-binding is a good example. Women were expected to have their feet broken and bound at a young age to make their feet impossibly small. This was considered dignified and often required for her to find a suitable husband. The Catholic missionaries who came to China tended to try and integrate into the society and tolerate its cultural practices. Protestant missionaries, on the other hand, were standard-bearers for Western cultural practices, and expressed horror at foot-binding. This led many Chinese to see the practice as bringing dishonor upon their culture. Anti-foot binding societies sprung up across the country, in which people vowed that they would not bind their daughters' feet, and their sons would not marry any woman with bound feet. The practice died out within a generation of the missionaries' arrival. Though Protestant missionaries were remarkably unsuccessful in their attempts at religious conversion, they achieved great success in bringing about a cultural one.

As society becomes more complex and interconnected, different ideologies with competing value systems seek hegemony. They do this largely through honor and shame. Awards, medals, and tributes are given to honor people seen as having contributed something worthy of praise. Shaming is done by "making an example" out of someone or something. Thieves could be sent to the stockades in full view of townsfolk, and adulterers were made to stitch "A"s onto their sleeves or coats. Shame also had material consequences: commerce often depended on honor, and people would not do business with someone who had been shamed and dishonored, either by their own actions or by their family.

Our current age tends toward economic explanations of human motivation. Not only do we ascribe human actions to self-interest, but we tend to see that self-interest as materially rooted. That people may do things for honor or glory escapes us, or we may explain these things as mere cover for greed. It is certainly true that honor and glory are a kind of currency that one may spend on material wealth: Alexander of Macedon gained immense wealth from conquering the known world, but purchasing power was not his reason for doing so. He wanted his name to live on throughout the land and through the ages. Honor, like wealth, can be passed down from one generation to another, but unlike wealth, you can, as it were, take it with you.

Law

Honor can be a messy business. Even without devolving into a blood feud or a duel to the death, having to defend one's family honor can be a matter that favors the strong over the weak. Honor can often require the strength to defend it with violence. As such, what honor demands may be in contradiction to what justice demands. A solution to this can be found through a formal legal process: instead of two parties avenging one another, a third party carries out the punishment. This third party must in some sense represent the collective will. They are not one party among many, but representatives of the society carrying out its own justice on behalf of all.

Such justice can be dispensed in an even more even-handed manner if there are standard criteria by which to judge disputes. Such standards exist by custom in pretty much every society, but with the rise of civilization, such standards began to be codified and written down. One of the oldest such codes in the archaeological record is the famous Code of Hammurabi. Many of the penalties it prescribes strike us as harsh today. Theft was punishable by death, as was adultery (at least for women), perjury, and taking a slave outside the city gates. For slander, one could be taken before the court and have their forehead marked (presumably by cutting the skin). Barbaric as these penalties seem to us now, they are essentially taking what honor demanded and placing them in the hands of an independent court, rather than let them be resolved through blood feuds.

Legal codes developed along with writing and the state. However, not all law requires a state. The Jews had the Mosaic law well before establishing the kingdom of Israel or Judea. The law was what bound them together as a people. It was their covenant with God and with one another. The Catholic Church followed suit by establishing a system of canon law, which in turn came to influence common law throughout Europe. The Muslim legal code of Shariah likewise functions outside of the state apparatus, though it in turn has influenced the legal constitution of some states.

The modern nation-state is based on the concept of the rule of law. This means that laws are supposed to apply equally to everyone. The law itself is sovereign over everyone including those who make the laws. The problem is that law abstracts from real-life situations, and their impartial application can often fail to take mitigating circumstances into account. This is why courts are necessary for litigating such cases. Yet allowing this leniency also means that pervasive social biases affect the enforcement of laws. Laws are ostensibly objective but can also have discriminatory effects because they apply equal standards to unequal conditions.

Law objectifies relations by creating explicit processes and rules. It seeks to cut through the ambiguity of navigating social relations and deciding how to respond to transgressions. However, as societies become complex, so too does the law. Interpreting the law becomes an area of specialization.

Judges are of course required to judge the merits of a case. But when the law becomes too complex for the common person to understand, it becomes necessary for specialists to represent the parties involved and argue their cases for them, giving rise to the origins of what we now call lawyers and the legal profession.

Contract

With law comes contract. Where simple agreements can be upheld by mutual trust between the parties, contracts require enforceability. Contracts prevail when trust and honor cannot be depended upon. Under an honor system, one who does not keep their promises will become dishonorable and lose face in society. But where people are too anonymous for such an honor system to work, social sanctions become insufficient, and legal sanctions must step in.

The enforceability of contracts requires exact language whose meaning can be interpreted in court as no more and no less than what is intended. This leads to the development of legal jargon that requires a legal expert to interpret. Of course, it is not always practical to have an attorney present for every contract that is signed, while the contract itself is drafted by lawyers. This leads to a power imbalance where the person signing the contract rarely knows exactly what they're agreeing to; think of computer software's Terms of Service Agreement, which most people rarely bother to read.

In most cases, there is little harm done, because the terms of the contract are not particularly objectionable to either party. However, for many transactions, one is cautioned to "read the fine print." The unscrupulous can often trick people into deals where the signing party agrees to far more than they bargained for. While laws can be passed to reign in such predatory contracts so that legal recourse is available to people, the way people most often avoid being taken in by them is, strangely enough, the honor system. There are reporting systems such as the Better Business Bureau, or websites where people can read or write a review, in which people can warn others about businesses that take people in in this manner.

Even aside from the epistemic imbalance, there is often a power imbalance in contracts. The one agreeing to the contract may be doing so under desperate circumstances. This happens particularly with debt, from mafia loan sharks to payday lenders to the World Bank and IMF. Predatory deals in the past could lead one into indentured servitude, a step away from slavery. Today, employment is done by contract, with terms heavily favorable to the employer and employment being deemed "at-will." Unions attempt to counteract this by organizing to give the workers a voice at the negotiating table.

There is a reason the "deal with the devil" is such a popular cultural trope. The devil, unable to attack people physically, must rely on tempting people away from salvation so that he can possess their soul. The devil therefore acts as the ultimate predatory lender, offering whatever power or benefit the person asks for in exchange for their immortal soul. This plays out not only in the afterlife, but in the person's own earthly life, in which all the power and resources they've accumulated come at too high a cost, and everything around them falls apart. Such morality tales serve several purposes, but what is notable here is how it reflects the way predatory lenders so often operate in real life. For example, developing countries who took on IMF loans to improve their infrastructure often find themselves in a kind of devil's bargain where their resources get privatized and bought out by foreign corporations.

Our modern notions of freedom are founded upon freedom of contract. The worker agrees to work for the employer for a given wage under given conditions; the debtor agrees to take out a loan and pay it back at a given interest rate in a given timeframe; the renter agrees to pay the landlord a given monthly rent. The idea is that so long as neither party is coercing the other through force or fraud, it is a valid contract that no other party has a right to intervene in.

This is what passes for freedom under such a concept. Never mind the fact that social relations do not happen in a vacuum: the two parties exist within a social system that intrinsically creates a power imbalance between the two parties that greatly limits the freedom of one vis-à-vis the other. Attempts to address these systemic inequalities are decried as "social engineering," as though the existing order fell from the sky with no such engineering at all. Such thinking reaches its absurd logical conclusion in the modern libertarian movement. Things like eliminating age of consent laws or allowing hard drugs to be sold to children are not beyond the scope of what some are seriously advocating with a straight face.

Even among moderate and progressive liberals, there is often a sense that "consent" is all it takes to make something good, or at least not bad. The concept of "informed consent" may be applied, as with age of consent laws or predatory loans, but there is still an economistic thinking that people individually pursuing their own personal preferences, however much such preferences may be warped by social conditioning, is what is best for everyone. Or, if they see a reason for curtailing such transactional relationships, they are seen as a limitation on freedom, however necessary, in order to pursue some countervailing good, such as order or security. They may see such limitations as themselves contractual, part of the "social contract" to which we all implicitly agree to by participating in society. Rarely do we question whether this transactional notion of freedom itself might be skewed.

Bureaucracy

Law and contract form the basis of bureaucratic authority. Max Weber recognized three types of authority. There is traditional authority, in which authority is passed down through cultural patterns, such as priesthood or monarchy. There is charismatic authority, which centers around the personality of the individual, such as a cult leader, prophet, or leaders of social movements. Often charismatic authority will become traditional authority when the movements they found pass on to the next generation. The third kind of authority is called rational-legal or bureaucratic authority.

In this kind of authority, power is invested in the office of the person occupying it. They have a particular administrative role to play, and they are granted the legitimate power to carry it out. Where the traditional authority figure is seen as somehow embodying the tradition, the bureaucratic authority figure is merely expected to be competent and qualified to carry out the duties of their role. The authority lies in the position itself, not the individual, and if they step down or are dismissed the authority passes to the next person to occupy that position.

The position exists by law or contract, spelling out what their duties are, who they report to, who reports to them, and what procedures they must follow. Modern states are founded on such bureaucratic authority as laid out by their constitutions. Politicians occupy their positions for given terms after being chosen by democratic elections. They then delegate other positions to their staff, hired to fulfill specific duties. Through the political process, laws are passed establishing various state agencies, whose leadership is politically appointed. These leaders in turn hire others to fill the various positions necessary to run the agency. Administrative roles and duties are distributed throughout the agency to fulfill its stated mission as its leadership sees fit.

Private organizations are also established through bureaucratic means. The entrepreneur obtains a business license and creates an employment contract for those they hire. If they incorporate, they establish the organization's corporate responsibility to the shareholders. A corporate charter establishes the corporation as a legal person, to be treated as its own legal entity independent of its members and with the authority to act within the parameters laid out in the charter document. Everything from non-profits to publicly traded multinationals to towns and cities can be incorporated by such a charter.

It is not only the administrators that become numbers

in the system, but also those accessing their services. Customers, clients, users all become quantifiable data that are accounted for within the system. The collection of data is an integral part of the process. Transaction records, balance sheets, and inventories form the structure of bureaucratic life. As bureaucracy expands into every area of life, quantitative information becomes the air we breathe. Our very consciousness shifts toward the quantitative at the expense of the qualitative. Quantity becomes what is truly real and thus of value.

Capitalism apologists often appeal to the free market as the antidote to bureaucracy. Yet it is precisely with the growth of the market that we have seen the growth of bureaucracy.[3] The quantification that characterizes bureaucratic administration is integral to the market economy. The development of private firms required the management of employees. Taylorism and Fordism were developed to perfect this system of bureaucratic management, in which discrete, repetitive tasks are analyzed to find the most efficient workflow. The assembly line involved treating each worker as a cog in the machine.

The Soviet-style command economy is the typical foil to which free market advocates point. What they neglect to mention is the extent to which this economy was influenced by Taylorism and Fordism. The state took over the role of capitalist but kept much of the rest intact. Production quotas and five-year plans are hardly alien to the corporate world. Through these techniques adapted from the American

---

[3] See Graeber, David. *The Utopia of Rules: On Technology, Stupidity, and the Secret Joys of Bureaucracy.* Melville House Publishing, 2016.

corporate world, the Soviet Union and later China utilized them to rapidly industrialize. The Soviet system was simply a rival form of megamachine.

The shortcomings of such a system were certainly bureaucratic failures. In order to appease their superiors, lower-level administrators had incentive to over-report production numbers. This skewed data in turn went into calculations for future production quotas. The result was production becoming overly strained and resources being misallocated. Yet while such top-down meddling may rightly draw our scorn, we should not think ourselves to be so above it. The concentration of the world's resources in a tiny number of corporations puts the Politburo to shame. The same people tend to serve on multiple boards of directors, meaning that the number of people making the decisions for global production, marketing, and distribution is astonishingly small.

Markets

Neoclassical economics has conditioned us to think of markets as the natural order of things. Yet several historical contingencies were necessary to create markets in the first place, and even more to expand markets to their current global scope. Internally, mutual aid has traditionally thrived among local communities, while trade and barter have existed between communities. Markets were established in an imperial context first through the standardization of weights and measures, then through the introduction of coinage, with which occupying forces were paid. The coins were demanded back as tribute, creating a demand for them among the occupied people and giving them a value for which they were traded.

Social institutions have always governed the size and scope of markets, what could or could not be traded, and how resources were to be allocated. Markets were traditionally understood as a specific place. The marketplace was a place of social gathering where farmers could sell their surplus produce, artisans could sell their wares, and traveling merchants could sell goods and oddities gathered from far off lands.

Markets were for end products, the result of one's efforts in creating or acquiring them. Notably absent from the market was land. Land could be inherited, homesteaded, granted by an authority, or conquered, but not bought or sold. The closest thing to this would be if a farmer defaulted on a debt, in which case they might have to give their land over to their creditor (though they might just as soon sell their children into debt bondage).

Debt bondage was one of the great concerns for civilizations of antiquity. Debt had the ability to totally transform the world of social relations. What was inconceivable without debt was normalized within it. It could justify theft and violence and turn free people into slaves. Cancellation of debts was an important policy tool in the ancient world. The Law of Moses mandated a Jubilee Year every 49 years to cancel debt that had piled up. Great rulers could curry favor with the population to bring them onto their side with debt cancellation. Debt could also be alleviated through devaluing the currency, thus relieving debtors of some of the value of their debt. Sadly, this does not work when one's debt is owed in a currency other than one's own, leading to hyperinflation.

Usury was considered a hostile force against which societies fought vigilantly. Nearly every major religion includes some prohibition against usury. While there are varying definitions, at its core usury is the use of money to make money. Profit and interest were certainly known in the ancient world. A merchant would take out a loan to buy goods in one market that he knew he could sell elsewhere at a profit. The lender was taking a risk by lending out this money, so they sought an "interest" on the profit. A farmer might take out a loan because they had a poor harvest that year. If they had a more successful year the next year, they could pay it back, but if they didn't, they could be driven further into debt, leading to debt bondage. The farmer was not taking on debt to make a profit, but only to survive. Charging interest on such a loan was seen as an egregious theft. We see today in the mafia loan shark what the ancients saw in the usurer. And like the mafia, usurers could still manage to do business and carve out a niche for themselves in society, but they were viewed as social pariahs.

Usury lies at the core of capitalization. Put plainly, capitalization is the discounting of present value in expectation of future gain. Capitalization requires commodification, which requires privatization, which requires quantification. That is, if something can be quantified, it can be owned. If it can be owned, then it can be bought and sold. If it can be bought and sold, it can be done so at a profit. The same processes of quantification and manipulation are done by states in order to tax and regulate society. Capitalization as a privatized process unfolded from the late Medieval era until the present, during which more and more segments of society were commodified and traded on the market. The cyclical crises of capitalism are often solved by innovating with some new market to commodify. New forms of intellectual property, debt instruments, and abstract assets are invented in order to continue the process of capital accumulation. Collateralized debt options, NFTs, and cryptocurrency are just a few examples of such abstract assets. Capitalism seeks the endless creation of assets through which power can continue to be accumulated.

Is it any wonder, then, that the ancients were so wary of this force? Could they not perhaps sense the uncontrollable powers of such a beast if left to its own devices? They could see a use for the market, and accorded it its due, but with a watchful eye. The terrors such forces could unleash lay just beneath the surface, waiting to erupt if given the chance. It was a fire that needed to be contained.

That fire has gradually been unleashed upon the world and devoured everything in its path. The marketization of life is slowly commodifying everything it can about modern humanity. Not only is our labor time commodified, but so is our leisure time. We turn to gadgets and mass media to fill an isolating void in our social life in which a sense of community has been lost. Even where community is to be found, it has been commodified. Whether it's bars, coffee shops, concerts, or festivals, most places where people gather and socialize cost money. The justification for this is given to us by the system itself via the ideology of consumerism: choice is a virtue. We *choose* these commodities. What we do not choose is the social conditions of our choices. We partake of these commodities while our very lives have been commodified, and we have lost sight of what has been lost. We have an online simulacrum of community, but this too is mediated by the market. We are losing a sense of what value can mean outside of the market.

States

We turn, then, to states and their formation. Max Weber defines the state as the monopoly of the legitimate use of force. The state is the entity that gets to define which violence is legitimate or illegitimate. Violence carried out by state actors has legitimacy by default, while violence against the state — including defensive or retaliatory violence — becomes terrorism. Stateless societies are not necessarily egalitarian. They can have charismatic leaders, caste systems, patriarchal gender roles, or gerontocracy, but what they don't have is an institution with the authority to impose its will upon others through violence. To be stateless means that public decisions require the willing participation of everyone involved. With the institutional authority of the state the sovereign can say, "Guards, seize him!"

Crucial to the state is the supposition that the power invested in the rulers does not simply inhere in them specifically but in the office they hold. A charismatic leader may claim the loyalty of millions, but when they die, that loyalty dies with them. Only by instituting rules of succession can that power outlast them. The state is the abstraction of power from the person. A head of state, whether a monarch or a prime minister, holds power by virtue of an institution much greater than them.

Much like commercial institutions, the state possesses

an inherent identity, and like them, it has an internal logic directed toward its own perpetuation and expansion. States occupied a core position over a peripheral sphere of influence long before the capitalist mode of production emerged. Powerful core states would seek advantages through trade and conquest to exploit the resources of the weak periphery. A world system emerged in which different regions rose and fell in power over the centuries.

With the rise of colonialism, Europe re-emerged as the core for the first time since the Roman Empire, right around the time that a process of financial capitalization was beginning to transform the continent. Around this time, European states also began to transform with the Peace of Westphalia. Prior to this, states had territory and spheres of influence, but there was nothing like what we now call borders. A state's power extended as far as they could and were always seeking to expand more. With Westphalia, however, states reached an agreement with one another to define and recognize one another's borders. Thus began the territorially bound nation-state.

The principle of Westphalian sovereignty established an international system in which states large and small would have their borders and sovereign territory recognized by other states. It established a principle of non-intervention in the internal affairs of sovereign states. While this seemed to limit the expansionist aspirations of states on the continent, it simply relocated them further away, as the push to colonize the Americas was already underway. Why was indigenous sovereignty not respected? Because their land was not recognized as a state. Statehood then becomes the precondition for legitimacy. Becoming recognized as a state involves adhering to institutional norms around sovereignty. One must have bureaucratic authority over a geographically defined area that is upheld through a monopoly of violence, and which in turn recognizes the geographically bound authority of other states. To gain autonomy as a state requires the recognition of legitimacy by other states.

Statehood also grants a degree of protection to citizens. Hannah Arendt wrote extensively on denationalization as one of the primary factors by which a targeted group is denied their rights. She noted that under Westphalian sovereignty, nationality is tied to "the right to have rights." Even under the most authoritarian regime, citizenship makes all the difference in terms of legal protection. Even under the most liberal democracy, denying the right of citizenship is the most straightforward way of creating exceptions to one's guaranteed rights and establishing a targeted group as outside the sphere of human rights. The state becomes simultaneously the primary apparatus of control over others and the sole means of protection from a world dominated by states.

Sociologist C. Wright Mills observed that the power elite define the conditions by which one can join their ranks. They prop up a self-serving myth of meritocracy, wherein one must be highly intelligent or talented to become one of them. Yet the knowledge and talent one requires is not necessarily real wisdom, but only those criteria that the power elite created for itself. Here we see how the Westphalian system applies this to the world system. The conditions of statehood are necessary to achieve protection and sovereignty under a system defined by nation-states. It necessarily rules out both the classic forms of empire and the kinds of confederation that were always its greatest threat. Autonomous zones such as the Zapatista-controlled areas of Chiapas or the AANES territory of the Middle East (also known as Rojava) exist outside the parameters of such a system.

Horizontalism

The state limits the imagination of what society can be. The logic of the state conditions the minds of its leaders, intellectuals, jurists, enforcers, and ultimately its subjects. Yet the contradictions of such a system also produce dissidents. Some of these dissidents may seek to conquer the system and overwrite it with their own logic. Such is the move that authoritarians on both sides of the political aisle tend to make. Others seek to carve out a different kind of political space, resulting in autonomous zones, communes, and mutual aid networks. These entities lack the advantages that come with political legitimacy, yet by virtue of that very fact, they are often invisible to the system. A system based on bureaucratic authority and chain of command has trouble even conceptualizing horizontal movements that do not depend on the leadership of a single individual. We see this in the conspiracy theorists who blame figures like George Soros for the spontaneous actions of horizontal mass movements like Black Lives Matter.

These horizontal movements defy the logic of the state. Organizers bring new people into the movement through mass demonstrations. Such demonstrations show people that they are not alone in their grievances. As individuals and groups take to the streets, they connect to one another.

In these connections, they form affinity groups that plan various direct actions with one another. Different affinity groups may coordinate their actions with one another for certain actions, but they do not operate under a single command structure. This proves difficult for law enforcement to infiltrate. If they take down one affinity group, that's maybe a dozen or so people at most. In the 1960s organizations like the Black Panthers had leadership that state enforcers could take out and cripple the organization in the process. Yet with horizontal movements, no one person is that important. A few people may go down, yet more come to take their place.

The growth of such horizontal movement can take the system by surprise. The state is good at maintaining its authority by lopping off the heads of movements that oppose it, but when they are effectively headless they can overwhelm the system. Such movement is painfully slow. Its glacial pace can make it seem impossible that change might ever come. Yet such movement is the only means by which authentic, lasting change can ever come. It is only in the exercise of the collective imagination — the mass actions taken by those who can conceive of a world other than it is — that the world can ever truly realize these possibilities.

What applies to direct action applies to direct democracy as well. There is a continuity between the two. For democracy to maintain its character, it must remain activist in nature. That is, it must have as its objective the continual transformative liberation of society. Such was the case with the establishment of the participatory budgeting process in the Brazilian city of Porto Allegre. This process, whose model has been copied in various cities throughout the world, created neighborhood budgeting committees that met to discuss what they felt the priorities were in their community that needed addressing. They sent a recallable delegate to take their concerns to the budget committee to finalize a draft of the city's budget. The process is repeated each year. Crucial here is the direct deliberation involved: it's not just an up-or-down vote, but an ongoing conversation. This is what real democracy consists of. In this scenario the recallable delegate is not simply a "representative" in the parliamentary sense. They are not there to enact their own platform, but merely to convey the agenda that they were sent for. These are the kinds of structures that foster democracy as an ongoing movement — a process in which we collectively reimagine what society can be.

Decentralization is important here, as only in smaller groups can this kind of face-to-face deliberation take place. Yet decentralization does not coordinate mass action. Decentralization simply means there are multiple nodes that are not controlled by a single central one. What is needed is a *distributed* network, such that each node can coordinate across multiple other nodes. Localism is another valuable aspect but can likewise be misconstrued. Localism is important because the local population centers of a city or municipality have more concrete existence than national and state borders that exist as abstract legal facts. Participatory democracy is most needed in our immediate surroundings in which we are already participants. Yet this localism must be paired with global solidarity. Only by uniting with others far from us can we work toward common goals on a global scale. These connections help us learn from one another and guide our own institutions based on the successes and failures of others.

The integration of local municipalities is achieved through confederation. Confederations such as the Hanseatic and Lombard League were able to challenge the might of the Holy Roman Empire. The Iroquois Confederation was an inspiration for democratic reformers in North America. Confederation has always been the great alternative to empire. Where empire seeks to control, confederation seeks to connect. Where empire is founded on force, confederation is founded on solidarity. It is the form by which people collaborate to uplift one another in the face of hegemony.

Kenosis

States, empires, patriarchy, capital, class hierarchy, racial supremacy, and other systems of domination stem from a *will to power* that seeks to subdue the world and reshape it in one's own image. Nietzsche claimed that the world itself is Will to Power. Indeed, if one studies Darwinian evolution, it seems that the competitive struggle for survival is the driving force behind all life. "Survival of the fittest" is a phrase coined not by Darwin but by Herbert Spencer, a sociologist whose mechanistic, hierarchical view of nature and society became known as "Social Darwinism," the official doctrine of the ruling class from the Gilded Age, which saw the rise of eugenics, to World War II, when its ultimate consequences were laid bare in the horrors of the Holocaust. It survives in varying degrees of subtlety in disciplines such as evolutionary psychology, sociobiology, realist international relations theory, and neoclassical economics.

Such a view suggests its own kind of Logos, one in which

assertion of will and mastery over others becomes the driving force behind all things. Social relations serve instrumental purposes such as survival of one's genetic material or access to the means for survival but having no intrinsic value. The universe becomes pure instrumentality — a resource to be manipulated by the exalted ego for its own ends. This is a kind of anti-Logos: the Logos of the Fall. The Kingdom of God is the world organized according to the Logos, so this anti-Logos is the Kingdom of Satan. Indeed, when Anton LaVey was writing the Satanic Bible, he drew heavily from such Social Darwinist sources as Ayn Rand and Arthur Desmond, author of the white supremacist treatise *Might Is Right* under the pen name Ragnar Redbeard. LaVey was an avowed atheist who claimed he only glorified Satan as a symbol, but in so doing he captured the essence of the Satanic impulse which has guided the struggle for power throughout history. Such systems are rarely so honest as to self-identify as Satanic; instead they wrap themselves in the cross and the flag. Yet they subject such symbols to the same instrumental value as everything else — a mere means to their own quest for power. In doing so, whatever explicit values or beliefs they claim, their true worship is directed toward the Prince of this World. Some worship his power, but we all must submit to it. The battle with the Powers and Principalities of this world is long and protracted, and none of us can escape its clutches.

Where the Kingdom of Satan seeks domination, the path of kenosis seeks connection. Rather than a one-way imposition upon the world, it seeks to converse with the Logos, listening attentively to where it guides us. There is a kind of organic unfolding that happens when this is done. Life develops in this way, not as a master plan but as generative morphogenetic fields that unfold adaptively within the environment. Every creature is a center of activity within a web of relations that is itself a center of activity. It is interacting fields in every direction. Every emerging field shapes the activity of the fields within it. It is not that the whole is greater than the sum of its parts so much as the parts are determined by the whole. Where mechanistic processes involve building up wholes out of parts, organic processes involve the development of parts out of the whole, as we see in the development of life in the womb from a single egg into a fully developed organism.

Our constructed environment obviously cannot develop in the same way. We cannot plant a seed that will organically grow into a society with harmonious institutions. Yet we can pay attention to these natural processes and construct institutions along the same lines. We must deliberately plan and act in the world, and we can do so in a way that develops organically according to the Logos. We bring our plan into the world not as a complete blueprint, but as a generative concept that unfolds sequentially within an environment. It finds pathways to achieve its purpose, finding where it can contribute to the harmony of the whole and building accordingly. Rather than master planners, we become humble servants in the realization of organic wholes striving to be borne by way of our creativity.

Organic institutions are living institutions because they facilitate the life of the community. Our lives are lived within institutions and are directed by the wholes they create. A vital institution will manifest a greater degree of life, while a moribund institution will destroy that life. The Kingdom of Satan is fueled by the spirit of Thanatos. It destroys life in various ways, sometimes through institutionalized violence, but also by killing the soul of this world, reducing everything to instrumental value and hollowing out our lives of community, connection, and purpose. To renounce this spirit, we must rediscover the life-affirming spirit of the Logos and build according to its ways.

5

Power

A typical story about the rise of hierarchy goes something like this: Long ago our ancestors lived in simple foraging bands of extended families, in which everything was shared and there was no class or hierarchy. Then agriculture developed, tying people to the land and leading to social stratification. Slavery, patriarchy, authoritarianism, and class hierarchy all followed inexorably from there. As Rousseau put it, we rushed "headlong into our chains." But archaeological records show otherwise.

The birth of social stratification seems to be a matter of rigidifying social relations that had, up until then, been subject to continual reinvention. As far back as the Upper Paleolithic people participated in elaborate burial rituals indicative of status. Yet this did not seem to manifest as a kind of class inequality in which one group was exploited by another. The bones of this period indicate an equitable distribution of nutrition and health. Moreover, these elaborate burials were often centuries apart: if the people they commemorate were leaders of some sort, it seems they did not create any sort of dynasty that outlasted them.

What we find instead is a kind of seasonality to social structures, with complex societies forming and then disbanding. Large gatherings for seasonal festivals would bring people together from far and wide. Such gatherings required some sort of governance and organization, but it would not necessarily be a rigid hierarchy. Officials could be appointed for specific duties, but when the season ended, so did their duties. Confederations of different bands and tribes would come together to organize the functions of these gatherings.

This pattern extended from the late paleolithic well into the agricultural age. Stonehenge is one of the most famous examples of a structure that served as a seasonal gathering point for Neolithic farmers. Rather than agriculture leading inexorably toward hierarchical organization, it is rather this flexibility in social structure that seems to have been lost at some point.

This flexibility also seems to mark the difference between hierarchy and domination. Hierarchical formations may emerge and then dissolve, but domination is an enduring structure. Hierarchies based on charismatic or traditional authority needn't imply a right to dominate, but they can become coercive through the emergence of a dominator mentality. This mentality does not happen in a vacuum, but spreads throughout society. It appears as patriarchy, gerontocracy, class, and dominion over nature. All these forms of domination emerge together as part of a single underlying phenomenon.

This dominance is underpinned by the power of the sovereign. Sovereignty is supreme authority over a territory. It has been justified by appeal to divine power, by noble blood, or by social contract, but it is always fundamentally rooted in the belief in the right of one or some to dominate others. This domination is portrayed as necessary, whether according to some cosmic law or human nature or some mythic origin story.

Even egalitarian societies tend to have a sense of *being* dominated by forces beyond themselves. The gods and nature spirits demand supplication and can enact harsh penalties for denying them their wishes. As humans have always stood humbled and overpowered by the forces of nature, so too have they understood themselves to be dominated by the spirits of nature. Ludwig Feuerbach claimed that religion was a projection of a society's own ideal of itself. Yet in a sense, it is the reverse: kings have always drawn their power from the gods. The gods held power that people usurped for themselves only later.

Cities

Some of the earliest cities maintained an egalitarian structure. Early megasites, such as Nebelivka which dates to 4,000 B.C., show signs of having been governed by councils of equals. Residential quarters would be organized into neighborhoods with their own assembly house where people would gather and work out their business. There does not appear to have been a central assembly house for all the neighborhoods. A more effective method could have been for one assembly house to send a representative to another neighborhood assembly house to coordinate action between neighborhoods.

Such egalitarian institutions were by no means the rule, but they existed alongside more centralized and hierarchical forms of social organization. Central leadership allowed for decisions to be made quickly and carried out efficiently. What the leader ordered would be done, and the finality of their word could be relied upon to settle disputes. This may have its origins in hunting parties in which coordination required a top-down chain of command. Such a hierarchy would find its completion once the hunt was over. It may have changed once their target went from game animals to human settlements, though raiding parties could be more costly in terms of casualties than hunting parties. A single raid might yield a number of crops, tools, and artifacts, but a longer-term solution would be to simply conquer the settlement and establish one's group as the new ruling class.

The Neolithic village would not inevitably lead toward social stratification from within but could make a tempting target for those seeking to impose a stratified culture from without. Many early cities seem to have been walled fortifications designed specifically to ward off such a fate. Once conquered, however, those same walls come to guard the new rulers, who seek to strengthen their positions through the establishment of standing armies and command over the economy.

The words "city" and "civilization" both derive from the Latin "civitas," referring to citizenship. To live in a city was to be a citizen of a particular political order. City life was characterized by a division of labor that allowed for commerce and trade between artisans and merchants, bringing a dazzling variety of goods to the marketplace. Civilization can be roughly defined as a social organization defined by city life. Understanding civilization therefore requires an understanding of urbanism. Cities are planned as systems of diverse parts made to work together. Living quarters, businesses, and government buildings all must be designed to flow together harmoniously, connected by infrastructure to deliver water, power, transportation, and goods, and conversely to adequately remove refuse.

Urban planning reflects an intentionality in its design. It exemplifies priorities and values. Cities have been built around religious worship, international trade, tourism, governance, and a variety of industries. They can reflect egalitarian or authoritarian attitudes and aspirations. They can grow organically around the needs of their citizens, or they can be designed in a top-down manner to reflect the priorities of their rulers.

In the Middle Ages, cities became a kind of refuge from the despotism of the feudal manor. People could move to cities to become craftsmen and artisans, joining a guild as an apprentice and working their way up to master craftsman. The medieval commune was a vibrant center of life for its residents. The winding roads and pathways could be confusing for an outsider but had their own kind of order in accordance with daily life. Roads were narrow, difficult to send an army through, but belonged to all people in common. A nobleman might have been able to ride his horse through the street but would still have to share the road with the blind beggar. The city wall was a kind of membrane that kept the community together, the gates ritually closing at night and opening in the morning, as if the city itself were breathing. The alleys and nooks provided shelter from the elements. Houses were stacked together, providing mutual insulation, with the bottom floor acting as a shop from which people worked and sold their wares. Many cities banded together to form defensive and commercial alliances such as the Hanseatic League or the Lombard League, the latter of which managed to challenge the power of the Holy Roman Empire.

But the advent of gunpowder made city walls more vulnerable to siege, and this communal way of life gave way to a more authoritarian regime. Kings and princes consolidated multiple cities under the leadership of a capital. The autonomy of the city gave way to the power of the nation-state, with borders defended by national armies. Cities once again became territorial institutions serving the sovereign.

The narrow roads of the medieval town evolved into broad roads built for horses and carriages, with pedestrians forced to stick to the sides. Where medieval houses had shops on the bottom floor from which craftsmen conducted business, towns were now lined with shop windows. The separation of work and home would progress with the development of capitalism.

Empire

Planned cities can be useful for empires. They offer a template that can be duplicated in multiple places, with roads designed for soldiers to easily march through and defend. Beginning in the 19th century, cities began to be designed to minimize the effectiveness of mass revolts, so that police could readily put down an uprising. While the city could be a cooperative affair, it could also be a crucial base of operation for centers of power. It was built upon the division of labor, requiring the import of food from the countryside. A centralized state proved a useful means of maintaining a favorable flow of resources.

A clear chain of command proved valuable in the military. The hierarchical state was essentially a military state. The sovereign commanded armies who disciplined the population into strict obedience. Military conquest brought a flow of goods to the empire, while also offering a path to advancement for the soldiers, who were rewarded for their loyalty.

The regimentation of military discipline was applied to the population to produce great wonders. Backbreaking labor and loss of autonomy was the price to be paid for the monumental achievements by which these societies could realize some semblance of immortality. The wonders of the ancients are with us today, and those who built them must have felt a great sense of civic pride in their accomplishments.

Empires are stages for creative destruction. Their conquest leaves graveyards in their wake and subjugates others under their rule, yet they have a unifying effect on the places they conquer. Disparate cultures with their own developmental paths might have had trade with their neighbors, but a conquering empire connected far off lands and created vast trade networks. With the rise of an empire, not only were goods and resources brought together, but ideas and cultures.

Yet while this cultural blending would leave its mark upon the world wherever empires arose, all cultures were not treated equally. The conquering empire was a hegemon into which all other cultures had to be assimilated. The imperial power could adopt fashions and customs from their territories, but they inevitably held a sense of their own superiority. They dictated which values and ideas their subjects had to adopt and thus instilled in them their own ideals by which to measure themselves.

Power does not drive creativity: it harnesses it, manipulating it for its own purposes. The one technology that belongs to empire is the power to capture the creative energies of the conquered. Whether that power comes as absolute despotism or the rule of capital, it has always been a parasite upon the human imagination. Empire is built by turning war into occupation. New territories are conquered, then occupied, and eventually integrated into the system. After conquest comes colonization, in which war is continued through other means. Force is replaced with the threat of force. The more successful the conquest, the less this threat of force needs to be acted upon. A conquest is complete once the conquered come to identify with their conquerors.

This means integrating one's subjects into the empire. One way to do this is economically. The tribute demanded from the colonies could be paid in currency issued by the empire, often with the sovereign's face stamped on the coins. The tribute owed created a demand for the coins, and the stamp on them let people know who their sovereign was. The coins circulating as currency meant some people could make a handsome living for themselves and would know exactly who to thank. A wealthy merchant within the conquered territories had an implicit stake in the empire's continued existence.

Political power could be used in the same way. In some

cases, the sovereign of the conquered territory could be kept in power as a viceroy if they pledged their loyalty to the new sovereign. Yet many a conqueror felt they could not be trusted and would have them executed so they could install their own ruler. The new ruler could be a military commander who served them well, or it could be a local figure who they felt they could trust. Even if they went with the former option, they would have to find some local loyalists willing to participate in the occupation in exchange for power and prestige. No occupation can hope to succeed in the long term without buying off some people.

Sovereigns have long made grand displays of redistributing wealth to their people. A poor farmer might prostrate himself before the king and ask for forgiveness of his debts, and the king would agree, his generosity on display for all to see. Such displays of magnanimity would later become institutionalized in the modern welfare state, in which the generosity is depersonalized from the sovereign to the system, but the logic remains the same. The modern bureaucratic state legitimizes itself through public services. Thus, the violence of the state is justified by displays of generosity. Individual acts of violence are tragic but transient, but violence combined with care tends to perpetuate itself. This is how abusive relationships work, and statecraft is a matter of maintaining such a relationship on a mass scale. The state establishes its power through violence, and then maintains that power by creating dependency.

Another useful tactic is to divide and conquer. Creating a caste system that favors one group of people over others means that the privileged group is incentivized to maintain that privilege instead of uniting against their common oppressor. Commoners and workers living under the brutal thumb of the oppressor will still fight hard not to join the slave class below. Notably, this played a major role in the development of race as a social category under colonialism. Poor whites, some of them indentured servants themselves, looked down upon the black slaves who were at the bottom rung of society. This space between them made them enforcers of their own oppression as well as those below. Power finds its lifeblood in such divisions.

Propaganda is essential to the maintenance of legitimacy. The victor portrays their own side as honorable, magnanimous, and legitimate, while the previous regime was portrayed as illegitimate, cruel, weak, and degenerate. Propaganda can be spread through art, music, poetry, literature. It can be especially powerful in the form of monumental architecture. From pyramids to skyscrapers, nothing shows off one's might quite like an imposing building that towers over others. Statues may exalt important figures, but buildings speak to the glory of the empire. A "bigger is better" attitude pervades authoritarian society. Great power demands a great empire, and a great empire demands great wonders.

Myth can be one of the greatest forms of propaganda, precisely because it operates on a subconscious level. Myths often contain a kind of sedimentary layer of conflicts and battles. The overthrow of the Titans by the Olympian gods suggests a time when a new Olympian-worshiping culture defeated another culture that worshiped the Titans. In Hinduism, one finds a rivalry between worshipers of Vishnu, originating from the Vedic culture of the Aryans, and followers of Shiva, with its origins in the native Dravidian culture. Rather than conquest, there is a kind of back-and-forth in their mythology in which one god will prostrate themselves to the other, recognizing them as the supreme god, which the other side will counter with another myth explaining this gesture away and showing why it is actually their god who is the supreme deity. The old gods may be subordinated, but their continued worship can be a form of subtle resistance, in which a battle of the psyche does what a battle of swords cannot.

It may even be said that authoritarianism comes first from myth before it finds its way into social organization. Stateless societies still conceive of themselves as subject to the coercive power of the gods, who in many cases were not so much worshiped as appeased. Kingship is, in a sense, the human attempt to become a living god. Sometimes this would be carried out through acts of arbitrary cruelty. The phenomenon of human sacrifice seems to occur most prominently in early states whose ability to govern was weak and therefore reliant on intimidation and fear. Earthly power was seen to derive from some heavenly power. When Christianity emerged in the Roman empire, this divine power took on a more demonic dimension. Satan tempts Christ with power over all earthly kingdoms. Yet there was also a sense that this power was not to be trifled with. For this reason, St. Paul frames it as a spiritual battle, in which rather than fight against the state directly, Christians were to resist the Powers and Principalities of this world. He also tells them that no kingdom has been established without God's permission. This is in accordance with the idea that God does not cause evil but permits it so that greater good may be accomplished. The kingdoms of the world are ruled by the Prince of this World, but his reign is already doomed by the coming of the

Son of Man, who will overthrow him and his kingdoms in the end of days.

Nationalism

However hegemonic, an empire can never completely overpower the human drive for autonomy and self-determination. The organic bonds of family and community will always be more real and exert a greater demand upon our loyalties. In many cases, the empire will leave these intact, so long as they have access to their resources. Yet in exploiting these resources, they can create upheavals in traditional communal bonds. The forces of occupation demand not only their resources but their labor. Slavery is one method for achieving this, but instead of owning the people, conquerors own the land and make the people work it for a living. Yet the land has a long memory. Stories are passed from one generation to another of the way things once were.

The more people are integrated under the hegemony of empire, the more they seek to hold onto their cultural heritage. The memories passed from one generation to another become a source of strength and courage for a subjugated population. Their customs, rituals, and creeds form a basis of identity, and within a conquered society whose way of life has become a commodity, identity becomes increasingly important.

What is today called "identity politics" is the logical conclusion of a world constituted by global hegemony and commodified relations. The uniqueness of one's culture becomes something to be tightly guarded. Often this defensiveness takes on revisionist tones that assume a kind of cultural isolation; on the contrary, even the relatively autonomous Neolithic village would have had cultural exchange with its neighbors. Yet such sentiments are a response to very real injuries and injustices, where one's traditional clothes, music, and sacred rituals become commodities to be consumed by their conquerors, even as one's own way of life is demolished and uprooted.

We must not underestimate the symbolic dimension of conquest and empire. The destruction or profaning of cultural symbols is one of the conqueror's favorite tactics. We see in places like the United States, Canada, and Australia the extent to which conquerors will go to eliminate the culture of those they seek to subdue. Efforts to retain their culture become acts of resistance, while the efforts of the colonizer to appropriate those symbols for themselves becomes new ways to perpetuate that colonization.

Not only can maintaining cultural identities serve as a form of resistance, but so too can forging new identities. The Ghost Dance movement of the late 19th century became a rallying cry to unite disparate Native American tribes in resistance to US occupation. Tribes that had previously fought one another were brought together by the prophetic religious movement in resistance to their common oppressor. Similar millenarian movements could be found in the Boxer Rebellion, or more recently in the Rastafari movement. And while such movements are typically unsuccessful in their political aims, they manage to embed themselves in the cultural imagination in ways that have lasting consequences.

Reclaiming traditional identity can be a powerful act of

defiance, yet in the process, there is a tendency to relive old rivalries and feuds and enact cruel vengeance upon others. The bitter memories of one's own people can be ample motivation to create bitter memories for others. Nationalism may first arise as a hope for liberation but can quickly sour into an authoritarian nightmare. There is no inhabited corner of the world that has not been touched by conflict, conquest, and oppression.

Beginning with the Peace of Westphalia, nation-states as we know them began to emerge. Westphalian sovereignty, as it came to be known, meant that a state was sovereign over its own internal affairs, and was expected in turn to respect the sovereignty of other states. "Internal affairs" were in turn defined by national borders, themselves an innovation. Previous states had territories, which were essentially as far as they could make their influence felt, but having a territory legally demarcated and respected by an international system was entirely new. This meant that those seeking freedom and autonomy were incentivized to establish a nation-state that would be recognized by other states.

Anti-colonialist sentiments can quickly turn into nationalism. Nostalgic appeals to one's ancestral homeland can become chauvinism for the Fatherland. Painful memories of past conflicts and humiliations can bubble up into violent outbursts of racism and xenophobia. A sense of solidarity among one's people can become a sense of superiority and supremacy.

We can see this process unfolding today in India, where a Hindu nationalist government seeks to undo the "foreign influence" of Christianity and Islam. India is home to almost 32 million Christians and about 195 million Muslims. Both groups have ruled India at different times, and both have plenty of blood on their hands. Yet these groups have also established lives and communities of their own and become part of the fabric of Indian society. When India gained independence, two predominantly Muslim areas split off and became Pakistan and Bangladesh. Yet as is all too common with nation-states, the national borders crossed areas that shared cultural history. Regions like Punjab, Jammu, and Kashmir cross the border between India and Pakistan, and ongoing territorial disputes reflect a long and conflicted past. Many Hindus carry bitter memories of the Muslim Mughal empire that once ruled over them, and now we find the Indian government encouraging mob violence against Muslims with nationalistic rhetoric portraying Hindus (and to a lesser extent Buddhists and Jains) as the "true" Indians.

Identitarianism can take on isolationist or expansionist dimensions, sometimes simultaneously. One must first in some way secede from the existing international order before they can begin to remake it according to their own designs. We see this in the Axis powers of World War II, each of which had seen a nationalist furor bring tyrannies to power out of feelings of national embarrassment, and from this nationalist furor, they sought to gain new territory for themselves: Italy invaded Ethiopia; Japan invaded China; and Germany invaded most of Europe. To do so required first a rebellion against the world order represented by the League of Nations and the Versailles Treaty.

Yet this same nationalist fervor can also lead an imperial power to disown its declining empire. We can see this in the US and Britain. The post-war world order brought the US to an unprecedented level of power, leading the self-proclaimed "free world" against the Soviets and their allies. NATO enlisted other countries under US-led military leadership and the Bretton Woods institutions created a financial world order that favored US interests. Through the CIA, dollar diplomacy, and the largest military the world had ever seen, the US created a new kind of empire. Starting around the 1970s, this world order took a particularly aggressive turn toward market liberalism through a series of trade deals, culminating in the controversial North American trade deal known as NAFTA.

The neoliberal world order was driven by Western corporate interests. It allowed them to exploit weak labor laws to build factories that offered low wages, and use a local labor force to manufacture their own products. Those products were shipped back to the US as cheap consumer products, crippling the power of labor unions and subverting labor and environmental regulations. National laws to support one's own population were overturned by this free flow of capital. There was a significant left-wing resistance to this global world order, including the famous "Battle of Seattle" in 1999. Yet just as this alter-globalization movement was taking off, the terrorist attacks of September 11 brought a cold chill upon it. Soon America had a new mandate: to defeat the forces of Islamic terrorism. In the name of the War on Terror, the US launched ill-fated wars in Iraq and Afghanistan that have tied up the US military in the Middle East and central Asia ever since. As these "forever wars" dragged on, not only the left but many on the right began to question this world order that they had once led.

Into this environment emerged Donald Trump, promising to "Make America Great Again," a slogan first used by first-wave neoliberal Ronald Reagan. Calling NAFTA "the worst trade deal in the history of trade deals" and capitalizing on the complicity of both parties in this neoliberal world order (especially his opponent Hillary Clinton, whose husband signed NAFTA, and who led a hawkish state department under Obama), he presented himself as a populist hero, defying the "globalists" who had ruined this country by eroding national sovereignty and made America the world police for an order whose benefits didn't trickle down to ordinary Americans. At the same time, he promised to bring the force of the state against a perceived degeneracy in the country, signaling that white Christian conservatives were the real Americans, and that he was on their side. He raged against immigrants — particularly Mexicans and Muslims — as well as the "cultural Marxism" of anti-racism, LGBTQ+ rights, and multiculturalism.

An irony of being at the heart of a world empire is that people displaced by that empire's own policies and conquest end up immigrating to one's own country. This influx of immigrants ends up making one's own citizens feel that their own land no longer belongs to them. They often feel "invaded," even though these immigrants are often there because the conquering nation displaced them from their own home. Their anger over immigration is often directed at "global elites" in what is almost invariably thinly disguised antisemitism. This conspiracism springs from a sense that what is wrong with the world is not some confluence of interpersonal forces but rather the deliberate machinations of some hidden cabal. In fact, the word "cabal" is derived from the Kabbalah, an esoteric system of Jewish mysticism.

Much could be written on antisemitism itself, and the

scapegoating of the "International Jew" and related tropes in which they are portrayed as a covert group of elites orchestrating world affairs. A great deal of resentment against the problems of capitalism becomes personified in the form of this "global elite." They act as a kind of sacrificial lamb for the sins of capitalism. Antisemitism is a peculiar type of prejudice that stands out from others in the way it figures into conspiracy theories. There are other ethnic groups with an overachieving "model minority" status such as Jains in India or the Chinese diaspora, but these groups have not inspired the same kinds of conspiracism as the Jews.

The history of the Jewish people is one of being scattered among nations. Yet bound by this common history and a shared covenant, they have maintained strong communal bonds across borders. Mutual aid networks between these disparate communities led to suspicions of dual loyalty, and the "international Jew" arose in the popular imagination. Brought up in the study and interpretation of the Torah, Jews enjoyed a high literacy rate, which gave them an edge in bureaucratic professions such as banking and law, as well as a lively scholarly tradition. This brought them close to the centers of power, with princes and other nobles using their services.

At the same time, in the Christian world, there was a great amount of religious antipathy toward the Jews, with church leaders teaching that they were cursed for the grave sin of deicide, collectively bearing responsibility for the killing of Christ, re-enacted every year in the popular Passion plays. This seething resentment, combined with the relative isolation of the Jews, led to widespread speculation, including rumors of secret blood rituals in which children were killed. This "blood libel" as it came to be known, became a rallying cry among the masses during great purges known as pogroms. The church largely discouraged this belief, yet there continued to be stories of children that had disappeared and were rumored to be victims of this blood sacrifice. These children were often venerated as folk saints.

The church had a paradoxical position: on the one hand, they taught a faith that defined itself largely against the Jews who had rejected their savior; on the other hand, they owed their religious heritage to these same people, whose God they believed to be the same God revealed to them in Christ. Moreover, as the largest formal institution in the world, it required a great deal of administrative and financial help just as princes and nobles had, and often turned to the Jews who were so well-suited to this work.

Jews learned that they were safest close to the centers of power and away from the masses. Yet their aristocratic benefactors could readily turn on them and release them to the angry crowds as a scapegoat for their own failings as leaders. They formed their own administrative class that clung close to the elite but could never actually occupy formal positions of power. Their administrative associations gave Jews an increasing role in the modern world, which was increasingly characterized by bureaucratic and financial power. The Jewish banking family known as the Rothschilds rose to prominence not only as financiers to the great European powers, but also serving in a great diplomatic role. The financial integration of Europe around this time also led to a diplomatic integration resulting in a period of relative peace between the powers that lasted until the first World War.

At the same time, the Jewish scholarly tradition underwent

its own modernization. The Jewish Enlightenment arose as part of the broader Age of Enlightenment sweeping Europe, emphasizing rationalism, secularism, and republican values. Jewish intellectuals sought integration into the emerging bourgeois society while still maintaining a sense of identity. Yet others sought a refuge for their people, giving rise to the Jewish nationalist movement known as Zionism that sought a Jewish homeland in Palestine.

Through secularism, nationalism, finance, diplomacy, academia, and law, Jews became associated with all things modern, especially with the rise of the modern bureaucratic nation-state. They became linked in the popular imagination with other modernizing influences such as the Jesuits or the Freemasons, or the short-lived Bavarian Illuminati. Modernity was a deeply destabilizing force, uprooting traditional ways of life, and its afflictions were blamed on these organizations, who were pictured as plotting in secret and orchestrating world events. These groups came to be synonymous with a nefarious group of "global elites." Today, words such as "globalists" or "elites" serve as dog whistles for these groups, often with the image of the international Jew at its center.

Class Struggle

A major political philosophy of global significance was born from the mind of secular Jew Karl Marx. Writing a generation after Napoleon had emancipated the Jews in Europe, Marx was a learned scholar in fields such as philosophy, history, and economics. He saw history as driven by the forces of class struggle, with capitalism embodying certain internal contradictions, creating an intrinsic instability it must always seek in vain to rectify. Rather than the conspiratorial views that centered Jews and secret societies, Marx's analysis saw class interests as guiding world events.

The bourgeoisie, having risen from under the thumb of feudal aristocracy, were now the ruling class. Their class interests were not a secret conspiracy, but a natural outgrowth of their relationship to the means of production, which they shared even while in vigorous competition with one another. The dispossessed proletarian class, who had only their labor to sell, held revolutionary potential as the people who not only worked in the factories but made and fueled the engine of industrial progress.

Marxism had a peculiar relationship with modernity. Though the rising exploitation and regimentation of daily life under capitalism had already come under great scrutiny by Marx's forbearers such as Robert Owen and Henri de Saint-Simon, Marx styled his critique as a scientific rather than moral one. Modernity was defined by the capitalist world order, and he predicted the eventual fall of capitalism and rise of socialism based on a dialectical movement of historical forces immanent within capitalism itself.

Because of this, Marx saw capitalism as a progressive force. Rather than hearkening back to a previous time, he saw the task of socialism to be one of bringing out its internal contradictions by further revolutionizing the forces of production while building a working-class movement to eventually seize the means of production. Marxism thus operated as an internal critique of modernity, while pushing the forces of modernity to their logical conclusion.

This philosophy was carried out in several revolutions of the 20th century, most notably Russia. Initially there were some impressive experiments in direct democracy: the "soviets" from which the Soviet Union derived its name were worker's councils through which workers could control the means of production and have a voice in their local communities. Yet they were soon overpowered by the directives of the party, who had an agenda of nation-building. The party created five-year plans that rapidly industrialized the country, making it a formidable enemy of the NATO forces led by the US. Yet in the process it became a form of state capitalism, with the state taking on the role of the profit-seeking capitalist.

The logic was that the forces of production had to be unleashed in order to accelerate the contradictions of capitalism. This acceleration meant the uprooting of traditional ways of life. Religion especially was treated as a leftover superstition that had to be overcome to pave the way for the new socialist man. Ethnic groups seen as "backward" were "re-educated" in a manner not dissimilar to what happened to the indigenous peoples of the Americas and Australia. We see this happening even today in China's Xinjiang region. Colonization and exploitation took on new guises and justifications under an ideology that was meant to oppose these things.

It must be said that Marx cannot be held fully responsible for the path that Marxism took in the past century. He believed in democracy: his idea of a "dictatorship of the proletariat" was never meant to be an actual dictatorship, but an expression of the power of workers governing themselves. Yet he is not entirely blameless. While perhaps not authoritarian per se, he was a strong promoter of centralization. His belief in a vanguard party led to a kind of hegemonic mindset in which instructing the masses in correct ideology became more important than listening to their struggles and working out collaborative solutions. What Marx said with subtlety, Friedrich Engels would say more bluntly: his essay *On Authority* handwaves the objections of the libertarian left by insisting that all production involves authority because of the coordination required. He claimed that a cotton spinning mill requires authority because workers would have to work in unison at fixed times, as though the workers could not work such things out for themselves or even choose to innovate with the process of production.

Most problematic was Marx's developmental mapping of history, in which different eras were divided into different modes of production that advanced in logically defined stages. He derived this map from American anthropologist Lewis Henry Morgan, whose modernist schema saw an evolution of societies from primitive hunter-gatherer bands to modern Western civilization at its peak. Marx stretched this evolution further and saw socialism coming next, with communism as its apotheosis. This is the source of accelerationist tendencies in Bolshevism and other authoritarian socialist movements that insist upon mobilizing the "forces of production," bringing people under the power of the megamachine in ways often mirroring Western colonialism. Marxism was only able to make headway in anthropology by dropping its ahistorical framework, which did not hold up when examining the rich variety of social formations. Only when Marxism is decolonized of its Western modernist assumptions can its liberatory potential be truly realized.

Police

The ruling class cannot maintain its power without enforcers. In the modern state, this is done by police. To understand the history of the police, it is necessary to disentangle the police as an institution from policing as an activity. Throughout history, societies have had some form of policing without an institutionalized police force. The most common form of policing is self-policing: Communities police themselves by looking out for their neighbors. Even in societies that have a professional police force, this is still the primary means of protection. The presence of others is often enough to dissuade people from doing things that might arouse suspicion or provoke a reaction. Jane Jacobs emphasized the importance of "eyes on the street" as the most basic security measure. Yet what is genuinely important is not the presence of people but the trusting bonds of community. Communities must have familiarity, with neighbors who know each other and see each other on a regular basis. Such communal bonds cannot be imposed from the outside; they require the organic unfolding of public space.

Law enforcement as a distinct profession has its genesis as some external authority over the community. Soldiers have traditionally performed this task. Conquering a territory is futile without occupation. Where the security of a community can be achieved by the community itself, sovereignty and occupation require enforcement. The sovereign requires loyal soldiers to carry out their agenda. These soldiers are stationed in the community not to protect the people but to protect the power of the sovereign. They may "protect the peace," but only insofar as threats to peace are threats to the sovereign. Their purpose is to prosecute crimes against the state, not against the people.

In the Middle Ages, feudal lords would hire a "shire reeve," a magistrate charged as manager of the manor and overseer of the peasants. This person would maintain the compliance of serfs and peasants, ensuring that they continued producing for the lord and abided by their dictates. It is from this position that we get the modern word "sheriff," which is known to us through the tales of Robin Hood and the Sheriff of Nottingham.

The overseers under America's plantation system carried out similar duties in upholding the slave economy. When a slave escaped, they were caught by a slave patrol. Meanwhile in the industrial North, the proletariat was prone to strikes and upheavals that threatened the profits of the capitalist class. Security forces such as the infamous Pinkertons were hired to break these strikes and bring labor to heel. Despite popular belief, these were not the first modern police forces. That distinction belongs to the Paris Police Prefecture organized by King Louis XIV of France to protect his absolute rule. The principle, however, remains the same. It is the armed enforcement required to carry out systems of exploitation and oppression.

The modern police force is essentially a standing army. What occupying armies do abroad, the police do domestically. The increased militarization of the police in recent years has driven this point home. Today's police are equipped not only with the latest assault rifles and body armor, but also tear gas, flash-bang grenades, sonic cannons, and even tanks. Some politicians on both sides of the political aisle will gladly fund these arsenals, believing that it is the people, not the state, that cannot be trusted with guns.

Policing includes several functions, including patrolling, investigation, apprehending suspects, interrogation, and crowd control. It is this last function that was key to the rise of the modern police force. With the rise of capitalism, unrest among the workers became a growing concern that disrupted the process of capital accumulation. Having a sheriff to arrest people was no longer enough. An organized armed force was required to put down rebellions and force workers back into the factories. From simple clubs to modern "less than lethal" methods like tear gas and rubber bullets, various means were devised to crush social movements and make society safe for capital accumulation.

Those involved in social movements become special targets for investigation and harassment. Even if they do not have enough evidence to convict prominent activists of a crime, they can conduct raids on their houses, pull them over randomly, arrest them on spurious charges, and detain them for non-existent violations. That such charges will not hold up in court is beside the point: the aim is to intimidate those who would rise up against the system. The convictions they obtain are but one subset of the vast system of repression they uphold.

Where past empires had armies enforcing the will of the sovereign, the modern nation-state is supposed to be based on popular sovereignty and consent of the governed. This enables the conception of the police as "public servants." In theory, they serve a government of, by, and for the people. This fiction obscures the power of vested interests, the various tools for suppressing the voting power of the people, and the intrinsically undemocratic implications of representative government. The state is inherently a structure of class domination that always serves the material interests of the ruling class. The more unequal a society, the more it depends on brute force to maintain that hierarchy. As neoliberalism tightens its grip upon the world, we see historically unprecedented levels of inequality, and along with it, an expansion of the security state. The invisible hand of the market becomes a visible fist in the form of the police.

This is not to say that the police never stop the "bad guys" as they claim to do. In any prison you will find plenty of rapists, murderers, and other violent offenders. Sometimes they will even go after members of the ruling class. Corrupt politicians, white collar criminals, and sometimes even police officers themselves are occasionally subject to official investigations that lead to arrest and prosecution, though often only because of strong public pressure. At their best, they simply carry out the dictates of the state, and serve the ruling class only in the abstract as a function of carrying out their duty.

On paper and in a properly functioning nation-state, the police serve the state as an institution rather than becoming a violent rogue agency. When the latter happens, as we have observed in recent years, there is a slide into fascism, with which the police share a common interest. The presence of police does not make a society fascist, but police are intrinsically a fascist force within society. A society can be considered fascist to the extent that it gives their police free reign to enact violence against their enemies. Fascism appeals to them by removing the checks on their power required to maintain liberal democracy and unleashing them on dissenters and targeted minorities. When fascism is ascendant but has not yet fully taken power, police will often collaborate with fascist gangs, allowing the latter to do the dirty work for them while they look the other way.[4]

Fascism

Fascism arose in the context of a battle against both liberalism and anti-capitalism. Where antisemitic conspiracy theories posited an international Jewry manipulating world events, Marx sought to mobilize the international working class as an engine of history. Those who clung to traditional ways of life saw an onslaught from all corners. The Rothschilds represented the liberal capitalist order that was uprooting traditional values and supplanting them with the logic of the market, while Marx represented the forces of revolution that threatened to overthrow systems of loyalty to family, nation, and traditional authority and replace them with class solidarity. As disparate as these interests may seem, they were all connected in the conspiratorial mind. Both liberalism and Marxism were viewed as disruptive forces against tradition, and both could be somehow tied to the nefarious Jewish world conspiracy. In the reactionary mind, both capitalism and communism were corruptions of a racial order based on loyalty to one's own people.

This worldview was brought together in a forged document

---

[4] In my years living in Portland, whenever the Proud Boys would come to town and were greeted by anti-fascist protesters, the police would let them brawl with bear mace, batons, paint guns, and all manner of other weapons, and only once the Proud Boys left would they declare an unlawful assembly and arrest the anti-fascists.

call the *Protocols of the Learned Elders of Zion*, purporting to lay out a Jewish plot for world domination, involving Freemasons, public education, the spread of atheism, usurious economic exploitation, and the subversive influence of Marxism. The Protocols remained relatively obscure until copies were brought west by fleeing White Russians, claiming that a Jewish plot had brought the Bolsheviks to power.

This conspiracy theory spread throughout the West. Henry Ford distributed 500,000 copies of the *Protocols* throughout the US. In Germany, the document influenced antisemitism among the Volkisch movement and mystical Aryanism, ultimately culminating in the Nazi party. Hitler saw in the *Protocols* a convenient scapegoat for Germany's humiliating defeat in World War I. The Jews, he contended, were a fifth column who had manipulated the war to bring Germany to its knees through the reviled Versailles treaty and the rise of Bolshevism. He also saw Jewish influence behind the communist uprisings within Germany under the Weimar Republic. He promised to bring Germany back to its former glory by defeating the forces of Judeo-Bolshevism, the enemy within.

Scholars struggle to define fascism. Marxist scholars have sought to define it by its class character as a petit-bourgeois movement seeking to usurp power from the wealthy hautebourgeoisie while also consolidating their own power over the proletariat. While there is some basis in this, fascism can sometimes present itself as a working-class movement like Marxism while appealing to conspiracism over class analysis. At the same time, fascism can present itself to the capitalist class as the only bulwark Marxist revolution in times of economic crisis and social upheaval. It can present itself as both anti-capitalist and anti-socialist, traditional and revolutionary, elitist and populist.

Fascism needn't necessarily adopt an explicitly racialist ideology as the Nazis did. What is important is that it draw a line between insiders and outsiders, such that the insiders are empowered to violently oppress the outsiders. Antisemitism may not always be explicit either, but it is inevitably implicit in the kinds of conspiracy theories by which whatever the present situation is explained. Even Jewish far-right movements can appeal to antisemitic tropes. Benjamin Netanyahu, for instance, has denied German responsibility for the Holocaust,[5] and his son Yair has accused George Soros of orchestrating Israeli opposition to the far-right Likkud party.[6] Zionism can be quite complementary to antisemitism, offering other nations a place to send their Jews.

People can often be confused by these apparent contradictions. The fascist gang known as the Proud Boys was at one pointed headed by an Afro-Cuban man named Enrique Tarrio and accepts other non-white recruits. Because of this, many in the media have been hesitant to call the movement white supremacist despite its promotion of conspiracies about white genocide and the "Great Replacement" theory. While non-white figures such as Vietnamese American pseudo-

---

[5] Botelho, Greg. "Israeli PM Benjamin Netanyahu Criticized for Saying Holocaust Was Mufti's Idea, Not Hitler's." *CNN*. Cable News Network, 22 Oct. 2015. Web. 17 May 2022.

[6] Sokol, Sam, and Ran Shimoni. "Soros, Nazis and Epstein: Yair Netanyahu Takes the Stand in Activists' Libel Suit." *Haaretz.com*. Haaretz, 24 Apr. 2022. Web. 17 May 2022.

journalist Andy Ngo support their organization, it seeks to brutalize immigrants, minorities, LGBTQ+ people, and anyone seen as subversive to their vision of Americanism.

How can such people support that same oppression that might just as easily be directed against them? The answer lies not in some logically rigorous definition of who is in and who is out. Those who join them in bullying others get to be part of their in-group. If one does not wish to suffer their wrath, they can join in on the bullying and become one of them. It is essentially the attitude of the schoolyard bully politicized into a mass movement. Conspiracy theory is the ideology that justifies their sense of oppression; bullying is the praxis by which they justify their own superiority.

The delineation of in-group and out-group is fundamental to setter colonialism. Settler colonialism involves the displacement of existing populations to make way for one's own people. Where the immigrant seeks accommodation in their new home, the settler seeks to remake it in their own image. Settler colonialism contains the seed of fascism, and in fascism it reaches its apotheosis. The genocide of Native Americans under the mantle of Manifest Destiny directly inspired Hitler's *Lebensensraum*.

Fascism involves an obsession with "degeneracy." Degeneracy is defined in terms of deviation from social norms. These norms are understood in terms of cultural hegemony and rigid gender roles. Obsessive fretting about ideals of manhood pervades fascist thought, and men who oppose them are portrayed as effeminate or unmanly. Manhood is seen in terms of willingness to inflict violence against others. Empathy and care for others are seen as signs of weakness.

Conspiracism, racism, bullying, and toxic masculinity do

not constitute fascism by themselves, but combined they form the essential framework. Yet trying to strictly define what is and isn't a fascist movement largely misses the point. Fascism is not so much an ideology with strict boundaries as an authoritarian tendency that can creep into public discourse. This "fascist creep" is a process by which this tendency spreads itself and pushes the Overton window in its menacing direction.

The fascist creep seeks a platform for ever more extreme positions that make their way into mainstream discourse. One may start with complaining about illegal immigration and border security, then otherize the immigrants themselves by portraying them as a criminal element that is dangerous to society, then call for open violence against them and justify genocidal policies against them. Each step is a shock at first that then becomes normalized by the next shock. Society does not fall to fascism all at once, but through this series of shocks that shift the ground from under one's feet.

Fascism takes advantage of the intrinsic weaknesses of liberalism. Liberalism promotes the free exchange of ideas as a sacred value. Yet this marketplace of ideas only works so long as people argue their ideas in good faith. Bad faith arguments are a staple of fascism: the fascist doesn't care if they're caught in a lie, because they have no need for consistency. All that matters is that they manage to induce their feelings of outrage and wrath in others. If a lie is repeated enough, people will start to believe it. The fascist does not seek to know objective truth. They merely posit what would have to be true in order to justify what they plan to do. They do this all while appealing to the liberal doctrine of "free speech." They don't care about defending their ideas so long as they can make the conversation about their right to express them.

For all its evasive tactics, fascism can also be surprisingly honest about its ambitions. Whatever plausible deniability they may try to invoke, fascists are quite clear about who their targets are, and they seek a world without them. Fascism takes refuge in audacity, and institutions trained in the norms of liberal democracy often have trouble taking such bluntness seriously. Authoritarian regimes operate through dual messaging: to the outside world and particularly to loyal sympathizers, they will present a benevolent face and deny any atrocities, while to their own people they will double down on their atrocities and make it clear what happens to those who cross them. Fascism appeals to a sense of transgression for people through its public vulgarity. Refusing to apologize offers a certain disaffected segment of society a sense of freedom. It offers them a chance to get back at a world they feel has wronged them by denying them their proper place within it. Its recruits often come from a place of emasculation and humiliation, and through fascism they get to be powerful and dominant. It offers them a kind of manna of domination from which they can unleash their destructive urges on everything, including themselves.

But totalitarian ideology cannot be satisfied with conquering the masses. It must conquer and subdue reality itself. It must present unreality as reality and the masses must really believe it, because only in this way can its power be complete. It is not enough for the masses to follow orders. For fascism, the party line must govern their entire reality. If they say two plus two is five, then all evidence to the contrary must be a conspiracy by some shadowy elite that must be destroyed.

Fascism invokes a nostalgic desire to return to a mythic past, yet it also constitutes the apotheosis of the modern nation-state. Liberal notions of popular sovereignty and social contract identified the state with society, rather than with its rulers, so the state was essentially the embodiment of the people. Yet the exact identity of "the people" is a matter of contention. With its territorial claims and construction of national identity, the nation-state has always had a vested interest in defining who is or is not one of "the people." Nationalism involves schismogenesis, the process of differentiating oneself from another. To define oneself as a nation is to define who is outside that nation. Fascism seizes upon a doctrine of who really belongs to the nation and seeks to root out all elements that are seen as foreign to it. It requires enemies to survive, and where necessary it will designate new enemies. The ability to conjure up new enemies is central to their ability to rule by fear. It is precisely the arbitrariness of totalitarian violence that makes it so effective. Once loyal party members can suddenly find themselves subject to show trials and summary executions.

Fascism would be nothing without enforcement, and for this it looks to a collaboration between public and private forces. Police have a natural sympathy for fascism based on a common set of enemies. The first police forces were created not to stop crime but to stop social upheaval. Strikebreakers and slave patrols arose to maintain systems of domination, and this legacy continues today. Police work appeals to those with a desire to impose their will on others and punish their enemies—exactly the impulses to which fascism appeals. As such, fascist groups have a long history of infiltrating and collaborating with the police. These fascist gangs do the dirty work that the police are prohibited from doing while the police provide cover for them. The police are still subject to the state, and while the state maintains some semblance of democracy they may still be called upon to arrest and punish them, but they still have sympathizers among their ranks who can do favors for them. As democratic structures weaken, the police become emboldened and go rogue, resisting every effort to curtail their power and subject them to democratic control.

Fascism is first and foremost a movement. It is not about the absoluteness of the state but of the movement that seeks to seize the state apparatus. Once in power, existing institutions are either replaced by or supplemented with institutions constituted by that movement. Competent state bureaucrats are replaced by party loyalists. Fascist paramilitary movements that previously collaborated with the police may gain official status as a new secret police. It is these loyal foot soldiers of the movement who are tasked with carrying out the greatest atrocities.

If the megamachine is one distortion of the Logos in which all aspects of human life are regimented, flattened, and drilled into submission, there is another distortion that is chaotic, destructive, and nihilistic. Fascism is a synthesis of the two. It is not mere despotism, but a nihilistic despotism animated by an intoxicating death drive. It is humanity giving in to its worst impulses. The desire for domination, cruelty, and supremacy supplants compassion, empathy, and solidarity. Rational discourse gives way to propaganda and bad faith. Critical thinking is overtaken by conspiracies that tell them to be afraid of the other and justify doing anything to destroy them. Fascism is the pinnacle of all that is evil, sinful, and cruel in human nature. It is the full realization of a Dark Logos; it is the Spirit of the Antichrist.

Popular Sovereignty

Liberalism is rooted in the idea of "popular sovereignty." This was a rather novel idea during the Enlightenment, one that pushed the traditional notion of sovereignty on its head. Sovereignty had always been understood as the legitimate right to rule over others. Yet popular sovereignty, based on the concept of a social contract, suggested that the sovereign ruled only by the "consent of the governed." This is a curious contradiction: on the one hand, it maintains the right of the state to rule over the people, but the legitimacy of their authority is derived from the people themselves.

The social contract is clearly an abstraction; no one signed such a document. We are born into it. The "consent of the governed" comes through the act of voting. The idea is that people come together to choose who will have authority over them. One might think that those who don't vote would thereby be considered not to have signed the contract, but since territorial sovereignty by its nature cannot be exercised over others on a strictly voluntary basis, those who do not vote for the winner are still expected to submit to them. Others claim that the social contract is implicitly signed by one's use of public infrastructure: if you use a road, you are agreeing to the political structure that made those roads possible. Roads do not require any one political system to be built— only labor and materials. This logic would seem to apply to any political structure at all, no matter how tyrannical, so long as it creates public infrastructure that people use.

Ironically, it was under feudalism that social contract took a more literal form. The vassal swore their military allegiance to a lord in exchange for land, along with any serfs attached to that land. The serfs, of course, were not party to this contract, but were simply tied to the land and served whoever owned that land; the feudal contract did not apply to those whose labor was at stake. Similarly, a worker today works for the same company even if it changes ownership, though in the latter case the worker can either quit or get fired, neither of which applied to the serf.

Liberalism abstracted this concept into a system that did not get rid of sovereignty but shifted its justification. No longer was it based on the sovereign's birthright, but found through the popular vote. The government is now supposed to represent the people who elected them. Yet this representation really meant a competition between elites for popular support. Such affairs are, at their heart, aristocratic rather than democratic. If one is truly chosen to represent the people, then the people themselves must decide on an agenda they would like to enact and then send their representative to convey those priorities in deliberation, with the decision-making power resting ultimately in their constituents. Under liberal democracy, however, the candidate sets their own agenda and attempts to persuade the people to choose it over their opponent's agenda. Deliberation is done by those elected, not by the ones who elected them. Even without the corrupting influence of special interests, gerrymandering, and voter suppression, such a system is unworthy of the name "democracy."

That this system *is* subject to such distorting influence reveals a deeper weakness. It makes politics a competition, and to make it a fair competition requires that all concerned play by an agreed upon set of rules and norms. Liberal democracy presupposes that those who compete are implicitly in agreement with its own values. This is what makes it vulnerable to fascism. The prize for this competition is none other than sovereignty, for which wars of conquest have been fought since the dawn of civilization. Checks and balances used to limit sovereignty require an implicit assent by those in charge of society's institutions. Liberal institutions assume a level of political neutrality among their leadership. They may be headed by government appointees, but those appointees are assumed to use their office for the fulfillment of their duties to the people. That they might instead serve their own ideological goals breaks our social contract, though this kind of system exploitation is inherent when that contract presupposes all actions are based in good faith. The more institutions are infiltrated in this way, the weaker the hold of liberalism becomes. This is what fascism aims to do: to seize the ostensibly neutral institutions of the liberal state and subvert them in the name of a partisan, anti-democratic agenda, in which power is sought above all else.

Liberalism attempts to tame the power of sovereignty through competition. Yet such competition also requires cooperation with a set of norms, such that those who wield power must in principle agree to such constraints. Just as businesses in competitive markets seek to corner the market and thereby limit competition, so too do those in competitive politics seek ways to gain a foothold on the competition by whatever underhanded means available to them. Elections present voters ostensibly with a sense of autonomy and control, but they serve as a honeypot for those who seek to wield power for nefarious purposes.

A genuine democracy must be more than electoral: it must be deliberative. Decision-making power must lie with popular councils, open to all, in which issues are discussed and deliberated with the aim of popular consensus rather than mere majority rule. Such councils would have the power to delegate authority over specific tasks, so long as that authority can be as easily revoked. Existing city councils could be transformed into administrative bodies, responsible for enacting the will of the people and maintaining public institutions. These councils would be formed at a municipal scale, and in the case of large cities may require even smaller scale councils that then send delegates to a larger council. Such delegates would bring decisions from these larger councils back to their local council for the definitive vote. Municipal councils could maintain relationships with other municipal councils to form confederations based on mutual interest. In this way, hierarchical power is replaced by distributed power, and "power over" is replaced by "power with."

Popular assemblies must be borne of mass organizing as an expression of popular will. Such assemblies may then seek political legitimacy by running candidates for city council who will recognize them as decision-making bodies to which the council itself would become accountable. Such assemblies must be open to all. While it is not necessary that everyone participate, everyone should have the opportunity to do so. Every accommodation should be made for disability, for conflicting work schedules, and for including marginalized voices. Such arrangements would not require some cataclysmic revolutionary break, but they would challenge the hegemony of the nation-state, whose very structure they would undermine.

This kind of popular democracy could produce a genuine social contract. People would agree on the rules that they themselves would follow and could renegotiate those rules when they aren't working. People are much more likely to follow rules that they have a part in creating. The law ceases to be an abstraction held over them by hegemonic forces and becomes instead a continuous negotiation of how to live together in harmony with others.

Direct action is continuous with direct democracy. A direct democracy requires participants who are dedicated to social transformation. They must develop a sense of politics, not in the sense of a set of partisan allegiances, but as a commitment to participation in the public affairs of their community. This commitment is expressed through activism and organizing, and for a popular assembly to succeed, that energy must carry over into it. Democratic councils and publicly owned enterprises alike can be taken over by profiteers and reactionaries if they are not founded in a sense of public engagement. Democracy, to be truly democratic, must be activist in nature.

The transformations necessary for such a society cannot be legislated into existence, but neither does it require complete disengagement with the public sphere. A proper engagement with electoral politics should be directed toward inscribing new rules of engagement between people and capital. It means running candidates for office who will establish popular power through democratic institutions, using the power of their office to redistribute that power to the people.

This redistribution of power creates the conditions for the transformation of society but does not by itself bring about that transformation. It takes concerted organizing effort to raise people's consciousness and mobilize them toward realizing the common good. Democracy is first and foremost a praxis. It requires engagement and pedagogy to truly be the work of the people. Statecraft manufactures dependency on the part of the population. Freedom requires that we unlearn this helplessness and take agency over the course of our society. This is not to say that all or even most people must participate in the democratic process. Popular councils may get by on the efforts of a dedicated few, seeing their ranks swell occasionally while discussing issues of widespread concern. But politics, in the truest sense of the word, must be transparent. What is important is that their doors be open to all.

Popular councils would create a powerful center for the emergence of collective intelligence. No master planner can account for all the needs and issues that arise for people, but a participatory process in which such issues are raised and deliberated allows them to be addressed organically at every step of the process. The administrative government acts in the service of this popular power, appearing before the council for regular progress reports and to collaborate on how to implement their agenda. Some trained facilitators may assist council meetings in developing amicable solutions, but they would have no more decision-making power than any other council member. In the process, the people themselves would become trained in the practice of democracy. The vested interests that set policy agendas today could finally be eclipsed by the revolutionary power of collective vision. An agenda of imposition would fade into one of organic unfolding.

Variations on such systems have included Porto Allegre's participatory budgeting system created by the Brazilian Workers Party, the Landless Workers' Movement (MST), the autonomous municipalities of the Zapatistas in Chiapas and Rojava in Northeast Syria. Historical precedents like the Paris Commune and the CNT-FAI abound, including older examples like Athenian democracy or the Iroquois Confederacy. None of these exactly fits the model described here, nor should they necessarily; the details of such a system would have to be worked out in real time according to local political and social conditions. Yet this set of principles can be used for constructing such systems, which in fact are revolutionary only insofar as they hearken back to a system that has been suppressed by the forces of empire and statecraft, but which re-emerges time and again throughout history. Such systems are in fact the immune response of the Logos reasserting itself against the incursions of the megamachine. It is through such horizontal power that human potential can be fully realized.

6

Markets

As empires grew and their reach expanded, keeping soldiers stationed in the territories to maintain imperial rule became a costly endeavor. In these conquered territories, a traditional system of trust and mutual aid ruled daily life — a kind of reciprocal altruism. Such reciprocal altruism is found almost universally among friends, who will share what they have out of enjoyment of one another's company.

This reciprocity requires bonds of trust, akin to a credit system. In such a system, an occupying soldier would be a great credit risk. With no ties to the land they occupy, and the locals for the most part not wanting them there, there would be little reason for people to help these soldiers with goods and services, other than those demanded in tribute. Keeping the soldiers fed and properly equipped required supply chains that were vulnerable to disruption and attack.

A solution was found in the creation of coinage. Coins evolved out of an earlier system of bullion, in which precious metals were fixed by state decree at a certain exchange rate. These metals served as a store of value that could be traded for goods and transported long distances. Yet within the population centers themselves, mutual aid was still the norm, and soldiers were largely excluded from it. The practice of stamped coins denominated as currency changed that.

Coins were minted with the emperor's face, letting conquered people know who it was that ruled over them. These coins would be used to pay the soldiers. In turn, they were demanded back as tribute. But why would the empire demand tribute in the form of something they themselves issued? Why would they scatter these coins throughout the empire only to take them back? The answer lay in the value that such demand generated. Because people had to pay a certain amount of coin as tribute, they had incentive to collect these coins. Because soldiers were the ones being paid in this coin, people now had reason to exchange goods and services with the soldiers. This also meant that as people collected more coins than they needed for tribute, they could spare their surplus in exchange for goods and services from others who also needed enough to pay tribute.

This is how the first markets emerged. Impersonal, quantifiable transactions overtook the informal system of mutual support that was the prevailing rule for human societies. Markets are one of the principal tools of colonization. Once a place is conquered, the traditional way of life that people relied upon is disrupted as its production and resources are integrated into larger systems of trade. Through tribute, debt, and taxation, subsistence economies are transformed into export economies for the empire.

Colonies that once knew autonomy and sovereignty became dependent upon their colonizers. They were forced into competition with other colonies to export their resources, and in return receive the goods needed to support themselves. In today's globalized economy, countries undergoing famine will continue to be net exporters because their economies are driven toward providing resources for other countries rather than feeding and providing for their own people.

Trade

The starting point of mainstream economics is trade. Classical economics began largely as an argument for free trade. The mercantilist approach of the time emphasized the importance of protecting domestic industry while pushing to open markets abroad. This led to a kind of zero-sum game in which nations sought to gain economic advantage over others by expanding their own exports while trying to limit imports. This was an outgrowth of the guild system. Guilds were secret societies that kept trade secrets and regulated supply chains, ensuring that they did not become economically dominated by outside powers.

This made sense at the level of the municipality, and it allowed multiple cities to enrich one another through confederation. With the birth of the nation-state, however, sovereigns sought to consolidate the power of the city and countryside into a single economic engine. The closed system of the medieval commune expanded its boundaries out to the political borders of the modern Westphalian state. These states, however, had contrived borders negotiated through treaties and based on what political scientist Benedict Anderson called "Imagined Communities." The municipality is an organic polity. It has porous boundaries created and maintained by its inhabitants, its surrounding environment, and trade with outsiders. The nation-state attempts to manage the resources under its command much like a general working out a logistical problem on the battlefield.

This system was heavily criticized by the physiocrats, a group of scholars in France during the mid-18th century. They saw in mercantile protectionism a category error: for them, the wealth of a nation was its land. It was the fruits of the earth — primarily agriculture but also mining and other such activities — that needed protection. It was this wealth that was to be captured and redistributed to the rest of the economy. Manufacturing was, for them, parasitic on real wealth; it was foolish to try and protect manufacturing industries, and the state should instead concentrate on its natural assets. The market for finished products would then regulate itself by means of *laissez-faire*, or non-interference, a concept inspired by and drawing from the Chinese idea of *wu wei*, or action through non-action. The physiocrats were greatly inspired by China's economy, which had a system of scholar-bureaucrats at the top and merchants at the bottom. The physiocrats believed that they had discovered the natural economic order, brought into harmony with the way of nature.

The physiocrats in turn were criticized by Adam Smith, the founder of classical economics. Smith developed the labor theory of value, according to which the value of a product is the labor one is willing to expend to obtain it. As production is collectivized through mass industry, the labor that goes into production would come to equilibrium with the labor consumers are willing to do to obtain the product. This leads to the familiar supply-and-demand curves of introductory economics.

Like the physiocrats, Smith advocated free trade. He believed that the free exchange of products between nations would mutually enrich both nations. His 1776 book *An Inquiry into the Nature and Causes of the Wealth of Nations* raised the concern that the bourgeoisie of one country might find it more lucrative to invest abroad, but believed they would be guided by local bias, as if by an "invisible hand," to invest in their home country. Though this term was used only once in the book, it came to be identified with a broader theme in his work, that of the mutual alignment of self-interest by the market, creating a kind of spontaneous order.

In fact, this is precisely what has not happened. What we have instead is a system of globalization in which capital traverses borders freely, siphoning wealth from wherever it can be found into the pockets of an international elite. Developing countries can be flattened by trade, becoming vassal states that can be easily abandoned as soon as capital finds it cheaper to produce elsewhere. This economic imperialism benefits a few core areas at the expense of all others. Over time, it leads to stagnation even in the imperial core, as the US has witnessed with outsourcing.

Smith and the physiocrats were not wrong to critique mercantilist protection, but they fell short in critiquing the nation-state form upon which mercantilism rested. It was all based on the fiction that a vast area united under a single government, currency, and national economy could function in the same way as the diversity of cities and regions that comprise that area. The nation-state attempts to smooth out the difference between its regions and develops policies that end up benefiting some parts at the expense of others.

According to urban theorist Jane Jacobs, cities perform the vital function of "import substitution." That is, as they import goods from elsewhere, they also develop the ability to manufacture those goods themselves, for which they in turn can find markets. Rather than two-way trade between exporter and importer, a thriving city will act as a kind of springboard for smaller economies. The benefits of trade are passed down a line of cities at different levels of development, each innovating to carve out their own niche in the trade network. These differences are flattened by the nation-state, which seeks to standardize its territory politically, culturally, and economically. Under such conditions, protectionism will benefit some areas and disadvantage others, as will free trade, but neither will distribute the benefits evenly because they are artificially bound together under a single polity.

In this way, empires sow the seeds of their own destruction. The conquest of other regions requires devoting significant portions of one's economy to maintaining a military; equipment is exported to troops stationed abroad, who then convert the conquered regions into colonies producing exports for the imperial core. In the process, they cripple the ability of their own cities to substitute these imports. Their cities stagnate and their empire collapses. Similarly, countries fall victim to a "resource curse" in which their overreliance on a single major export leaves them vulnerable to systemic shocks. They must be able to diversify their economy to become resilient over the long term, and to do so requires that their cities develop a springboard trade system with other cities so as to form stable trade networks.

In the end, it is not nations that trade, but people. The

organic polity of the city is the site at which these particularities come to the foreground: only there can we find the kind of improvisation that is needed for genuine development. As consumer products become cheaper and more widely available in our increasingly globalized world, the ability to maintain resilient economies stagnates. Only by transcending the hegemony of the nation-state can this be overcome.

Commodity

Markets involve prices, and prices require quantification. Mutual aid requires no such quantification. A sense of reciprocity means that everyone takes care of everyone else, so no one needs to worry about getting ripped off or shortchanged. Such concerns only enter the equation when bonds of trust are lacking. As David Graeber put it, "Who was the first man to look at a house full of objects and immediately assess them only in terms of what he could get for them in the market? Surely, he can only have been a thief."[7] Market relations prevail when interpersonal bonds are not strong enough to ensure reciprocity.

Where mutual aid is the rule, there is no distinct economic sphere. The exchange of goods and services is nothing other than a social interaction between people. The goods themselves are of secondary importance to the relations they serve. In traditional marketplaces social rituals exist

---

[7] Graeber, David. *Debt: The First 5000 Years*. New York: Melville, 2011. p. 386

around market transactions to maintain this social element and avoid the pure objectification of market relations. We see this in cultures where haggling is still a common practice: a vendor names their starting price while the consumer names their price, and they haggle until they agree on a final one. It is often when the argument comes down to a difference of a few cents that it becomes most intense. This ritual gives the market transaction some semblance of social relation it would otherwise lack.

This personal touch mostly disappeared with the rise of chain stores and supermarkets. The economic has been pried away from the social and overtaken it. Instead of trying to maintain social relations in the face of an impersonal system, the objectification of the market has pervaded all of society. Materialism is economic before it is metaphysical. The process of commodification degrades human relationships even as it enchants the commodity. The commodity becomes an idol by which our own humanity becomes alienated. It becomes the mediator of all human relationships. Where economic transactions once existed as extensions of social bonds, now our social ties themselves become reduced to transactions. The person becomes replaced with *homo economicus*, a rational calculating creature pursuing its own self-interest without regard to social ties, reduced to a set of wants to be fulfilled for the right price.

The mystery of the commodity was the starting point of Marx's analysis of capitalism. The commodity, he said, was plagued by a contradiction of two values. On the one hand, the commodity has a use value for the person using it. This use value is wholly qualitative and subjective, varying based on the needs and intentions of the person. The same knife can be used to cut vegetables, whittle, carve one's name in a tree, or kill someone. On the other side of this is exchange value — the value of the commodity on the market. A storeowner keeps an inventory of commodities not for their personal use, but to sell to customers for a profit. An object can have use value without any exchange value, but there can be no exchange value without use value.

Exchange value, according to Marx, is determined by abstract labor. The price of a commodity represents the amount of labor required to procure it. Supply and demand represent respectively the labor that goes into creating a commodity and the amount of labor that people are willing to expend to get the commodity. As demand changes, production changes to match it. The exchange value therefore represents the overall distribution of labor dedicated to its production and consumption. Marx used the term "commodity fetishism" for the reifying illusion that a commodity has some intrinsic value, rather than value of the social organization of labor embodied in it.

Graeber builds off Marx to develop what he calls an anthropological theory of value. In examining the ritual practices of different cultures around objects of exchange, he finds that it is not only production but also exchange that can contribute to an object's value. As an object passes from one owner to another, it is this history that grants it an aura of value. We see this with the crown jewels of England, whose value lies not so much in the gold and silver with which they are made, nor the labor used to produce them, but precisely in their historical association with the British monarchy. We see this also when we get a book signed or a memento autographed by a celebrity. Family heirlooms and the like hold value for us precisely because of the memories and traditions associated with them. What we call "sentimental value" guides far more of our lives than a quantitative economic analysis could show us.

Marx's labor theory of value claims to be an objective measure of labor hours while Graeber's anthropological theory of value presents an irreducibly cultural and even personal dimension of value. The price system under capitalism involves the capture of value through differential power. The capitalist sets the price based on discounting present value. What this means is that the commodity is sold for a price that is expected to yield the highest long-term returns.

That set price is determined through differential accumulation— firms compete for monopolistic control of the market, judging their success not in absolute terms, but relative to their competition. The maneuvering itself defines the competition, even when it does not result in total monopoly. Capital is nothing other than power held over the economic sphere. The degree to which one holds capital is the degree to which one can bend others to their will.

To discount present value in expectation of future value is to have a vested interest in shaping that future value, and this is achieved through sabotage. In the context of the market, sabotage is best understood by economist Thorstein Veblen's distinction between business and industry. Industry is the productive activity of human creativity, and it is an inherently collective process. Even a craftsman working alone in their workshop is drawing from the accumulated knowledge of others. Business, on the other hand, is concerned with pecuniary distribution. The value created by industry must be commodified and restricted to be privately expropriated by the capitalist class. In other words, industry must be strategically sabotaged. This is done by restricting the collective nature of industry. Patents and copyrights force competitors to produce needless workarounds to what would otherwise be shared collective technical knowledge. Integration of industry through mergers and acquisition increases one's price-setting power, and with it the power to shape the future in a way that will help realize those future gains.

Debt

Civilization is defined by cities. It is a pattern of social organization in which there is a flow from the rural periphery to the urban center. This expands into the imperial model in which peripheral cities serve the interests of the capital. From there we get the "world system" as described by sociologist Immanuel Wallerstein, in which countries can occupy the core or periphery.

The bustling life of the city offered a cornucopia of exotic delights. Merchants would travel from far and wide to sell their wares. They would borrow money to buy goods in one place and travel to another place where they were scarce and sell them at a profit. The lender would seek some return on their investment in the form of an "interest" or share of the profit. When lending to merchants on their commercial ventures, charging interest was a matter of shared risk. Yet lenders at times were predatory, charging interest on something that did not come with a profit for the borrower. For example, a farmer whose crop failed that year might need a loan to make it through the current one. If a lender charged interest on such a loan, it meant that the debtor would have to produce a surplus above what they lost to break even.

If they failed to make good on that surplus, they would have to borrow more, delving further and further into debt, until the debtor essentially owed their life to the lender, often rather literally. With nothing left to mortgage, they might simply sell themselves to the lender as a debt slave. More likely, they would put their wife or children up as collateral, and when they were unable to pay off the loan, they would be the ones sold into slavery.

Debt has a way of turning morality on its head. Because the debtor agreed to take on the loan, behaviors that would normally be considered abhorrent become justified in the name of collecting on the debt. People could be deprived of their land, their possessions, and their freedom on the premise that they owed something to the other person. This justification of exploitation based on a contractual idea of consent continues to be one of the leading ideas of the modern ethos. Yet in ancient times there was a rebellion against this insidious phenomenon. This kind of exploitative lending, known as usury, would be repeatedly condemned by religions throughout the world. Such condemnations can be found in the teachings of Plato, Aristotle, Moses, Muhammed, and Gautama Buddha.

While there seems to be no consistent agreement on what exactly constitutes usury, the condemnations against it all share a common recognition of the degrading effects such exploitative loans had on human life. Usury had a vampire-like quality in which the usurer was sucking the life force out of the debtor. Usury was a demon that threatened to tear apart the fabric of society. Middle Eastern societies would often periodically forgive non-commercial debts, typically at the coronation of a new king. This was developed by the Israelites into the Year of Jubilee. This periodic debt forgiveness was essential for maintaining order. Such measures helped prevent the kind of boom-bust cycle that plagues modern capitalism.

Today, the assumption that a debtor must pay off their debts is sacrosanct. True, there are regulations about how much creditors can charge, debtor's prison has been abolished, and the banks can count on getting bailed out in the event of an economic crash. The people themselves can only count on default or bankruptcy, but even then, the student loan racket has ensured its own immunity from that loophole. Debt is the real driver of the modern economy. Each person is like a crop from which debt is to be continually harvested. The creditor class finds ever-new ways of extracting debt until the whole system collapses, but not before they have found a way to save themselves in the process and reboot the system.

Property

With permanent settlements, people can control the land by restricting access to it. This is first and foremost done collectively through the establishment of territory. Territoriality exists for both humans and animals, but the concept of property involves more than this. Where territory is simply a sphere of influence, property is something quantifiable, fungible, and excludable. It is distinct from usufruct, in which one has the right to the private use of something for some duration of time. Property may be recognized by convention but is generally upheld by legal title.

Territory historically belonged to the sovereign. The whole of the kingdom was whatever fell under their power. Property allows for the subdivision of sovereignty, such that individuals and families can have territory for themselves, subject to the law of the sovereign. Property could be bought, homesteaded, or granted by the sovereign. It was this latter practice that allowed a sovereign to buy people's loyalty or forge alliances.

Inheritance is a primary concern for property. Patriarchal family structures depend upon the passage of property from one generation to another for the maintenance of power. Marriage plays a significant role here. In traditional societies, marriages were often arranged by wealthy and powerful families to secure strategic alliances. Marriage could be narrowly viewed as a means of accumulation and a stabilizing territorial force, as evidenced by the phrase "keeping it in the family." The matter of who exactly would get the inheritance was also a matter of patriarchal norms. Typically, the eldest male child would inherit the estate. Daughters would be married off and younger sons might serve in the military or priesthood.

Under feudalism, land ownership was practically synonymous with the state. The term "landlord" comes down to us from this era when the owner of the land was literally a lord. A lord would grant his vassal a fief in exchange for their loyalty and service. A fief was a property title that included land along the serfs who worked it. The serfs would pay a portion of their crop to the vassal who would render military service to the lord. This military service could then lead to conquest of new lands which could then be dispensed to vassals.

Property once referred only to land, but by the Middle Ages land was recognized as a special case of property, known as "real" property. Personal property was produced by human effort and exchanged on the market, but real property was a portion of nature's bounty over which one exercised some degree of sovereignty. Yet it was understood that sovereignty was conditional: all things ultimately belonged to God. Property was not an absolute right, but a conditional privilege to be used for the common good. It was justified on the basis that having a territory of one's own gave one incentive to look after it.

What was not so common until early modernity was the buying and selling of land to different owners, especially at a profit. A serf or tenant farmer gave their lord some portion of their harvest, and a medieval burgher might live in collective housing, but the idea of facing eviction for non-payment of rent would have been a rarity prior to modernity. Under capitalism, the interaction between real estate and banking drives credit bubbles that inevitably burst and bring the economy to a crash.

This tendency toward cyclical crises, once known as the "boom-bust cycle" but now euphemistically known as the "business cycle" has been one of the defining features of capitalism since its inception. The various explanations of this cycle have been offered along rigidly ideological lines. Marx explains it in terms of crises of overproduction based on the tendency of the rate of profit to fall. The Austrian school explains it in terms of malinvestment due to fractional reserve banking. Neoclassical economics has

Real Business Cycle theory, which explains it in terms of exogenous shocks. What seems clear, however, is that this cycle appears wherever capitalist property relations meet debt financing.

Debt itself has become an asset to be traded and capitalized upon. The 2008 Global Financial Crisis saw the fallout from complex debt instruments that collateralized mortgage debt. People's mortgages were bundled into assets that were speculated upon by Wall Street investors. The result was a handful of people getting rich off those just trying to have a place to live in. The very ground on which we walk has not escaped the clutches of usury. The commodification of housing has become the driving force of the economy. Developers, private equity, and hedge funds buy up housing for speculative purposes and bid up rental prices as high as they will go, leaving millions unable to afford to continue living in the cities they call home.

Slavery

One of the most ancient forms of property is the ownership of human beings. Slaves were traditionally obtained through capture in battle, through debt, or as legal punishment. Slavery formed the backbone of ancient civilizations, from Greece to Persia to Rome. Not all slaves were assigned to drudgery: some could be treated as beloved household members, and some could even attain great social status. Yet what set them apart was that their lives were not their own. The master could do what they wished with their slave, up to and including killing them.

During the Middle Ages, slavery was largely eclipsed by serfdom. To be sure, serfdom shared many similarities with slavery: a serf could be bought and sold, but only together with the land to which they were bound. The lord also had certain duties to the serf, providing them protection while allowing them enough of their own cultivated land to provide for themselves and their families. Serfdom itself began to decline around the 11th century and suffered a death blow after the Black Plague wiped out one-third of Europe's population, freeing up a great deal of land for cultivation. It moved further east and was only abolished in Russia in 1861.

With the rise of colonialism, slavery came back with a vengeance. When Columbus landed in Hispañola, he set about enslaving the indigenous population, forcing them to mine for gold. Enslavement of indigenous peoples was tried in numerous places throughout the New World. But these slaves knew the terrain better than their European owners and were able to escape back to their tribe. The import of slaves from Africa proved to be more fruitful. The European demand for slaves was so great that slavery became the basis for their entire economies. To keep up with demand, warfare with other tribes skyrocketed, and slavery became the punishment for even minor legal offenses.

The slave economy worked in tandem with the wage economy. The cotton picked by slaves in the South was spun into fabrics by factories in the North. It also kept a check on wages from rising too much. For both wages and slavery, the cost of living was a limiting factor. The master had to provide food and living accommodations for the slaves, while the capitalist had to pay their workers enough to sustain them. The workhouses of England provide an interesting middle ground: established by the Tudor Poor Laws and later reformed under the Speenhamland system, they were houses where the able-bodied poor were sent to live and earn their keep in a factory setting. In theory, they could exit these institutions and seek employment elsewhere, but in practice it became a form of indentured servitude.

When slavery was abolished in the United States, the prison system took over. The same black people who had worked in the plantations were rounded up and arrested under frivolous pretenses and sent to work in chain gangs. Prison labor to this day provides commodities for all manner of economic sectors today. There is even a sense in which it is voluntary: prisoners prefer to work jobs because it gets them out of their cell and gives them something to do while they serve their time. They even get paid, albeit at a much lower rate than minimum wage laws generally allow. Yet this is quite literally a captive labor market, and their choices are deliberately constrained. Furthermore, they are frequently barred from seeking the same kind of work when they are released from prison. The plantation system is still alive and well and will continue to find new guises until we demand an economy free from exploitation.

Debt slavery remains common in many parts of the world. In certain countries, entire families are indebted to a lender for generations. Children are forced to work off the debts of their parents, which prevents them from going to school and getting an education that might help them escape their state of poverty and would then incur new debts themselves in order to survive. In 2014, The International Labour Organization estimated that every year about $51.2 billion is made from forced labor.[8] For now in what we call the "first world," debt protections exist to prevent people from this kind of hazard, but if there were ever a push to bring back slavery, rolling back these protections would surely be one of the primary methods for doing so.

Slavery pervades the black market today with human trafficking, sexual slavery, forced labor, and commercial sexual exploitation. Industries using unfree labor include mining, agriculture, manufacture, domestic work, and the illegal drug trade. Tough immigration laws are often exploited to smuggle people into a country who have nowhere to turn and must submit to their exploiter's demands. Children are often trafficked for forced labor, for adoption, or sexual exploitation. Chinese firms in the Congo extensively use child labor in their cobalt mines. The illegal organ trade often exploits immigrants, homeless people, and others in desperate economic circumstances. The commodification of the human body is the logical conclusion of commodification as such.

Forcing people to work has always been one of the classic dilemmas for the ruling class. Slavery is one such method for doing so, but the cost of caring for slaves can be expensive, and the cost of keeping them from escaping even more so. The control of land offers another alternative. Serfdom allowed the purchase of land along with the serfs so that the serf's life remained much the same regardless of who their lord was. Taxes and tribute provide an even more subtle

---

[8] "How Profitable Is the Exploitation of People? Sadly, Extraordinarily so." *International Labour Organization*, 28 May 2014, https://www.ilo.org/newyork/voices-at-work/WCMS_244965/lang---en/index.htm.

form, creating a debt that people must work to pay off. This method created the first markets and was used repeatedly by colonial powers to create export economies to supply the imperial core. The history of civilization is the history of these attempts to control the labor of others. A liberatory politics must seek to understand this process and actively resist. Only a world without forced labor can be truly free.

Commons

While the medieval view recognized the utility of property, there was also a sense of shared resources that were for everyone: most common land today in Europe is pastureland for grazing, but open fields for planting and harvesting were also once common. As private plots of land increased, the need for shared land and resources remained a mainstay of society. Agricultural land was not the only thing held in common. Fisheries, forests, waterways — these all belonged to the people in common. Even today, as much as capitalist property relations have encroached upon our lives, there is widespread understanding that such things belong to the public and should not be subject to private profit-seeking interests.

The commons suffered a catastrophe starting in the late medieval era. The enclosure movement was the gradual process by which common land was seized by private landowners to increase their own yields. The conquest of the commons left behind many peasants whose subsistence farming had left them with a modest but sustainable existence, forcing them to work other people's land for a wage.

This process was accelerated under the Tudor dynasty in England. In breaking with the Catholic Church, Henry VIII closed the monasteries that had provided essential services to the poor and confiscated them for the Crown. The Church had served the poor institutionally through its almshouses, and by encouraging its members to be charitable toward the poor. With the closure of the monasteries, it became necessary for the state to take over these functions. This was done through the enactment of "Poor Laws," which treated the poor as a problem to be managed.

The Poor Laws delineated between the "deserving" and "undeserving" poor. Those deemed ineligible to work due to age or infirmity were licensed to beg as they had before, while those caught begging without such licenses could be flogged or sent to the stockades for their first offense and executed for their third offense. For those willing to work but unable to find employment, workhouses were created. These workhouses provided room and board to go along with a highly regimented life while setting a floor for wages. They were operated at the local parish level, restricting freedom of movement and creating a "poverty trap"— once one entered a workhouse, it was exceedingly difficult to leave.

The enclosure of the commons marked the beginning of colonialism. Before the European powers had the chance to pillage Africa and the Americas, it was their own people who were robbed of their livelihood and forced to assimilate into the capitalist machine. Many of the conquistadors and pioneers who sought a new life for themselves in the New World were fleeing immense debt and hardship in the old country. The opening of these lands for settlement provided a relief valve for wages, preventing them from falling too low.

"Seeking a new life" was the cliché of the westbound settler. In their new homes, the settlers imposed more blatant forms of theft and dispossession than they themselves had suffered back home. The indigenous peoples of the Americas lacked the strict view of property rights that the settlers had, and so their territory was seen as up for grabs. The Spanish missions offered food and accommodations, but much like the English workhouses, the price was often forced labor that could be impossible to escape.

The pillage of the commons continues to this day. Oil companies are given capture rights over fields they discover, entitling them to not only the oil in the ground but also the land on which it is found. Companies like Nestlé seek to privatize the water supplies in locations throughout the world. International financial organizations such as the World Bank and IMF use debt leverage to impose privatization on countries they lend to, and the US military has a history of using brute force when such negotiations fail.

Intellectual property marks a particularly insidious example of capitalism's encroachment on the commons. If ever there were a natural commons, surely the realm of ideas is one of them. None of our ideas are completely original. We must all learn and absorb countless ideas from all around us to combine them into something truly innovative. Intellectual property is often justified on a utilitarian basis as encouraging innovation, but if it does so, it is only because the capitalist economy requires that innovators must seek a profit for themselves in order to live.

Such innovation is often directed not toward social usefulness, but toward working around the patents of others. Because information is intrinsically shared knowledge, inventors often can't help but step on the patents of others. This results in patent-trolling against upstart companies, and a kind of patent arms race among established companies. Moreover, patents have been used to entrap small farmers by making them dependent on GMO crops and prosecuting them for saving seeds, as they would normally do with traditional crops.

Economists have developed their own mythology about the commons. The "tragedy of the commons" is supposed to occur when a common resource becomes over-exploited by common resource users pursuing their own gain. Overfishing and overgrazing are commonly cited examples. The phenomenon is certainly real enough, but the solution usually pointed to is placing the resource under the control of a single entity, private or public.

Elinor Ostrom overturned this assumption by studying various forms of commons management by users of the resources themselves. Such an idea ought not to have surprised people: the commons had been collectively managed by societies throughout history. The capitalist usurping of the commons is what is truly new. Ostrom outlined eight design principles for management of common pool resources: the resource must be clearly defined; appropriation and provision of the resources must be adapted to local conditions; resource users must be allowed to participate in decision-making processes as much as possible; effective monitoring must be done in a way that is accountable to resource appropriators; there should be a system of graduated sanctions for those who violate community rules; means of conflict resolution must be cheap and easy to access; community self-determination must be recognized by higher-level authorities; and for larger common pool resources, there must be multiple layers of adjudication.

Common pool management systems along these lines have developed time and again across cultures throughout the world. The workings of such systems can take on a multitude of different forms for different purposes, but they have at their heart a collaborative spirit. We do not need masters to divvy up the world for us: people have always found effective ways of sharing. The commons and democracy go together. If the commons falls into the hands of a single individual or entity, it ceases to be the commons. The history of the commons is the history of people cooperating to maintain it.

Guilds

While the serf plowed the lord's fields, the medieval town was filled with workers who organized together according to their crafts. The organizations they formed, known as guilds, were initiatory structures in which one would have a chance to hone their craft under the tutelage of a master. They would be assigned to simple tasks at first, working on more complex projects as they advanced through the ranks and training those below them. Such organizations had a hierarchical character, but they were an internal hierarchy, based on proving oneself with one's skill. From apprentice, one could advance to journeyman and so on all the way up to master. Being a member of the guild meant sharing a stake in it and its fortunes. It existed for the benefit of its members and the perfection of its craft.

Solidarity was the foundation of the guild. Members swore

binding oaths and would back one another in feuds with opposing guilds. They would keep "trade secrets" to their crafts, ensuring that they would not fall into the hands of rivals. Guilds from different trades would form networks and supply chains with one another, working together to govern entire towns. They set standard wages and labor practices, provided medical care and pensions in old age, planned the infrastructure and civic activities of the urban center, and controlled trade with outsiders. Together, they governed an urban commons.

Where ancient civilizations used slave labor to build their great monuments, the guilds that built many of the great cathedrals of Europe were composed of free men who took pride in their craft and shared their rewards in mutual solidarity. They experienced their work as rewarding not only in the pay they received, but in the joy of perfecting their art. There is all the difference in the world between the mindless drudgery of repetitive tasks and the creative engagement that the guild craftsman enjoyed in their work.

The guild in many ways resembled a modern union or cooperative, but they exercised the hegemony of a cartel. There were those who resented their price-fixing and their barriers to competition. Such things would later plague capitalism, and similar concerns led to some of the first anti-trust laws against the guilds. Yet because the guilds belonged to their members collectively, the benefits of such monopolistic tendencies were widespread.

The guild system offers us many lessons today, both positive and negative. They give us some idea of what a cooperative economy might look like. They show how business can be conducted based on horizontal networks rather than exploitation and conglomeration. They show how a teacher-student relationship can exist in place of the employer-employee relationship, so that one advances based on skill to become a master craftsman themselves. The communal cities in which guilds were based managed to form confederations with one another that offered an alternative to kingdoms and empires, and today offer the most promising possible alternative to the nation-state.

At the same time, guilds existed mostly to serve themselves and their own members and did not offer much help to outsiders. They had internal solidarity, but those outside the guild were of no concern to them. Their members sought to make themselves equal to nobility, furnishing privileges for themselves. There was a kind of proto-proletariat in the medieval city that existed outside the guild system, and while they did not live under the thumb of capitalist exploitation, they also did not enjoy the benefits of the bourgeois guild members. Political participation was limited to guild members, and often only the elite ones at that. And while in theory any journeyman could work his way up to master craftsman, in practice such promotions were often deliberately scarce.

Guilds existed within the context of feudalism, and although they offered an alternative to the feudal order they never directly challenged it, nor did they offer much help to the serfs who continued to labor under it. Their greatest challenge to feudalism was in fact when feudal lords began turning to this merchant class for loans to finance their wars, working around the system that had furnished them with knights and armies up until then. In this way, some of the earliest foundations of capitalism were laid.

Cooperation

Worker coops today operate in a similar spirit to that of the medieval guild. The workers collaborate to decide how to operate their business, and they decide how the profits are divided among their members. The prospect of a coop-based economy has been raised several times by various economists; there is no reason a coop cannot be operated as efficiently as a capitalist enterprise. In fact, democratic control over the profits means they can be directed where they're needed rather than lining the pockets of those at the top.

However, coops operating in a capitalist economy tend to compete with one another just as for-profit capitalist enterprises do. There may be internal solidarity, but the spirit of competition still drives business. An alternative is to form cooperative networks in which they mutually support one another against for-profit capitalist enterprises. Unfortunately, when capitalist enterprises do this, it's called a cartel, and there are anti-trust laws on the books to prevent this kind of thing from happening. While such laws are applied sparingly to major corporations due in large part to regulatory capture, it seems far more likely that such laws would be applied disproportionately against those seeking to challenge the for-profit capitalist paradigm. There are some subtle examples of this: credit unions have formed networks that allow customers of other credit unions to use their ATMs without a service charge. Nonetheless, the barriers to such cooperative networks are considerable, and if successful, it could lead to the situation of the medieval guilds all over again, with those inside the cooperative network reaping the rewards and privileges not enjoyed by those on the outside.

For this reason, Murray Bookchin suggested that cooperatives should be based not at the level of the business, but at the municipal level. This means that those within a given municipal jurisdiction would have control over production, deciding what gets produced in what quantities and how it's distributed. This allows for a more democratic solution than the Soviet-style command economy while avoiding the competitive tendencies of the capitalist market. The spirit of solidarity would extend beyond workers into society itself.

Yet if we look at Ostrom's guidelines for common resource management, we can see room for multiple levels of adjudication. The work site is one level of adjudication in which the immediate concerns of the workers can be addressed. Another is the immediate community in which the worksite operates. Another is the community of businesses, while yet another is the community of producers and consumers. There are multiple overlapping communities, some local and others non-local, and democratic institutions must be developed to address each of these levels of community.

The idea of there being a "work site" is itself somewhat of a modern invention. The separation of work and home for most of the population is something historically new that emerged with capitalism. Farmers have long lived on the land they cultivate, medieval craftsmen often had a workshop in their own home, and shopkeepers would live on the floor above their shops. Some may have had occupations that took them outside the home, such as traveling merchants, but the kind of daily commute most of us have today would have been unthinkable for most people throughout history.

In certain trades it makes more sense for workers to gather

in a common space rather than working separately from their own homes, but these could be distributed within one's local community. Part of the reason for our current situation is that rather than working in an industry, we work for a company. We commute to a job where we do a particular kind of work that could just as easily be done somewhere closer to us, but it happens to be where our employer is located. We may then seek out employment with a different company and have a different commute to do the exact same kind of work.

From an efficiency standpoint, this is madness, a madness that only makes sense for a system in which one company is competing with another. In a cooperative economy, workspace would be continuous with living space, and work itself would be continuous with the rest of life. Markets under capitalism are understood in terms of supply and demand, yet this is only applied to goods and services. To demand not only commodities but a better way of living is taboo, and those who do so are scorned as dangerous radicals — and wholly replaceable ones at that.

Cooperation is a natural state. It takes a great deal of political and economic power to disrupt the natural cooperative spirit of humanity. That power can be undermined to the extent that new systems of cooperation are forged. Mutual aid societies, worker self-management, popular assemblies, and confederations of municipal governments can all forge systems of cooperation that overcome the bonds of the capitalist power game used to bind us into its trap. The common bonds of humanity can be realized once we appreciate what we have to gain by choosing cooperation over competition.

Money

Some question whether markets can ever be truly democratic. They argue that money inherently leads to exploitation. Money as an abstraction of goods and services accumulates to those who can sell their goods and services effectively. While this may have a meritocratic ring to it, is this truly a just system? There has long been recognition that the elderly and disabled who are unable to work should be provided for in some way, though our current system of social security is woefully inadequate for such a task. Even under a well-funded social safety net, such people still receive the bare minimum of money, simply because they are incapable of the kinds of activities necessary for earning more.

There is nothing particularly virtuous about being a skilled salesperson. Most sales tactics are highly manipulative, and multi-level marketing schemes are veritable cults. More subtle manipulation is done through advertising. Consumer demand is never simply a given. There are always people looking to mold tastes to their own benefit. Moreover, there are those who seek money through dishonest means. Some resort to outright theft, while others resort to fraud, pushing elaborate schemes to swindle people out of their money. The more sophisticated among them, however, resort to usury. They find ways to manipulate money to make more money without providing any tangible goods or services in the process. Through predatory lending and speculation, their skill lies in accumulating money for themselves, but there is nothing meritocratic about such a process. They are simply skilled thieves manipulating the system to enrich themselves.

How might a cooperative economy address this? First, whether we abolish markets outright, it is imperative that they be contained. Under capitalism, the market has come to swallow up everything in its wake. Everything in our society has been commodified and capitalized, and we will never have a free society until this process is reversed. We must make social need rather than pecuniary interest the driving interest of society. There must be democratic oversight over markets, including their size and scope. Decisions must be made about what aspects of society should and should not be subject to market forces. Cities could be transformed into communes, becoming a common storehouse of resources for all to use.

It is also possible for money itself to be subject to democratic control, making it serve public interests. This can be achieved particularly through the democratic control of credit. Credit unions are a small step toward this, but they are still embedded within the profit-seeking capitalist context wherein loans are given out based on the expected return of profit. While credit unions may avoid some of the riskier speculative loans that major banks engage in, they are still profit-seeking enterprises.

The French anarchist Pierre-Joseph Proudhon proposed a more radical idea, known as mutual credit. Mutual credit would operate as a public good. Under such a system, everyone is both creditor and debtor, mutually lending to one another as needed. The ledger of credits and debits balance each other out, creating an elastic money supply that discourages hoarding, interest, and inflation. While mutual aid is often contrasted with money, it essentially operates like a credit system, in which people help each other out on the premise that they too will be helped when they need it. Mutual credit essentially extends the principle of mutual aid into a money economy. It operates on the principle of "from each according to their ability to each according to their need." This too may be undesirable under certain circumstances. Money requires quantification, and quantification can sometimes spoil the spirit of mutual aid. When people are counting their debts to one another, they are keeping tabs in ways that erode the kinds of communal bonds that mutual aid tends to presuppose.

Markets have a certain impersonal element to them. The vendor and customer are likely to be strangers, and once their transaction is complete, they each go their separate ways. When friends engage in market transactions with one another, they will often give one another a special deal if it is in their power to do so. They balance their need for compensation with the value of their friendship, so that profit becomes a secondary consideration.

Mutual credit can therefore supplement less formal forms of mutual aid for transactions in which such communal bonds cannot be relied upon. Marketplaces would be places where vendors sell their wares to strangers, who could buy them using mutual credit in the form of something like an interest-free credit card. There could be spending limits on such cards, decided upon democratically by the people. There could be a system whereby one's account balance gradually "regenerates," and one simply waits to spend that much money again. Rather than accumulating debt, debts could naturally disappear over time.

On a larger scale, mutual credit could be integrated with a municipal bank used for public expenditures. In this way, credit at every scale could be placed under democratic control. Rather than a means of exploitation used to enrich a few at the expense of many, credit could become a commons for the benefit of all. Combined with decommodification of housing and distribution of the means of production, a democratic economy could decide the size and scope of markets, while the market itself would belong to the commons.

Spontaneity

The free market has long been conceived by its proponents as a kind of Logos. As we've seen in this chapter, Francois Quesnay based his idea of *laissez faire* on the Taoist concept of *wei wu wei*. Adam Smith spoke of how the interests of different laborers were brought together as if by an "invisible hand" by their own self-interest. Friedrich Hayek spoke of the "spontaneous order" that emerges from a market system, which efficiently distributes the planning decisions among producers and consumers.

The consequences of our own market-driven society seem to clearly contradict this. Of course, many libertarians complain that what we live under is "corporatism," not capitalism. They are quick to point out the numerous state interventions in the market for the benefit of corporations, such as granting drilling rights to oil companies or massive bailouts to banks. They are not wrong to point out such state interventions as an intrinsic feature of our current economic system. Where they are wrong is in assuming that this goes against the logic of capitalism.

Capitalism was born of massive state intervention in the

economy. It involved the formation of the nation-state to uphold a system in which international capital markets were possible. It involved the enclosure of the commons in order to force people out of the pastures and into the assembly lines. What's more, it created an unstable system prone to boom-bust cycles in which each crisis could only be solved by a new form of commodification, which in turn could only be aided by the state.

The myth of a pure "free market" was always aspirational, and never corresponded to the actual history of capitalism. As we shall see in the next chapter, capital is inseparable from power. Yet in perceiving a kind of Logos at work, these thinkers grasped something important that transcends the logic of capitalism. Capitalism is often contrasted with state socialism, in which production is centrally planned, yet the heavily monopolistic form of capitalism we see today is centrally planned in ways Stalin could only dream of. It is precisely insofar as markets lead to monopolistic concentrations of power and distort human needs that they deviate from this Logos.

True spontaneity can emerge only when people are liberated from the market. When people are secure in their living conditions, able to meet their basic needs without work, they can instead devote their labor to tasks that inspire them. They can learn new skills, practice new crafts, or work on projects they always wanted to do but previously didn't have time for. They can read, socialize, make love, celebrate, spend time with family and friends, and create the bonds of genuine community. This is the true essence of life.

Our current paradigm is blinded by its emphasis on production and consumption. A plate that is only made once is washed countless times. Most labor is not so much production as maintenance, whether maintenance of efficiency, health, cleanliness, well-being, relationships, or community. It is our relationships that are the true object of labor. Commodity production and consumption should be mediated by those relationships, yet under capitalism it is the commodity that defines our relationships.

It is within this social nexus that true spontaneity can emerge. People influence, learn, collaborate, compete, and inspire one another. These interactions form a synergistic creative space in which ideas can emerge and feed off other ideas. This collaborative space can advance knowledge not only in the arts and sciences, but in practical know-how or technics. Creativity is fundamentally collective. Knowledge, culture, and technology should all be shared by all.

We must find an authentically spontaneous order, one in which power is distributed efficiently among all the stakeholders in production. An authentic socialism would not concentrate the power of planning in the hands of the few but distribute it in such a way that production serves the common good. Markets may have a role here, but only insofar as they operate within a larger system that prevents these concentrations of power. Only with a deconstruction of power can the Logos truly be realized.

7

Capital

Markets in the Middle Ages were dominated by guilds, but they could never exert full hegemony. There were always merchants and lenders who worked for themselves as well as independent artisans and craftsmen, and the power and prestige of the nobility was threatened by that of the guilds. Their riches lay in their land holdings and the taxes they levied on them. Some were known as "robber barons," charging people for access to resources they controlled. Such were the type of exploiters against which Robin Hood was said to rebel. The same label would later be applied to the cutthroat industrial capitalists of the 19th century.

These profit-seeking nobles - including wealthy merchants who purchased their titles - sought to make business ventures to compete with the guilds, which exerted monopolistic control over much of the production in trade. Those seeking to bypass the hegemony of the guild system and set up their own enterprises looked to the countryside. There, people could take their capital and organize trade networks of cottages producing goods and selling them at a profit. In these "cottage industries," a capitalist would subcontract work to these cottages and receive a profit for themselves.

After the Black Death emptied out the feudal manors, leaving yeoman farmers where there were once serfs, a movement began to privatize this common land in what became known as the enclosure movement. This left many peasants without land to make a living for themselves. They provided a steady stock of labor for these cottage industries, which through the development of technology and centralized labor management systems developed into the factory. Where the guild craftsman would apply their training to create finished works reflecting their skill and creativity, the factory worker was assigned a small, repetitive task that numbed the mind and drained the soul. This was not a natural evolution from feudalism, but a counter-revolution against a situation that had empowered workers and peasants and threatened the power of the feudal hierarchy.

Wage labor has existed in some form since antiquity, but it took on a new life under capitalism. Where the slave was considered human livestock and the guild worker was an initiate into an order, the wage worker represented labor as something abstract: an asset in which to invest for profit. Wages are a per-unit commodity of abstract labor to be purchased from the worker. This differs from a contractor who agrees to a particular job and carries it out. The contractor still controls their labor and does the job according to their standards. By contrast, the wage worker sells their working day to the capitalist, and while they are "on the clock" they are beholden to work according to the rules and standard set by the employer.

The factory owner was not a worker who worked their

way up through mastery of the craft, as one would find in a guild, but rather an investor who used their capital to buy the machinery and hire dispossessed workers willing to exchange their labor power for wages. Their goal was profit, and if the workers saw some share of that profit, it was only when the general level of wages rose due to competition, forcing the owner to spend more money to retain them. This also meant that when labor was abundant, wages would fall.

The process of dispossession through enclosure, which Marx called "primitive accumulation," ensured a steady supply of laborers into the factories and the control of the capitalist. In fact, it produced a surplus of labor, Marx's "reserve army of the unemployed," allowing them to suppress wages by limiting access to the means of production. This pool of unemployed people meant that workers could be readily replaced, with the ever-present threat of hunger and poverty hanging over their heads.

Sabotage

Thorstein Veblen saw that one of the principal functions of the capitalists was not to increase industry but to strategically sabotage it. Their aims are primarily monopolistic, and only incidentally productive. They seek profit, but they do not "maximize" profit so much as they deploy it in the pursuit of power. Full employment is far more productive than maintaining a pool of unemployed people, and would even be profitable for everyone. Yet these shared profits would threaten the relative power of the capitalist. Thus, artificial scarcity is maintained. Capital will gladly take a pay. Administrators increase their own salary rather than investing it in more production. Bureaucracies retroactively render themselves necessary because nature abhors a vacuum. Business elites create and manage the institutions by which people are admitted into their ranks. Power is not isolated to one individual but circulates among a group of people. Yet it also must also maintain a hierarchical distribution. Capital operates by restricting the distribution of power and maintaining the structures by which it is perpetuated.

Capitalism has a well-known growth imperative, in which economic output must grow indefinitely. In a Marxian critique of political economy, due to technological innovations there is a tendency of the rate of profit to fall. As technology enhances the productive power of labor, the amount of labor required as a ratio of capital would decrease. Commodity value, he claimed, was tied to the amount of abstract labor necessary. Therefore, over time, there should be a decline in average rate of profit coinciding with the decline in necessary labor power. John Maynard Keynes envisioned something like this bringing about a "euthanasia of the rentier," in which declining interest rates would eliminate the speculative aspects of capitalism and lead to a new era of social investment. However, Marx saw that capitalists had an arsenal of tools in their belt to counteract this. Capital must continually expand its productive base by extracting more materials, growing the labor supply, opening new markets, collateralizing capital into abstract forms, and increasing labor exploitation. This growing throughput applies increased stress on the environment. There is no infinite growth on a finite planet.

So how does this square with Veblen's idea of sabotage? Marxian analysis claims that capital really is increasing production, yet Veblen's analysis suggests that capital sabotages production. How can this be? We've seen this growth firsthand as neoliberalism has opened capital markets throughout the world and globalized production, but Veblen would say that what has grown is precisely sabotage. We see growth in the division of labor, the bureaucratic multiplication of tasks, the abstraction of capital into financial assets, the creation of new wants through advertising, the canalization of product demand through branding, the commodification of not only nature and labor but of ideas and virtual entities. Along with this also comes the growth of the security state, as imperialism is used to maintain global order and the police and surveillance state is expanded domestically to squash dissent. It is, in other words, a growth of waste.

This waste is apparent in the workforce. David Graeber describes a phenomenon of what he calls "bullshit jobs," which effectively have no social benefit other than to pad the pockets of capital. First are the "flunkies" such as receptionists and administrative assistants who serve to make their superiors feel important. Then there are "goons" hired by corporations to fight the "goons" of other corporations, such as lobbyists, corporate lawyers, and telemarketers. Next are "duct tapers" who make temporary fixes to problems that could be solved permanently. Next are "box tickers" such as survey administrators and corporate compliance officers who create the illusion that something is being done when it is not. Then there are "taskmasters" such as middle management who manage and create busy work where none is needed. For every "bullshit job," there may also be real jobs that uphold the bullshit job. A telemarketing firm might have an office where they hire a janitor who does real work but is only doing so because of the bullshit jobs they support. A secretary might end up doing most of their boss's job for them, because it is their boss that has the bullshit job.

This multiplication of meaningless tasks does not contribute any greater value, surplus or otherwise. It is what John Ruskin called "illth" as opposed to "wealth." What it does is simply extend the control of capital over our lives. Workers who are confined to an office for 40 hours a week do not have time to organize and agitate for a better world. Those that do have such time face an increasingly militarized police force ready to crack their skulls. It is not enough for capital to control land, natural resources, and the means of production. To maintain this control, they must extend it into our daily lives. The factory system itself became popular not so much because it is more efficient than the guild system, but because it broke down the specialized skill of the worker and made them easily replaceable. The factory has now been spread out into the city, and the wealth we create in common is captured through algorithms, debt leverage, and rentier speculation.

Finance

The control of capital extends beyond one's own factory or institution. The stock market allows individuals to trade shares in companies they would otherwise never set foot in. This distributed ownership means firms can sell not only goods and services, but also their own future profits.

The distribution of stock in companies seems on the surface to democratize capital ownership: anyone can buy a stock, which entitles one not only to a share of the profits, but also a vote in the company in proportion to one's shares. Yet such shares are highly concentrated at the top. An employee may have a 401k or even a personal portfolio, but such things pale in comparison to the amount of controlling interest the wealthy have over the global economy. Moreover, the same people often sit on multiple boards of directors, and multiple companies are owned by the same parent company.

There is a tendency in economics to treat stocks as "fictitious capital," having a derivative value that is dependent upon the "real economy." Yet this confuses the nature of capital. Capital is by its very nature abstract. It is the result of a process called capitalization. Capitalization is simply the discounting of present value in expectation of future gains — in other words, using a commodity to make a profit. That commodity could be a manufactured good; it could be a tool used to make other goods; it could be the factory in which those goods are made; it could be land on which the factory is located; it could be the firm that owns the land or a separate firm that owns the factory.

Capital is an abstracting process rooted in quantification. An object that can be quantified can be owned. An object that can be owned can be bought and sold. And an object that can be bought can be sold at a profit. Capital therefore has a metaphysical component to it. It is an emergent consequence of a relationship with nature based on quantification, objectification, and domination. The moment we ate the Fruit of the Garden, we took the first step toward capitalization. Capitalization itself is a process that has unfolded since the late Middle Ages and accelerated since. Phenomena like derivatives, short-selling, and futures markets are simply logical extensions of the entire concept of capital. The expansion of capital is the constant quantification and abstraction of new sources of profit.

Firms trade on the stock market as one of many commodities whose futures can be bid upon. The bets both predict the future value of assets and affect that value. If a large enough group of people invest in a stock, that stock's value will increase, and by investing in it, those people are betting that this increase will happen. Keynes once compared this to a newspaper beauty contest in which contestants are asked to choose the six most attractive faces out of a selection of a hundred photographs. To win the contest, one must come closest to guessing the six finalists. To succeed at this, one must choose not the six faces that one personally finds most attractive, nor the six faces that everyone else finds most attractive, but the six faces that everyone will expect everyone else to find most attractive. In this manner, the stocks that people most expect everyone else to bid on will be the ones whose price does in fact go up. Because expectation plays such a major role in the stock market, it is subject to sudden shocks based on the news of the day. It also creates a feeding ground for manipulation.

Capitalization means betting on future value, and the best way to predict the future is to influence it. Capital therefore is always in search of ways to exert power over the course of world events. If people can make the future bend to their will, they can make their bets pay off. They seek to influence government policy, technological research, consumer demand, and availability of resources. They seek to stake out their monopolistic control of society and expand it while guarding it against competitors.

Firms engage not in free competition as economic models often presuppose, but monopolistic competition characterized by differential accumulation, in which different firms seek an edge on market share through acquisitions. Production plays a much smaller role here than orthodox Marxist theory tends to assume. Expanding production may result in increased profits, but it is easily matched by one's competitors, making any competitive advantage short-lived. Attempts at cost-cutting, either through efficient technology or deliberate budget slashing, inevitably result in a short-lived advantage as competitors follow one's example.

Far better to expand the size of one's firm by incorporating other firms into one's enterprise. Mergers and acquisitions do not intrinsically affect production one way or another: production can continue to be done by the same people when ownership changes hands. In fact, mergers often come with layoffs, increasing market share and maintaining output while decreasing the number of bodies tasked with production. Mergers and acquisitions increase during times of economic expansion, but if too many people are trying to "beat the average," stagnation occurs, and recession sets in. Recovery occurs as new forms of capitalization emerge to provide a new market to be sought after by monopolistic capital.

Corporate CEOs may get large salaries, but the real money is in stock options. This allows them to buy or sell stock in the company they run based on how they expect it to perform in the future. There is ample opportunity for manipulation, in which one makes these bets based on information otherwise concealed from the public. This practice, known as insider trading, is illegal, and people have gone to prison for it. However, without whistleblowers or other leads, it is easy for it to pass under the radar, and because it can be so hard to prove what someone knew at a given time, the government often doesn't care.

Colonialism

Capitalization demands expansion, and historically this meant colonization. The year 1492 marks the birth year of globalization. Upon landing on the island of Hispañola, Columbus saw that there were immense quantities of gold, and he enslaved the local Arawak people to mine it for him. His brutality was legendary even among his contemporaries, but it set the stage for a pattern that would repeat itself time and again. A race to conquer the world began, with Spain and Portugal initially dividing the spoils between themselves.

A dividing line was made granting most of the New World to Spain while giving Africa to Portugal. In Africa, the Portuguese found mighty kingdoms willing to sell them large quantities of slaves. A huge market for these slaves developed in the New World. Slaves from Africa were taken from their homes and brought to this new continent of unfamiliar territory and with nowhere else to go. France and Britain later joined this scramble for the world, along with others like Belgium and the Netherlands.

The Netherlands, however, was less in need of a land empire when it was able to build a financial empire. Dutch bankers had been financing the Spanish Reconquista against the Moors, and the Spanish crown was deeply in debt to them. The gold that Spain brought back from the New World went straight into servicing that debt, and a massive wave of inflation erupted in Spain, while Dutch coffers overflowed.

The British combined the military expansionism of the Spanish with the financial power of the Dutch. The Bank of England was established as the first central bank, allowing the British to finance their colonization efforts throughout the world. British companies used the conquered territories to establish enterprises, from the founding of Jamestown by the Virginia Company of London to the Company Rule in India by the East India Company. This public-private partnership would become a defining feature of British imperialism and laid the foundations of global capitalism.

These enterprises required local inhabitants to do the work. Many refused to do so: Indigenous peoples often lived an idyllic agrarian lifestyle growing perennial crops that required a minimal amount of work, unlike the more intensive European farming methods. The inducement to work for European plantations proved futile even when high wages were offered. Europeans complained about how "lazy" the people were, and contrived ways to make them work. Enslaving everyone by force was too costly, so policies were designed to leverage people into debt servitude. The British implemented a "hut tax" in their African colonies, taxing each household or "hut" a certain amount payable in currency, labor, or grain stock. The result was that people had to work for their colonizers to pay back this debt.

Land was privatized and the commons abolished, just as it had been in Europe. Conquered lands belonged to the crown and were granted to favored European speculators. The process of primitive accumulation made commodities of the land and natural resources. People who had lived on the land for generations now had to pay a landlord for that privilege. Traditional horticultural practices that supplied food for the local population were replaced by large plantations run by outsiders. Regional economies were transformed toward an export-based system in which a single cash crop was grown for global consumption. The result was a massive loss of autonomy for these colonized lands, who would remain economically dependent on their colonizers long after officially gaining their political independence. Upon gaining their independence, these countries inherited the debts of the colonizers who had opened markets there. They took on new loans to pay for these existing loans, ensuring they would forever remain tied to their colonizers.

The separation of agriculture and industry further increased this dependence. Natural resources were exported to the imperial core, where they were used for manufactured products that were then sold back to the colonies for more profit. Farmers could no longer make their own tools, so they became dependent on their colonizers for the very means of making a living. This system of dependency was served by an international finance system leveraging usurious loans to the peripheral colonies that brought wealth back to the imperial core. The periphery was to export only raw materials. Only the core was allowed to produce finished goods. Traditional forms of craftsmanship were uprooted and destroyed, to be replaced by the factory model of a subservient proletariat. This form of sabotage would repeat itself in multiple iterations throughout the history of capitalism, following a pattern of what David Harvey calls "accumulation by dispossession."

Hegemony

As capitalization expanded, empires themselves began to let loose the chains of statehood and nationality to become a single global empire of capital. The stock market allowed people to invest remotely in the resources of other countries. People who have never set foot in a country can invest in their real estate market, bidding up housing prices and putting rent and homeownership out of reach of people who live there. International loans often come to low and middle-income countries with conditions involving the privatization of their resources and opening up of their capital markets. This leads to a form of neocolonialism in which their resources are funneled to wealthy investors in the Global North.

What's more, loans intended to improve a country's infrastructure end up going to foreign contractors, so that the wealth flows out of the country. The result is a huge subsidy to these corporations, paid on the backs of these countries seeking to improve the lives of their own citizens. This quick flow of capital in and out of a country makes it extremely difficult for the development of industries by their own people. Thus, the ones building factories in these places are also foreign investors. The people become wage laborers for the colonial powers, enriching them and seeing the profits flow out of their own country and into the pockets of the Western bourgeoisie.

The new imperialist power first and foremost serves an

international capitalist class that has captured the state apparatus and uses it to maximize their own profits. Some states benefit more than others by their relative position to either the core or periphery, but the capitalist class ultimately knows no national allegiance. There is no homogeneous group dictating world affairs according to some grand conspiracy. Rather, there is a class of elites competing with one another for power in its myriad forms. They use political donations to affect policy in ways that benefit their bottom line, which may go against another industry's bottom line. They compete with one another in the political sphere as well as the market.

Capitalists seek to limit their competition as much as possible, in politics as much as the market. Firms are constantly bought out by other firms, so that it's never quite clear where the money is going. It can be exceedingly difficult to boycott a company that owns a wide variety of different brands under one conglomerate. Such monopolistic tendencies were once targeted by anti-trust legislation, but policy and enforcement has grown lax to the point of near obsolescence since the 1980s. The result is a more unequal distribution of wealth than ever before.

Even in countries with strong antitrust and campaign finance laws, states still depend on corporate interests. They are seen as "job creators" who keep the economy going. States must therefore compete with one another to create a business-friendly environment to attract investors. They naturally still want to make sure that their constituents will vote for them, which means passing compromise measures to satisfy the people enough to keep them coming to the polls. However, in a profound sense, the capitalist class simply has more votes than them. The people must therefore vote for which corporate-friendly political platform is most suitable to them.

The fundamental rule is that capital eats first. This is not to discount the real differences between political parties. This is not a matter of candidates being "in the pocket" of corporate interests, though that happens as well. It is not about crafting legislation specifically with the good of capital in mind, though that too is common. An adamantly pro-worker party could fight for all manner of legislation to benefit workers, but only to the extent that it doesn't interfere with the mandate for capital accumulation. If capital is no longer able to expand and accumulate profit, then the entire system is thrown into disarray.

Philanthropy can be yet another form of monopolization. Some elites will make a show of donating to great causes that make them look like positive contributors to society. The Gates Foundation, for example, has as its mission enhancing healthcare around the world and eliminating poverty. However, in doing so, it ends up setting the agenda for the countries in which it operates, pushing what the foundation thinks is best for people. No one elected this foundation or its founders to determine healthcare policy in the Global South. No vote was held to determine that it should guide economic development in all the countries where it operates. Such things are at the discretion of the organization's leadership to use its donations for their prerogatives.

Think tanks propagate their ideological visions of what the global political and economic order should look like, and if those ideas happen to align with financial power, they can expect plenty of funding. They can spread their influence through the media, whether through direct ownership of networks, sponsorship of programs, or having public intellectuals appear on news programs to argue their case.

The university is a prime spot for spreading influence. Universities occupy certain parts of the public imagination as centers that radicalize influence; while this may have some truth in some humanities fields, it is not the case for STEM fields. Engineering or computer science labs can get vast amounts of outside funding, and become career tracks for the corporate world and the military-industrial complex.

The social sciences are not immune to these influxes of cash, most notably economics. The field of economics is not completely unified, and there are departments where one can find heterodox views taught, but by and large economics is dominated by the Neoclassical school. This school has become the foremost propaganda arm for the Neoliberal world order. They produce the experts that join these think tanks and create a consensus that the interests of corporations are common sense. Some more progressive-minded economists become Neo-Keynesians instead, but while this school argues for more steering of the economy through public spending and tax policy, they still ultimately do so with the capitalist class in mind.

Economists are to the modern state what the high priests and seers were to the ancient God-kings. They attempt to read the signs of the times to advise politicians as to what set of policies will guide the way to prosperity. These policies tend to align with what became known as the Washington Consensus. This was a consensus, not between the different countries of the world, but between Wall Street, the World

Bank, and the IMF. It is a view that advocates privatization of resources, opening of capital markets, and market liberalization as the key to growth, which itself is treated as the highest good. The result is debt peonage, turning the borrowing countries into vassal states.

John Perkins recounts his experience as an "economic hitman" who would come to a country with a resource coveted by the capitalist class and offer them a loan. If they accepted, capital would come into the country and restructure it to extract their wealth. If they refused, they could instead fund an insurgency against them, hiring "jackals" to overthrow them and prop up dictators that would serve their interests. If this failed, a military invasion would be the last resort, as we saw in Iraq. As he describes it, "If an EHM is completely successful, the loans are so large that the debtor is forced to default on its payments after a few years. When this happens, then like the Mafia we demand our pound of flesh. This often includes one or more of the following: control over United Nations votes, the installation of military bases, or access to precious resources such as oil or the Panama Canal. Of course, the debtor still owes us the money — and another country is added to our global empire."[9]

Then there is of course the hegemonic influence of religion. The version of Christianity taught by colonizers has tended to be self-serving. This is especially evident today in Evangelical Christianity, which has spread throughout Africa and Latin America rapidly over the past few decades. Evangelicalism follows other forms of Protestantism in its emphasis

---

[9] Perkins, John. *Confessions of an Economic Hitman*, Berret-Koehler Publishers, San Francisco, CA, 2004.

on individual salvation and the primacy of Scripture but has become particularly notable in its preaching of Prosperity Gospel. Prosperity Gospel is a theology that promises earthly prosperity in exchange for worship. Through this vehicle, the Washington Consensus becomes not merely an ideological imperative, but a religious obligation. Private property and free markets become the means by which the Kingdom of God is to be realized.

This cult of Mammon appeals to people because it promises a change in their own circumstances that seems more immediate than the long process of social change. This form of Mammon worship has found its way into New Age spirituality through the concept of a "Law of Attraction" which allows one to manifest whatever one desires through the power of positive belief, effectively turning consumerism into a form of worship. This spiritual narcissism has spread rapidly through cult-like multilevel marketing schemes that promise people a quick way to the riches they desire for the price of recruiting others into their pyramid scheme.

Profit

Marx analyzed capitalism as a system defined by a set of internal contradictions. These contradictions are not the kind of logical contradictions one finds in formal logic such that A = -A. Such contradictions are necessarily a logical impossibility, and therefore cannot exist in reality. The contradictions that Marx discusses are of the Hegelian type: mutually antagonistic forces within a given system that give it an internal instability. The contradictions of a system can never be resolved. Instead, the system must continually maneuver itself to find some sort of balance, which it cannot maintain without maneuvering in another direction, as if trying to stay still on a unicycle. However, the contradictions come from multiple directions, and the system inevitably loses its grip and falls into crisis.

A central contradiction for Marx was between use value and exchange value. The use value of a commodity is the value that it has for the person possessing it, while the exchange value is what it can be bought and sold for on the market. The producer creates commodities not for their own consumption but to sell them on the market to consumers. Exchange value is driven by supply and demand, but demand is not straightforwardly equivalent to use value. The same item can have a wide variety of use values but only one exchange value. A knife can be used for chopping vegetables, carving wood, or committing murder. Its exchange value is indifferent to its various uses.

Yet through the process of capitalization, the use value of something is simply its discounted future exchange value. This is what happens with speculative assets. People buy something at one price with the expectation of selling it at a higher price. This becomes particularly problematic when the asset also serves a vital use value. Consider housing: People need a place to live, so a house serves a vital purpose for them. But as more people seek housing, demand for it rises, driving up the price. In response, speculators buy up houses not to live in, but to turn around and sell at a profit.

This happens with all manner of natural resources such as water, minerals, or fuel sources. It also happens with essential services such as health care or public goods. The contradiction is between the uses people have for goods, especially ones essential to their survival, and the demand for profit. Extracting profits by withholding scarce resources or creating artificial scarcity is known as rent-seeking. Rent is income earned from possession rather than production. The rentier seeks to corner the market and monopolize resources.

A segment of the economy known as the FIRE sector is defined by rent-seeking. It stands for finance, insurance, and real estate. These industries do not provide goods and services so much as they control access to them. They are gatekeepers who keep resources artificially scarce. Such controlled access may be necessary if the resource in question is naturally scarce or finite, but doing so based on the profit motive leads to outcomes that benefit the profit-seeking few at the expense of the many. The FIRE sector is at the very center of the economy today. The days of the industrial factory have been surpassed by an economy of private equity, real estate speculation, debt leverage, and data mining. Factories still exist largely in the Global South, but even so, they play a smaller role in the global economy.

Profit distorts human needs and desires. In addition to creating artificial scarcity of essential resources that people rely upon to survive, it also incentivizes the creation of wants where none existed before. Consumption becomes not simply about satisfying one's needs, but about finding new needs to be satisfied. Consumption and production must both rise for the capitalist to maximize profit. Consumerism is the consolation the worker finds for sacrificing most of their waking hours toiling away to labor for another. The demands of wage labor keep us separate from the bonds of community we might otherwise enjoy.

Wage labor produces alienation, in which the work we do is not our own. The artisans of old would produce their own products to sell on the market at a price they set. Under wage labor, the worker is tasked with creating goods or performing services at the direction of the capitalist, who then sells it on the market and pays the worker a fixed wage out of the profits. The worker is effectively lending their labor to the capitalist, and the capitalist is their debtor, yet labor laws have been arranged to obscure this debt-like structure by giving the capitalist all the privileges that would normally go to the lender rather than the borrower. The capitalist then becomes a "job provider" rather than the worker being a "labor provider." At no point does the worker control production. They work at the discretion of another to produce products that are not theirs. Their lives do not belong to them, so whatever free time they have is spent in the pursuit of possessions. As most of one's wages go toward rent and other essential expenses, whatever commodities or entertainment one can purchase with what's left are a welcome distraction.

In mainstream economics, the idea that price signals accurately represent real needs and wants is still taken at face value. At the very least, it is treated as the baseline from which "distortions" must be corrected. Nothing is more emblematic of this than the practice of measuring national economies by Gross Domestic Product, or GDP. GDP simply measures the total amount of money exchanged in an economy. It doesn't matter if that money is spent on food and shelter or booze and gambling — GDP measures the *cost* of economic activity. It tells us nothing about what is gained for that cost.

If one were to try to measure the benefits accrued to a society, one would seek to minimize cost relative to those benefits. Instead, the cost becomes the very measure of those benefits. Breaking it down into GDP per capita remains a measure of cost rather than benefit. The problem is that benefits are qualitative rather than quantitative, and economics only knows how to deal with quantity. The economy should serve values that transcend itself. The power of capital has served to distort values in such a way that society is made to serve the economy.

The capitalist seeks profit not as an end in itself but as a means to power. In cases where power and profit conflict — and there are several — they will always choose power. Capital is intrinsically obsessed with control. To control the market is to control the future, and to control the future is the dream of all tyrants. Capital is the modern-day successor to the empires of old, seeking to conquer one another and control one another's territory. Capitalization has ushered in a new era in which empires can be bought rather than conquered by the blade. The conglomeration of firms and hegemony over institutions has expanded power in ways that the likes of Alexander the Great or Genghis Khan could only dream of. We now live under the global empire of capital.

The United States is currently the leading superpower whose military might secures this empire of capital. Yet it would be a mistake to simply equate the US government with the power of capital, as so often happens in anti-imperialist discourse. Capital by nature knows no borders. It is loyal to no country, but seeks to remake states in its own image. To the seat of empire, it offers a flow of cheap goods to be consumed. Yet it can also support production of finished goods in one country while drawing raw materials from the periphery of empire. This was the model of classic imperialism and was true of the US until the neoliberal era starting in the 1970s. A similar pattern is emerging today in China with its Belt and Road Initiative.

State actors within the empire of capital can find themselves in the core or the periphery. Core states such as the United States benefit from a concentration of capital that funds a privileged standard of living. Other states find themselves dependent upon them for capital, and become export markets for natural resources or manufactured goods that cater to the consumption demands of the core states. These states form the periphery. There are also semi-peripheral states that are dependent upon the core but are themselves able to exert some regional hegemony of their own and form their own mass consumer markets.

The US now finds itself in a position where its manufacturing is largely focused on the production of weapons for the maintenance of its empire. Meanwhile, an increasing amount of work is in the service industry, which is more immune to outsourcing. The rest consists largely of administrative tasks. The spread of capital markets throughout the globe involves the proliferation of paperwork, administering the flow of capital, property claims, financial accounts, payrolls, legal claims, store inventories, and so on.

Capitalism's growth imperative should not be understood in purely physical terms. Rent-seeking always outpaces production. The drive toward differential accumulation multiplies the abstractions on which firms can speculate to seek an edge on their competitors. Physical resources are simply a means toward this monopolistic edge, and capital will first seek to hoard them before putting them to use in production. The latter they will do only to the extent necessary to keep up with their competition.

We have an energy crisis not because renewables cannot be as profitable as fossil fuels but because fossil fuel companies have so much vested power and hegemony that they are unwilling to concede. Oil companies could theoretically switch their investments over to renewables and still make a profit, but will not do so at the cost of letting go of the market power they have staked out as an industry and more importantly, against one another. The reckless waste of resources under capitalism is a cost of war between capitalists.

Crisis

Core states use their power to enforce the international economic order and ensure that the demands of differential accumulation continue to be met. Yet all these efforts cannot hold off the inevitable cyclical crises built into the system. Capitalist accumulation is differential, requiring a constant imbalance in the market that allows for companies to gain a competitive edge over one another. With everyone trying to beat the market, eventually this competitive edge smooths off and results in stagnation, with firms selling off assets in an attempt to stay ahead of the falling profits of their competitors.

It should be emphasized that the institutional structures of capitalism work in such a way as to obscure the fundamental capacity of the economy. There are still people who need goods and the capacity to produce them. What has been lost is simply the capitalist's ability to maintain their profit margins. The profit motive demands that people lose their livelihoods rather than let profits fall. Profit motives are relative, not absolute: even a falling rate of profit can be good for a firm if their rate of profit falls slower than everyone else's.

There is a dichotomy between circulating capital and fixed capital. When capital is invested in the production of goods and services, it has a relatively short turnaround time. Yet if capital is invested not in producing goods for consumption but in bidding up speculative assets, no new wealth is created. The investors take on debt in the hopes that the profit gained from these assets will exceed the debt they must pay off. Eventually a point is reached where the debt can no longer be paid off. This happens particularly often with the housing market. Housing prices are bid up at the same time that people need to live in them. When people can no longer afford housing, the productive sector of the economy suffers, as workers must make longer commutes to get to work and have less money left over for buying consumer goods. The return on this speculative investment slows down as this contradiction reaches its limits and the debt can no longer be paid. Financial instruments serve as both risk managers and asset speculators, blowing up the bubble even further, and ultimately creating an even greater crisis.

When crises hit, the government intervenes to restore order. Attempts are made to "prime the pump" by injecting money into the economy to boost consumption. Stimulus checks are sent out in the hopes sales will increase and make businesses profitable again. Public works are used to boost employment. Yet because of the cardinal rule that capital eats first, stimulus plans often involve bailing out the speculators who created the crisis in the first place. The 2008 Global Financial Crisis saw toxic debts bought up by the government to keep banks afloat and get them lending again. Debt relief that could readily improve the lives of ordinary citizens is the exclusive privilege of the financial elite.

Capitalism never actually solves its crises; it simply moves them around. Capital makes use of geographic inequalities to produce surpluses in one place and sell them in another. It's a familiar paradigm: new areas are developed by exploiting older ones. New markets are created through capitalization and a gold rush occurs for these new assets until stagnation sets in, precipitating a new set of assets. We see this today with the development of cryptocurrency and NFTs: a whole digital economy had to be created to create an even greater level of abstraction from which capital could continue its accumulation. Attempts to gamify every aspect of human life are like a heroin addict looking for an intact vein. Only by this constant reinvention can capital continue to resolve — and perpetuate — its crises without rendering itself obsolete.

The instability of capitalism comes from the fact that it requires an imbalance, but this imbalance is built upon credit, which is intrinsically dynamic. Feudal lords did not need to continually seek out new serfs and land titles to continue financing their lifestyles. They owned the land outright, were entitled to a portion of what their serfs produced, and did not have to worry about paying anything back. The capitalist, by contrast, takes on debt to finance their enterprise, and must make a profit on their investment in order to pay back what they owe and come out ahead. If the drive to get ahead of their competition isn't enough to motivate the capitalist, the need to get ahead of their debts will do the trick.

Capitalists seek ways to stake out a passive revenue stream that will ensure profits. However, they face competition from other capitalists seeking to stay ahead. To come out ahead means not only for one's revenue to exceed expenses, but to gain a monetary edge. Yet the tendency is for such comparative advantage to level off over time. Much like the boom and bust of cryptocurrency and NFTs, newer forms of speculative asset must be invented just to satisfy this never-ending drive to gain a competitive advantage.

Public Sector

There is some rationale for propping up existing businesses; it's easier to revive businesses that are struggling than to finance the creation of new ones. But public sector work can often fill this gap through temporary infrastructure spending, or more long-term agencies. Some countries will nationalize certain key industries, which allows them to run at a loss during times of economic crisis and continue keeping people employed.

Critics of nationalization claim that such state monopolies destroy innovation, whereas a free market allows for competitive industries to invent new products and innovations without interference. Even if this was the case for one particular industry, there are certain sectors of the economy that lend themselves more toward public management, and in many cases have perverse incentives under the profit motive. The FIRE sector is a great example. Its activities are entirely rent-seeking by nature, and any "innovation" in them is guaranteed to be an innovation in extraction, not production. Of course, as we have seen this applies to productive industry as well: Veblen's distinction between business and industry sees business as extractive by its very nature, controlling production and innovation through strategic sabotage. State enterprise often fares no better because of its concern for centralization and standardization, which is why democratization and decentralization are imperative.

Nationalizing private industries has some benefits, but it is still done by state actors that yield to the influence of capital. They still obey the mandate of capital accumulation, even if it is not their own profits they safeguard. The answer lies in democratization of both the private and public sphere, which in the process would dissolve the distinction between the two. The FIRE sector would most immediately benefit society by being pushed into the public sphere, but it is merely one step toward a more cooperative economy for all. The democratization of the economy means the transformation of the economy away from a growth-based profit motive toward a socially based economy that serves human needs.

Land and natural resources belong to the commons, and their private appropriation serves monopolistic industries to the detriment of everyone else who must use them. Private companies managing them for profit do little more than hold them hostage for a ransom. Their gains are entirely extractive, not productive. The unearned gains of the landlord were a particular polemical target for classic liberals such as Adam Smith and David Ricardo, who saw their rent-seeking as destructive to the innovation of the market. This critique reached its apex in the late 19th century with Henry George, who saw in land monopoly the source of poverty itself; instead he promoted a single tax on the full unimproved value of land as a solution to a vast variety of social problems. His solution still left the land itself in private hands, but the profit from it was rendered to the public sector. Yet getting the profit motive out of it is only a small step toward the liberation of land. It also places far too much faith in assessment and taxation to overcome the entrenched power of the rentier class, who will inevitably find workarounds and ways to leverage their holdings. Only a system of usufruct and collaboration can produce truly democratic communities in which the land belongs to all.

Insurance provides a safety net to manage risks. Private insurance makes sense for private business transactions involving shared ventures or protecting a purchase. Yet insurance often involves public goods that are grossly distorted by the profit motive. The abysmal health care system in the US is a prime example of this, though past experiences in areas like fire protection offer other significant cases. Safety nets are first and foremost a matter of public service. Once the need for these public goods have been met, private insurance can play a supplemental role, but it's dangerous to let it take the lead.

Finance is a particularly devious creature, perhaps the most closely identified with capitalism itself. Finance provides the service of *liquidity*, converting real goods and services into an abstract form that can more easily be transferred and aggregated to purchase other goods and services. This is a basic function of the money form. Credit extends this liquidity across time, allowing parties to obtain larger sums of money for a project to be paid off later. The investment may be in a profitable enterprise, in which case the lender may have some "interest" in a share of the profit. They could also be commercial loans in which the interest is simply an upward transfer of wealth. Or it could be some speculative asset such as a house, which is both a commercial purchase and a profitable investment, yet which produces nothing of its own.

The role of finance in allocating wealth is not so different from that of the government. The difference is that the government allocates their spending according to legislative priorities, whereas banks allocate spending according to what will bring in the most profit. A government doesn't need to be profitable — in fact, it makes no sense for it to be so. Government spending is the source of all the money in the economy, so the government must operate at a deficit. Without such a deficit, no savings or profit could occur in the private market. Government money is vertical money, spending money into existence. Bank credit is horizontal money, moving liquidity around through double-entry bookkeeping. In both cases, there is a common misconception about the way in which money is issued. It is assumed that government spending comes from taxes, whereas bank loans are made from deposits. In reality, taxes come from spending and deposits come from loans. In both cases, the spending is limited not by the amount of funding, but by the resources available to be mobilized.

Yet the essential difference remains one of profit versus policy. Policy may be influenced by profit-seeking industries, but the government itself earns no profit. Corrupt politicians seeking to line their pockets or elicit campaign donations to get re-elected are a constant moral hazard in countries without sufficient campaign finance laws, but the government as an institution cannot by its nature be a profit-seeking entity. If the government serves the profit motive, it is the profit of the ruling class, not the state itself.

There is no reason that profit must be the deciding motive in any social investment. The same credit systems that support Fortune 500 companies could support networks of worker co-ops. The decisions about what gets funded could be in the hands of the people. If we had a truly democratic economy, people could decide what their communities look like, what kind of industries to support, and what kind of development takes place. Currently, that kind of democracy exists neither in the public nor private sphere.

The private sphere is often praised as decentralized and diverse compared to the public sphere which is subject to a state monopoly. Yet what both spheres lack is a communal autonomy and self-determination. What we have now is a private sphere using credit for profit-seeking enterprises while communities depend upon vertical public spending that serves those same private interests. A distinction must be made between the profit-seeking interests influencing both private and public spending and the social needs that are currently neglected by both.

A promising alternative lies in municipalism. Municipal services are of course already provided in the form of garbage pickup, electric and plumbing utilities, and public transit. Yet the development of municipal industries could be a promising frontier. Since municipalities are by definition local, they could develop industries based on the local resources available. Such industries could be geared toward providing jobs and resources to the local population and selling the products to other municipalities, building confederated alliances.

These industries needn't be centralized into a single factory or warehouse. Depending on the industry, they could develop small-scale machinery that can be used at home or in decentralized locations and lent to people to produce for the collective bounty. Whether such small-scale producers would get an hourly wage, a monthly salary, a commission, or some combination thereof would be a matter for public deliberation but would likely depend on the type of work involved. What is important is that it is placed within the public realm of democratic control and in direct antagonism to the prerogatives of capital accumulation.

The municipality thereby facilitates the equitable distribution of the means of production while also acting as a clearing house for the exchange of products. The profit motive is averted, and a democratic ethos pervades not only public governance but economic life as well. In this way, the municipality becomes a commune. It is essential that democracy be extended as much as possible in such a system. Politics cannot be the realm of a professional elite but must be a praxis of and by the people. The power to deliberate policy and planning must lie in the hands of the people themselves.

Socialism

Socialism has been defined in various ways: as government control over the economy; as an economy that serves social interests; and as worker control over the means of production. Though these various definitions may butt heads, there is a continuity between them. The point of workers controlling the means of production is not so much about the workers receiving the full product of their labor, which essentially comes down to asking that they be paid more. The point is that so long as the means of production are in the hands of capitalists, the logic of capital accumulation reigns supreme, and the economy will serve that interest.

Only when workers have control of their own labor can they direct that work toward social purposes beyond the profit motive, and build an economy based on cooperation rather than competition. When that kind of workplace democracy becomes the norm, it can spread to the public sphere and create real democracy there as well, while withering away the distinction between the two. This is what Marx meant by a "withering away of the state": as private and public functions become more democratized, class distinctions disappear, and along with it the distinction between public and private sphere. State authority and economic subjugation give way to communal self-determination.

Marxist-Leninists have generally held that a worker's state is necessary for this transition. The workers must first seize the machinery of the state and redirect its activities toward the replacement of capitalist production with socialism. In the process, the state itself becomes subject to the demands of capital accumulation, essentially becoming one big capitalist enterprise. State propaganda tends to idealize work as some noble calling for the good of the state; workers are encouraged to offer up their labor for the glory of the revolution. This, of course, does not fundamentally change the nature of their work, but merely glamorizes it. The real payoff must ultimately come when global capitalism is finally defeated. Only then can the worker's state wither away into full communism.

In matters of economic policy, there is often little difference between these revolutionary socialists and the democratic socialist parties in Western parliamentary systems. Both seek to nationalize key industries and support generous welfare programs while also supporting expansionist producerist policies. For democratic socialists, of course, the disadvantage is that as members of a multi-party system rather than a one-party state, they are not always in power, and when they are they must form a governing coalition with other parties, often making compromises in the process. Yet such compromises are at least done in a democratic spirit, however hampered by special interests. The compromises of state socialism, however, are an acquiescence to the systemic hegemony of global capital. The socialist state attempts to beat capitalism at its own game, accumulating capital for the sake of creating its own counter-hegemony. The liberation of the worker becomes identified with the good of the state, and only at the end of this struggle will they be able to rest. The democratic socialist may or may not adopt this Marxist eschatology but tends to be more concerned with what they can do to advance the cause of the working class while they hold power, though both groups must compromise their ideology in order to maintain their power.

Another pathway is that of revolutionary syndicalism. The Industrial Workers of the World called for "One Big Union," in which all workers could be organized by industry and united in common cause against their bosses. They would, in this way, "create a new world in the shell of the old." The union, it was hoped, would become the site of political and economic decision-making, replacing the power of both the capitalist and the state. Such a system was tried and nearly succeeded in Catalonia in 1936, only to be defeated first by leftist infighting and then finished off by Francisco Franco's nationalist forces.

Such a pathway to self-determination may not even be that relevant anymore. Under the current system of global capitalism, the factories have been outsourced to other countries, and can readily be relocated again if capital finds the local conditions too unfavorable for their interests. In core countries where traditional production has largely been displaced by service jobs, these service jobs can and should be unionized. Even with high levels of union membership, however, such an economy would still be dependent on exploited labor from peripheral countries, who in turn will find it difficult to organize if production is switched to yet another country with more favorable conditions for capital. Given the enormous role of the FIRE sector in today's economy, a radical unionization effort would have to involve the unionization of service workers, tenants, and even the homeless and unemployed. In other words, we would have to organize not only workplaces, but the whole of society.

Under these pressures, "seizing the means of production" is less imperative than rebuilding them. In doing so, it will make a great deal of difference as to what form they take. It's one thing for workers to take over a factory and claim it as their own, but if we are building a new economy for the people, we should question the factory model altogether. Before the factory, there was the workshop. A workshop could be a communal center where workers produced things together or it could be part of one's own house. A combination of both could help empower people to produce for their own needs and those of their communities. The proliferation of small-scale productive technology could help people create products for more immediate use rather than relying on extensive supply chains. Raw materials would still need to be traded, but information could flow freely so that the know-how and technics for making different products could be spread throughout the world.

With such productive forces at the fingertips of the whole population, we arrive at the free association of producers — communism. To get there requires liberating our institutions from hegemonies that structure our lives around capital and state power. This means examining how institutions cultivate subservience, passivity, and hierarchy, and how they could be restructured as convivial, pedagogical, and liberatory. We have seen how money, property, and utilities could be transformed in this way. Another such institution deserving special consideration is technology, to which we now turn.

8

Technics

Technology is essential to our identity as a society. It is the primary metric by which we measure other cultures of past and present. Often all we have left of ancient cultures are artifacts, and we use these to categorize how "advanced" they were. But those artifacts are measured against what we see as advancements in our own modern society; this measurement also ignores that some of the most important innovations are cultural and structural. Social technology precedes material technology. The artifacts that we call technology are the products of an important social institution called technics.

Technics can be understood as "know-how," and it is this capacity for reproducing knowledge that constitutes a society's true technical prowess. When a society's manufacturing base is destroyed in wars or natural disasters, it can recover remarkably quickly if technical knowledge is preserved. Such knowledge exists in even some of the most "primitive" societies in their understanding of edible and medicinal plants, their methods of tracking and navigation, and proficiency in hunting and fishing. Toolmaking is knowledge of this kind, but only a subset of such knowledge leaves a physical trace.

The ancient megamachine of regimented workers was every bit as much a machine as one made with gears and pulleys. People work together as moving parts in a seamless whole. It is similar to a hunting party or military unit functioning in lockstep with one another, or a dance troupe performing a coordinated piece, or factory workers at an assembly line. The mechanization of the body precedes the creation of other tools to assist in the process.

Such mechanization is an extension of our natural tendency toward habit and muscle memory. Ritual comes from this same tendency. Yet where ritual creates meaning, mechanized labor creates products. We consciously learn skills that then become automatic, and in the process make higher-order decisions on how to deploy these skills. When we learn to drive, we must think about shifting gears, accelerating and decelerating, checking mirrors and blind spots, and so on, but eventually these things become ingrained to the point that we are able to listen to the radio, converse with friends, and even let our minds wander while still performing all the mechanical functions subconsciously.

When one engages in a craft, such automatic habits combine with conscious planning. The craftsperson sees the end product in their mind's eye and applies their skills toward achieving that goal. Not so with more regimented labor. Under the megamachine, each person performs a specific function to carry out the plans of someone else. The worker acts as the hands of the master. Their own intention and vision are left out of the process entirely. Even this can have a certain dignity when the worker believes in the master's vision, as when creating a great work of architecture in which one can take civic pride. It is another matter when the worker is alienated from even this, selling one's labor power for a day's sustenance, the final product belonging to the master to sell for their own profit. Work under such conditions becomes a burden, a cost one bears to survive.

Technology has the capacity to enhance our creative powers, but it can also overpower us and subsume our very humanity into the machine. It can overtake not only our lives but our values, measuring success and progress by the standards of the machine. Such standards mean that productivity and output are seen as goods in themselves, rather than the means for realizing social goods. Consumption is the other side of this value system. As production becomes the supreme virtue, consumption becomes the primary consolation. Production and consumption join forces against their common enemy: leisure.

Leisure is nothing less than the enjoyment of life. Leisure often involves forms of labor, as when pursuing a hobby, or physical exertion, as when engaging in athletic activity. Leisure is not wholly separate from work, but rather involves work on one's own terms. Leisure can be incorporated into productive work to the extent that one is able to enjoy one's own creative autonomy over the process and a shared interest in the results.

Artisanal craftsmanship can be a perfectly leisurely hobby. It offers the satisfaction of meditative activity, an outlet for one's creativity, and a pedagogical pathway to developing one's skill and attaining self-mastery. It is for this reason that artisanal crafts had to be usurped by capitalism.

Colonialism involved the destruction of traditional crafts so that only core imperial powers could produce manufactured goods using the factory model, which kept workers from attaining the satisfaction of self-mastery afforded by such a personal touch.[10] The factory model alienated workers from their creative energies and turned work into drudgery. When production came back to the colonized world, it was under the factory model, which offered none of the consolations of the ancient crafts that had been destroyed.

Elements

The capacity for making tools precedes our own species. Fashioning tools out of one's environment has been observed in apes, corvids, and numerous other animals. The earliest known stone tools were fashioned by the hominid species *homo habilis*. These tools were likely used primarily for butchering raw meat as this species had not yet tamed fire: meat would be tougher to cut up, making such stone tools all the more useful. Similar stone tools could also be used for cutting wood, though we have little way of knowing what wood tools and constructions might have existed in the past, since they would rot away with little trace long before our present era.

Later species such as *homo erectus* developed sophisticated stone tools alongside the critical harnessing of fire. Archaeologists still aren't sure if they had the ability to make fire on

---

[10] The destruction of India's textile tradition to make them dependent on British textiles was among the injustices that Gandhi protested.

their own or were simply able to capture it and use it for their own purposes, but even the latter represents a significant advance in technics. Fire embodies the very principle of creative destruction. Like a living creature, it consumes matter to create energy.

Fire was an engine of transformation throughout human history. Fire allowed people to shape their tools and weapons, cook food, boil water, warm up in the cold, and illuminate their night. Fire in the hearth, the forge, the candle and oil lamp, represented a constant companion and a looming danger.

The ability to cook food allowed for a revolution in nutrition: it could kill off parasites and foodborne illnesses, and make certain foods more digestible. The overall effect of cooking was to allow people to get more out of the food they ate and spending less time trying to seek and consume it.

The fireplace had a central place in the community. Sitting around a campfire continues to hold a hypnotic power over us. Its warm glow soothes and enchants. The fire kept predators at bay, yet also attracted some curious company. A popular theory suggests that wolves attracted to the smell of cooking meat may have waited along the outskirts of encampments for scraps, leading to the domestication of the dog. Whether or not this is the case, we can certainly credit fire for the domestication of humans. The stories and songs and rituals done around the campfire formed the essence of human culture.

As people created permanent settlements, the fireplace moved indoors to become the hearth. The center of communal life became the center of domestic life, and the hearth became the symbol of the domestic sphere itself. Household deities were worshiped around the hearth. Cooking became an integral part of culture. One of the most readily identifiable cultural signifiers is its native cuisine.

If the hearth was the sign of the home, the sign of the workshop was the forge. The first application of the forge was ceramics, especially pottery, which had a direct effect in underpinning storage capacity. The storage of grains was particularly important, as it allowed for an accumulation of surpluses that could support non-agricultural endeavors. It also allowed for the saving of seeds, helping people to replant crops each year and spread their crops into new areas.

This storage capacity was essential to the agricultural revolution. Early states were essentially grain storage facilities with an army to protect them. Political anthropologist James C. Scott spoke of early "grain states" where the growing of grain by farmers and its storage in centers of power formed the basis of political authority. Grain makes an excellent basis for taxation: it is visible, divisible, assessable, storable, transportable, and rationable.

The forge presented the next iteration in the use of fire, with the ability to modify the temperature of the fire to hammer out the impurities of metals and mold it into shapes for tools, weapons, armor, or construction. Metal tools were stronger than wood and more malleable than stone. Such tools proved valuable extensions of the human body. Farming, logging, construction, and craftsmanship all saw a whole world of new possibilities.

Farming was revolutionized by the plow. The work of multiple people tilling the soil could now be done by a single person operating a plow pulled by horses or oxen. Thus, larger fields could be cultivated by fewer people. A new division of labor developed, with men doing the plowing while women stayed inside the home to perform the domestic duties of cooking or sewing. The digging of canals further expanded agriculture and created a greater resource base with which to feed a complex society.

Construction materials became more readily available. Rocks could be quarried with metal picks. Trees could be chopped down with metal axes and saws. Lumber could be used not only to build houses, but to build scaffolding for more monumental architecture. Fortifications could be built to defend cities and frontiers from attack, and weapons of war could be forged to attack and subjugate others.

All of these advancements taken in total created a certain "legibility" that allowed for the kind of accounting and assessment that was integral to state formation. This legibility was realized in several ways, from the city planning to the standardization of family names. Bureaucracies always work through the simplification of complex phenomena. Human societies develop customs and practices that are legible to their own members and forge community bonds but are inscrutable to outsiders. An administrative power must standardize social patterns in order to absorb people into its system and control them.

The administrative state grew out of a need for logistical planning arising under this new phenomenon known as civilization. The ability to create finely crafted tools went with the ability to regulate and administer a stratified society. Classes and castes grew to ensure that there was a reservoir from which to draw the differing forms of labor needed to keep the system going.

Obtaining metals involved extracting them from the

ground, a task not suitable for free men. This was a task for slave labor. The mines were fraught with dangers, from collapses to toxic fumes and any number of respiratory diseases. Miners would sleep in the mines, sometimes going months at a time without seeing the light of day. Where the agricultural worker encountered life in all its vitality, the mine was a place of unforgiving raw matter. For the miner, matter is a given quantity of this or that substance, no different from any other quantity of that same substance taken from another mine. The aggregate quantity of substances to be molded and crafted into tools and artifacts becomes the model of a certain way of seeing the world. The mine is the birthplace of materialism. The need for slaves to mine the metals drove campaigns of conquest, and the metals they mined allowed for the building of new weapons and armor to equip the armies and help them conquer yet more territory and take new slaves.

The Bronze Age was the birth of empire. Mining, metal, slavery, and empire all went together. A mode of production came together based on the enslavement of war captives, forging of weapons, exploitation of farmers, and the tight discipline of the military machine. The megamachine served a sovereign who acted as a living god, the state apparatus itself a manifestation of divine power. The sovereign was at the helm of this massive machine whose greatest end was the glory of their own power.

The War Machine

The military was the first megamachine. Troops with the

discipline to operate as a cohesive unit were able to conquer more easily. Armor and weapons develop in tandem, with defensive and offensive equipment mutually surpassing one another. As city walls and defenses develop, so do siege weapons. The continual investment in military technology helps one stay ahead of the game.

The creation of weapons immediately birthed an arms race. New technology is readily adopted in weapons of war. With other economic activities, one may maintain a concept of "good enough," but in military matters, one must always keep up with external threats. No matter how peaceful one wishes to be, defending oneself is a necessity of power.

Those skilled at conquering gain greater access to resources, and in turn use those resources to strengthen their military and conquer more territories. Much like the profit that the capitalist keeps reinvesting, for empires, conquest begets conquest. With a powerful enough army, one can often avoid a fight, as territories willingly surrender and submit rather than face destruction.

Not all militaries follow the machine model, with soldiers as the engine of empire. Some are proud warrior cultures whose warriors charge into battle seeking glory and honor. The soldier-warrior dichotomy can be found throughout history: the Roman legion vs Germanic and Celtic tribes; Athens vs Sparta; the British army vs Scottish Highlanders. One might think the Mongol hordes were an exception to this, but in truth, Genghis Khan organized a highly trained and disciplined armed force out of what had once been a warrior culture. The Vikings were a warrior culture, and while they terrorized villages throughout Europe and the Near East, they never built an empire.

The war machine involves more than just weapons and tactics. It also includes logistics, transportation, surveillance, communication, medicine, cryptography, and espionage, among other areas. Because of this, military technology often trickles down into civilian life. We can see this with such technologies as computers, internet, jet engines, satellites, and weather radar. To be a military society is to be a technological society.

As militarism summons this technological boom, it mechanizes society. The need to keep the troops fed, supplied, informed, and ready to deploy necessitates that civil society become regimented, surveilled, regulated, policed, and disciplined. The Roman empire constructed roads between its territories to facilitate troop movements just as the interstate highway system was created to move troops anywhere in the country at a moment's notice. Mass surveillance has become an increasingly pervasive part of our lives. Commercial enterprise functions on the basis of a regular work schedule to which workers are expected to adhere.

Police are thought of as separate from the military, but in truth they are a standing army used against one's own citizens. The police may indeed be "peacekeepers" who maintain "law and order," but it is the law and order as decreed by the state, not the people. Military-grade weaponry is readily adapted to this domestic military. Police forces as such are only a couple centuries old, but the policing of conquered territories by standing armies is as old as empire itself. In the modern era, the conquered territory is not just on the outskirts of the empire, but within its very heart. The conquered are the subjugated classes of society, and the police exist to keep them under the thumb of empire.

The carceral state extends the machine through the practice of human warehousing. Prisoners provide a cheap source of labor that was once provided by slavery. Where prisoners of war once provided slave labor to work the mines, today's prisoners are captives of a war on the subjugated classes. Marginalized communities are patrolled by police, facing search and seizure on the flimsiest of excuses while being profiled as a criminal class. When accused of crimes, they are often pressured to accept plea deals, which puts them into the system as people to be tracked and surveilled and kept out of certain sectors of employment. Meanwhile, prisons serve as something of a solution to housing shortages. The housing market can be devoured by speculators while those dispossessed by the system can be readily housed and fed in correctional institutions.

The security state is a powerful engine of commerce. Conquest has always served as a means of extracting surpluses to fuel further expansion; capital does the same thing today, with the support of the military-industrial complex. The army, police, prisons, surveillance, tech, bureaucracy, and finance all form a framework for the extraction of wealth and maintenance of a global class system. The forces of empire break down boundaries while building up barriers. They take all that is unique and personal and subjugate it to the machine.

Power

The ancient megamachine showed just how powerful a purely human machine could be. Accentuating this was animal power in the form of strong livestock such as horses and oxen. Muscle power, both human and animal, was the chief engine of civilization. This included human livestock in the form of slaves, who powered the great empires of history, as well as the coercive might of the military. Muscle power, combined with smart engineering, built the pyramids and numerous other ancient wonders.

The human harnessing of water and wind are tied together, from the earliest irrigation systems to aqueducts to complex hydraulic systems to sails on ships. Cities and other population centers tended to be built next to major waterways, allowing supplies to be shipped via boats. Water and wind were passive forces to be redirected, while human and animal power formed an active force to be applied where needed.

The use of windmills for mechanical purposes is known as far back as ancient Mesopotamia. Windmills saw a vast expansion during the Middle Ages, when they were used to grind grain and pump water. Around this time, the watermill also came into maturity. It was a time when these natural forces in one's own environment could be utilized in a way that harmonized with the landscape. It saw advances in optics, woodworking, and craftsmanship, with new ways of organizing labor for mutual benefit.

Social historian Lewis Mumford dubbed this age of water and wind the "Eotechnic" age. Power and production in this age was not for its own sake, but for the enhancement of life. Water and wind were renewable and could not be monopolized. They allowed nature to take care of repetitive tasks while freeing up the hands of workers for more creative pursuits. Later, hydraulics allowed for the development of the first mechanical clocks. Automatons using the same interlocking gears and precision-timing mechanisms were often featured in elaborate clock towers. Such automatons inspired Descartes to develop his mechanistic metaphysics. The clockwork universe would eventually overtake the consciousness of an entire civilization.

Water, fire, and air were all brought together in the development of the steam engine. The earliest steam engines existed in ancient times: they were used to operate automatons, open doors automatically, and perform other tricks meant to wow temple worshipers. Yet it was only at the end of the 18th century that commercial steam pumps came into being. They were used in mines and to pump water wheels to power textile machines. The steam engine developed further over the course of the next century to become the symbol of the Industrial Revolution, or what Mumford calls the Paleotechnic. Trains were one of the most visible manifestations of this. The steam locomotive vastly reduced the limitations of time and space. Instead of months, people and supplies could now move across a territory or continent in a matter of days — weeks at most. Steamships could forge new ocean trade routes without depending on the wind. The world became much smaller. It was around this time that capitalism started to come into its own. The shrinking of the globe meant its openness to the movement of capital.

These steam engines required a heat source, and that source was coal. Mines were flooded by the new industrial proletariat. The mines were owned by private companies, who often owned the town as well. Houses, stores, even churches, were all owned by one company. Some company towns would even issue their own currency that could only be spent at the company store. The miners may not have technically been slaves, but their lives very much belonged to the company. As a result, coal mining towns were dens of poverty: to this day in places like West Virginia, coal companies are often the primary job provider and exert an enormous influence over local politics and people.

The industrial regime was fueled by a drive to be bigger, faster, stronger, and more expansive. Production became the measure of man. As productivity advanced, the power of the worker waned. As the machine amplified the power of workers, it diminished them in stature. The machine was the means by which the worker enacted their own servitude. Steam power required centralized, large-scale production, with a central heat source to power all the machines. With the development of electric power, a more distributed system became possible, what Mumford refers to as the Neotechnic age. Electric power does not dissipate as much as thermal power, so factories had more flexibility in how they arranged their production line. Where the steam engine had to occupy a central position on the factory floor along which production units had to be placed, with electricity each machine could have its own electric motor that could plug into any outlet.

Global capitalism can be understood in terms of the abstract power of capital and the telecommunications systems that make it possible, but remember the power of fossil fuels pumping through the veins of our system. Modern patterns of settlement are built around automotive transportation. People commute vast distances to work, sometimes losing hours of their day. Fossil fuels made the regime of growth possible, beginning with the Industrial Revolution and continuing to drive it to the point of oblivion. To regain balance requires slowing down the engines of production and building a socioeconomic and technical regime at a human scale.

Energy

The reliance on coal continued from the age of steam to that of electricity, though it was exported outside of the factory into the power plant. Coal power remains one of the most common energy sources in the world. It is also one of the leading sources of air pollution and carbon emissions.

Yet electricity can be produced in a variety of ways. The splitting of the atom created untold power, initially for destruction. Nuclear scientist Robert Oppenheimer, upon seeing his atomic bomb unleashed, lamented, "Now I am become death, destroyer of worlds." Yet the power unleashed in Hiroshima and Nagasaki was also promoted as a revolution for powering the world. Nuclear energy gives a huge bang for your buck once it's up and running, and gives off neither particulates nor carbon dioxide, but only steam. However, such a calculus is deceptive without taking account of the costs, both financial and environmental, of commissioning and decommissioning. An underrated factor is also the amount of water needed to cool the reactors. It requires large-scale mining of uranium, often in the Global South under conditions of extreme exploitation. Then there is the matter of storing nuclear waste, which has a half-life of thousands of years.[11] Such issues led to popular opposition to nuclear power in the 1970s, and people remember this as causing construction of new plants to grind to a halt. In the worst-case scenario, there are the nuclear disasters of Chernobyl or Fukushima. However, by the time of disasters like Three Mile Island and Chernobyl, the business case for nuclear power had already been lost and investor confidence collapsed following rising construction costs, plants failing early on, and heavy reliance on subsidies. The narrative blaming protesters serves to shift the blame for a failing industry onto public outcry over genuine safety concerns. These safety concerns will only grow as climate change brings more unpredictable weather such as tsunamis and wildfires.

New generations of nuclear energy seek to solve these problems by reprocessing nuclear waste as new fuel, and using molten salt reactors that run at higher temperatures which don't require the level of coolant that traditional nuclear does, making them more secure from meltdown. There is a shift toward downsizing nuclear toward smaller nuclear batteries that have lower operating costs. Yet while the costs are lower, output falls even lower.[12] Nuclear, it seems, lends itself toward greater centralization, and does significantly worse as a distributed technology. This is a problem because centralized production is more vulnerable

---

[11] Barron, Robert W., and Mary C. Hill. "A Wedge or a Weight? Critically Examining Nuclear Power's Viability as a Low Carbon Energy Source from an Intergenerational Perspective." *Energy Research & Social Science* 50 (2019): 7-17. Print.

[12] Ramana, M. V. "Small Modular and Advanced Nuclear Reactors: A Reality Check." *IEEE Access* 9 (2021): 42090-2099. Print.

to being shut down all at once, whereas distributed systems can remain resilient when one or more parts shut down.[13]

Energy sources are all around us, forming an ecosystem of power. While electric power is relatively new as a public utility, energy harvesting is as old as life itself. Plants use the power of the sun to photosynthesize, producing nutrients that are consumed by other species that are in turn consumed by other species. A farm is essentially a solar energy collection system. As we have seen, wind and water also have longstanding pedigrees that predate the electric grid. So much of the modern power paradigm is geared toward power *generation* when there is already so much power to be *harvested*. Capturing this power for energy requires an ecological approach to technology, and a diversity of sources is key to maintaining a steady supply of energy.

Hydro power was widely used in the twentieth century, but the construction of massive dams often had devastating environmental consequences, disrupting food chains and radically transforming ecosystems. There are more small-scale distributed forms of hydro power that avoid this, known as micro-hydro, which can be incorporated not only into rivers but even in plumbing systems. Geothermal energy could be placed along tectonic plate boundaries making use of the natural heat under the Earth's crust. It is cleaner, more cost-effective, and more reliable than coal or nuclear, but it has limited applicability due to geological factors, and can cause hydraulic fracturing, which can contribute

---

[13] McDonald, Samuel Miller. "Is Nuclear Power Our Best Bet against Climate Change?" *Boston Review*. 31 Jan. 2022. Web. 17 May 2022.

to earthquakes. Solar power has the advantage of being clean and decentralized. Solar panels can be installed on any rooftop. However, they only work when the sun is shining, so there's a window of time in which this energy can be collected. The efficiency of solar power has increased by leaps and bounds since its introduction, as has the ability to store energy, and has become much more cost-effective. However, typical photovoltaic panels rely upon rare earth metals whose mining operations are every bit as destructive as coal. Wind power is one of the top energy sources today. It's clean and efficient, but like solar, it is an intermittent energy source, only working when the wind blows. Such intermittency is not as much of a problem with proper storage systems, but even without them, energy use can be timed for peak hours, and use of multiple different sources provides greater systemic resilience.

A whole panoply of energy sources can be discovered if one looks around. Cogeneration allows one to extract energy from processes that give off heat as a byproduct, or to siphon off heat from energy generation. This can be useful for fuel cell batteries, composting, waste incineration, fermentation, and any number of processes. Hydraulic systems such as plumbing can add turbines that produce electricity from the water pressure. Kinetic energy can be harnessed from several sources by putting piezoelectric sensors under roads or dance floors. These are all minor energy sources that pick up extra power at the margins, and are not sufficient as a main power source, but the more of these sources we are able to tap into, the more resilient the energy grid will be. This stacking of functions can improve overall efficiency. The ability to derive energy from other processes that we already use means putting our resources to optimal use.

The distributed integration of these elements constitutes a strategy known as "soft energy paths."[14] This strategy involves distributing different kinds of energy sources according to where it can be optimally collected, stored, and redistributed. The "smart grid" that distributes energy to where it's most needed helps overcome intermittency issues with certain renewables such as solar or wind. Micro-hydro can also serve as a counter-weight to solar since there is often increased water flow during the winter. The use of fuel cells for energy storage adds an extra level of resiliency.

The harvesting, storage, and distribution of electricity are not the only aspects of the soft energy path. There is also the need to power down and use less energy. Energy efficiency is incrementally addressed in buildings as a supplemental consideration taken up after a building has already been designed. This is largely because architectural design and engineering are often done separately. The architect takes aesthetic and social functions into account when designing the building before handing it to the engineer to figure out how to make it work. Smart design can tunnel through the cost barrier by making use of passive solar, cogeneration, and efficient airflow, among others.

If efficiency in building design is important, urban design is even more so. A well-designed city integrates the needs for power along with transportation, water and sewage, and waste disposal in ways that flow seamlessly with the lives of its residents. The smart grid is part of this, but having easy

---

[14] Lovins, Amory B. *Soft Energy Paths: Toward a Durable Peace.* Harper & Row, 1979.

access to services in one's community is essential. American planners often envy their European counterparts for the well-designed public transportation systems the latter have; the real dichotomy is not so much between driving and public transportation as it is between driving and walking. Walkable spaces are the key, with public transportation as the vehicle to take people from one walkable space to another. The closer people live to their place of work and essential shopping supplies, the less driving they have to do. Keeping all such essentials within walking distance was of course a necessity until the twentieth century, so smart planning often means planning as if driving was not an option for most people.

To use energy wisely, we must learn to work with nature. This means looking for natural sources of energy that can be put to use, but also finding ways to use less of it. The uses of sun, wind, and water, as well as gravity and biomass that preceded the age of electricity, can still be applied today, while also capturing that energy for electricity and storing it for later use. Traditional methods of building and planning made optimal use of the resources around them because they lacked the technology to power the kind of heavy machinery we now enjoy. We must relearn the way previous generations got by without electricity, and then supplement that with energy captured from a variety of natural sources.

Renewable advocates are quick to make the economic case for this transition. They point to the energy savings that could be realized, the resiliency that these technologies provide, and the profitability that they promise for business. All this is true enough, but so long as we live under the dictatorship of capital, any savings realized in this way will only go toward further accumulation. Increasing the efficiency of a process only leads to increased use of that process to realize more gains.

Perhaps this is why nuclear energy is so often taken more seriously as an option than renewables. Renewables call on us to work within the limits of what nature provides, but nuclear is a technology geared toward accumulation. It may allow for that accumulation without the direct carbon emissions of coal, but its logic is one of continued centralization and authoritarianism. It is the most convenient technology for business as usual. Continued accumulation, regardless of how efficient it is, no matter how clean the power source, can never be truly sustainable.

Industry

The Industrial Revolution plunged civilization into a world of black skies and a layer of soot. Lung disease was rampant, and acrid smoke permeated the air. At the same time, however, improvements in sanitation reduced water-borne diseases and dramatically cut down on child mortality. This led to a massive population boom, which in turn created an immense pool of workers and the overcrowded slums needed to house them. Children filled mine shafts and women labored in crowded textile factories. The "Satanic mills" described by William Blake devoured the natural world and corrupted the human soul.

Advances in textiles pushed demand for cotton. The cotton gin, which was meant to save on labor, ended up making cotton a much more viable commodity than ever before. Slave markets exploded with new demand. More slaves were needed to pick more cotton to spin more thread and create more clothing. Around the same time, the idea of fashion as we know it today came into being. Certainly past eras had known fancy clothing, particularly for the aristocracy, but the idea of clothing going in and out of fashion from one season to the next would have been nonsensical to a person living a century earlier — clothes were worn until they were either outgrown or fell apart (and even then, only after they could no longer be sewn back together). Yet because capital must always seek to create the demand for their products, the fashion industry became a way to ensure that the new middle class would keep buying clothes year after year.

When slavery was abolished, a system of sharecropping took its place, effectively a new form of serfdom. This too was displaced by the industrialization of agriculture. Drip irrigation, sprinkler systems, harvesting machines, and several other innovations had a radically transformative effect on the economy. At no time in history has a civilization had such a small portion of its population working in agriculture. It was the industrialization of agriculture along with the introduction of electrical power that essentially completed the Industrial Revolution and paved the way for a new technical regime.

The Industrial Revolution enhanced the productivity of the worker several-fold, but in this new neotechnic age, machines replaced the worker. Industrial agriculture displaced the worker from the farm and led to a mass influx of workers into the city, where factory jobs were abundant. Then automation displaced the worker from the factory. For a while, this was seen as a positive development: with machines taking over the work of human labor, it would liberate humanity to pursue other goals.

However, what replaced productive work was not leisure but service work and layers of bureaucracy. The new factories were not those that produced car parts and electronics, but burgers and fries. The old factories were shipped overseas. Interestingly, they often became more low-tech in their new countries than they had been originally because the lower cost of labor meant fixed capital was at a premium, where before it was labor that was at a premium. Today, factory production is spread throughout the world, with parts of the same products being produced in different factories in different countries before finally being sold as finished products. The modularity of the process means that production occurs wherever is most convenient for capital.

Miniaturization is the paradigm of the neotechnic phase. The computer is the greatest exemplification of this. There was a time when a whole office building would have one computer. Today, not only do offices typically have a personal computer for every worker, but the same person might have a laptop, a tablet, and a smartphone as well. We live in an era where the distinction between different electronics is dissolving into a myriad of different screens of different sizes with similar computing capacity.

Technology under this regime becomes more a matter of facilitating the production and transfer of information. Before the internet, this was done primarily through paper, delivered across the globe through an international postal service. In the digital age, information can travel instantaneously to anywhere: every computer, server, satellite, and cell tower comprises so much infrastructure constituting this global web of information that it is never simply located in any one node.

In principle, this decentralized network should be more amenable to decentralized organizational structures, but in this new era, information is yet another commons for capital to colonize. Capital seeks to monopolize the infrastructure of this vast network, buying up competitors and their patents to extract rents from them through intellectual property. In the age of social media, users themselves are free sources of information, data points to be sold for profit.

Intellectual property was first developed as a way to facilitate trading of information between firms. Guilds operated by trade secrets, which members swore solemn oaths to protect. This kind of disciplined loyalty could not be counted upon by early capitalists operating with hired wage laborers working under them; such workers were loyal only to their paycheck, which they could just as soon get from another employer looking for a competitive advantage. A firm copying the technology of another enjoys its benefits without the cost of developing it. Patents and copyrights allowed a firm to make a profit off the use of their technology and information by charging a fee for their use.

Such claims required a vast legal apparatus to uphold, which in turn required the development of the bureaucratic nation-state. In the modern digital age, nation-states themselves operate as part of a vast network of nodes in which capital operates. States nominally have the sovereignty to determine their own laws and regulations regarding intellectual property and other aspects of this information economy. However, capital seeks standardization in these laws, which it achieves through international banking systems and free trade agreements. The free flow of capital and international enforcement of intellectual property rights constitutes a global mandate for which countries can face harsh sanctions for violating.

This decentralization also happens in workplaces, with workers divided into teams and individuals often operating relatively independently within a firm. There is a creative dynamic between nodes in the network that produces all the innovation and value. Capital simply captures this value and sells it as its own. Firms themselves are bought up as vassals of larger conglomerates. The extraction of resources, the production of commodities, the development of technology — all of it takes place in a vast global network ruled by a global rentier class. Capital is not committed to any one form of organization, but rather seeks to leverage whatever fissures can be found within any given organization for its own power. It will seek to curb innovation to the extent that it disrupts its power, but will find ways to filter it into forms that are amenable to their continued rule.

It is worth recalling Veblen's distinction between business and industry. Industry is concerned with material production. It is an intrinsically collective effort, if only because productive knowledge is collective. Every invention is built upon a vast background knowledge developed by countless others. Every product uses products that others have created or resources that others have extracted. Even the lone artisan in their workshop is drawing from a collective system of knowledge and production that is beyond quantification. Business, on the other hand, is concerned only with pecuniary distribution. Business takes the collective effort of industry and seeks ways to profit from it. This includes rent-seeking tactics to strategically sabotage industry. Business will allow industry to operate to the extent that it can extract this profit, and intervene with it to the extent necessary to maintain artificial scarcity and class hierarchy. In this way, business is parasitic upon industry, and thus is the greatest impediment to it.

Appropriate Technology

The socialist approach to technics has largely been to intensify the technics of the capitalist order. The Soviet Union and China industrialized rapidly using the technocratic management methods of the capitalist West. Marxist theory has often focused on unleashing the forces of production to accelerate the tendency of the rate of profit to fall. Under this logic, a form of state capitalism is practiced under the premise of accumulating surplus value for the worker's state and bringing out the internal contradictions. The surplus value is used to fund an extensive welfare state similar to that of social democracies, but the need for growth and accumulation remains.

This is promissory socialism: the people are assured that the exploitation of their labor is done not to enrich the capitalist class but to build a socialist system in which the means of production will finally belong to them and they will no longer be alienated from their labor. A post-scarcity society is sought, in which machines will do the work for us, and people will be free to pursue leisure and recreation. Yet all the while, the workers are subsumed into the same megamachine as those living under capitalist regimes. The machine instills a sense of servility in the worker that is not alleviated in the least by declaring it the People's Machine.

An alternative approach seeks to release work itself through a more liberatory approach to technology. This approach, known as appropriate technology, seeks to use technology to satisfy needs rather than promote accumulation of surpluses. Instead of seeking to maximize efficiency in producing as much as possible, it seeks to optimize the work process and final product for the community involved. It thereby seeks to reorient production away from the capitalist growth imperative and toward communal values that serve the common good. The result may appear either "high tech" or "low tech," but it is not arbitrarily so: it simply places the good of the person at the center, and uses whatever tech is best suited to such a purpose. Such technology is designed to be an extension of the creator rather than rendering them servile to the machine.

This involves a decentralized approach, in which technology makes optimal use of local materials, local energy sources, and local labor to produce goods and infrastructure for the local community. Trade and information networks are maintained, but rather than structuring the community to serve those networks, it adapts those networks to serve the community. Production serves the community first, and only then produces surpluses to be traded with others. It is the same global network, but the nodes are built up, rather than subsumed to the empire of capital.

In his 1973 book *Tools for Conviviality*, Ivan Illich uses the term "conviviality" to describe a harmonious relationship with technology. Convivial technology is technology that enhances our creative powers rather than replaces them. The problem with technology is we sought to make it our slave, and in the process we became enslaved. We become free to the extent that we treat technology as our collaborator rather than a servant. Technology is convivial to the extent that it is accessible to everyone, that it requires little specialization to use, and that its use is directed by the user. Convivial technology tends to be small-scale, which is to say, human scale. It works with us, not for us.

Illich identifies five ways in which technology can disrupt our lives. First is environmental, in which large-scale technology stresses the environment beyond its carrying capacity. Next is radical monopoly, in which a technology entrenches itself into society in such a way as to render itself a necessity. Then there is overprogramming, in which the technology lends itself to overspecialization and professionalization. Next is polarization, in which structures and institutions are built that include some and exclude others, creating dominator hierarchies between the haves and have-nots. Finally, there is planned obsolescence, creating a technological rift between past and present.

Similarly, there are five characteristics of convivial technology. First is connectedness. This looks at how technology shapes interpersonal relationships. This means ensuring that production and supply chains don't rely on the exploitation of others, and that it enhances social bonds rather than eroding them. Second is accessibility. This means making the technology adaptive to people with different physical and mental abilities; simple to use so that it will not be controlled by a small elite of experts; and available for whoever wants to use it. Third is adaptability. This is the extent to which it can be reused, repaired, or modified to reduce wasteful consumption as much as possible. Fourth is bio-interaction. This is the effect the technology will have on ecosystems and living organisms, seeking a closed-loop economy in which inputs are minimized and waste is recycled and reused as much as possible. The fifth and final aspect is appropriateness for the task performed. This means that time and material inputs should be aimed toward human ends rather than the mechanical efficiency of the megamachine.

It is not that one can or should have a society that makes exclusive use of convivial technology. Some technologies simply do not lend themselves to such flexible, personal use, yet may still be useful enough to keep. Every society will have its own balance to strike between convivial technology and what we may call "rigid" technology. The point is that such decisions should be made in a democratic manner that respects the whole of human life, rather than just the profit motive. We must awaken from the stupor of technocratic life that has taught us to value production, efficiency, and growth, and make wiser decisions about how we augment and experience human life.

Appropriate technology has a social context. It flourishes under certain environments. When cities develop in a healthy and sustainable manner, they foster ingenuity through the process of import substitution. Appropriate technology is adaptable, modular, and practical. It is, in other words, the kind of technology that a human-scaled economy will tend to produce. It is authoritarian technology that interrupts this process and occupies space with dominator hierarchies. Appropriate technology, therefore, simply needs the right liberatory space in which to flourish, and it will do so.

Freedom

The current technical regime perseveres by forcing the population into wage labor, alienating people from their own creative abilities. It is therefore crucial that we establish an irreducible minimum. That is, we must guarantee each person a minimal standard of living, including food, housing, credit, education, and leisure: people must be secure in their basic needs so that they can pursue more valuable and creative tasks. Some may choose to do nothing, and simply live off the dole. This should not be a problem, as the proliferation of unnecessary work is precisely what maintains the destructive engine of accumulation. It is in fact necessary to eliminate these unnecessary jobs from the economy, and doing so requires that we guarantee a livelihood without work. In 1930, John Maynard Keynes predicted that, in 100 years' time, a 15-hour work week should be sufficient for the needs of the economy; today that figure is likely much less. We can afford to have most of the population do nothing productive and still sustain the needs of everyone.

However, most will find they are not satisfied with watching TV all day and would instead discover their own creative pursuits. They may study philosophy, write poetry, play a musical instrument, plant a community garden, learn a new skill, hold festivals and banquets, or pass their knowledge on to others. They would also have more time with their families, friends, and neighbors, to cherish the moments that truly matter. Relationships would take a higher priority than commodities, and care work would be valued over productive work. Effort that once went into production could be redirected toward celebration, incorporating festivals and gatherings into the life of the community. Aristocracy traditionally enjoyed such privileges, going so far as to disdain work. They would practice fencing, go horseback riding, wrestle, joust, throw lavish parties, and practice art and music. Such things are also the common lot of societies that have little if any hierarchy. Such societies also share the burden of farming, hunting, cooking, building, and other such necessary activities, but these would be shared in a sense of comradery and play. This can be our lot as well.

Universal basic income would be a part of this, but UBI under a private housing market would simply transfer that income into the hands of landlords. It is therefore necessary to decommodify housing and establish a usufructuary economy in which the municipality acts as a commons from which to draw for all available resources. A library-like system of free lending would allow for sharing of resources and minimize reliance on the market. A municipal credit system controlled by the people would allow for purchases in local markets and collective funding of large projects for the benefit of all rather than the narrow pecuniary interests of capital.

We must establish what urban sociologist Henri LeFebvre deemed *the right to the city*. This means that the social space currently occupied and commodified by capitalism becomes the common inheritance of all. People must have equal access to municipal resources, public space, and contributions to public decisions. The city must belong to all its inhabitants. A right to place, to community, to common resources must be shared by all. Undertaking the responsibility of solidarity, everyone has the right to find in the city the conditions essential for their political, economic, cultural, social, and ecological development. Everyone must have the right to participate in the formulation, definition, implementation, fiscal distribution, and management of public policies and municipal budgets. To ensure the wellbeing of all its residents, the city must assume the realization of projects and investments to the benefit of the urban community.

Ensuring this right to the city is essential to the liberation of work. By establishing the city as a usufructuary commons, an irreducible minimum can be established whereby people are free to pursue their own passions when liberated from wage labor. Freed from the confines of capitalist production, a new technical regime can emerge based on the free association of producers. Technology can then be built with flexible uses to address local needs. A democratic techne can emerge which enhances the creative abilities of all and facilitates a more leisurely society with more time for social relationships, creative pursuits, spiritual practice, and self-realization.

Science

Science and technology share an interesting dialectical relationship. Technology puts scientific discoveries to use, but it also enables new scientific discoveries to be made. Perhaps the most advanced science of the Middle Ages was that of optics, which enabled the first corrective lenses, but also enabled tools for enhanced viewing such as binoculars or telescopes. Telescopes were initially used for seeing far off distances, but it was Galileo who turned it toward the heavens. It is this repurposing of frivolous leisure that often drives technology, just as a child-like curiosity drives science. Play comes before practicality, and practical solutions are developed in the process of imaginative exploration.

This play joins thought and action. One ponders a hypothesis and then attempts to solve the puzzle of how reality might behave if that hypothesis were true. This, of course, is the goal of scientific experimentation. However, not all science is experimental. Some sciences, such as paleontology, involve excavation, which is a real-life process and not a lab experiment. The past has already happened and we cannot wind back the clock to watch it unfold differently. While chemistry may be deployed for the purpose of dating a fossil, the overall endeavor is more akin to detective work than controlled experiment.

Because we take science to tell us meaningfully reliable things about the world, there is a tendency to view it as disinterested and overly rational, bracketing off any values, emotions, or imagination. Yet it is in fact a highly imaginative endeavor. It is one in which one's imagination is spurred by some curiosity and set about on a quest to satisfy it. It is not disinterested but intensely interested in the phenomena it examines. It is furthermore rooted less in conscious reasoning than in praxis and tacit knowledge.

Tacit knowledge is key to understanding science.[15] Everything we explicitly know is grounded in some intuitive know-how. We are always reading some sort of map while interpreting it as we move. To read the map is to know how

---

[15] Polanyi, Michael, and Harry Prosch. *Meaning.* The University of Chicago Press, 2012.

to read it. To interpret it is to know how to make inferences. To move is to translate that inference into action. Science shines a spotlight on phenomena, but for everything it puts in the spotlight, there is a wider field of tacit knowledge supporting it. What is tacit is subjected to a new spotlight, but the field of tacit knowledge continues to recede from view. Scientific discovery is a matter of converting tacit knowledge into explicit knowledge. Hidden implications to previous research become apparent in subsequent research and become subject to new testing.

A collective field of tacit assumptions constitutes a paradigm. The paradigm determines how knowledge is arrived at, what counts as knowledge, what gets measured or ignored, and how results are demonstrated. Experimental results are interpreted according to the paradigm within which one is working. Sometimes there is a single prevailing paradigm, as with Newtonian mechanics, while other times there are competing ones, as with modern theoretical physics.

Paradigms can run deeper than that, however, and constitute a type of techne. As there are authoritarian or democratic technical regimes, these technics can show up in scientific discourse and research programs. There is a type of science that approaches nature as a vast mystery to be explored with great reverence and humility. Nature is understood in terms of its cycles and diversity, in order that humans can adapt to it and thrive within it. Along with this comes a view of the human as a dynamic agent integrally connected with the environment. This paradigm is ecological, pluralistic, and based in wonder.

There is another paradigm that is authoritarian and patriarchal, viewing nature as a resource to be exploited and bent to the human will. As it seeks to assert human dominance over the natural world, it empties out the human subject. Humans are reduced to complex machines programmed to behave in particular ways based on biological self-interest. Genes, neurons, and other "hard" coding are the engines that shape human destiny, not anything resembling agency, freedom, or social relations. Freedom is understood as rational utility-maximization. This type of science sees humanity itself as something to be rationally managed. Technocratic planning is the order of the day, and hierarchical organization is seen as the natural order of things. When a managerial approach extends to the whole of humanity, exploitation becomes the very law of nature, seizing what one must to get ahead. Life becomes a struggle of the fittest, with cooperation a mere convenient and temporary strategy to advance one's own interest.

This is nature as megamachine. It is the extension of the megamachine into the cosmos, indeed not unlike the ancient megamachine of the Bronze Age. Much like the court astrologers and seers of that age, the science of the megamachine interprets nature with the goal of preserving power. The power of patriarchy, exploitation, and racial supremacy are upheld in the name of science. The gods have become depersonalized, reduced to a set of inviolable "laws of nature" that determine how the world runs and *must* run, and all suggestions to the contrary are wishful fantasies contrary to the order of the things.[16]

Changing our social structures, therefore, requires a shift in our relationship to nature. We must cast off the chains of technocratic, managerial, patriarchal domination. We must rediscover nature in her mysterious relational presence. We must rediscover the human subject as a center of embodied connection. We must rediscover society as a collaboration that we co-construct and can choose to construct differently if we have the will to do so.

None of these values contradicts the available scientific evidence. They simply reframe how we evaluate the evidence and teach us where to look for new evidence. They offer us new horizons for understanding our place in the cosmos. They will unite the rationalized human object with the actualized human subject. We will find ourselves, as Stuart Kauffman puts it, "at home in the universe."

In *Two Suitors: A Parable*, historian Richard Tarnas posed the following scenario: Imagine that you are the universe, and two suitors are trying to court you. One treats you as if you lack any intelligence or purpose, inferior to himself, and relates to you as if your existence is merely of instrumental value to him to exploit you for your resources. The other values you as an intelligent, worthy being with your own

---

[16] One can see this in evolutionary psychology, sociobiology, and a trend toward neurological and genetic reductionism, particularly with respect to IQ and various forms of human achievement. This mode of science was of particular interest to Jeffrey Epstein, whose generous donations to Harvard funded such research. Evolutionary psychology's reduction of human behavior to reproductive fitness worked well for a man who sought to seed the human race with what he considered to be his superior DNA, and who viewed young girls as vessels for male fertility.

values and purposes. He seeks to draw himself closer to you, to know your inner depths and mysteries. Which suitor would you choose?

This is a science of liberation. It will seek to understand what freedom looks like, how to relate to nature as community, and how to relate to one another as full persons in mutual connection. These things may be scoffed at as unscientific, subjective, or outside the realm of science. Yet this is only true of a science that accepts a priori the fact/value distinction, presupposing a valueless universe onto which value is, to the degree that it exists at all, projected upon the universe by subjective human habits. In contrast, we can understand value as something arising within the world itself, expressing some mysterious facet of the Logos.

9

Cities

The built environment is an extension of ourselves. All animals shape their surroundings in some way, but humans take it to another level. Human settlements may be temporary, setting up camp in a given location until the seasons change, game animals migrate, or livestock needs new pasture, then picking up and moving elsewhere. Others build permanent settlements with continuously occupied structures from one generation to another. Permanent settlements allow for more people to live in one place, becoming more socially complex as they expand.

Over millennia, the nomadic way of life has been eclipsed by that of permanent settlement. As a result, there is a common assumption of a developmental trajectory from the former to the latter, as though nomadism is the more "primitive" form of culture: we speak of societies and their technological advancements in terms of being "civilized." Yet history is not so simple. The foraging and pastoral peoples known to us today are largely nomadic, but this is partly due to most of the fertile lands being settled or subsumed, and non-agrarian peoples must contend with marginal lands. In the time before agriculture, people inhabited all manner of environments, and the more fertile ones afforded residents with abundant food without having to move around. There was a limit to how big such settlements could grow without depleting the food supply, but several naturally abundant places were available for a global population much smaller than our own.

As discussed in previous chapters, some of the first cities were ceremonial. The Göbekli Tepe site in southern Anatolia was a vast temple complex where humans settled for at least part of the year. The same flexibility that allowed nomads to pick up from one hunting ground to another also allowed people to switch between being nomadic for part of the year and moving into large settlements for other parts of the year.

Houses were often built in a circular formation, with a center for communal activities. The firepit that held a central place in the Paleolithic developed into the hearth in the Neolithic household, which took on a religious significance. While life may have been simpler in many ways, people in this era achieved astounding feats of monumental architecture such as the megalithic sites of Stonehenge or Göbekli Tepe.

In the time before the rise of cities, villages and towns were not isolated from one another. We have evidence from the Stone Age of expansive trade networks spanning entire geographic regions. Settlements across vast distances shared a common culture and were in constant communication with one another. The growth of cities is often seen as a kind of expansion, but it's more of a contraction — cities pull people into their orbit.

Contrary to evolutionist models in which people develop

inexorably from small bands of hunter-gatherers to complex settled societies, people have always had the capacity to make and unmake social structures according to their needs. Technics apply as much to social structures as to tools and artifacts, and the dawn of the megamachine went with the rise of authoritarian structures. The rise of the state was characterized not by people running headlong to their chains but rather through a calcification of structures so that authorities that once existed seasonally became permanent fixtures.

Community

Some of the earliest cities were egalitarian. Çatalhöyük was a proto-city where houses were stacked together and accessible only from the rooftop, allowing for easy communal defense. A similar situation presents itself in the early settlement of Jericho. Many of these proto-cities seem to have arisen out of a sense of mutual defense. The city walls formed a kind of permeable membrane that fostered the good of the community inside while minimizing external threats.

Cities could serve many purposes. Sometimes they were located near important natural resources. They could be geographically important trading centers, particularly seaports where goods could arrive from far away. Sometimes their origin was less pragmatic and more cultural: pilgrims traveled to religious centers from distant lands to trade not only goods but also ideas and practices. Whatever their origin, cities were places of material and cultural exchange.

Feeding a city requires agriculture. In proto-cities, there

was enough surrounding farmland for the inhabitants to provide for themselves. However, as larger cities developed, a division of labor grew between city and countryside. The city became dependent upon the agricultural surplus from the country. In return, the city provided a commercial center where goods could be produced and traded, allowing the country-dweller access to resources they might not otherwise have. Yet there was a clear asymmetry: the city needed the countryside much more than the countryside needed the city.

These cities were founded on solidarity. People would come together around trade, defense, and mutual aid. Their roads were built not for the passing of armies, but for daily commerce. Winding paths traversed houses and workshops where people sold their wares. Roads were designed around buildings, rather than vice-versa. Such conditions were meant to be lived in, not passed through. If one visits ancient or Medieval cities today, one can easily get lost in the maze of winding roads that split off in seemingly random directions. Yet for those who lived there, there was an organic order to this layout. It is an order built for its residents, not for visitors.

A living city emerged from a living process, and buildings were predominantly vernacular. That is, they were built using local knowledge without professional guidance. If someone wanted a house and there were none available, they could simply build one wherever there was room. Houses doubled as worksites, and were often stacked next to one another similar to modern townhouses. The compactness of this development maintained a comfortable microclimate that protected people from the elements. Each new building was designed to blend in with its surroundings, unfolding naturally in a kind of conversation with the environment.

In modern urbanism, design and construction are strictly separate, with planning taking place in a studio and then carried out by a construction crew. By contrast, under the guild system the master builder would work on-site with the rest of the crew, guiding the building toward completion. Having eyes on the ground allowed them to adjust the plan as needed so that the final form was best adapted to its environment, not unlike how biological forms are able to develop along different adaptive pathways. The result was structures that had life and vitality, something which speaks to us to this very day.

Whether professionally built by a guild or constructed in the vernacular, buildings that possessed this quality of organic unfolding permeated the entire city. These places had life because they unfolded according to the principles of life. And precisely because of this, they brought life to the community, with streets made for bustling, convivial activity. People felt a sense of belonging that is lost under modern urbanism. People now travel long distances to visit these places and experience the kind of vitality that they never experience back home.

Infrastructure

We live under the shadow of industrialism. The Roman grid re-emerged in the Renaissance and became the pervading feature of modernity. The modern city is built around commercial and industrial interests. Every road, every bus route, every tram line, is built for the purpose of ferrying people to and from work and transporting supplies from one location to another.

Though the conviviality of the medieval commune is lost, the modern city is more integrated than ever. Houses are no longer simply structures built up wherever there is space. They must connect to the electric grid, water and sewer systems, roadways, waste disposal systems, and other utilities. Utilities have always played some part in cities, but the march of technology has led to an increasing variety of services that the municipality can and must deliver to its residents.

Human settlement has always followed the availability of water. The first towns were settled along riverbanks, which provided not only for crops and drinking water, but also transportation, first of people and later of materials. Irrigation allowed expansion into places that did not naturally have enough water to sustain the population. Water was also used for industrial purposes from an early age, notably in the forging and smelting of metal. The development of watermills allowed the natural flow of water to be used for milling, rolling, and hammering, powering industries such as lumber and textiles. Hydraulics were used heavily in the Industrial Revolution, including the heating of water to produce steam power, which came to define the age. Hydraulics are still widely used today in the mining of minerals and the operation of industrial machinery. Influent and effluent flows continue to play a central role in countless industrial processes.

We tend to think of water as one utility and electricity as another, but they are integrally connected. Electricity powers a vast system of pumps in a city's water system. Dams play a critical role in bringing electricity to rural areas, while power sources such as coal and nuclear that rely on the generation of heat use enormous amounts of water to cool their equipment, risking meltdowns if these systems go awry. These power sources use more water than agriculture, not counting the water used to mine the minerals they consume.

A city is an ecosystem, and it must be wise in its use of resources. Drought and famine have killed off more than a few once-mighty civilizations. There needs to be an elemental balance for a civilization to thrive in harmony with its environment. We must be mindful of throughput — the flow of resources into and out of our social and technological systems — to ensure the larger environment around us can sustain it.

Soft energy paths such as wind and solar take advantage of natural flows. The wind and heat of the sun are used in ways that minimize strain on the surrounding environment. Whereas dams cause mass disruption in an ecosystem, micro-hydro power can make use of natural waterways without significantly disturbing them, and can even be applied to parts of our own water distribution systems, especially wastewater. The more distributed and scaled down these systems are, the less they throw the ecosystem out of balance, and the more fail-safe systems there are in case any one part goes out of commission.

This passive principle, in which natural flows and processes are attended to and utilized with as little brute force as possible, also applies to buildings and roads. The use of local resources for building materials cuts down on transportation costs and encourages a conservationist ethic toward one's surroundings, encouraging that what is taken from the environment is replaced at a sustainable rate. The layout of development should reflect both the natural advantages of location and social factors that emerge from patterns of settlement.

Utopia

Cities have always figured prominently in utopian schemes. In a sense, the city has its origins in utopian thought. The Greek *polis* gives us the root form of what we today call "politics." It was the site of all sorts of political experiments and visions about the ideal society. Athens and Sparta were both experiments in types of political order. The former was the birthplace of democracy, while the latter gave us regimented military society. In Athens, we have a system in which the body politic takes shape as a society of equals ruling together, where public discourse shaped policy. The public in this system only included a minority of people who lived there, excluding women, slaves, and foreigners. Yet those included within it were peers, none better than another. They chose leaders by lottery, drawing lots to choose who would exercise executive functions for limited periods of time. In Sparta, the body politic consisted of a warrior class, with another class of non-citizen residents, and a third class of slaves known as helots.

Plato produced one of the most famous pieces of utopian literature with the *Republic*, which depicted the ideal polis. For him, the polis was the means through which people could strive toward the Form of the Good. He imagined the stratification of the ideal society into different classes, with Philosopher Kings ruling with wisdom, followed by soldiers and auxiliaries, and a third class of commoners who, unlike the other two classes, were allowed to own property. Wary of the logic of the market, Plato saw how property provided one form of power that must be kept separate from political power. He sought a kind of meritocracy that would direct people toward the Good by overcoming the corrupting influence of financial and familial influence on the structure and exercise of power.

Aristotle analyzed the strengths and weaknesses of different forms of government, including despotism, oligarchy, and democracy, seeing virtues and flaws in each, while discussing how each can degrade and give way to another. Throughout all these forms, however, he saw the polis at the center. He saw politics as emerging from ethics, and ethics as ultimately directed toward the polis. Virtue, he claimed, was directed toward living together with one another, which meant inhabiting the polis. Man, he said, is by nature a political animal.

The Roman grid arose as an ideal for the administration of the empire. Its perpendicular lines crossing one another to create segments of a city allowed them to plan these settlements from the ground up. Indeed, many such settlements began as military encampments, with buildings replacing tents as the camps transformed into permanent settlements. Such settlements were laid out with different quarters serving different functions in a total system whose ultimate goal was upholding imperial rule. They offered a blueprint that could be replicated in each new territory they conquered. Wherever they went, they would make the conquered territories Roman.

This central planning approach has influenced countless would-be utopias ever since. The twentieth century saw numerous attempts to construct a "city of tomorrow" that takes an engineer's eye to the problems of the city. Such social engineers often have a brilliant mind when it comes to accounting for throughput and environmental flows. They may seek to make completely self-sustaining settlements, such as Paolo Soleri's Arcosanti, optimize the city for traffic flow, such as Brazil's capital of Brasilia, or seek to "scientifically" plan cities such that technology does the work for us, as in the Technocracy movement and its offshoots such as the Venus Project.

A panoply of wide-eyed visionaries throughout history have believed they possessed the special key to designing the perfect city, from the Garden City movement to Le Corbusier's Radiant City. From the City of God to the City Upon a Hill to the City of Tomorrow, the city has been both the subject and object of idealistic dreamers since the dawn of civilization. Most city planners don't have nearly such robust ambitions, yet they proceed with a similar single-minded focus, usually one geared toward generating revenue for the city or for the private interests they represent. Whether utopian or profit-driven, such planning inevitably leaves those who are most affected by their decisions out of the process.

Planning

What these schemes don't account for is the element of spontaneity. Some urban planning may actively try to suppress the spontaneous elements of the city, attributing to them all the shortcomings of our current environs. Capitalists critique socialism as the ideology of central planning and coercion, while lauding their own belief in spontaneity as a virtue of the free market. Friedrich Hayek spoke of a "spontaneous order" produced by market signals that could not be replicated through central planning because of all the tacit knowledge distributed throughout the population. Yet if Hayek's criticism applies to state planners, it applies just as much to large concentrations of capital, whose economic prerogatives override the concerns of the community.

Under a modern planning regime, developers come into a city or community with a proposal for some project designed to bring in revenue. Residents may or may not get a say in the matter, and if they do it is a simple yea or nay vote. If they say no, they do not get a say in what gets built instead. It is assumed that whatever needs their community has will be met by the free market meeting their demand. Yet we see from phenomena such as food deserts that the needs of many communities, particularly those with less purchasing power, are not being met.

Jobs tend to be concentrated in commercial districts, while sprawl pushes people out to marginal sites. Those seeking gainful employment must take increasingly long commutes just to make ends meet. For many, this means relying on public transportation, if it's available. Even in municipalities with good public transportation, many jobs are located outside of their reach, creating a major barrier for those who can't afford one. The separation of work and home is a relatively recent development brought about by the enclosure of the commons and the growth of industrialism. As the factory replaced the workshop, workers became a factor of production to be managed, rather than the subjects of production.

Instead of a visionary planner's grand design or a profit-driven free market, cities need real local autonomy and collaborative planning. Someone busy commuting to one or more full-time jobs just to make ends meet is not likely to have the time or energy to take an active role in planning and managing the community around them. It is difficult to manage when you are being managed. What is needed is not only jobs, but a community of people with whom to produce and exchange goods and services.

Jane Jacobs saw diversity as key to a thriving city. Like so much modernist folly, current building practice involves flattening of difference and imposition of monotony. Developers will clear an area to construct entire neighborhoods at once using formulaic designs. They build long streets first, then construct the buildings to fill in the land between them. Residential and commercial zoning are clearly separated, with roads and freeways for cars to take people from one to the other. Such neighborhoods, Jacobs argued, are not only dying but already dead, and waiting for the corpse to putrefy.

A diversity of residential and commercial buildings means a neighborhood becomes a place where people not only go home at night but where they actually live, work, and meet one another. A constant flow of foot traffic keeps eyes on the street and prevents certain forms of crime. There is considerable evidence that violence and property crime are strongly curtailed by this continuous communal presence.[17] This concept, also known as "natural surveillance," is a crucial component of an approach known as Crime Prevention Through Environmental Design (CPTED). A meta-analysis found that such approaches could decrease robberies between 30 and 84%.[18] A mix of old and new buildings allows the new buildings to be dedicated to more intensive enterprises while the older buildings can be put to uses that require less overhead such as community spaces, art galleries, or pop-up shops. Shorter blocks, more footpaths, and smaller frontage areas allow for a greater diversity of uses and more free flow of people in and out of a neighborhood.

Fostering the connections to produce a vibrant community requires a gradual process of unfolding. Like a forest, there is a kind of ecological succession to neighborhoods in which new growth complements but does not replace the old. Each new addition to the neighborhood is a center that can either support or clash with other centers, creating or diminishing wholeness. In this way, the community unfolds as an ecosystem.

When cities unfold organically, they create positive space. Positive space is space that has a welcoming, respectful center, and each center supports other centers to create a

---

[17] See National Institute of Justice. "Social Ecology of Community Crime Prevention." National Criminal Justice Reference Service, 1998. and Fadhila, Syifa, and Nurliani Yulia Lukito. "Surveillance and Architecture, Analyzing the Idea of Eyes on the Street." Evergreen, vol. 7, no. 1, 2020, pp. 132–137.

[18] Casteel, Carri and Corinne Peek-Asa. 2000. "Effectiveness of crime prevention through environmental design (CPTED) in reducing robberies." American Journal of Preventive Medicine 18(4S): 99–115.

coherent whole. When positive space is present, people are drawn to public spaces to gather, converse, and enjoy life together. In an age where social media is bringing people across the globe together digitally, we are losing the local connections that are necessary for real community.

Residents are not mere passive consumers of housing. They are crucial for producing healthy communities. Cities clear slums by forcefully displacing existing residents to make way for new construction. But to regenerate the community into a thriving place requires long-term residents who stay and contribute to its livelihood. A mix of old and new residents is as crucial as a mix of old and new buildings. Long-time residents help improve their communities by building a life for themselves there. This allows for new housing and businesses to move in, not as large hegemons that displace people, but as smaller gradual improvements that create stronger centers and enhance the greater whole.

A healthy community needs food, health services, spaces for children to play, and beautiful, nurturing surroundings. Transportation is also a need, but all too often, transportation is prioritized to move people outside their community. A community is not a true community if it does not have these kinds of essential resources and services. It is just a storehouse for workers, serving the production needs of capital. Large roads and freeways cut through communities rather than build them up. Even rail lines and other public transportation can prove detrimental if they are prioritized over walkable spaces and close-knit communities.

As public spaces are closed off and emptied out, we increasingly become strangers toward one another. It becomes more difficult to make new friends, and existing friendships are maintained more online than in real social interactions. Daily life involves moving from closed-off apartments or segregated suburban homes into cars, where people are separated from one another, then into office buildings where they experience most of their in-person social interactions among people who are paid to be there, then finally go home and watch television or chat online or through texts. To socialize requires effort. One must make plans, go out to bars, clubs, and events, but there is little of the intimacy found in bustling city streets where community is found on a daily basis.

Completely self-sufficient communities are neither realistic nor desirable, but they should seek to build a diverse local economy within their trade networks. Trade is good. Not all goods and services can be produced in one place, and people's lives may be enriched by a variety of goods available from elsewhere. However, communities can be flattened when transportation is prioritized, making them little more than stops along the way from point A to point B. Cities were traditionally designed to stop traffic so that commerce and communal life could take place, but the modern city is designed to be driven through with as little slow-down as possible. Communities must cultivate their own potential in order to fully benefit from connecting and engaging with other communities. This holds at all levels of community, from the immediate neighborhood to the city and municipality to all levels of organization. Only then can a "community of communities" flourish.

Planning cannot be left to the professionals alone. Their expertise will inevitably serve some interest other than those of the people living there. It must be a communal effort. Lewis Mumford suggested getting children involved, with surveying integrated into education. Education today serves the purpose of preparing people for jobs to serve the interests of capital accumulation. An alternative approach to education could focus on raising people to be contributing members of their community. The community survey could be tailored in an age-appropriate manner, where younger children learn simpler aspects of it, and as they advance, they become progressively more capable of assessing the community's needs and bringing them to the table for collective planning.

Participatory democracy gets a bad rap. People think of angry NIMBYs yelling at town hall meetings and assume that's what local democracy is. Such sessions have little to do with democracy. Democratic governance is not about arguing between fixed positions and going with the majority so much as a pedagogical process of shared learning and deliberation in which problems are addressed through creative problem solving. Community meetings that seek "input" merely offer a platform for the loudest voices in the room. Community planning, however, challenges them to work with others. Properly facilitated, such meetings can tap into the collective intelligence of the group to develop novel solutions to problems. Such solutions may then be copied by other municipalities, allowing for useful ideas to spread organically, while poor planning techniques will have no institutional hegemonies to enforce them. Participatory democracy is fundamentally pedagogical. It trains people in the art of democracy. Citizenship is a praxis to be cultivated.

Direct action is the foundation of direct democracy. Popular challenges to structures of power prefigure a type of society in which these structures no longer rule. Squatting, blockades, sit-ins, and occupations all represent an assertion of autonomy and a refusal to be silenced. Such actions will not bring a revolution in one fell swoop, but if successful, they can extract concessions from the system and, in a death by a thousand cuts, bring greater democratic power to the people. Radical planning means organizing with an eye to extracting such concessions from the system that improve the life of the community.

Property

In the post-war era, home ownership became the driving force of American life. Owning a home became a way to carve out one's own piece of the world and be a lord and sovereign over one's own piece of land. Over time, a home became a stepping stool toward a bigger home and greater luxury. People took out mortgages on homes not for the home itself but for profit they hoped to make off it. Real estate became the path to wealth and status, even as real production was outsourced to other countries. The McMansion phenomenon became the ultimate reflection of this rat race, creating a simulacrum of real wealth and status commodified for public consumption.

That's just individual ownership, however. The real estate market is a massive global industry in its own right driving this private market. Private equity buys up homes en masse, speculating on their rise in value. Landlords will leave units vacant for years at a time holding out for renters who can afford higher rents rather than lower rents to fill them more quickly. Developers will buy up properties and flip them, displacing incumbent tenants for new higher-income renters. Real estate is bound up with finance, creating a global apparatus of rent extraction and debt. The city has eclipsed the factory as the primary site of capitalist exploitation.

Despite numerous tax incentives, home ownership remains unattainable for much of the population, who must rent instead. There is a great deal to be said for apartment living: many have pleasant decor and great amenities like a pool, sauna, or gym that would be prohibitively expensive as a private homeowner. Collective living has an ancient pedigree, and the benefits are bountiful. The problem is that renters are subject to rising rents that can price them out and force them to live elsewhere, an inherently unstable environment. The increase in land values that brings profit for the homeowner can spell disaster for the renter.

Henry George proposed to address this situation by taxing the full unimproved value of land, effectively turning everyone into renters. The homeowner and landlord would pay the state the same increment that the renter must pay to their landlord. This is meant to encourage the development of more housing in high-demand areas, effectively easing the burden on land values overall and decreasing the increment that renters and homeowners alike would have to bear by minimizing the "leapfrog effect" whereby development is scattered and land developed unevenly due to speculative withholding, and thereby cut down on urban sprawl.

The idea is to force landlords to develop, yet there would still be a fire under the renter and homeowner's feet, and they would have to wait decades for any benefits to trickle down. Job loss, medical crisis, or major debt could still force someone out of their home. The capitalist housing market is one of precarity, and while land value taxation may improve things at the margins, it does not alter the underlying property relations that divide renters from owners. It shuffles around development by filling in underdeveloped areas, but it does not fundamentally address affordability, livability, or security of tenure. We cannot fix the housing crisis without limiting the power of landlords and developers. Rent control, social housing, right to counsel, tenant right to purchase, and good cause eviction are but a few of the steps needed to work toward the ultimate decommodification of housing.

Efficient urban development using land value capture can fund community planning, but we must make housing available to all regardless of ability to pay. We must abolish the distinction between landlord and tenant, between owner and renter. Abolishing evictions would force us to start treating housing as something other than a commodity. The redistribution of rents can take non-monetary forms, in which all contribute as they are able toward the well-being of the city.

Squatter communities like the favelas of Brazil demonstrate that when people have security of tenure, they will continue to improve their communities. Multi-story houses are built to house new generations of residents. All this is done without the help of developers, architects, or planners. The knowledge required to build communities is distributed throughout society but is all too often inhibited by property rights and the pecuniary logic of the market.

The separation of work and home exacerbates these problems. Office buildings used for jobs that can be done at home are superfluous, even more so for the "bullshit jobs" described by David Graeber. Shifting from the capitalist wage model toward decentralized and cooperative production would free up a vast amount of space currently dedicated to commercial enterprise. Office buildings could be repurposed for residential use or replaced altogether. Community centers and marketplaces can be integrated into the buildings where people live.

What is needed in housing is what is needed in labor: organization. Tenants must organize to demand more affordable housing. In place of private developers driven by large capital, they must demand municipal developers that work directly with tenants. Unhoused populations must likewise organize. They must make their voices heard as agents of their own destiny, rather than merely a problem to be cleaned up. Even homeowners facing exploitation by predatory banks are part of this struggle. Urban planning and development belong under the power of the people, away from the hegemonies of capital and the bureaucratic state.

If the prerogatives of capital accumulation can be overcome, people could have more say in the type of public buildings they would like to build. More resources could be devoted to enjoyment, recreation, and leisure. For every billionaire who owns their own private pool, golf course, racetrack, art gallery, yacht, or island, could we not devote some portion of such resources for public consumption instead? Our lives were meant to be spent in more than just toil. There is no reason we cannot produce enough for everyone's needs and have plenty of time and resources left over for festivals and revelry. When the pursuit of endless accumulation ceases to be the basis of our economy, we can rediscover how to live lives of joy and comradery.

Security

For people to thrive in a city, they must be safe. In modern society, this task has been entrusted to the police. As police budgets become bloated with militarized weapons, we see widespread protests against the violent excesses of policing and demands that the police be defunded. This sentiment comes as a shock to those who believe that police forces have always been a necessary feature of society, and not a fairly modern development rooted in American slavery.

The functions of policing include patrolling, investigating, apprehending suspects, and crowd control. Crowd control becomes a social need only when society is divided against itself through antagonisms of class, race, and other social hierarchies. Combined with other methods of harassing and intimidating dissenters, the police serve the purpose of upholding not the safety of the public but rather a social order based on class domination. Their patrols serve to intimidate targeted communities, keeping people on their toes about running afoul from them. Just as imperial armies occupied conquered territories, so do police occupy and surveil the communities of marginalized ethnic groups.

Such communities have a paradoxical relationship with the police. They must depend on them for safety precisely because they are prevented from developing their own safe communities free from the meddling of the system. Their communities are economically segregated and cut off from opportunities to better themselves. Success in such a community means leaving the community. Police will readily respond to a call from a wealthier neighborhood but are unlikely to patrol such neighborhoods. In marginalized communities, on the other hand, they patrol them relentlessly but will take an excessively long time responding to calls. Their pervasive presence in such communities is meant to bust people, not keep them safe.

In marginalized communities, chronic unemployment can lead people to seek illegal sources of income such as drug-dealing, sex work, and property crime. Such high-stakes enterprises not only lead them afoul of the law, but also make people less safe from one another. Gangs form to protect one community against another and to protect the profits of their members. The criminal justice system compounds these problems. Someone in prison cannot be there to raise their children, so those children grow up in single-parent homes or are sent to foster care. Cash bail makes freedom from incarceration a luxury for those who can afford it. Employers are hesitant to hire convicted felons, so those who have been to prison often have trouble finding work when they get out, and without any better options, they return to their illegal trades from before. This compounds the already constant stress of poverty, in which a state of constant precarity keeps people on edge.

To liberate these communities and make everyone safer, security must become a communal affair. Enforcers for the state will always serve the class interests of the state. Economic justice is required to ensure a more equitable distribution of wealth, creating opportunities for these communities to develop their own local economy and provide opportunities for its residents. Healthy communities that develop organically are better able to maintain eyes on the street and thus keep the neighborhood surveilled not by Orwellian machinery but by a thriving community. Yet even in the most prosperous communities it is necessary to keep the community safe from dangerous individuals. The first step in dealing with them should be de-escalation. Social workers trained in mental health are much better candidates for dealing with such situations than an officer trained to arrest and detain people.

Where force is required, trained community members are better candidates for dealing with such problems than agents of the state. Police rarely come from the communities they patrol, and when they do, they often have a much different relationship to it than other residents. Yet we must still be wary here, for vigilante neighborhood watch organizations can often be as violent and repressive as the police due to personal biases. Police work of any type tends to attract a certain type of person, with a desire for power and a binary us-versus-them worldview. A gang-like loyalty develops between them, forming the infamous "thin blue line." It is important, therefore, that the responsibility for community defense be distributed as widely as possible, rather than entrusted to a few self-selected individuals.

In egalitarian communities such as Rojava, policing is a form of community service. Rather than a permanent hired police force, community members are called up for a period of service, after which they step down and another community member is called up to serve in their place. This ensures that those who are policing at any one time will in turn be policed by others in the future, so whatever punishment they exact may come back to them if they're not careful. It also means that everyone is trained to defend their community, and so will be more prepared to defend it at a moment's notice without relying on law enforcement.

Some may worry about the proliferation of guns in such communities. They trust in a specialized police force with assault rifles, but trusting their fellow citizens with such firepower is a bridge too far. Notwithstanding a long list of victims of police violence[19], from Oscar Grant to Breonna Taylor to George Floyd to Philando Castille, it is possible to keep guns off the street but available for public use. A public armory could be accessible to those with the credentials, such as those serving in a community militia.

We must shift to a system of justice that is transformative rather than carceral. As with planning, justice should be a communal affair. A restorative approach asks: who has been hurt, what are their needs, whose obligations are these, what are the causes, who has a stake in the situation, and how can the stakeholders be involved in addressing the causes? Yet restorative justice is not yet transformative justice. Where the former addresses a wider community of stakeholders, the latter goes beyond the criminal justice system and addresses the social structures that produce injustice. Alternatives to policing and incarceration are important, but they are both downstream of alternatives to crime. When people are secure in their basic needs, a major source of conflict is removed. When they live in thriving and nurturing communities, there

---

[19] Nearly 1,200 people died from police violence in 2022: Marks, Andrea. "The Year Just Started and Cops Have Already Killed At Least 7 Unarmed People." *Rolling Stone*, 31 Jan. 2023, https://www.rollingstone.com/culture/culture-features/tyre-nichols-unarmed-cop-death-shooting-1234671669. Accessed 13 Mar. 2023.

is less incentive to prey upon that community. The system isolates us from one another, turning us against each other through artificial scarcity and social divisions. When we are struggling under stressful and degrading conditions, we tend to cling more strongly to what divides us.

It is crucial that people have freedom of association. This requires that people have free and secure housing available. Abusers will often use economic power to maintain control over the abused. If their victim could simply move out and live on their own, this would undermine that power. Giving them that option by making free housing available for all would do wonders to increase survivor autonomy. The necessity to work for a living restricts our freedom of association by locking us into a regular routine dealing with the same people every day, including those we may have conflict with. People deal with bullying, abuse, and sexual harassment because they need their paycheck. Our servitude as workers and renters is reinforced by such humiliating abuse as we are forced to tolerate. However much companies may make a show of taking such abuse seriously, they cannot offer a true remedy to it because doing so would undermine our dependence on such jobs in the first place. If we guaranteed a basic standard of living for everyone, people would not have to make such humiliating compromises.

The ultimate prerequisite for keeping a community safe is that it be a real community. Systems of power are maintained by finding ways of capturing and disrupting communities so that they will be dependent on the core centers of power. In ancient times this was done by slavery, tribute, and occupation. In the modern age, communities face housing and financial discrimination such as redlining, police patrols and surveillance, school-to-prison pipelines, cycles of incarceration, food deserts, gentrification, hostile architecture, car-based infrastructure, and multiple other barriers to their organic unfolding. Healing requires a kenotic path in which barriers are removed and assistance offered, but the development must unfold from within, led by its own community members.

Beauty

An underrated dimension of public life is the aesthetic. Beauty is often treated as a luxury, something to be consumed privately. Beauty is said to be in the eye of the beholder, and therefore something to be left up to personal taste. It is true that beauty is not measurable; it is stubbornly qualitative in a way that, more than anything, defies quantification. It is also true that people have different aesthetic preferences. Yet while such preferences are subjective, they are not arbitrary. People can and do argue about the artistic merits of works of art, based on intersubjective criteria about what a work expresses, what feelings it evokes, and what statement it makes. One person may prefer jazz while another prefers heavy metal, but they can agree on the aesthetic content of each.

Beyond desire, beauty is a basic human need. Dreary and mundane surroundings take a heavy toll on our psyche. People need more than food and shelter. They need to experience harmony and wonder. Natural beauty is one way in which this need is met. For those who can't get away from the city, parks and gardens can help fill this need, as can the integration of plant life into the urban landscape. The rural village has little need for such green spaces — they are to be found all around. The city must plan such spaces and make them accessible to all. These spaces provide much-needed relief from stress, and greatly contribute to the public's mental health.

Our eyes are always scanning our surroundings, picking up on different environmental affordances. If a scene is too plain, our senses feel atrophied and numb. If something is chaotic or out of proportion in the environment, we may feel a sense of dissonance. In nature, there is a continuity of proportion across different scales like that of fractal geometry. This scalar coherence is an intrinsic property of life, and as organisms we are drawn to this quality in nature. Traditional architecture had a similar scalar coherence that was abandoned by modern architecture in favor of simple, streamlined shapes. The result is a landscape deprived of life. Modern buildings have a dull flatness to them, while postmodern buildings may have a chaotic structure to them that is more grating than pleasant.

Architecture builds upon natural beauty with created beauty. Some of the first architectural marvels were megaliths built from surrounding stones. Religion and aesthetics have gone together for as long as we have evidence of either, from the ornate burials and temples of the Paleolithic to the world's great cathedrals, temples, synagogues, and mosques. The need for awe and wonder lies at the root of art and religion alike.

Humans have always felt a sense of their finitude in the face of the immense vast wonders around them. Pyramids and ziggurats were among the earliest monumental buildings of civilization. They mimicked the majestic beauty of the mountains. Mountains have long held sacred value to religions throughout the world, from Olympus to Sinai to Kailash. They reached up to the heavens and conveyed their might, as the early pharaohs and kings sought to do. Modern skyscrapers convey a similar imposing aura. Scale plays a profound role in the human psyche; to seek that scale was none other than to storm the heavens and seek divinity for oneself. The tower of Babel offers us a reminder of the hubris in this endeavor.

The ostentatious palaces, manors, and castles of the ruling classes are sites of exquisite architecture. The luxurious decorations within are for their own enjoyment and for conducting official business, but the estate itself becomes something for the public to admire. Their indulgence becomes a vicarious source of public enjoyment. There is a strange kind of populism to this conspicuous consumption: this kind of public indulgence is relatable to a public that would want to do the same things if only they could afford to.

The dwellings of common folk may not have the same grandeur as the great mansions and palaces of the rich and powerful, but they can be glorious in their own right. If one visits any number of pre-industrial villages, one can find avenues of brightly colored houses creating a lively atmosphere and rich vitality. Such homes possess a continuity of style that manifests a sense of local culture. There is grandeur not so much in any individual building but in the cohesiveness of the whole neighborhood, which exists as a community rather than simply an aggregate of homes. These are not merely places to live, but places in which life is lived together.

Public squares where people gather, where vendors sell their wares, where children play, where musicians and performers busk for tips, all show signs of a community that is alive and thriving. A beautiful community is one in which life is truly lived and not merely endured.

The modern urban environment is a dreary, soulless landscape that takes a heavy psychic toll on us all. Billboards, identical corporate franchises, walls of glass and concrete collide as an oppressive force to dull the imagination and limit our ability to function as anything more than cogs in this vast machine. If the architecture of our cities strives for "realism," it is only because we have lost the imagination to picture a better reality.

The problem lies in the way we conceive of order in utilitarian, mechanistic terms. Christopher Alexander suggests that the key to beauty lies in the interactions of centers. Centers interact with other centers to create a harmonious whole, and this applies at the level of the building, the neighborhood, the town, the region, and so on. As Alexander notes, this principle applies to life itself. The mechanistic view of life obscures this holistic perspective of life as the harmonious interaction of centers. Life follows a Logos which, when pursued properly, can be applied to human settlements, and bring life to them as well.

The life of a community is found in the relationship of centers. The natural order is founded on a complex relationship between centers of activity. Cells are centers that form organs that are centers in the organism that is a center in an ecosystem, and so on. This organic order depends upon mechanism, but it is not mechanical. Our built environment is not exempt from these principles. A well-designed living space will feel more *alive*. Good architecture and urban design will have a more lifelike quality that invites more conviviality from the community.

The present landscape of mediocrity and disharmony is barely a century old. Modern architecture's origins were once quite different and held great promise. The Victorian era saw various neoclassical revivals seeking to harken back to the Old World, as if to compensate for the "satanic mills" that blackened the landscape with smoke and soot. Toward the turn of the century, a new style called Art Nouveau emerged, which sought to incorporate floral patterns and organic forms along with classical elements and ornate ornaments.

After the First World War, this gave way to Art Deco, a cosmopolitan style incorporating influences from sources as diverse as China, India, Persia, Egypt, and Central America. It became the first truly global architectural style and became synonymous with the optimism of the time period. The first skyscrapers were built using this aesthetic, including such marvels as the Chrysler Tower and the Empire State Building. Art Deco and Art Nouveau together represent a path that modern architecture could have taken, but a new set of orthodoxies developed that set it on quite a different course.

Louis Sullivan coined the phrase "form follows function," meaning that building design should follow a practical form based on the function it is meant to serve. In an age of skyscrapers and steel construction, the older layouts of buildings no longer seemed to apply, and a design principle was needed for new buildings going forward. Sullivan himself was no enemy of embellishment, and quite often added ornamental flourishes to his utilitarian designs.

Yet others combined this principle with that professed by Adolf Loos in his essay "Ornament and Crime." Loos was decrying the ornamental flourishes of the Vienna Secession, an Art Nouveau movement in his native Austria. He advanced a moralistic argument that ornament was a "crime" to architecture that made it subject to obsolescence, and decried it as "degenerate," comparing it to the Papuan practice of tattooing. He argued that Western man must have the moral strength to resist such degeneracy and embrace an austere aesthetic with no need for flourish. That Loos died a convicted pedophile adds a certain irony to his racist argument about "degeneracy," but the argument seems to have stuck with architects for the better part of a century.

Modern architecture involves a business model in which architect, engineer, and construction crew are each involved in separate parts of the process. The architect designs the building in a studio, often using a scale model that gives them a bird's eye view of the building, but doesn't give them the perspective that comes with having eyes on the ground. The engineer then figures out how to make it all work properly, then the plan goes to the construction crew to build it. There's a strong incentive for turnover, where a building is built cheaply and swiftly so the client can begin generating profit and the architecture firm can move on to another project. Cheap materials that wear out quickly necessitate repairs down the road and often the destruction of the building within a couple decades, but this is rather the whole point: capitalism generates profit through planned obsolescence. There is little incentive to build beautiful buildings that will last.

Traditional architecture followed a pattern language based

on complexity, harmony, and order. A building would exhibit patterns at different scales from smallest to largest, providing information to the eye from multiple different perspectives. The different scales would harmonize with one another in a fractal-like pattern, exhibiting scalar coherence. Life itself is built like this: our bodies have scalar coherence from mitochondria to cells to tissues to organs all the way up to our bodies themselves. Cultures that had no contact with one another developed their own architectural styles exhibiting this same order, not because they were consciously aware of this pattern, but because humans are instinctively drawn to it. At smaller scales, the building materials themselves would sometimes provide the pattern, such as the wood of a log cabin.

Christopher Alexander suggests there is a certain "quality without a name" exhibited by buildings that follow this pattern language closely. Later he came to identify it with what he called "the I," meaning not the individual self but something like the Hindu idea of Atman. When we find it, this quality speaks to something deep in our soul. It is the trace of divinity hidden within creation. As created beings ourselves, we have this quality — the *Imago Dei* or "image of God"— that we are then able to recognize in other things. It is that quality of life which is present in living organisms and is likewise present in human artifacts, buildings, and institutions to the degree that they follow the path of the Logos. This quality cannot simply be planned but unfolds organically in a process of reciprocity between building and environment. It involves a process of building up strong centers to create greater wholes. Strong centers are developed through relations with other centers. Scalar coherence strengthens these relationships between centers. All life is organized as an unfolding relationship between centers, and architecture that follows the same principles also exhibits life.

This quality emerges in a common vernacular. Vernacular architecture is not a single architectural style, but a way of doing architecture. Every part of the world has had its own local vernacular styles that look wildly different from one another but share a kind of living quality that is missing from the modern city. Vernacular architecture uses local materials and expresses something unique about the location. It speaks to the local history, tradition, and culture. Its beauty is not a matter of gaudy excess and expense like some royal palace, but the quaint charm of a place with a history and a unique character.

Where vernacular architecture unfolds, modern architecture imposes. Using scale models, the modern architect pays attention to the larger scale with little attention to smaller scales and almost no attention to intermediate scales. The result is mind-numbing, dull, and uninspiring, sometimes intentionally so. Architects who boast of "realism" fail to understand the biological instincts that made classical architecture so appealing. Postmodern architecture seeks to reintroduce complexity and pattern but often does so without an understanding of this pattern language, creating structures that simply increase tension and anxiety. In understanding the organic principles of wholeness and order, we can see that ornament is not truly separate from function. An organic order will have an ornamental quality, and properly integrated ornament will serve a function in the way the building is experienced. Ornament is often viewed as something extra, but ornament properly understood is simply another center used to strengthen other centers. It is every bit as functional as any other part of the building because the building must function as a field of centers.

Throughout history, people have built their own homes. The knowledge for doing so was widely distributed. A common pattern language was shared by all. People living in favelas or shantytowns today often build one wall at a time as they can acquire the resources. These individuals live at the fringes of society, in a precarious position in which they risk being evicted, whereas the medieval burghers had the support of their community. The communities they built in this way had a liveliness to them that has been lost in the modern age of planned landscapes. There was a pattern that persisted amid all the variation, and this combination of pattern and variation is what gave it this vitality.

Planned buildings such as cathedrals and guildhalls were collective endeavors. The master builder had the grand design in mind, but the pattern language was understood by all the builders involved. It was a pattern that involved the whole community for whom the building was intended. The master builder was part of the construction process itself, working onsite so that he could get a sense of the building's place and function in the community. Even with the overall layout in mind, the design itself was a process.

What connected these large projects with the homes that ordinary people built was that everyone shared a pattern language. The professionalization of building has created a situation in which architects have their own individual pattern language that is not only not shared with ordinary people, but that they jealously guard from one another, leading to a fracturing of aesthetics. Attempts to recreate a consistent order through building codes or mass-manufactured housing often make the problem worse, because they lack the connection to the lived experience of the community that a common pattern language brings about.

To revive this pattern language, we must learn to build through dialogue rather than imposition. Architects must become part of the building process itself, and the pattern language must be shared among all the construction workers. Something akin to the guild system, wherein the architect acts as master builder working with the other builders on-site, would vastly improve the life of buildings. An understanding of the harmony and scalar coherence at the heart of this pattern language must be revived. Yet the technical complexity needn't be precisely understood so long as one pays attention to the unfolding of centers. The pattern needs to be understood only to recognize what we already know instinctively.

Municipal developers could operate as a public service working with the community to find out what needs to be built and involving them in the building process. Architects and construction crews would work together on-site to help guide the building as it unfolds. The community should be allowed to participate in the process so that the knowledge of how to build can be spread throughout society for the benefit of all. When building becomes common praxis rather than the specialized domain of the few, the communities we build can serve all who live in them. The life of buildings must be maintained so that they can emerge as structures that support life.

We can build beautiful communities for all if we understand the principles of order found in nature and collaborate to build this beauty together. Instead of rationalistic planning, organic growth can be realized if we allow it to emerge. Authentic communal autonomy requires overcoming the aristocracy of homeowner associations, the exploitative control of landlords, and the authoritarianism of central planners so that spontaneous organic development can be allowed to unfold.

Countryside

Cities do not exist in isolation. City and country constitute an integrated whole, at times antagonistic, other times cooperative. Urban issues about public transportation and housing are largely irrelevant to the countryside, where population is sparse and maintaining buses and light rail are impractical. Rural land is, of course, where most farming is done. The crops and livestock grown in the countryside provide food that is shipped to cities, while those in the country rely on manufactured products and services from the cities and industrial centers.

Conventional wisdom sees rural farms as preceding cities. The story goes that agricultural surpluses were first necessary to allow for concentrated populations and division of labor. Jane Jacobs challenged this logic. She posited that cities came first and provided a springboard from which agricultural development could follow. Cities perform the function of import replacement, where people start producing something locally that was once imported, contributing to the diversity of goods and services. This includes food as much as it does manufactured goods. The discovery of Göbekli Tepe confirmed Jacobs' intuition. The ritual importance of the site preceded the development of agriculture, and from this center sprang the gradual development of the countryside.

Under capitalism, however, we have seen an emptying of the countryside into the cities in a process of urbanization. Where cities were once a springboard for rural development, they are now processing centers for rural refugees. People who once worked as farm workers and tenant farmers have been pushed off the land by industrial agriculture and land monopoly and now live in slums or on the streets. Nearly a quarter of the world's population lives in slums, and that number only continues to grow as inequality becomes more acute. Under this system, cities fail to perform their vital function of differentiation of work, and instead become centers to concentrate and exploit the poor.

People move to cities to find jobs. With few options for work in the country, they move to cities to find work and support themselves. Yet high rents keep most out of decent housing, so slums spring up along the edge of the city. In the Global North, strong zoning ordinances and police enforcement prevent the formation of slums, so we get homelessness instead. Those who can't find work get by with panhandling, busking, and social services. As more people move to bustling metropolises in search of work, landlords raise rents accordingly and push more people into homelessness.

These are all consequences of the capitalist drive for endless accumulation. The enclosure of the commons forces people dependent upon capital to support themselves. They are likewise dependent on landlords to keep a roof over their head. The dispossession of land, exploitation of labor, and extraction of rent all work together to keep a population of people subservient to the power of capital within these urban empires.

A much different pattern of development would be possible by reclaiming the commons. The decommodification of housing, open access to the means of production, and provision of a basic standard of living for everyone would allow people much greater freedom to spread out, and take a great deal of pressure off of large cities. Socialists have long identified the separation of town and country as one of the primordial divisions of labor. Under the free association of producers, the population could be distributed more evenly and efficiently. Metropolitan areas facing housing crises could shrink to more manageable populations and open new areas for farming, while the countryside could see small-scale industry enrich their material and cultural life.

Methods of farming could change significantly as well under such conditions. Modern farming is heavily industrialized, producing cash crops using monocultural methods involving genetic modification, fertilizer, and pesticides. Apart from being destructive to the environment, such methods are highly capital-intensive and thus unsustainable. An influx of population to the country could allow for more labor-intensive methods in which a larger community could participate seasonally while still having time to participate in non-agricultural production.

A great deal of interest exists for small farming. Farmer's markets and farm-to-table dining are major attractions in big cities. But small farms can be a big economic risk, and a major burden to run by oneself. What is needed is not a collection of small, family-owned farms to compete with the large corporate farms. A more resilient system can operate as a decentralized network of farms mutually supporting one another. Just as small business is not the answer to big business, small agriculture is not the answer to big agriculture. What is needed in both cases is distributed power and mutual aid.

We do not want population creep to encroach on sensitive natural ecosystems, but this is even more reason that people should be liberated from the constraints of production under the current division of labor. The point is not to forcefully relocate people, an authoritarian measure that would have disastrous consequences. The point is that the current disparity arises from concentrations of productive power that need not exist, and that a significantly different pattern could emerge under more liberatory conditions.

The proper balance of city and country is distorted by the territorial state. States may enter free trade agreements or engage in protectionism of local industry, but either strategy is likely to harm cities relative to the countryside or vice-versa. It is also likely to favor certain cities over others. The success of small polities in East Asia such as Hong Kong, Singapore, and Taiwan is in large part because their small sizes minimize this flattening effect. A city, freed from the control of the territorial state, can regulate its imports and exports more smoothly, allowing for import substitution to build up a local economy. Successful cities like this are then able to generate surrounding towns and villages that support the urban economy while also enjoying benefits from the city. An ethos of cooperation replaces one of competition and exploitation.

The cultural effect of such a redistribution in the United States could be considerable. So much of our culture wars today involve disputes between "coastal elite" urban dwellers and rural "flyover country" denizens who cling to reactionary ideology. A redistribution of population would bring both groups into closer contact with one another and influence social development in a more even-handed way. It would liberate the urban underclass from unaffordable conditions in the city while freeing the rural poor who lack work opportunities. Modern capitalism has produced massive alienation not only from our labor but from one another. It is time we start healing.

10

Empire

The rise of capitalism is tied to the rise of nation-states. For the sake of accuracy, I should note that I am using a somewhat loose definition of "nation-state." There is the technical definition, in which nation and state are congruent, enshrining certain norms into law such as a national language and a national identity based around a particular dominant ethnicity, with other ethnic groups expected to conform and assimilate. Under such a technical definition, the United States, for instance, does not qualify.

Here, the term is used more broadly to describe a territorial regime with Westphalian sovereignty, and this is how I will be using the term here. The system of Westphalian sovereignty granting each state its own exclusive territory marked by legally defined borders requires the recognition of other states who mutually agree to respect one another's territorial sovereignty. This system has changed over time, but even as the world becomes more globalized and integrated, its system of internationally recognized borders remains as relevant as ever. Nation-states are far from abolished, but we can say that they have been relativized. Nations do not work for the sake of national capital so much as global capital, and those that do not go along with this are subject to sanction.

Nation-states have a way of rewriting history so as to make themselves seem inevitable; a kind of national mythmaking is a necessary characteristic. Any given place possesses a history of conquests, migrations, trade, war, intermarriage, and other contacts between different cultures. A single city might have a history of occupation by several different empires. What the nation-state does is collect these diverse threads and create an imagined community based on a territorially enclosed space and connect that space to that diverse history. It causes us to think of that past in terms of the present political formation.

Nation-states flatten differences. They unite disparate entities under a single national banner and set of policies. Different cities, towns, and regions have different economies with different needs. Uniting them under a single national economy subject to a unified set of policies will inevitably harm one region at the expense of another. Whether the nation pursues free trade or protectionism, one region will lose out compared to another. They erode the autonomy needed for every region to pursue its best interest, and prevent cities from performing the essential function of import substitution which is critical to their development.

Nation-states and private property share a similar logic. The same land can see its ownership change hands countless times over its history, just as multiple flags may be flown over it, both often as a consequence of the same wars of conquest. Both can also occur without changing who lives there. Medieval serfs might see themselves and their land subject to one lord and then another. Property and national borders are both abstract lines drawn over concrete entities for purposes of control and domination.

The kenotic alternative to property is usufruct: private use without ownership. The alternative to the nation-state is confederation: organic relations between populations based on cooperation rather than control. A confederal system would not erase history, but free it from the confines of the nation-state, embracing the broader movements of cultures and people. Both involve a shift from territorial control to human relationships. It follows that the abolition of one necessitates the abolition of the other. A Soviet model of socialism in one country must necessarily be hypocritical insofar as it maintains borders that separate it from the rest of the world. Lenin advocated national liberation, but he was consistent with this only to the extent that such national liberation movements sided with the Soviet Union. A true liberation movement must look beyond the nation-state itself.

National borders are invisible boundaries that exist by law, not nature. If one looks at the Earth from space, one does not see a world carved up by national borders but clusters of cities and towns. Confederalism is the form that fits this natural order of human settlement, centering political sovereignty in the population itself and relying on social bonds rather than state coercion to connect these places to one another.

Nation-states have poisoned any hope for solidarity between peoples. An us-versus-them mentality infects the discourse. On one side there are those who throw their support behind the imperial aims of the West as guardians of liberty who will neglect or excuse the countless crimes against the people, such as overthrowing democratically elected governments and installing dictators friendly to corporate interests. On the other side are self-proclaimed "anti-imperialists" who so distrust the aims and ambitions of the West that they reflexively side with whoever is against the West, with a willingness to discount, rationalize, deny, or willfully ignore evidence of atrocities by these countervailing powers. Pitting state powers against one another is a convenient way to erode solidarity between the people living in these countries. Propaganda goes both ways, and a healthy skepticism should be maintained toward all powers and authorities.

Empire

The Westphalian system has evolved into what Michael Hardt and Antonio Negri call "Empire" (with a capital E). That is, from the imperialism of traditional European empires, we now have a global system which doesn't negate the nation-state but relativizes it so that rather than expand their own individual empires, nation-states compete for greater relative status within this Empire. According to this theory, all modern wars are essentially civil wars. This is not to say that the entire Empire directly participates in these wars, but the system as a whole has stakes in every war. This also means that political representatives are accountable not only to their national politics and national capital, but also to the global system of capital.

The emergence of this Empire corresponds to a shift in global capitalism. The old paradigm of industrial production has shifted to an information economy. Of course, industrial production still occurs, but the production itself has become informationalized. Think of modern agriculture, where the gene sequences of crops are patented and privatized. The term "biopiracy" has emerged to describe the malicious appropriation of knowledge and genetic resources from farmers and indigenous communities via monopoly control and patents, but this is an insult to pirates. Pirates steal private property, but these practices steal from the commons in the name of private property. Intellectual property has existed since the beginnings of capitalism, but the new global economy is fundamentally based on the ownership and manipulation of information.

The intimate details of our lives have become commodities to be traded. Social media sites harvest the personal information of their users and sell it for profit. The insurance and financial sectors profit by gamifying every detail of our lives, betting on outcomes and influencing the system to guarantee payouts. Michel Foucault refers to this management of human life as "biopower." Traditional sovereignty is based on the power of life and death, in which the sovereign can decide who lives and who dies. With biopower, however, life is not simply given or taken, but managed — and the Empire of global capitalism is a biopolitical machine.

This system cannot be maintained in one country without the cooperation of others. Free trade agreements and global institutions flatten differences between nations to allow for the free flow of capital and ensure global recognition of these property claims. The crop patents of a company in the United States must be upheld against their use by farmers in India. No single country can manage such a system of control, so a polycentric order of global control had to emerge.

Under the Empire, war ceases to be a state of exception and becomes the rule. Martial metaphors like the War on Poverty are used for addressing social issues, but the War on Drugs involves actual military adventurism. These wars on abstract concepts have no definite endpoint, so they become permanent social fixtures. War becomes a matter of international policing. War as a state of exception has traditionally permitted the suspension of freedoms and authoritarian rule. War as a permanent fixture thereby shifts even the most democratic societies toward authoritarianism.

The Empire has a hybrid constitution that combines elements of many political systems, including monarchy (rule of the one), aristocracy (rule of the few), and democracy (rule of the many). It is neither a worldwide government nor a unified command and control organization. The current constitution places the United States in the position of monarchical head of this existing international order. The position of king does not provide one the ability to rule according to their whims and desires. Instead, this global force serves as the protector of financial markets around the world. Not only does the US military defend its national interests, but it also serves as a global police force, preserving the neoliberal world order in order to guarantee the unhindered movement of capital. Intergovernmental organizations such as NATO uphold US hegemony, but at the same time they oblige it to act in support of other member nations.

The dominance of the dollar has enabled the United States to act as the financial capital of the globe: the International Monetary Fund and the World Bank both maintain offices in the same building as the Federal Reserve and the United States Treasury. But Hardt and Negri believe that the significance of this position is declining, and see a developing vacancy in this role. While some see another contender such as China filling this role, they see the role itself as receding in importance. It is not just that the United States no longer enjoys exclusive rule over this global order, but no nation *can* rule over it.

The dominating nation-states, major companies, and supranational institutions make up the aristocratic component of the system. There is a great deal of competition for dominance within this realm. The fundamental features of this system are unaffected by the various people vying for critical positions since those players do not change. The nationalist movements on the extreme right, which are represented by figures like Trump, Bolsonaro, or Modi, do not seek to disengage from the existing international order as much as they attempt to organize their support in order to advance up the international hierarchy.

The democratic component is made up of a jumbled assortment of factors. It includes non-state militias such as Blackwater and other mercenary groups, religious organizations, non-governmental organizations, private corporations, and the media. This form of governance by the many is democratic only in the narrowest sense: it provides some semblance of representation, but there is no opportunity for directly challenging the authority of the system. Any and all efforts of this kind to resist will inevitably be appropriated by the Empire.

The 2003 invasion of Iraq represented an attempted coup by the United States against this world order. The Bush administration and its neoconservative agenda sought to reassert American unilateral power over the aristocratic power of the international community. One can point to several missteps that led to its failure, but the attempt was doomed from the start. Even from its privileged position as global police force, the United States could not go it alone. The biopolitical Empire of global capital cannot be managed by a single imperial power.

The 2022 invasion of Ukraine by Russia is more than just a local territorial dispute: it is a challenge to the global order itself. Aleksandr Dugin, a political theorist associated with Russia's far-right movement, pushes for an alternative world order that is built on multipolarity. This refers to a balance of power between regional states as opposed to one dominant superpower. In place of NATO's Atlanticism, he proposes Eurasianism, which involves a return to a realist "sphere of influence" politics in which Russia would have hegemony over the areas that are next to it. There is some debate about the degree to which Vladimir Putin is directly influenced by Dugin, yet it is unmistakable that his views coincide with those of the Kremlin. Russia is not permitted to pursue a restoration of their previous imperial rule, that of the Soviet Union. Instead, they plan to overthrow the established order to put themselves at the head of the pack. This attempt to rewrite the global order is unpredictable, but the Empire will likely remain in some form, with its contours undergoing a dramatic metamorphosis.

There is no peace in having one state unilaterally withdraw from the Empire, least of all the one tasked with its enforcement. The US military operates as the police force for this order, and other nations depend on it for their own protection. The Empire has plenty of blood on its hands, but much like capitalism itself, it cannot simply be abolished by removing its most powerful members. The Empire is a network with multiple nodes, and can easily survive a changing cast of characters. Already the countries of Europe are seeking to arm themselves to reduce their reliance on the United States for military assistance. The socioeconomic order depends on this flexibility; to overcome this, a whole new order must be built from within.

The Empire is incapable of changing itself. It is only possible to replace it, and the thing that takes its place may or may not be a relative improvement. It is impossible to build a liberatory international system solely through the military force of nation-states; rather, it must be developed from within by its subjects. Even now, we are witnessing a major realignment of the global order in the global response to Israel's genocide in Gaza, and an opening for an alternative order. It is necessary for a horizontal movement to arise from within the Empire in order to cause cracks in the system and ultimately take control of it.

Multitude

A counter-empire must be constructed, founded on what Hardt and Negri refer to as a "politics of multitude" to combat the hegemony of the Empire. The multitude does not seek a singular goal but rather a variety of goals that include racial, gender, economic, and ecological justice. It is a constellation of causes that has come together to fight against the forces of the Empire that are flattening the world.

The multitude is not a mass, a crowd, or a collective. These terms all imply a kind of undifferentiated unity, while the multitude is irreducibly pluralistic. Class reductionists of the Marxist tradition have traditionally sought to unify the proletariat, which necessarily excluded not only the bourgeoisie, but also the "lumpenproletariat" consisting of criminals, vagrants, and sex workers, whom Marx and Engels dismissed as unthinking and reactionary. The proletariat's class status as workers was seen as the key to their revolutionary potential. Marxists have long supported feminist and black liberation struggles, but often from an analysis that sees these as epiphenomena of an economic struggle between workers and capitalists.

With respect to identity-based struggles, Marxists tend to see the role of the vanguard party as connecting these struggles to class struggle, which is understood as the economic "base" underlying the "superstructure" that these struggles confront. Some Marxists outright dismiss these struggles as "distractions" from the class war, conveniently centering the oppression of white cishet male workers over the particular concerns of other marginalized identities. Even non-Marxist leftists such as Murray Bookchin, who sees an intersectionality of oppressions, often tend to emphasize the need for unity and shun the "divisiveness" of identitarian struggles.

In contrast to the proletariat, the multitude is envisioned as a diverse plenitude of subaltern identities existing within the framework of the global capitalist order. Hierarchies of race, gender, religion, and sexual orientation all produce oppressed groups whose interests and experiences vary significantly, but who share an experience of subordination under the global capitalist order. The multitude is a class concept, but it entails an expansive concept of class that is as much political as it is economic. The various forms of oppression are exploited by the Empire, not strictly based on labor and production, but by privatization of the commons, which the multitude produce through their complex interactions. Every social hierarchy is a form of sabotage that can be exploited by the ruling class for power and profit. One can even say that capital accumulation is nothing but the reproduction of social inequality. It is true that identity-based struggles fail to be revolutionary if they remain at the level of identity. They must instead begin at the level of identity and seek the abolition of the conditions that construct that identity, as was the trajectory of such black radicals as Malcolm X and Huey P. Newton. The multitude is a creative force that can develop a new society based not on the domination of one group over another, but rather on the collective empowerment of all individuals.

We are witnessing the expression of a multitude as a result of the convergence of a variety of movements, including those advocating for racial justice, environmentalism, and the empowerment of women and sexual minorities. These movements all pursue their own causes, but increasingly perceive their interests as crossing and harmonizing with other movements. The multitude's ability to network and communicate across borders and cultures allows it to build global alliances and movements that challenge prevailing hegemonies and create alternative social and economic models based on principles of solidarity and the commons. A "movement of movements" begins to emerge. The multitude, because it produces the commons, has the ability to fight the privatization and commodification of the commons.

Just as industrial capitalism constructs the proletariat, neoliberal capitalism constructs the multitude. It creates a fragmented working class by dividing workers based on their skills, education, and income levels, weakening the collective bargaining power of workers and makes it difficult for them to unite and fight for better wages and working conditions. It privatizes public services such as education, healthcare, and transportation, resulting in increased inequality as those who can afford to pay for these services receive better quality care than those who cannot. It promotes deregulation of markets, which allows corporations to operate with minimal oversight. This results in a concentration of wealth and power in the hands of a small group of individuals and corporations, further marginalizing the multitude. It promotes individualism and self-interest over collective action and social responsibility, creating a culture where individuals are encouraged to pursue their own goals at the expense of others.

As capitalism has evolved, so too has the nature of work. The rise of the service sector, the gig economy, and other forms of flexible, precarious work have blurred the lines between work and home, extending the power of the capitalist into our personal lives. Global supply chains and outsourced production have deterritorialized the factory and extended it over the whole of society, weakening labor protections and expanding worker competition across the globe. The assembly line has become an assembly network. As the floor has gone out from under workers in the global North, people are pushed into low-wage service jobs and meaningless bureaucratic "bullshit jobs." Women, people of color, and other marginalized groups may face additional challenges through hierarchical systems that surveil their activities, gatekeep opportunities, and regulate behavior. These differential hierarchies not only divide the underclass but disperse them across the globe.

This dispersal undercuts the strength of the multitude as workers. But vulnerability also allows them to create new forms of resistance based in solidarity, cooperation, and empathy. Workers understand the experiences of others who are also marginalized or oppressed, and this understanding can be used to build powerful, effective networks. These networks are powerful because they are based on a shared understanding of the experiences of oppression and exploitation, and a commitment to working together to challenge these structures of power.

When Karl Marx was analyzing industrial production, he saw how production had already been collectivized. Workers on the shop floor managed each aspect of production under the authoritarian management of the capitalist, but because of the collective nature of their production, they had the capacity to seize the means of production and run the factory themselves. Under the Empire, collectivized labor has spread across the planet. This labor is increasingly immaterial, involving management of information, knowledge, communication, and relations. Capital encloses and privatizes these immaterial forms of labor, which one does not even have to be employed to perform, allowing for increasing precarity. The multitude thereby constructs the commons through shared knowledge, networked production, cultural production, and the digital commons. In resisting the privatization of the commons, the multitude can liberate it and run it for themselves.

The modern city is the new factory. The city is a commons constructed by all who live there. Economists are accustomed to thinking not in terms of the commons but of "externalities." An externality is an indirect cost or benefit to a third party from the activity of another party or parties. There are positive externalities such as research and development whose benefits exceed those captured by the developing firm, as well as negative externalities such as pollution or antibiotic resistance. Another way of putting this is that externalities are those things that escape market relations. Externalities are precisely the production of the commons. The goal of capital is to privatize benefits while socializing costs, and the prevailing wisdom of market economists is that both should be privatized. The reverse path would be to reassert the commons. We are all involved in the production of the commons, so we are all entitled to its benefits, just as we are already made to pay its costs. For this reason, the city is the site of resistance for the multitude.

The multitude must focus on developing new forms of resistance based on horizontalism and decentralized power. This means moving away from hierarchical models of leadership and instead developing networks of cooperation and communication that allow for a more democratic and participatory form of resistance. Bridges must be built that recognize the interconnectedness of different struggles, developing new forms of solidarity that cut across traditional boundaries of race, class, and gender.

The Old Left, represented by the Russian Revolution and the labor uprisings of the 1930s, involved masses of people directed by central party leaders seeking to seize state power.

The New Left of the 1960s saw a shift toward the model of the guerilla fighter, exemplified by Che Guevara. There is something more decentralized about the guerilla, dispersing into the forest to swarm state armies. At the same time, however, guerilla movements are still typically ruled by centralized hierarchies. This structure inspired movements like the Black Panther Party and the Red Brigades. Later we see a new transitional form of resistance in the Intifada beginning in 1987. Here, there is still centralized leadership from organizations, but there is a move from the military structure of the guerillas to more dispersed network forms.

With the Zapatistas, we see a guerilla movement that is also a dispersed network model. This indigenous movement did not seek to seize state power, but created their own autonomous zone while also spreading their message to the rest of the world via online communiques. Where Lenin sought to export revolution by military force, the Zapatistas sought to spread revolution by example, encouraging others to follow their lead. The alter-globalization movement followed suit, setting the stage for a new form of resistance exemplified by the Arab Spring, Occupy Wall Street, Black Lives Matter, Me Too, Idle No More, the Climate Strike, and any number of other decentralized social movements.

Within the nodes of the Empire some are more powerful than others, but the network as a whole is robust enough to resist attacks to any one node. For this reason, those who oppose the Empire must organize themselves into a network. The modern Empire, in contrast to those of the past, does not have an outside. There are no barbarians waiting outside the city walls to take over the Empire and make it their own. The opposition must emerge from within as a movement that is more dispersed and distributed than the Empire itself.

The multitude is distinguished by a swarm-like intelligence that exceeds the sum of its parts. The complex interactions are pedagogical in nature, facilitating collective learning. This swarm intelligence serves as the foundation for deliberative democracy. The democratic assemblies of a new political order are built on the foundation of dispersed social movements networking with one another.

The multitude must fight against the Empire as a dispersed constellation of forces establishing the commons wherever it can. They must construct a system of usufruct and mutual aid wherever there is private property. They must establish democratic governance in those areas that are currently ruled by autocracy. Their lack of central command structure, together with the rich variety of its members, is one of their greatest strengths. While organic leadership may emerge as needed, it does not rely on any single vanguard that can be targeted and taken out. The vanguard emerges not as a permanent position, but as a function that may arise when needed. Anything the Empire is unable to simplify, flatten, or reduce is beyond its ability to control. The multitude harbors the germs of the Empire's destruction, but it must be willing to act.

Struggle

The multitude is not inherently progressive. For all the liberatory social movements that have been born of their struggles, there have also been reactionary uprisings as well. The world saw this with horrifying clarity on September

11, 2001. The World Trade Center, a perfect symbol of the global Empire of capital, was attacked using airplanes, the preferred global means of transportation. The culprits were quickly identified as Al-Qaeda, a terrorist organization of radical Muslim jihadists. Al-Qaeda emphasized centralized decision-making and decentralized execution. Its leaders articulated the ideology and strategy, but semi-autonomous units would carry out their own attacks, seeking official approval for any large-scale operations. Osama Bin Laden captured the Western imagination as its leader, but his leadership was of a mostly charismatic and symbolic form. Their decentralization was their strength. Their use of the internet to radicalize people allowed them to create terror cells in countries throughout the world.

As the American military machine began its costly wars in Iraq and Afghanistan in the name of fighting terrorism, ISIL and ISIS developed out of Al-Qaeda's operations in Iraq and Syria, attracting recruits from across the globe through similar online outlets. They claimed territory for themselves within the power vacuums. Wherever they went, they slaughtered Christians, Jews, and Muslims they considered heretical or apostate, while enslaving and raping women. Using the decentralized tactics of the multitude, they pursued fascist ends.

This is the terrifying underbelly of the multitude. The networked non-local forms of resistance become the means to extend power rather than combat it. The information networks that facilitate communication can also disseminate lies and propaganda. Conspiratorial movements like Qanon provide a simulacrum of democratic participation by giving their followers a sense of being together on some world-historical mission to uncover the truth. Such conspiracy theories take advantage of the Empire's hegemony to present their own "alternative facts." The multitude rightly distrusts the Empire, but this distrust creates openings for propaganda with the flattering premise of being in on some great secret. It also offers convenient scapegoats, such as immigrants or social movements, presenting them as machinations of some ominous elite rather than genuine expressions of resistance by the multitude.

Using social fissures in the Empire to turn the multitude against itself is a key strategy for modern fascist movements. Russia has made extensive use of cyber warfare to influence elections in other countries, electing far-right candidates who usurp the rule of law and run corrupt regimes for personal gain. The new form of global fascism has plenty of similarities to the fascism of the 1930s, but there are some key differences. Classic fascism relied on the "Big Lie" that gave people a grand narrative to explain everything, but the new fascism relies on continuous lying that renders truth meaningless. They don't have to convince people of the truth of their lies, they just need to make the truth a matter of partisan opinion.

To believe in truth is a radical act. As the police state escalates its war against black and brown communities and pundits conjure public panic about trans people, any resistance to this monstrous state of affairs is cast as degenerate "wokeness," which is itself the great enemy that must be eradicated by any means necessary. People are being primed to commit atrocities, and we are moving headlong into a time of nightmares.

As the multitude is produced by capitalist modernity, so too are different resistances to it. One of these manifestations is anti-modern. This is found in various forms of religious fundamentalism, nationalism, and reactionary movements. These anti-modern movements do not simply represent a return to premodernity. They are very much creatures of modernity produced by its flattening hegemony. Even the post-truth manifestations of modern fascism do not simply accept a postmodern relativizing of truth, but rather weaponize it to assert one's own truth without argument. One can see, for example, evangelicals spreading an aggressively capitalist version of Christianity as a missionary religion, or anti-immigrant nationalism violently enforcing the borders that capital uses to sabotage labor and maintain dominance. Anti-modernity thus becomes a tool in the colonizing power of modernity itself.

The rebellion of postmodernity offers little in the way of resistance to modernity or anti-modernity. Its critique of grand narratives and deconstruction of dominant discourses are essential corrections to the colonizing grand narrative of modernity, but its resistance consists of little more than intellectualized ironic detachment. What is needed is an alter-modernity. The mass movements around the turn of the millennium were described by the media as "anti-globalization," but they came to describe themselves as "alter-globalization." Far from opposing a globalized world, they challenged globalized *capital*, and in its place they sought an alternative globalization based on the global commons. In a similar way, alter-modernity seeks an alternative form of modernity that values pluralism and embraces principles of social justice, environmental sustainability, and cultural diversity. By building a movement of movements that connects their struggles together, the multitude can seize the potentials of the globalized world to build a global commonwealth.

For Hardt and Negri, the key to doing this is through love. Love, they insist, should be understood not simply as a feeling, but as a political concept. Love is a matter of grounding ourselves in a deep sense of empathy and compassion for others. We must see the struggles of others as our own struggles. We must be careful of love, however, as it can be distorted and corrupted. Evil is not a matter of lack of love so much as distorted love. Love can take an insular form, such as toward one's family, race, or nation, creating in-groups and out-groups. It can also take a form that seeks to impose unity, eliminating or minimizing differences. An authentic love of neighbor means love of alterity. We must love others not for being like us but unique from us, and embrace distinction without hierarchy. Love means welcoming the stranger in our midst, recognizing their value on their own terms.

Love is closely tied to the commons. We see this even in love's deficient and distorted forms that promote such commons as family or nation. An expansive love must move us beyond such limited allegiances to embrace our fellow beings: the great faith traditions teach that universal love is the highest good of all. The market encloses the commons and reduces people to utility-maximizing individuals, but wherever there is love, we see the construction of the commons. Love encourages us to share resources with others and work together for mutual benefit. Empathy for one another encourages us to view others through an egalitarian lens, as fellow human beings deserving equality and dignity.

Love motivates us to challenge dominant oppressive systems, moving us to acts of great courage and conviction in standing up for the oppressed.

Confederation

The multitude can establish a confederated order by constructing horizontal links among themselves. A confederation is an older type of government that existed long before the nation-state. Throughout history, the choice in human organization was empire versus confederation. Whereas an empire is established by military conquest, a confederation is established through social cohesion. When people come together to build their own stable community and join forces with other groups in order to grow stronger, this is the beginning of a confederation. They engage in mutually beneficial trade, support one another militarily, and collaborate on common endeavors.

Every member of the confederation can exert some level of influence over the others, but nobody is required to comply with the reforms proposed by anybody else unless they reach a consensus among themselves. This makes it possible for more beneficial changes to spread, while allowing more problematic changes to be contained without being imposed on a widespread scale. This results in the development of a learning mechanism that enables evolution to improve the fitness of social systems through adaptation to varying environmental conditions.

The variety and development of novel forms of collective identity generated by the multitude has the capacity to promote grassroots democracy and local sovereignty, which may contribute to the establishment of local assemblies, forming the fundamental building blocks of democratic confederalism. Resistance to power structures can create a society based on social ecology, participatory democracy, and a shared commitment to the common good. The multitude can throw the sovereignty of the nation-state into question and pave the way for the construction of a decentralized political and economic framework.

With the use of a scalable system in which smaller community councils send delegates to larger level councils, it may be possible to exercise direct democracy while discovering the most effective means of resource distribution. Consider this: if every person on the planet formed a council consisting of twenty other people, and each of those councils sent a delegate to a higher-level council of councils, which in turn sent its delegates to a higher-level council, and so on and so forth, it would only take eight levels to cover the entire population of the world. It may be possible to build councils out of existing governmental institutions by switching from a system of representation to one of delegation, transferring decision-making authority to the multitude.

The transfer of sovereign authority from a government to democratic bodies is crucial at the most local level, but similar reforms can be implemented at state, regional, or national levels. The multitude must organize to create participatory local assemblies. Electoral candidates could emerge from this organization. It is necessary that they be held accountable to this group. Following their election, these candidates would attempt to change city councils so that they cede more authority to democratic structures.

Elections could be reformed to replace a representational system with a system of delegation. The will of the people is brought to the council to be enacted, and any changes must then be brought back to the local assemblies for approval.

Every level of government has the power to cede its sovereignty to the people and democratize its institutions. A nation-state under progressive leadership could use its power to grant greater recognition to people's assemblies, encourage democratization of municipalities, and remove forms of state sabotage that privatize the commons. In no way does this necessarily mean they *will* behave in this manner. Such help should be welcomed when offered, but it should not be relied upon. Organizing should focus on building movements, from which counter-institutions can be built while existing institutions are transformed and democratized. We cannot rely on the existing system to save us, but we don't need to start over from scratch.

It is critical that power be distributed from the bottom up, rather than the other way around. The democratization of society must ultimately be led from below, but it may accept support from above in the form of radical politicians, so long as these politicians are willing to hand over power to the people rather than pretending to speak for them. Confederalism offers the possibility of broadening the scope of this organization, with the goal of supplanting the Empire of nation-states and global capital.

Antonio Gramsci distinguished between a war of position and a war of maneuver. The war of position is a slower process in which one attempts to advance one's cause by working within pre-existing legal and political frameworks. The war of maneuver, on the other hand, is an attack on the system that employs extra-legal or illegal strategies, such as direct action or revolution, and it may include a greater degree of confrontation and conflict. Both approaches should be considered in the pursuit of confederation.

As a result of the confederation linking the numerous autonomous movements that make up the multitude, an alternative world order is formed. It generates the possibility of unity amidst the existence of diversity. It emphasizes equal dignity amidst differences, and the right to self-determination in opposition to the forces that seek to homogenize people under the banner of the nation-state and the all-encompassing hegemony of the Empire.

The community of communities is not structured like a Russian doll, with one level within another inside another inside another and so on. It is an extensive web of arborescent and rhizomatic structures that are connected to one another in a web-like fashion. Community is both permeable and pliable, but it is also more real and tangible than any legalistic or bureaucratic barriers that are established around people. Community is something that is inherent to the human spirit, which is why, despite the fact that servitude and alienation may attempt to beat it out of us, we still inherently strive to be a part of one.

Intercommunalism

The Soviet Union was an attempt to create a counter-Empire. Vladimir Lenin's goal was not simply to create a revolution in Russia. Russia was to be the starting point of a global revolution: once a revolutionary government was established in Russia, it was to be an organizing point for other revolutions throughout the world. Leon Trotsky expanded this idea of permanent revolution, arguing that the revolution must look outward toward the transformation of the world and overthrow of global capital. Only then could socialism be achieved. Joseph Stalin, on the other hand, suggested socialism could be constructed internally within Russia. Trotsky and Lenin were closer to Karl Marx on this point, but even they assumed that this global project must be undertaken through national liberation movements, creating independent states.

The effect of this was the Cold War, in which the United States and Soviet Union vied for influence over national governments, engaged in proxy wars and espionage, and sought internal control over their own people. Far from fearing the Soviet Union, the United States greatly benefited from this balance of power. Each side's denunciation of the other served more to keep their own people in line rather than threaten one another. It is commonly believed that the United States won the Cold War, but in fact they lost — the goal was never to win, but to keep it going.

The approach of the left during this time was proletarian internationalism. This meant supporting national struggles for liberation against colonialism and capitalist hegemony. The revolutions in China, Korea, and Cuba were all rallying points for the Western left, as were the anticolonial struggles in Africa throughout this time. Whoever resisted the American empire was hailed as a hero by the international socialist movement.

There were some problems with this, however. For one, this solidarity was broken by feuding between the socialist powers themselves. The Sino-Soviet split of the 1960s created a schism among Western socialists, with some supporting the Soviet Union while others sided with China. It also gave people a blind spot with respect to the oppressive policies of these anti-Western governments themselves. The CIA certainly sought to undermine these regimes with propaganda, but this became a standard excuse to dismiss any criticism of them as counter-revolutionary fabrications, no matter what the source. The victims of the Soviet gulag, the Cultural Revolution, or the Orwellian police state of North Korea could all be summarily dismissed as Western lies. Even dictators who in no way identified as socialists, such as Syrian dictator Bashar Al-Assad, have enjoyed cover from Western leftists on the basis of being "anti-Western."

International politics since the Cold War has remained a matter of taking sides between one faction of states or another. One must either align with the West or its enemies, thereby dismissing the atrocities of one or the other. We certainly cannot dismiss the existing balance of power, and the West no doubt deserves to be taken down a notch, but we must not delude ourselves that this way leads to liberation. The Empire feeds upon this double bind, since whoever emerges victorious will reform the Empire in their own interests rather than abolishing it. The Empire offers no third option: we must create one ourselves.

An alternative approach was proposed by Black Panther leader Huey P. Newton. In 1974, before the term "globalization" was popularized, he spoke about how capitalism had already eroded national boundaries through the forces of economic neo-colonialism. It had created a state of "intercommunalism." It would no longer suffice to be an "internationalist" because the nation-state was already in decay. It was rather a matter of deciding which kind of intercommunalism one sought. The Empire of capital had created "reactionary intercommunalism," and so it was the duty of radicals to create a "revolutionary intercommunalism." Just as workers banding together to form unions could help counter the hegemonic power of capital at a smaller scale, so could revolutionary communities from different regions form confederations that could counter the power of global capital.

The concept of intercommunalism invites us to view the world not as a collection of nations but as a network of communities. We shouldn't be asking ourselves which violent state to assist in their battle for power; rather, we should be asking which communities we can back. We have an obligation to express our solidarity with the impoverished and downtrodden people of every nation. That might require us to back the fights of individual nations, but we shouldn't lose sight of the fact that the problem extends beyond the borders of individual governments. There is a danger when any leader, party, or state becomes "too big to fail." The movement must stay true to the cause of liberation.

Repression at the hands of Empire gives the multitude its identity. This repression extends to both national governments and grassroots social movements. Intercommunalism provides us with a framework that enables such nations to be conditionally supported as a subaltern group seeking liberation, while at the same time recognizing subnational liberation movements. It is imperative that we transcend the power battles of the Empire and build an alternative within it. Diverting our attention from constructing the counter-

Empire of the multitude, the Empire reduces us to picking a side in its power games.

We must build local democratic power while supporting others in doing the same, thereby weakening the nation-state while forging networks across national borders. These bonds can grow through trade and mutual defense, including volunteer militias that can be called into action to defend allies under attack. These defensive alliances could circumvent the power of NATO along with other great powers. The relevance of national borders will gradually fade as a new kind of political paradigm displaces it, based on complex relationships rather than bounded regions of land. Solidarity networks could traverse state lines and create a revolutionary intercommunal order.

It is all well and good to issue solidarity statements for those fighting for liberation, but we must also build institutions. The world order of the Empire has non-governmental organizations such as human rights groups, charities, and environmental groups that operate internationally. A revolutionary transformation of such institutions could lay the groundwork for a new confederal order, establishing new democratic structures for managing the global commons.

Commonwealth

Neoliberalism and globalization have had a synergistic impact, resulting in the development of a new type of social organization referred to by Hardt and Negri as a "republic of property." This particular social structure arose as a result of the interaction of the two ideas: the privatization of natural resources and the concentration of wealth and power in the hands of a relatively small, privileged minority. Wealth encompasses more than just monetary assets; it also includes access to medical care, educational opportunities, and even interpersonal interactions between people. The republic of property takes all that is collectively produced and seizes it for private profit and power.

The state's role in this political system is analogous to that of an agent for the ruling class; the state is tasked with preserving property rights as well as the interests of the powerful and wealthy. This system is inherently undemocratic because it restricts people's access to the resources they need to survive and advance, and it concentrates an excessive amount of power in the hands of a relatively small group of people. In other words, the nature of this system prevents people from participating in democratic decision-making.

The only way to break free from the property-based republic is to build a new social order based on the commons. Resources are controlled collectively, and distribution is determined by taking into account the needs of the society as a whole. The people must build this new social order from the ground up, by establishing new forms of governance and decision-making that prioritize cooperation and mutual aid over individualism and competition.

In the emerging political era, the commons is the primary site of political struggle. The commons is understood as land and natural ecosystems as well as the products of human creativity: immaterial labor such as ideas, information, and cultural content are intrinsically common, and it is only the sabotage of the ruling class that allows them to be privately appropriated. Where capitalism emphasizes private property and state socialism emphasizes public property, the commons is the negation of property. In one sense it belongs to everyone, but in another sense it challenges the very notion of its belonging to anyone. Its paradigm is not one of ownership but of usufruct. It is not owned but rather collectively managed and maintained for the good of all.

In a similar way, the democracy of the multitude is not sovereignty. It is the negation of sovereignty. Even the "popular sovereignty" on which bourgeois democracy rests cannot contain the democracy of the multitude. Democracy and the commons go together. To create the commons is to create systems for collectively managing it. To have sovereignty over the commons, whether through private property or state ownership, is to negate its status as commons.

No exact system for democratic management can come from a single blueprint. It too must emerge democratically, taking account of local conditions and including the voices of diverse interests. Democracy is a continuous process by which the commons comes into being, as well as a process by which it reproduces itself. Democracy is an adaptive organic structure that is subject to constant revision as needed to better suit its purpose.

The global commonwealth can only emerge from the multitude, a vast and diverse network of people involved in global campaigns against capitalism and for social justice. This will occur when the multitude transforms into a global commonwealth. The ability of the multitude to create new forms of resistance and organization, as well as new political and social relationships outside of the framework of existing institutions, distinguishes it from other types of social movements. The multitude is an amalgamation of many social groups, communities, and organizations that have joined forces to create a more democratic and equitable society.

The "commoning" process, which refers to the collaborative administration and use of shared resources, allows the global commonwealth to emerge from the tangle of entities that it currently consists of. This process entails the creation of new models of governance and decision-making that are based on cooperation and mutual aid rather than individualism and competitiveness. Elinor Ostrom's principles for governing the commons call for multiple levels of adjudication. Local resources could be managed directly by the people who live there, while other common pool resources of a more global level will require a polycentric approach. The structures of such management systems must be negotiated by the multitude, but they can start from the structures that already exist. The communication and information management systems currently privatized by capital are run by the multitude, and from them the infrastructure of a new commonwealth can be built. The commonwealth will be built upon the ruins of the republic of property.

State power is founded upon domination, and must be replaced by civic power which is founded upon participation. The civic dimension, what Jürgen Habermas calls the "public sphere," is the forum for the multitude. The concept of citizenship has become a legal abstraction used to identify one as belonging to a nation-state, but in its original sense it implied a sense of participation in the affairs of the polis. We must revive the polis as a site for democratic governance of the commons. Where the Empire and multitude come to blows, the Empire justifies itself by military while the multitude justifies itself by democracy.

Democracy

For much of Western history, democracy was a dirty word. It was seen as an affront to the natural order of things, in which the elite ruled over the crowd. Democracy was viewed as mob rule, a terror on par with the Huns and the Vikings. America's Founding Fathers were adamantly against democracy, even as they opposed the monarchy as well. What they sought instead was an oligarchy of white male property owners, an elite truly worthy of ruling. Viewing democracy through a positive lens has roots in the movements challenging that oligarchy, such as feminism and abolitionism. It was really only with the rise of communism and fascism that democracy became a central aspect of America's self-image, precisely as a foil to the authoritarianism of these other systems.

America was never really a democracy, but it at least tried to justify itself by appealing to democratic principles. Now democracy is attacked from several directions. One of these directions is the market. Fiscal liberals see the market as the organ of collective intelligence, sending signals to facilitate the optimal distribution of goods and services. The "invisible hand" is far wiser than us mere mortals, for it knows not merely what we *think* we want, but our "revealed preferences." The people are only trustworthy as consumers, not as voters. In the latter capacity, they might vote for more entitlements for themselves, draining the treasury and destroying the economy. Some might even compare it to democracy, encouraging everyone to "vote with their dollar." Unspoken is the fact that "one dollar, one vote" is a far cry from "one person, one vote."

Another attack on democracy comes from the self-styled technocrats, techno-populists, and techno-fascists. These are the smartest guys in the room, the whiz kids who know exactly how society ought to be managed. The tech industry is full of such men (almost always men): they know the "one weird trick" to make society function best, if only people would listen to them. Of course, they don't really need society to listen to them. They just need society to hand them the keys so they can run a tight ship without the troublesome meddling of the rabble. Sure, some may have to be displaced, policed, and incarcerated in order to achieve their designs, but that is a small price to pay for progress, and those who stand in the way of progress are the enemy.

A third frightening attack comes from the rise of global fascism. Fascists consider themselves to be the natural aristocracy, in whom authority should be bestowed by right. They value democracy exactly to the extent that it benefits them, and no further. If they win an election, the people have spoken. If they lose, it was clearly rigged, and must be resisted violently. The term "reactionary" aptly describes the tantrums of this set, for whom the only reality is that they are always right. When the world contradicts them, it is the world that is wrong. Those who see the world differently than them do not count, and must be silenced at any cost.

Whither democracy? Is there something to be said in favor of popular rule? Do people actually have the capacity to govern themselves?

Have you *met* the average person? Most people are not particularly wise or progressive. Many are selfish, hateful, and shortsighted. This is why Leninists have always insisted on a vanguard party to guide the masses toward class consciousness. Mao Tse-Tung even tried to modify this concept in a more democratic direction with his concept of the "mass line," in which party leaders would go out to the masses to learn their needs and concerns, then translate them into the Marxist framework. But the ultimate decision-making authority was in the party itself.

If the people were to have such authority, would it be two wolves and a sheep deciding what's for dinner? Would they vote to execute gay people, legalize lynching, or euthanize the disabled? Such risks should certainly be taken seriously. But it's important to remember that such violence is typically enacted *against* democracy. The Ku Klux Klan carried out a protracted campaign of terror to destroy democracy in the South, particularly for newly freed black people, but also any white sympathizers they might have. People remember how "state rights" were invoked against federal interference to protect the civil rights of black people, but we must also remember that segregationist policies were themselves profoundly anti-democratic. Urban technocrats today even have the gall to accuse communities of color resisting gentrification of being "segregationist," as though autonomy over their own communities was in any way equivalent to the second-class citizenship that segregationist policies reduced them to.[20]

It is the denial of democracy that must be resisted — the attempt to shut people out, whether on the assumption that they don't know what's good for them or that they will go against one's own interests. It is not that everyone has the right analysis or the right ideas; it is that the process of deliberation can bring forth the best ideas through the collective intelligence of the group.

Democracy involves process, and this often requires facilitation. A skilled facilitator can draw out the answers from the people, encourage participation, and address power dynamics. They do not make decisions for the group, but help the group come to a consensus. It is a pedagogical role, helping the group learn from one another. Paulo Friere's radical pedagogy is not meant merely for school children: it is the process by which the multitude learns to govern itself.

There is also something to be said for checks and balances. The checks and balances in the US Constitution are meant to curb democracy in favor of the propertied elites. However, there can also be checks and balances that protect the interests of marginalized groups. In Rojava, in addition to the neighborhood councils that decide policies, there are also women's councils that have veto power over any proposals these councils make. This helps secure women's rights in a region with a long history of patriarchy. Similar councils can be made for marginalized ethnic, sexual, or

---

[20] One finds this sentiment often in the so-called "YIMBY" (Yes In My Back Yard) movement, where "incumbents" who currently live in a neighborhood, no matter how poor, are often treated as a privileged elite unjustly discriminating against newcomers who move in and drive up rents.

gender minorities.

The multitude constructs the commons, and in so doing constructs the means for governing it. The foundations for a global commonwealth are already being built. We must simply seize it by resisting the republic of property and reclaiming the commons. The commonwealth is our shared inheritance, and we must guard it from all usurpers. Fortunately, we do not have to go it alone. We have each other.

11

Ecology

For decades, climate change has lingered in the background like an Eldritch abomination, lying in wait to bring about destruction and devastation. We are now in an unprecedented moment when we are reaping the consequences of a disordered relationship with our environment while living through the greatest crisis ever faced by humanity. Never has our way of life been a matter of such consequence.

The Earth has previously gone through periods of climate change and mass extinction. Some geologists classify our current era as the Anthropocene, an epoch in which human activity has been the driving force on soil, climate, biodiversity, and other ecological indicators. Science indicates that we are currently in the sixth great mass extinction, known as the Holocene extinction event.[21] Yet these previous crises were never caused by a species that had the self-awareness to do something about it. Some identify the

---

[21] It still pales in comparison to the Permian extinction event, which killed off some 81% of marine species and 70% of terrestrial species.

agricultural revolution of the Neolithic as the beginning of the Anthropocene. Others see a later origin with the Industrial Revolution. Whatever the case, we have tipped the balance in a way that endangers our future as inhabitants of this planet.

Ecology is often used interchangeably with "environment," yet the environment is only one aspect of what ecology studies. Ecology is fundamentally about relationships, the complex interactions between the elements of an environment that produce a dynamic equilibrium. Ecology is a young academic discipline, but it hearkens back to something that our ancestors intuitively understood. It goes against the reductionist tendency of the various technocratic sciences, and instead takes a holistic approach to systems.

Ecology includes our own relationships with nature, as well as with one another. We are participants in our own ecosystem, and we must understand our own contributions to it, both positive and negative, to understand how to optimally maintain it. Ecology is a matter of interconnected systems mutually supporting one another to create a dynamic balance. Our bodies are ecosystems composed of organs that are ecosystems of cells that are ecosystems of mitochondria, each iterating upon the thing before it to create life.

If there is confusion between nature and ecology, it is because ecology is how nature works. It is the complex interaction of centers to create dynamic wholes. This is important because far too many people under the banner of ecology advocate a "return to nature," by which they mean removing the layers of human artifice until we are stripped of technology and civilization. Yet we are products of nature; we must learn to think ecologically. This means applying the study of nature to how we live and construct our societies. We must not turn our back on progress but re-conceive progress in ecological terms.

Metabolism

Nature functions in cycles. Calcium, carbon, hydrogen, mercury, nitrogen, oxygen, phosphorus, selenium, iron, and sulfur are among the chemicals cycled through the atmosphere, lithosphere, hydrosphere, and biosphere. Our lungs cycle oxygen into carbon dioxide. Our digestive systems break down nutrients into waste products. Life is dependent upon inputs and outputs, and imbalance in either can break down the whole system, causing problems for our health.

Metabolism is fundamental to all life. The interaction between the elements of an ecosystem constitute a metabolism unto itself. Life must maintain a dynamic equilibrium. It must be flexible and adaptable to avoid being thrown out of balance. A living system requires a negative feedback loop, where if the system is pushed in one direction, there is a regulative system that pushes it in the other direction to maintain this balance. A disturbance in such a system can readily be absorbed so that balance can be regained.

A positive feedback loop, on the other hand, builds upon itself in a self-reinforcing manner. A small disturbance can multiply throughout the system, throwing the whole thing into chaos. Examples of this in nature include a hurricane or a stampede. Similarly, mob mentalities operate on this principle, such as a riot or a run on a bank. Positive feedback loops can be good for something that has a terminus, such as the process of blood clotting to heal a wound, but when the overall system is trying to survive positive feedback can be deadly. Cancer is a positive feedback loop running through the body.

Both types of feedback loop can be found in the economy. Supply and demand are supposed to work as regulative factors in the price system, creating a negative feedback loop that stabilizes prices. However, asset prices operate on a positive feedback loop. An increase in stock price signals to other investors to buy up that stock, increasing the price and attracting more investors, until the bubble bursts, causing a mass sell-off of the same stock. When this reaches a large enough scale, it results in mass unemployment, business failures, and social unrest. The only way the system's managers know how to respond to this is to try and steer the feedback loop back toward growth.

Yet growth has an ecological cost that we are reaping at an alarming rate. If we do not learn to curb the need for growth, we will throttle toward our doom at an ever-increasing velocity. The call for "degrowth," once a fringe position, has slowly crept its way into the economic mainstream. Its call to curb intensive resource extraction and industrial activity is often slandered as "austerity" that will burden ordinary people, but in fact it means freeing them from the oppressive weight of the megamachine. Fewer work hours, less commuting, and more leisure time to enjoy with family and friends are fundamental components of degrowth. Degrowth involves a commoning process, in which what had previously been privatized and commodified becomes the common inheritance of all. The commons makes us so much richer than property ever could.

Critical to this endeavor is the concept of throughput. Throughput is the flow of resources from extraction to waste product. What is important to understand is that the economy operates as a subsystem within our ecological domain. Too much throughput strains the environmental systems upon which it depends. Nature can provide us the resources we need, and it has waste sinks that can process waste products, but these only have so much capacity, and the more we strain them, the more unstable the whole system becomes. Stability means not using non-renewable resources at a faster rate than they can be replaced by renewables, not using renewable resources at a faster rate than they can regenerate, and not creating waste at a faster rate than waste sinks can absorb and process them.

Marx explained growth based via the tendency of the rate of profit to fall, suggesting that for the capitalist to counteract this tendency, they must continue to expand production. Yet Veblen observed that the primary function of capital is not production but sabotage. How can we reconcile this with the observable fact of growth? Economists Shimshon Bichler and Jonathan Nitzan suggest that what grows is precisely sabotage: companies subsume other companies, the security state expands to deal with rising inequality, bureaucracies grow, advertising targets people to fill the void in their lives with consumer products, fast fashion and planned obsolescence pile up in landfills. Economic growth is the growth of waste.

Growth is dominated by speculative assets and abstract accumulation. Derivatives, mergers and acquisitions, intellectual property and the like account for a large portion of growth, even as rates of production and extraction slow down. Yet so long as these monopolizing tendencies continue, they will squeeze the resources needed by people to increase their own market power. The result is marginalized populations being pushed out toward marginal lands, using marginal resources and pressing against the ecological limits of their surroundings, all while more productive resources are hoarded by speculators. To achieve sustainable throughput, we must address resource distribution.

Degrowth is not about running our existing economy on less throughput, nor does it mean living in poverty. On the contrary, it is precisely the drive for accumulation that leaves so many impoverished today. Under capitalism, surpluses are reinvested in further growth. In pre-capitalist societies, however, a surplus might go toward a large feast. A degrowth economy is one in which the surplus belongs to everyone: all are guaranteed a minimum standard of living that includes decent shelter, nutritious food, and access to the commons.

Population

The metabolic dynamic applies to our population as well. Political demography and population policies are rife with authoritarian, eugenicist, and ecofascist ideologies, seeking to control the population of the poor through measures like abortion and sterilization. But a population tends to level off on its own when people are not struggling to survive. Japan, France, and Germany have already seen their populations level off and even decline in some cases as a result of generous cradle-to-grave welfare policies that create a sustainable standard of living for their populations.

Demographic transition — the transition from high birth and death rates to low birth and death rates — tends to track with factors such as women's education, affordable healthcare, urbanization, and wage increases. The status of women is particularly relevant. Where women are viewed as objects to be possessed, as vessels for a man's children, as the means for his sexual satisfaction, that will lead to one population level. If, on the other hand, they are viewed as persons unto themselves, as agents in their own lives with their own goals and purposes, that will create an entirely different outcome. Population stability follows from freedom and liberation.

In countries that have dropped below replacement levels, the aging population is dependent upon a shrinking working population. This is often remedied by attracting more immigrants into the workforce. However, this has led to ethnic tension and increased nativist politics. Immigrants are weaponized by capitalists and politicians. They fill the rolls of labor considered too dirty or intensive, but they make a convenient scapegoat when popular anger erupts against economic hardship. The average citizen would be content to use immigrants for their labor and not have to deal with them at any other time. Yet the fact remains that immigrants are real human beings with their own lives, families, and interests, and a policy of accommodating them only to the extent necessary to make them work for everyone else is not sustainable. They and their cultures must be welcomed and embraced by their adoptive one.

The standard of living afforded to the retired population could be expanded to the entire population if we shifted away from capital accumulation and toward an economy of mutual aid and usufruct. The amount of work required to meet everyone's needs is much less than that required to meet capital's need to expand indefinitely. It can be distributed among the population into manageable amounts that allow people more time to look after the more important things in life, like caring for family and building supportive communities. The burden placed upon young people working to support the elderly could be much lighter and more meaningful.

Immigration allows people the opportunity to encounter and learn from one another's cultures. Yet we must also address the refugee crises that lead many people to emigrate in the first place. The much maligned migrants at America's southern border, for instance, are being driven from their homes by the mass violence of drug cartels meeting the demand for illegal drugs bought by American consumers. The US government's War on Drugs and the black market it spawned have left a trail of blood across Latin America. NAFTA and the CIA have left their own devastating impacts for good measure. The conditions these people are fleeing are very much the product of American foreign policy. So too with African and Middle Eastern refugees in Europe.

Hardt and Negri identify mass migration as an insurrection against the Empire. The Empire uses the apparatus of the nation-state to make borders porous for capital while closing them off to labor. Those who cross borders despite the law implicitly challenge this order. The ruling class understandably fears this insurgency, for it undermines the basis of their power. They have orchestrated a cruel counterinsurgency, from the concentration camps in Europe to the detention centers at the US-Mexico border. The reasons for migration are intensely personal, as people flee from war zones, famines, and crime-ridden failed states. Nevertheless, they present a challenge to an unjust world order.

We must build solidarity across these borders, between center and periphery, to stop the exploitation of the periphery while supporting those fleeing that exploitation. Reparations are owed to these victims of imperialism. Yet the greatest gift we could give them is sovereignty over their own lives and communities. Intercommunal organizations must help liberate the oppressed in all corners of the world. Only then can we truly encounter one another as neighbors and not as exploiters and the exploited.

As with other factors, population is an issue of throughput, which means that the limits to population are relative to environmental conditions that are themselves in flux and can be affected by our own activity in positive or negative ways. A greater population can be sustained to the extent that food supply can keep up and the waste products we create can be absorbed back into the ecosystem. Whatever we do to heal the earth is also for the sake of the people living here, who must not be treated as ends in themselves and another factor to be controlled. We must preserve our common home for the common good.

The carrying capacity of the Earth is a function of our relationship to it. Our current economic system is unsustainable under any population. A more democratized system could feed many more. It is often conjectured that we have thus far managed to avoid a Malthusian collapse only due to the innovations of the Green Revolution, without which we would be living in squalor. This is demonstrably untrue.

Such methods are suited to getting higher yields of a single crop at the expense of the rest of the ecosystem, whereas higher yields overall can be produced by planting a variety of crops within the same space.[22] This local diversity not only reduces fuel costs and prevents food from going to waste, but creates a resilient ecosystem in which life can flourish. Industrial agriculture has spread across the globe not because it is efficient but because it is monopolistic. These capital-intensive methods allow for the accumulation of greater wealth by disempowering farm workers, but regenerative methods could have higher sustainable yields that renew the soil in the process.

A higher population does not just mean more mouths to feed. It also means more hands to work the fields. In *Fields, Factories, and Workshops*, Peter Kropotkin went to great lengths to demonstrate how, with such labor-intensive agriculture, England could produce enough food to feed its entire population. The capital-intensive agriculture that has come to characterize the current regime is not, in fact, the most efficient way of growing food, but rather the most efficient way of extracting profit from food production. When we look at population, we must consider that people can contribute to the common good as much as they can take from it.

One can easily point to countries with low population growth and high standards of living compared to countries with higher population growth and lower standards of living

---

[22] For more information on the history and effects on the Green Revolution, see Baranski, Marci. *The Globalization of Wheat: A Critical History of the Green Revolution*. University of Pittsburgh Press, 2022.

and assume that population is the causal factor here. Little notice is given to the exploitation of the latter for the benefit of the former. Within the periphery, vast quantities of farmland are owned by a small latifundia who use it for corporate agriculture when it could produce more and better food for their own population through small-scale polyculture. High populations of exploited workers are good for the capitalist: those they don't hire belong to the reserve army of the unemployed, driving wages down and keeping the rest in line.

Much of the conversation around "carrying capacity" is entangled with the costs of continuing the accumulation of capital and has little to do with the costs of providing for people's livelihoods. How many resources go into stock markets, business trips, policing the poor, wars of aggression, advertising, daily commutes, yachts, gas-guzzling vehicles, sprawling suburbs with single-family housing, or skyscrapers full of meaningless paper-pushing jobs? We could easily do without all of these, but because they are priorities for capital, these resource expenditures count toward the "carrying capacity" that implicates all of us. If the rule of capitalism is "capital eats first," we would surely all be better off if we let capital be the first to starve.

Property

One of the great obstacles to an ecological society is unequal access to resources. In countries like Brazil, wealthy latifundia own extensive tracts of land, while small farmers must turn to more marginal land to grow crops and raise cattle.

To do this, they resort to cutting down the rainforest. It is all too easy to place the blame on these farmers while ignoring the economic factors that led them to that situation in the first place.

The logic of growth is a refusal of distributive justice. Its premise is that the rich can take a greater share of the pie so long as the pie itself continues to grow. If the poor have enough scraps after the rich have taken their share, then who could complain? One may even point to a reduction in rates of extreme poverty, even as inequality continues to grow. Yet there can be no infinite growth on a finite planet. The poor who work the mines, pick the fields, log the forests, and manufacture the products may find their wages rise even as they fall further behind their corporate masters. These gains come at the cost of a toxic environment that is increasingly inhospitable for all of us, particularly the poor.

Property rights, to the extent they exist, must extend from the common good. It may be to everyone's benefit for people to have some land for their own use, but when this principle is extended to benefit one person at the expense of another, we can be certain that property has run afoul of its purpose. This was recognized even by one of the central figures in creating the liberal capitalist understanding of property. John Locke, who believed that men were endowed with natural rights consisting of "life, liberty, and property," added the proviso that the right to property could only be guaranteed if there was enough land of equal quality available for everyone.

In asserting a natural right to property, Locke was breaking with the Natural Law tradition he was invoking. The Scholastics supported property as a useful institution insofar as it gave someone a piece of land to tend as one's own, giving them a stake in its continued stewardship. Yet they would never imagine claiming property as an essential human right. They recognized all too well how easily it could conflict with the right to life. Their faith also taught of the grave sins attached to the desire for accumulation. The church taught that property is an ephemeral thing: all the world belongs to its creator, and we are but stewards of creation passing through on our way to eternity. All property ultimately belongs to God, who offers it up for the benefit of all. On the last day, we will have to answer for what we did with what was given to us.

Property subject to the common good becomes usufruct. Progressive legal theory treats property not as a right, but a "bundle of rights." This means that it is a social relation involving not only the property owner but the community in which they are embedded. The community has a stake in the social and environmental effects that come from the owner's use of property. However, this bundle of rights can be expanded to a universal right to the commons, in which the ownership rights are transformed into rights of use.

Economic and ecological justice are deeply intertwined. Property cannot take priority over humanity. All that we have is not ours to keep, but to use for the betterment of all. The burden of protecting the environment is overwhelmingly hoisted on those who have the least. Shall we be exploiters that use people and nature alike for our own short-term gain? Or shall we be stewards who live together with people and nature as one common family and pass our common inheritance to future generations?

Agriculture

Industrial agriculture represents one of the most consequential forms of economic activity. The "industrial" aspect of agriculture certainly deserves some analysis of its own, especially given that the Industrial Revolution itself has its origins in the textile industry and the sheep-farming practices that supported it. Yet the transition to agriculture was more gradual than is often imagined. Hunter-gatherers had plenty of occasion to notice how plants reproduce and would have learned how to help the plants they harvested regrow each season. It is also a misconception that such foraging societies would have necessarily been nomadic. The foraging societies that survive today are nomadic because they have been relegated to marginal lands that have a smaller yield, and therefore must wander from one place to another to gather enough food to survive. It was not so for those societies that had a claim to the more fertile lands. We can see this in the Pacific Northwest, where fishing provided one of the main food sources for a society living in permanent structures.

The use of cultivated crops did not necessitate the abandonment of all other means of obtaining food. Societies continued hunting and gathering while also planting and harvesting crops and raising livestock. Certain crops became staples that provided enough calories, proteins, fats, and carbohydrates to provide a baseline of nutrition for people's energy needs. The domestication of animals allowed for a steady supply of meat, eggs, and dairy, but perhaps more consequential was the labor it provided. Whereas the use of hoes to till the soil required communal involvement, the plough allowed for larger plots to be tilled by fewer people, creating the conditions for centralization of agriculture.

Soil may appear lifeless, but fertile topsoil is crucial for human survival, and we neglect it at our peril. Throughout history civilizations have been felled by drought and famine. Soil is a living ecosystem, full of microbes that break down organic matter into nutrients that feed new lifeforms. Nutrient cycles are as essential to our lives as breathing. Maintaining these nutrient cycles means maintaining biodiversity and respecting natural limits. Agricultural practices that involve tearing up the soil end up depleting this vital resource. Crop rotation, no-till farming, and permaculture are several innovations people developed to work with these cycles and allow soil time to regenerate.

The trajectory of the Industrial Revolution, however, has been toward intensification of agriculture through inputs of fertilizer, pesticides, and herbicides. Rather than work to maintain nutrient cycles, it seeks to replace them through chemical fertilizer to increase the yield of crops several-fold. Pesticides are then used to remove unwanted plant and animal life that feeds upon the crops. In recent years, genetic modification has been used to make the crops immune to the chemicals being sprayed. These three factors are part of an arms race against conditions of our own creation. The repeated fixation of nitrogen into the soil does not heal the soil, but simply defers its inevitable collapse for another growing season. Chemical runoff leaks out into groundwater and surface water, flowing out to the ocean, creating coastal dead zones.

The problem with industrial agriculture is that it is more industry than agriculture. It relies on quick fixes at every turn rather than thinking ecologically. It is true that growing a field of crops with fertilizer, pesticides, and herbicides will give one a greater yield than the same field without those inputs. Sri Lanka discovered this the hard way when their government banned the use of chemical fertilizer and pesticides in 2020, reversing the policy within a year. To farm successfully without these inputs requires farming ecologically, using symbiosis between crops to create resilient systems.

Animal agriculture has also expanded at an unprecedented rate. Until recently, the average person might expect to eat meat once a week at most. Livestock grazed in open fields, fertilizing and compacting the soil, then moving on to other pastures while the plant life regenerated. Today, thanks to increasing demand due to government subsidies, livestock are raised in tight conditions on feedlots, producing mass quantities of environmental waste and requiring several acres of land devoted to feed for stock.

The issue of animal agriculture is often framed in mathematical terms, calculating the amount of land required to grow enough feed for each animal. Yet this calculus leaves out the environmental benefits that livestock can contribute, playing a crucial role in regenerating the soil. The problems of animal agriculture are a subset of the larger problems of industrial agriculture. The environment for growing plants and animals is treated as a separate sphere in competition with the surrounding environment.

Nature does not grow a single plant or animal in isolation. It grows ecosystems, with multiple species interacting with one another in ways that support nutrient cycles upon which each organism is dependent. It uses ecological succession to enrich the soil and allow for new plants to grow, along with animals to consume them and fertilize the soil, allowing for a greater variety of plants and wildlife to grow, and so on. The first stage of ecological succession is one in which "pioneer species" move into fertilized soil and grow. Typical agriculture tends to try to keep the ecosystem at this stage by tilling the fields and harvesting all the crops at once. This degrades the soil, which must be replenished, whether by crop rotation, leaving it fallow or, as in industrial agriculture, continuing to use more fertilizer.

Biodiversity is a fundamental principle of ecology. Monoculture is antithetical to nature's telos: it creates an adversarial relationship between crops and nature. Regenerative agriculture, on the other hand, harnesses nature's natural creativity by paying attention to its patterns and working with it. It involves building relationships with the local ecosystem and cooperating with it symbiotically. What is cultivated is not only crops but the means for sustainably growing crops in perpetuity. It is an endlessly pedagogical experience, in which we learn from the environment through continuous communication as a member of an ecological community, tuning into the Logos of the biosphere.

Permaculture follows the process of ecological succession. Because monoculture tends to keep the ecosystem at the first stage of succession, the permaculture grower can simply build off existing fields by adding perennials, which then make way for shrubs and trees, until an entire food forest comes about. A compact area can host a vast variety of crops that mature at different times of the year, thereby allowing the grower to have year-round income. Because the species nourish one another in a complex web of life as they would in the wild, the natural metabolism of nature is able to function and there is little to no need for fertilizer. A core principle of permaculture is the stacking of functions, which means that each element of the farm has multiple functions to maximize output from minimal input, copying nature as much as possible.

Organic agriculture has developed a thriving niche, but what tends to get overlooked in this discourse is the people who work the fields. "Farmer" has developed associations in the popular imagination with hard-working, salt-of-the-earth people living in harmony with the land. In fact, the term has its origins in control over the labor of others. When we speak of "farming out" a task to someone, we are approaching a more accurate description. Nor is this a mere matter of "big" versus "small" farms. Industrial agriculture has in fact spread itself through the same "small" farms so often eulogized in our political discourse. Industrial agriculture was not developed by corporations buying up all the big plots of land so much as through direct marketing of fertilizers, pesticides, growth hormones, and other industrial products to farmers who used them along with generous agricultural subsidies and tax breaks to become the new latifundia. It operates like a franchise, selling the means for setting up an operation and dumbing down the process so as to require no meaningful knowledge of natural cycles or ecological principles.

It is the farm *workers* who have been systematically neglected in all this discourse; they who were driven off the land through the development of farming machinery. The global trend toward urbanization is not some natural law based on the inherent advantages of cities. It is the response of billions who have been displaced because unlike the farmers whose fields they worked, they did not own the land and could not reap its profits. Farmers compose only a small portion of the rural population, but they hold enough power to write local tax laws heavily in their favor. The rest are driven to trailers and mobile homes if they can even find work to afford housing. Otherwise, they must seek new opportunities in the city. A free peasantry must be liberated through land reform that returns the fields to those who labor in them.

Industry

Technology is alternately damned and praised as the cause of and solution to our ecological crisis. The Industrial Revolution radically transformed society at a rate unheard of at any other time in history. Farming was among the first industries to be industrialized, reducing the number of people involved in agriculture and creating a food surplus to feed a growing urban population. Factories spread across the urban landscape, spewing toxic black smoke into the air. Rivers turned to sludge. Whales were hunted to near-extinction for their oil. Forests were cleared and fisheries picked clean. Capital's drive for limitless growth was built upon a technological base that made it possible and necessary.

Each crisis has been met by regulations meant to mitigate the impact. The regulatory state arose as a vast bureaucracy to curb the excesses of industrial capitalism. This mentality of "curbing the excesses" of capitalism became central to the modern liberal identity. The enemy was unfettered, unregulated capitalism — but never capitalism itself. The spirit of competition, of entrepreneurialism, is seen as a positive thing, while also recognizing that these things lead to their own undoing through monopolistic tendencies, which liberals seek to regulate against. Libertarians, for their part, blame the problems on "corporatism," not capitalism, complaining that the spirit of competition and entrepreneurship is hampered by regulation and market interference, and if we could get the state out of the way, then capitalism could truly work for all of us.

The left tends to treat capitalism as the root problem while leaving industrialism in place: if the workers could take control of the factory and run it themselves, then the problems of industry would fade away. Yet the factory itself is built on an authoritarian model and continues to make society in its image so long as it remains the dominant paradigm. Technology can be authoritarian or liberatory depending on whether it funnels people into predetermined pathways or expands our horizons, allowing for greater conviviality and freedom in our creative abilities. Authoritarian technologies impose upon the environment, both natural and human. It imposes where liberatory ones adapt. Rather than serving human needs, authoritarian technology reorganizes human society around servicing its needs.

Capitalism cannot simply be reduced to greed on the part of capitalists. People made profits before capitalism, but they kept the surplus for themselves, buying fine clothes and jewelry and surrounding themselves with luxury. The emergence of the factory model and reliance on credit saw a developing imperative to reinvest profit into continued growth. Industrial technology demands to be fed and uses humans to do it. Exploiter and exploited alike are subsumed under the logic of the machine.

The megamachine is social before it is mechanical. Technical artifacts presuppose a form of social organization to produce them. Under the megamachine, this means division of labor and systemic exploitation. This exploitation extends to humans and nature alike. The skies of Victorian England were darkened by black smoke from the textile mills spinning cotton picked by slaves in the Americas on land stolen from indigenous peoples while selling to the colonized people of India, whose own traditional textile crafts were banned under British rule. Capitalism is an outgrowth of colonialism, which has always involved the colonization of both land and people.

A different technical regime is possible, in which technology extends the creative powers of the people rather than molding them into cogs in the machine. However, this requires a different form of social organization. Conviviality in technology requires a similar conviviality in our institutions. Technology must serve human ends rather than upholding the power of capital. We must overcome the hegemony of authoritarian institutions and build participatory forms of organization to create a liberatory mode of production.

The megamachine keeps us servile, locked in endless drudgery that keeps us from exploring our creative gifts. A significant amount of work is totally unnecessary to human flourishing, serving only to secure power for the ruling class. We must overcome this stranglehold by capital through an irreducible minimum, in which the basic needs of all are guaranteed. Work and play could seamlessly intertwine, as work is made into a social activity and play is directed toward developing skills and hobbies. A shift from commodities to relationships would stop the needless expenditure on endless accumulation. Surpluses would remain, but rather than reinvesting in growth, it could be directed towards the community to be enjoyed by everyone. A sense of joy in community could fill the void of dissatisfaction upon which consumerism is built.

The creative projects people would explore when guaranteed this base level of security could be individual crafts or collective enterprises. Rather than factories operated under a wage contract, they could instead have workshops where they come together to collaborate on projects. Rather than a fixed schedule set by an employer, workers could set the schedule themselves according to what is convenient to them. They could work on the same project continuously throughout the week or they could have several different projects going on at the same time. They could shift between individual and collective projects as it suited them or take time off and do nothing at all. A lottery-based system of community service may be instituted for essential tasks that lack sufficient volunteers, but most undesirable jobs are products of a system in which the priorities of capital come first. Under a free society in which the people's prerogatives come first, such tasks could be modified using different technology or institutional design to be more pleasant, less degrading, or rendered obsolete.

The megamachine shapes urban development. Placing a Roman grid over the city, leveling the landscape to make room for grand designs, using centralized baseload power sources, the technocratic urbanist lays out his grand vision without having to leave his office. The land is developed for the purpose of reaping profit from the people who live there. Toward this end, wetlands are filled, neighborhoods are bulldozed or gentrified, and roads and freeways are built over natural habitat, all with the goal of extracting profit from people. A city that prioritized people would unfold organically according to local priorities. People would develop their neighborhoods piecemeal, building where there is room and fitting in with the local environment. There would be some need for large-scale planning, such as utilities and public transportation infrastructure, but these could be planned by popular assemblies open to all.

A distributed renewable energy grid would make use of the environment rather than overpowering it. Urban development would likewise involve streets, buildings, and infrastructure following natural patterns of settlement. When an area is settled organically, it first follows natural contours such as watersheds or slope breaks, and from there follows cultural patterns of development that flow from the lived experience of the people.

Community

There is a common idea that human influence on the environment is necessarily bad, and that the goal of sustainability should be a matter of reducing human impact as much as possible. But there is nothing to stop us from impacting the environment in a positive way. There is evidence that the Amazon rainforest, often referred to as the lungs of the earth due to the amount of carbon dioxide it cycles out of the atmosphere, was actively cultivated and shaped by human activity.

No other species has studied ecology. They have all fit into their ecological niche by acting according to their nature. We have fallen away from the Logos, yet we have developed the intelligence and insight to understand what we have fallen away from. If humans have upset the ecological balance, so too can we improve it. We have fallen from the prelapsarian grace of being creatures of instinct. We have modified the world in reckless ways that currently place us on the precipice of our own extinction. Yet the opportunity exists to make an impact that is positive rather than negative.

To respond to ecological collapse by simply trying to reduce our impact would still doom us all. We must actively work with the Earth to build a more bountiful and beautiful world. Even as we threaten the biosphere with unprecedented destruction, we understand better than ever what natural processes can heal nature. Through regenerative agriculture, rewilding, appropriate technology, and emergent urbanism, we can not only stop but begin to reverse the harm we have done to this planet. Carbon can not only be sequestered but restored to natural systems that nurture life. The discourse around climate change can too easily lead us to think of carbon as intrinsically bad, forgetting the vital role it plays in all biological systems.

The factors that keep us in a hostile and exploitative relationship with nature are the same that keep us in a hostile and exploitative relationship with one another. It is the logic of a system oriented toward dominator hierarchies, short-term gain, and limitless growth. Only by addressing the skewed logic of this system can we hope to solve the problems of our relationships to one another and to our environment.

Social ecology is based on the principle that social problems and ecological problems are interconnected. Society is a kind of ecosystem, embedded within the natural ecology. Indeed, both "society" and "ecology" are terms we use for sets of relationships, one between humans and one between organisms. Yet humans are organisms, and our own network of relations includes the human and non-human. Does "society" not include our pets, livestock, crops, climate, topsoil, carbon sinks, and biodiversity? Do these things not all affect our social conditions? Does our ecosystem not include farmers, urban planners, transportation, trade networks, and industrial output? If anything, the Anthropocene has simply thrown light on the fact that these things have always been interconnected.

Deep ecology tends to address this by subsuming the social into the natural, emphasizing the need to see ourselves as part of nature. Yet such an approach tells us little about how the rupture occurs in the first place and how to fix it. Its prescriptions tend to be subtractive in nature, limiting human influence as much as possible. Social ecology, on the other hand, starts from the premise that nature is already social. Nature is understood not as some great sea in which we are all but drops, but as a complex network of relationships, of which our human relationships are an integral part. Deep ecology asks us to view nature in non-anthropocentric terms, but social ecology asks us to examine our relationships with each other to better understand ecological relationships.

Peter Kropotkin's studies in zoology, history, and human geography anticipate some aspects of social ecology. In *Mutual Aid: A Factor in Evolution*, he discussed the phenomenon of mutual aid among species and then looked at its history among people, showing a continuity between the two. He challenged the prevailing Darwinian paradigm of evolution that emphasized competition as the prime mover in evolution. He did not deny that competition played a role in natural selection, but he emphasized the way that group selection operated on the need within a species to cooperate with one another for mutual gain. A species must struggle for survival within its environment to be able to eat and avoid being killed, yet one of the primary ways they can do this is through cooperative behavior. Competition is necessary within a species, particularly with respect to sexual selection, but the struggle for survival must first be understood as a mutual struggle.

Even between species, symbiotic relationships abound. Flowers and pollinators are an obvious example. Our own gut bacteria upon which we rely for digestion comes from sources outside of ourselves. Plants form mycorrhizal bonds with fungi, creating rhizomatic networks that process and recycle soil nutrients while acting as a kind of ecological nervous system that detects changes in the environment. A widely accepted theory suggests that eukaryotic cells first developed through a process known as symbiogenesis, in which single-celled organisms absorbed other single-celled organisms, which then developed into specialized organelles. Amid the competitive struggle for survival, nature also plays a harmonic symphony.

When we resort to systems of domination, we use others as a means to an end. It results in what Pope Francis, in his encyclical *Laudato Si*, refers to as "throwaway culture," in which people such as the poor and elderly are discarded when they are no longer useful to others. Throwaway culture extends to nature as well. Under capitalism, a forest is only valuable for its timber. True to his namesake, His Holiness urges that instead of viewing nature through the lens of dominion, we should see it as a family, which indeed is what evolutionary biology tells us. This encyclical derives its name from the famous *Canticle of the Sun*, written by the other Francis. This song expresses praise for "Brother Sun," "Sister Moon," "Brother Wind," "Sister Water," "Brother Fire," and "Sister Mother Earth." This may strike some as pantheistic, but Saint Francis was using these affectionate words not to express worship, but familial love. All of creation is one family, born of the same divine source.

Indigeneity

Capitalism is an extension and outgrowth of colonialism. The enclosure movement began the colonization of the European countryside before it was inflicted upon the Americas. Traditional ways of life that had sustained free peasants for centuries were wiped out as they were forced off their land and left with nothing but their labor to sell to the highest bidder. The peasant was historically tied to the land. They shared a knowledge of seasonal cycles, the medicinal properties of native plants, and the local ecology. They had a sense of belonging to the land, not only being *from* it but *of* it. This was lost when they were forced off the land and into the factories.

The war on indigenous people and the war on the environment have always gone hand-in-hand. The mass slaughter of the bison is a well-known example. The eradication of indigenous farming methods is less widely known. The imposition of European property rights onto societies that had completely different property regimes allowed for the theft of their land, which was worked by slaves to further exploit its resources. To this day, indigenous territory is a frequent target for mining, pipeline construction, fracking, and a whole host of dangerous and destructive activities. It is precisely because indigenous lives are so devalued that their land is seen as uniquely exploitable.

A view of indigenous people developed in the European imagination as not really having an innate culture, so much as being part of nature. On the one hand, they were understood as "primitives" who did not have the gift of civilization. On the other hand, some took a romantic view of them, as "noble savages." It is certainly true that such people had a kind of folk wisdom about their natural surroundings, as did Europe's own peasants prior to their displacement. But this was not a matter of being "primitive," but simply being embedded in their environment as an ecological community.

A great deal of indigenous knowledge was deliberately erased by European settlers. Why was it that this image of natives as primitive hunter-gatherers captured the popular imagination when Europeans knew perfectly well about the Aztec and Inca? The idea that the native represented some primitive stage of development was part of a deliberate propaganda campaign to dismiss claims made by the natives themselves. On land that is now Canada, the Jesuits recorded their encounters with the Huron in journals which were read widely throughout Europe. Within these journals, we find not simply the preaching of the Jesuits toward the Huron, but the frequently intelligent and articulate responses they gave. Modern descendants of Europeans may expect that the Jesuits in these encounters were like earlier versions of us, while the Huron were an alien culture we would not recognize. Yet what we find in the journals is many ideals we would now tend to identify with being spoken by the Huron in response to the values of the Jesuits which seem quite foreign in comparison, particularly with respect to freedom. The Jesuits insisted on the value of authority and obedience, convinced that a strict hierarchy was necessary to maintain society. The Huron had different ideas, ones which are much closer to the modern democratic ideals we now embrace.

David Graeber and David Wengrow argue that many of the ideas of the Enlightenment were influenced by these indigenous beliefs. Yet the freedom they spoke of presented a danger to entrenched systems of power, with often more radical understandings of democracy and freedom than we moderns have come to accept, so a system of social evolution was proposed. It was necessary to bracket these ideas as some primitive stage of development from which we emerged into civilization, sacrificing this freedom in exchange for order and complexity. In this scenario, their freedom and equality was a kind of prelapsarian innocence to which we tragically could not return. This idea has stuck in the European imagination ever since, cautioning people not to get too attached to the ideas they encountered in such writings.

The picture we have of the Americas prior to European contact is itself highly skewed. European diseases killed off about 90% of the native population before Europeans even had the opportunity to explore inland. We know that civilization arose in Mesoamerica among the Olmec, Toltec,

Maya, and Aztec. What is less commonly known is that in what is now the United States, a similar civilization existed. Known as the Mississippian culture, their art and jewelry bore a striking resemblance to that of their neighbors to the south. Their cities and temple complexes were built of earthen mounds rather than stone and they had no known writing system, but they made copper jewelry and flint weapons, grew maize, and traded with other tribes including the Pueblo peoples west of the Rocky Mountains. This civilization, described in the writings of the Spanish explorer Hernando de Soto, fell apart after being devastated by European diseases. Their descendants formed numerous tribes, including the Choctaw, Cherokee, and Seminole. Some maintained oral traditions connecting their ancestry with the mounds left behind, while others lost their elders to disease and had no cultural memory of it, contributing to the European myth that the "mound builders" were an entirely separate race.

Between this culture, the Mesoamerican cultures, the Iroquois, the Puebloans, the Inca, and the Amazonian cultures that cultivated the rainforest, the Americas were hardly lacking in advanced civilizations. Yet without the colonizing effect of industry and capitalist property relations, they maintained a connection to their natural environment that could only be destroyed by the proletarianization of the peasant class and the bourgeoisification of the elites. Conquest is older than civilization, but colonialism is a process of commodification. People are turned into commodities in order to produce commodities, and in the process are taught to turn nature into commodities. The spiritual ties with the land are severed, and a treasure trove of ecological knowledge is destroyed with it.

Yet indigenous people continue to pass this knowledge from one generation to another in defiance of their colonizers. Despite displacement, slaughter, and marginalization, they retain the cultural wisdom that comes from a sense of belonging to the land. Their struggles have been struggles for the land and the ecological balance it requires, as we've seen in the Standing Rock protests against the Keystone XL pipeline. Indigenous people have long sought to protect their land, recognizing that their well-being is utterly dependent upon the well-being of the ecosystem. It is indigenous lands that have been specifically targeted for extractive industries by colonizers. That is why they are natural allies in ecological liberation: their fate is tied to the fate of the ecosystem. They feel the brunt of the extractive policies of industrial society. Their subjugation and exploitation is inseparable from the subjugation and exploitation of the Earth.

Indigenous rights are fundamental to environmental justice. The tacit knowledge of the land is more than can be written down in books. Indigenous people had an intuitive understanding of ecology long before it emerged as an academic discipline. They have long histories of managing wildfires, maintaining soil fertility, and preserving biodiversity. The ecological crisis we face today is in large part a result of the systemic valuing of technocratic knowledge over the ecological wisdom lost with the onset of industrialism, and which indigenous peoples have struggled to maintain in the face of colonization. Only by allying with indigenous peoples throughout the world and learning from their ecological wisdom can we hope to overcome these challenges.

The restoration of indigenous sovereignty is crucial for

both social liberation and environmental renewal. Indigenous people have shown time and again that they are better caretakers of the land than the forces of capitalist modernity. The Land Back movement means returning tribal lands and restoring their autonomy. Some object that this amounts to a kind of reverse racism, a "blood and soil" nationalism in which white people will be forced off the land. This straw man fallacy ignores the lived reality that European colonizers violently forced indigenous people off the land and exploited their resources. Indigenous peoples have traditions of land tenure that do not involve such exclusivism or enclosure, nor the border nationalism of nation-states. Restoring their traditional territories to them and recognizing their sovereignty is a step toward a future in which we too will no longer be colonized by the ways of the nation-state. In decolonizing the land, we must also decolonize our own society and ways of life.

Transition

Our best estimates say that we have less than a decade to avoid the worst effects of climate change. We are well into the era of climate catastrophe: summers are filled with raging fires that devour the landscape; hurricane and monsoon seasons grow longer and more intense; and winter storms are reaching places that have never had to deal with snow. Agrarian land is drying up and soil fertility is dissipating. Some say it's too late for us, that what we are looking at is, if not the end of humanity, at least the end of civilization.

Can we still make it? We ultimately have no choice but

to act as if we can still make a difference, and assume that whatever we are currently doing is not enough. I have tried to convey a long-term vision of what kind of society we might strive for, but we don't have time to wait for that society before we act on the crisis at hand.

The good news is that as terrifying as the climate crisis is, the process of ecological repair is easier than most think it is. There is a natural cycle of ecological succession by which ecosystems develop. Ecological restoration is often a simple matter of getting that process started. Swales and terraces can catch rainwater to allow plants to grow. Trees can be planted in mountains to catch cloud moisture and bring rain to arid landscapes. Bushes and hedges can catch runoff and reduce flooding. Regenerative farming can fix nutrient imbalances, sequester carbon back into the soil, and reverse climate change. If we do these things while curbing throughput and moving to a post-growth economy, we can begin to reverse climate change within a generation.

The catch is, we must change the fundamental basis of our economy to do this. We cannot solve the ecological crisis from within the capitalist system. The profit motive and the growth imperative it produces are antithetical to the survival of life on this planet. However, we can do things here and now to stop the bleeding and buy ourselves time. There are some industries that have a vital role to play. We just need the political will to stand against the special interests blocking our path.

The framework of a "Green New Deal" has been floated in recent years. It is not so much a specific set of policy proposals as a platform for addressing the scale and scope of the ecological crisis. At the heart of this platform is a recognition of the interconnections between the ecological crisis and economic inequality. Like the original New Deal, it involves a series of public works projects to boost employment while addressing pressing infrastructure needs. It seeks to create and support "green industries" to take the place of the dirty fossil fuel and petrochemical industries that currently dominate our economy.

The creation of a smart grid is required. The less load there is on existing power sources, the easier it will be to switch to renewables. Retrofitting and weatherizing buildings, installing a distributed network of renewables, and developing better public transportation are all important steps. Energy storage systems could be installed to compensate for periods when energy production is low. High-speed rail could connect cities to one another with much less fossil fuel emissions.

Another important aspect is carbon capture. Agriculture must abandon its monocultural paradigm and switch to a regenerative model that will not only capture carbon but also replenish the soil while expanding the food supply for all. This can be done through the gradual introduction of perennial crops while reducing reliance on annuals. Restorative practices replenish ecosystems, so there is potential to expand farming into new territories that not only do not compete with natural ecosystems but facilitate their regrowth. The side benefits of this include not only food supply but biofuels, medicine, fabrics, and building materials. Several technological fixes have been proposed for carbon sequestration and may have some role in helping to mitigate climate change, but by far the greater task involves utilizing the forms of sequestration nature already provides to an optimal degree.

These measures would all face opposition from fossil fuel companies and other heavily polluting industries, but they could at least conceivably pass with the right elected leaders and sufficient popular pressure behind them. The idea of the Green New Deal emphasizes investment over restriction. Simply limiting industry would give capitalists the credible talking point that it would destroy jobs for the workers. This is what has kept places like West Virginia under the rule of coal-mining companies for so long. The investments of the Green New Deal would mean reorganizing industry around the monumental task of averting climate catastrophe while becoming more resilient against it. New "green jobs" could help work against the hegemony that many polluting industries continue to exert at both a local and global level. Yet green jobs are a small measure compared to the elimination of jobs through universal basic income. We must free people from compulsory work in order to shift from a society of production and consumption to one of relationships and conviviality. Work can become a creative act of joy rather than one of necessity. We must free people from the exploitative trap of forced labor so we can experience a life of genuine community.

We can do all these things even as we build local power, creating direct democratic councils and forming confederations with other municipalities. Building local power involves many of the infrastructure improvements that a Green New Deal would already entail. The network of renewables and microgrids that could be installed could contribute to greater local self-sufficiency, while political self-determination could be built up through mass organization.

The mix of federal aid and local organizing can move us toward building resilient communities. The organization of workplaces and formation of co-ops can go together with the building of cooperative housing and community land trusts. None of this would suffice to create a clean break with the capitalist nation-state, but it sets the stage for such a break. The more we build local autonomy, the more we create the conditions for breaking with the existing political and economic order.

The most important thing we need to do is *less*: less work, less commuting, less consumption, less waste. That opens the possibility of doing so much *more* that is truly meaningful: creating art and music, developing skills, learning, socializing, celebrating. This destructive system of exploitation causes endless, needless waste; we must stop it in its tracks in order to achieve genuine freedom.

All it takes is one spark to bring about this break. A mass movement can spring up overnight. Alter-Globalization, Occupy, Idle No More, Standing Rock, and Black Lives Matter are just a few of the mass movements we've seen erupt within recent decades. The conditions are ripe for more to come. Each one helps create the groundwork for the next. Getting the infrastructure and organization in place ahead of such a movement makes it more likely to create a lasting impact that will help us transcend the present era.

These movements need not be excessively large to achieve meaningful action. Climate change is heavily lopsided in its causes, with the wealthy few tipping the scales far more than the desperate measures of those who have the least. As such, its infrastructure can be strategically targeted by acts of sabotage with minimal impact on the average person. This is often denounced as "ecoterrorism," but such acts in no way imply the loss of human life. To sabotage a pipeline, to block the effluent of a polluting industry, to blockade a logging operation in an old growth forest — far from nihilistic acts of violence, these are life-affirming acts of hope. It is out of great love for humanity that one is driven to risk their freedom for the protection of future generations. When the media portrays such acts as "terrorist" or "criminal," ask whether the act in question constitutes an attack on life or an attack on Empire.

A double movement is essential for social progress: On the one hand, the positive movement of developing alternative means of living; on the other, the negative movement of obstructing the rhythms of the existing system so that a new system has a chance to take root. The latter is often a great deal more visible. Those marching in the streets engaging in property destruction tend to attract a disproportionate amount of sensational media attention. The constructive aspect is just as important, though crucially, that too can suffer the stigma of criminality when it runs up against propertarian concerns. Defying the rules that restrict our agency over our own lives will inevitably be met with resistance, through propaganda as much as by force. Yet we must all be mindful that we are subject to a higher law, one that stands above the laws of man because it is the true law of justice. This law is the divine Logos, and before its dictates we must ultimately bow.

12

Thriving

Not by bread alone do we live, but by family, friendship, community, love, and purpose. If our society has failed at meeting even the basic material needs of everyone, it has failed all the more in everything else. The great boast of our civilization is that it has provided us with so much *stuff*: even a low-income family living in a cramped apartment will have electricity, running water, a microwave, refrigerator, television, computer, and cell phones. This multimedia world contains wonders that previous generations could only dream of. Movies, television, social media, video games, and virtual reality can transport us to all manner of escapist realms of fantasy and hyperreality, but we cannot escape the loneliness of modern existence.

These technological advances have given us a plenitude of distractions, but no real fulfillment. Instead, we have the relentless pursuit of consumption. The French term *jouissance* means "enjoyment," but the psychoanalyst Jacques Lacan used it to describe a particular phenomenon of enjoyment. We compulsively "enjoy" things like television, video games, food, alcohol, drugs, and sexual pleasure, but that does not mean we get satisfaction. We enjoy them the way we enjoy scratching an itch, yet we continue to scratch until it is bloody and raw.

Pleasure and pain can easily fade into one another. We can overindulge in pleasures and become sick or burned out. Or they can come too easily to us, losing the appeal they had when they were just out of reach. We have a need to be challenged. We place higher value on that which comes to us with great difficulty. A world of toil and hardship is certainly a miserable world to live in, but so too is one in which we have nothing left to strive for.

We are not called to a life of mere pleasure, but of happiness and thriving, what Aristotle called *eudaimonia*. There is nothing wrong with pleasure itself. A eudaimonic life could hardly be one with no pleasure at all. It is rather a proper orientation to pleasure and desire, in which our desires are rightly ordered and directed to our greater good. With this orientation, happiness is not about getting everything you want but about wanting the right things.

Consumerism has distorted our desires to grasp at fleeting pleasures that pass as quickly as they come to us, only for us to seek another fix by consuming more. Moreover, it does this while capitalism robs us of the kinds of goods conducive to genuine thriving. We are thus offered an idol of false happiness in lieu of the real thing. We are presented with an aspirational lifestyle of better living through possessions and entertainment while we waste away at meaningless jobs isolated from one another. There is no sin in enjoying television and video games, wearing the latest fashion, or having prized possessions, but these are junk food pleasures, offering no lasting nourishment to the soul.

Degradation

Industrial society offers us the worst of both worlds. We have a seemingly unending supply of consumer products at our fingertips, fostering a world of quick fixes and instant gratification. Meanwhile, we spend the better chunk of our waking lives at work doing mind-numbing, menial jobs that leave us weak and drained. The eight-hour workday was designed for single-income households where one person stayed home and cooked. Instead, we tend to have two-income households where neither person has the time and energy to prepare full meals. Today, we have fast food and cheap microwavable meals. These cheap calories temporarily satiate us on diminishing budgets as rents gobble up an ever-greater share of our incomes and home ownership prices soar beyond the means of most.

Consumer products fill the void of an isolated world where our lives are not our own. They give us a semblance of agency in a world where our time is sold for a wage to pay someone else for the land we live on. We may escape this drudgery by going out and spending money on catered social experiences. We may go to a bar and pay for drinks while striking up a conversation with others or to seek potential sexual partners, or go on a date to a movie or restaurant, or we might even escape our daily lives altogether for a couple weeks by going on a vacation. We consume community and experiences just as we consume products. Everything in our lives is quantified, packaged, and sold to us as so many commodities.

We are funneled into a rat race to "get ahead" in life even as the goalposts recede further and further beyond the horizon. The megamachine trains us for the dual purposes of productivity and consumption, leaving many to ask, "Is this all there is?" We are the most depressed generation in history, and SSRIs alone aren't going to cure what ails us. As our planet convulses with the death throes of its dying ecosystems, a small handful of billionaires and corporations run every aspect of our lives, police murder black and brown people with impunity, and people are forced to take second jobs and side gigs to pay their rising rents, a sense of hopelessness has pervaded our cultural zeitgeist.

Our modern way of life is not working for us. We know instinctively that something is wrong, that we weren't meant to live like this. We wake up to one or more alarms, drink our morning cup of motivation, go to one of possibly two or three jobs, get some fast food because we're too tired to cook, go to bed and do it all over again. And that's for those of us lucky enough to have work and a place to live. Homeless encampments grow as rental prices become further out of reach. They are dealt with not as people struggling with a problem, but as a nuisance that needs to be swept away by the strong arm of the state. The crushing stress of our condition enhances our inhumanity toward our neighbor. We fail again and again to summon the solidarity with our fellow human beings that is necessary if we are ever to escape this wretched condition.

Could we not say that this system is degrading even for those who benefit from it? The Abrahamic tradition insists that extreme wealth and power not only robs the dispossessed but corrupts the soul of its possessor. Power over others is always precarious. It must be asserted and jealously guarded. It is a highly competitive position: one has power or wealth only in comparison with others, so to maintain one's position requires the restriction of competition while thwarting the attempts of others to do the same. Set against one's fellow man in a contest of hostility and greed, it is the soul that is ultimately consumed.

Dignity

Of the liberatory frameworks that seek a different way of life, Marxist materialism has exerted an extensive influence. Marx's analysis of capitalism is surely more exhaustive and extensive than any who came before him, and the standard against which any subsequent analysis must be compared. Marx sees something in the condition of the working class that is degrading. People are alienated from their labor, which they sell to produce a product that they do not own for the capitalist class that sells it back to them as commodities. Their labor power becomes surplus value at the hands of the capitalist, who reinvests it in the expansion of capital. This alienation afflicts the worker, making them estranged from the world their labor built.

Yet in its scientific pretensions, Marxism fails to offer an account of the human dignity that is violated by this arrangement. The historicism of Marxism treats human nature as malleable, formed by our material conditions. Given this, there is no obvious reason why the worker should rebel at their condition, except insofar as it may threaten their material needs. What is significant for Marx is not so much the oppression of the worker as the "contradictions" of their position within capitalism. He was far from unconcerned about the ethical dimensions of capitalism, but his "scientific" socialism could not account for it. Labor is needed to produce the commodities that the capitalist must sell, yet the worker must also consume these commodities for the capitalist to make a profit. The capitalist is caught in a double bind: if they pay the workers the full product of their labor, there will be no surplus for them to make a profit, but if the workers do not have the money to buy their products, they will also fail to make a profit. Therefore, capital must do a tightrope walk of continuous expansion, finding new labor markets to produce products, and new consumer markets to sell them. It is in this intrinsic instability that Marx saw capitalism sowing the seeds of its own destruction.

To truly understand the destructiveness of this system, especially if we hope to build something better, we must understand the injury it causes to the soul. We must have some understanding of what it is to be human in order to know what we need to truly thrive. Simply opposing capitalism does not guarantee that what we create in its place will be any better. Self-proclaimed revolutionaries will center their entire politics around hatred of elites, with little in the way of actual care and empathy for the oppressed. Indeed, much of what passes for left-wing discourse simply amounts to apologetics for dictators opposed to American interests. Such strictly adversarial politics are inevitably reactionary, and lead several people from the far left to the far right, whose lack of empathy and victimhood complex lie at the center of their politics.

A liberatory politics must begin with a recognition of

human dignity. To recognize human dignity is to recognize that which we seek to liberate. Dignity is much more than mere survival. While basic needs such as food and shelter are essential to human dignity, it is not by bread alone that we live. Many ruthless dictators have boasted low levels of malnutrition and high levels of literacy while maintaining a stranglehold on their people, choking out any of their aspirations beyond serving their own cult of personality. The dignity of human life extends far beyond bare existence to the fulfillment of our true nature. We must secure for everyone the means not only to survive but to thrive. Our current system offers us so many commodities and distractions, but not those things that feed the soul.

This consumer society has inundated us with a utilitarian logic that makes happiness a matter of satisfying personal preferences, even as a multi-billion-dollar advertising industry assaults us from every angle to warp our preferences in the service of profit. Because these desires can never be fulfilled, and by design are continually created, happiness is treated as something always just beyond the horizon. A new car, the latest smartphone, a bigger house, the latest fashions — these things do not give us true happiness, but we are made to be unhappy if we don't have them.

So long as happiness is reduced to limitless desires, society has an excuse not to provide for the happiness of all. Limitless purchasing power, if such a thing were feasible, would be a disaster for the planet. Indeed, it is the near-limitless purchasing power of the ultra-wealthy that endangers us. Yet even as we devote enormous resources to satisfying their wants, we still tell ourselves the timeless half-truth that money cannot buy happiness.

The problem is that with this commodified utilitarian vision of happiness, we do not have a clear vision of what happiness entails. What is the good life? What must a person have in their life to achieve that deeper sense of fulfillment known as *eudaimonia*? In some ways, very little. Mystics from several wisdom traditions have taken vows of poverty in pursuit of spiritual enlightenment, forsaking worldly possessions to find true happiness in the contemplation of the infinite. Such a lifestyle is more than most of us can bring ourselves to do. Yet the need to go to such extremes stems partly from a society that produces so many false substitutes for happiness while offering so little of the real thing.

We need to construct a society in which it is easier to be good. Capitalism encourages us to think in terms of pecuniary interests. It commodifies relationships, encouraging us to treat one another as means to an end. It not only encourages greed and acquisition, but measures our very worth as human beings on our capacity to accumulate. If we had a society based on mutual aid and the commons, then traits like sharing and compassion would be encouraged and rewarded.

Family

What we need in our lives is connection, meaning, and purpose. We are not isolated individuals, but persons embedded in a community. We are born physically attached to our mothers, and it takes the act of another person to sever this connection. Before we emerge as individuals, we are part of a family. From womb to tomb, our lives are connected with others.

Some societies are indistinguishable from family. Foraging bands are often extended families traveling together. Tribes met up on different occasions and people would intermarry into other bands and join them, but the basic fabric of society is based on kinship. Extended families are the traditional means of support for people. The elderly and infirm would be supported by family members who could work. Taking care of those who cannot support themselves is one of the major breakthroughs in human evolution. The prolongation of human life into old age meant that the elderly who could no longer provide physical labor could provide for the younger generations in other ways, sharing their wisdom and passing down stories from one generation to another. They were able to provide *cultural labor*, maintaining the community's ties with its past. Children would play with their peers, and older children would look after younger children. Peer learning plays a crucial role in child development that is often underrated in the context of the modern nuclear family. After infancy, relationships with other children in adjacent age groups tend to play at least as significant a formative role as our relationships with our own parents.

In other societies, multiple families live together, with different families enjoying higher or lower social status as families more than individuals. Some families gain aristocratic status while others become pariahs. The development of inequality is often imagined in terms of some gaining more property than others, but this is an oversimplification: traditional societies tend to be driven by honor codes, and the inequality in property may be a product of the honor and prestige accorded to different families. Under feudalism, for example, one could gain land by having noble status conferred upon oneself, perhaps by being knighted. While ambition and greed have certainly been with us as far back as we can tell, to see sheer acquisitiveness in this process of stratification is to read modern capitalist ethics back into pre-capitalist societies.

The city provides an alternative social arrangement, not eroding familial relations but creating an atmosphere in which one would have daily interactions with people outside one's family. In the bustle of the city, not only different families but different cultures come together and exchange not only goods but ideas and values. Cities offer spaces for creativity, including the capacity to reinvent oneself. In this way, cities are centers for the creation of persons.

The city can provide one with a kind of anonymity with which one can develop a new sense of identity, building a new life. This can be useful for people whose family life is less than ideal. Family is supposed to be a source of emotional and material support, but all too often family is precisely what people need to escape from to meet their own needs. Cycles of abuse are perpetuated from one generation to another, and it takes stepping out on one's own to truly confront this pattern and put a stop to it. Patterns of abuse are often cultural as well. Our own society has made significant progress in the past 50 years in recognizing the harm of hitting children, but there are far too many people who still use corporal punishment. Many people, especially in the LGBTQ+ community, are forcibly kicked out by their family, having no choice but to find a new life for themselves.

In the face of such circumstances, people do not abandon family altogether, but create families of choice. Any account that truly wishes to affirm the value of family must recognize that family can take these different forms. These newly formed bonds of love and nurturing are not opposed to biological families. In leaving abusive family situations and forming new families of choice, people will often go on to have their own children and create their own family lineages with a new set of values. We are social as well as sexual beings. We create progeny not only by reproduction but by adoption and nurturing. It is in the family context, regardless of the type of family, that values are imparted, and our immediate needs are met.

The history of humanity is the history of people coming together to form new social relations. Societies and cultures are not static things, but constantly evolving entities that undergo upheaval, splitting and reorganizing throughout history. Familial structure is one of many points of variance between cultures. Rituals and practices have always existed for adopting those from other cultures into one's own culture as family. It is of course within these family groupings that sexual relationships would develop, thereby bringing about offspring and family in a hereditary sense, but the system of heredity is itself defined within a given family paradigm.

We must develop an expansive love for the human family. This is what religion at its best teaches us. We are all family to one another under the infinite love of God. We must ultimately recognize the family of creation. All life on Earth is one family, and it is from this perspective that we must look after and treasure our common home. To say this is not to deny the struggle for survival, the conflicts that inevitably arise, or the violence that is sometimes unavoidable, but it does call us to recognize that we are bound by blood to our collective flourishing.

Formation

The goal of society should be the perfection of the person. For this, we must revive the concept of the polis. Prevailing political discourse today centers around how much of a role the government should have in regulating people's actions or intervening in the economy. Any pedagogical role for the public sphere is relegated to institutionalized public education. Such education is oriented not toward the formation of the person, but preparation for the job market. To the extent that the concerns extend beyond the economic, they tend to be nationalistic, instilling in children a narrative about the history of their country and their place in it that serves the ideological purposes of the state.

The modern school system is modeled after the factory. Children are funneled into classrooms, taught a standardized curriculum, given homework and tests to ensure they are learning the same material, passed through a series of grades sorted by age group, and sorted out into either universities where they earn further credentials or directly into the job market. The primary result of this model is the regimentation of life: the mechanized world of the standardized work week, wage labor, busy work, and consumerism. There are so many ways in which our society is mechanized and regimented, but the education system is where it begins. Its primary function is the discipline and regulation of the student.

There have been several critiques of modern schooling.

Standardized testing faces a significant amount of criticism these days. Class size is an issue people have taken up to offer children a more personalized classroom experience. Many critique the "school-to-prison pipeline" of schools in low-income minority neighborhoods. Even homework and grades have been challenged as unnecessary systems that do nothing to help children actually learn.

These systems *do* help children learn, but what they learn is how to be complacent within systems of power and authority. To help people develop into fully formed individuals, we must change our entire model of education and embrace a liberatory pedagogy. We must abandon the "funneling" model in which children are crowded into classrooms and given standardized lesson plans. Instead, they must be brought out into the world, given hands-on experience, connected with skill-shares, academies, and mentors. The funnel model must give way to a network model.

The funnel model focuses on credentials, which are a poor reflection of actual knowledge and mostly serve to gatekeep. When we get out into the workplace, we find that most actual learning is done on the job. To the extent that learning does occur in school, it is mainly because that is where children spend most of their time. School does not instill in children a desire for learning; that comes from an innate curiosity about the world around us. It imposes a specific style of learning, and for those children who are not predisposed to that style, they are conditioned to dislike learning as a result. If anything, standardized curriculum is a hindrance to natural curiosity.

Only when education becomes a commons to explore rather than an agenda imposed from above can it truly be liberatory. Only then can it also be transformed into the lifelong process it should be, rather than a childhood rite of passage. Learning is something we must continue throughout our lives. Instead of having to choose some specialty that we pursue the rest of our lives, we should be able to spend our whole lives learning new skills, practicing different crafts, and acquiring knowledge from a wide variety of disciplines.

Specialization has its place alongside generalists who can build connections between different specialties. In our present society, it takes a special kind of autodidact to be a generalist, because academia and the job market alike are geared toward specialization. A more open model would balance specialization with generalist knowledge by not locking us into a given career track upon which we depend. We currently have a "learning track" that becomes a "career track." Academic journals are locked behind ludicrously expensive paywalls. Specialized knowledge is hidden away from the public. We are constantly asked to "trust the experts" while being denied the resources to educate ourselves. Even when such resources are available, they are always side hobbies we pursue when we aren't working ourselves to death. A new kind of open-source academia must be created in which scholars share their work across disciplines, rather than funneling it into specialized journals. The doors of learning must be opened wide for all, abolishing gatekeeping in education so that we can all enrich our understanding of the world.

A life of learning is a far nobler organizing principle of society than a life of work. From early childhood, we are naturally curious beings. Learning is something we seek out because we see that knowledge and understanding are goods unto themselves. It is the instrumentalization of knowledge and reason that has made them tedious chores that must be forced upon students. Freed from the need to work for a living, work could instead become an educational experience in its own right, taken on freely as one learns a hobby rather than as a compulsory requirement to meet one's basic needs. Education, liberated from its institutionalized setting and technocratic logic, would become a means of personal formation. Educational theorist Paulo Friere critiqued the "banking model" of education, in which knowledge is "deposited" into the student. He proposed instead a model of problem-based learning, which respects the student as a source of knowledge, not merely an empty vessel. Such a process makes learning a dynamic process which draws out the student's tacit knowledge and not only teaches them information but helps them learn how to learn.

Freed from its nationalist and economistic context, education could be more of a pursuit unto itself. The guilds were educational for their members, who enjoyed a surprising rate of literacy. The first universities were themselves a kind of guild dedicated to the intellectual disciplines, the goal of which was not job prospects outside the university, but the full cultural cultivation of the person. Education must overcome the instrumental logic of our time and work toward the goal of self-actualization.

Democracy itself is a pedagogical process. Deliberative processes tap into the collective knowledge of the crowd as they problem-solve to come to equitable solutions. In the process, not only do people learn from one another, but they also learn the art of citizenship. This is a citizenship, not in the patriotic or nationalist sense, but in the civic sense of the polis. In learning how to govern ourselves, we become more fully realized individuals.

Mimesis

The trend in modern philosophy is to treat ethics as a matter of personal choice. The individual choices we make are to be evaluated by some objective metric. There is a utilitarian approach that measures these choices by the sum total of pain or pleasure contributed by one's actions. The Kantian approach insists upon duties and rule-following based on a categorical imperative of consistency and regarding people as ends in themselves. There have been several iterations of these, but the goal they have in common is to create some sort of objective moral calculus that can tell us definitively what is right or wrong in any given situation.

This search for a "science of ethics" offers little in the way of actually becoming better people. A strong argument may convince us to change our position on a given moral issue, but there is so much more involved in the formation of conscience. Real-life situations will inevitably be more complex than any formula or thought experiment can prepare us for. When we make a moral choice, we do so in the context of our own personal history, our relationships with the people involved, and any number of social and cultural factors that cannot be reduced to a formula.

We are likely to find moral guidance not in rational arguments, but in art, literature, and myth. In the context of narrative or allegory we see actual characters with their own background, upbringing, biases, strengths, and weaknesses, facing real struggles and dilemmas. Characters in stories give us examples to look up to, scenarios to relate to, and cautionary tales of what not to do. We do this in real life, too. We have role models that we look up to, peers that we relate to, and authority figures that guide us.

We are mimetic creatures. We learn not only how to act, but also how to think, how to feel, and what to want. Consumerism is based on advertising making us want a product by convincing us that others want it. This is how we keep up with the Joneses. Yet this also works for higher, intangible goods. Codes of honor work by mimesis. We see something in the wise and upstanding that we wish to emulate.

Society cannot properly regulate itself solely through incentivization. It is not enough to reward the good and punish the bad. We must set examples for one another. We must tell stories of great people who have gone before us. We must have heroes, role models, myths and legends. We must also strive to be role models for others. The way we live our lives signals to others how we permit them to live theirs. This is not a matter of some Kantian categorical imperative, but a recognition that our actions and habits are not isolated from the social world around us. Our actions are statements of values. What we do expresses what we value, and signals to others that they should share those values.

The mimetic nature of desire constitutes a central problem for René Girard, considered the founder of mimetic theory. Mimetic desire applied to excludable goods means that some will attain those goods at the expense of others, creating mimetic rivalry. This mimetic rivalry looms as a constant threat to undo society by plunging it into civil war. This, according to Girard, creates the need for scapegoating. This scapegoating can take the form of a sacrificial victim. The scapegoat mechanism has been developed differently by different societies throughout history. In some cases it manifests as human sacrifice, yet it can also form the basis of monarchies, in which the sovereign is ritually separated from the rest of society. It can also take religious forms. Girard saw in the crucifixion of Christ not only the ultimate sacrificial victim, but one who in His perfect innocence reveals the innocence of the sacrificial victim as such, undoing the logic of scapegoat mechanism.

This upsets the equilibrium on which society is based. This undoing of sacrificial logic does not imply less violence. The sacrificial logic remains strong in the privileged attitudes of those who blame the victims of systemic violence such as refugees and the homeless, yet its subversion means there is also a tendency to identify with the victims. Those who take up this cause lead the charge in this moral revolution, yet they have also created a new vocabulary in which oppression can mask itself. It is now more common for the oppressor to present themselves *as* victims. Ideas like the "gay agenda" or "reverse racism" present the liberatory movements of oppressed groups as if they were themselves impositions by a conspiracy of powerful elites. Such conspiratorial forms of victim-stancing see an "agenda" forced on them to accept others who are not like them. Conveniently, such groups tend to claim that they alone are the most oppressed, and refuse to recognize the oppression of other groups, let alone express solidarity with them. It is therefore not enough to claim victimhood, but to be in solidarity with the marginalized and oppressed as such.

To avoid the sacrificial crisis, it is important that mimetic desire be directed toward virtuous goods such as community, family, friendship, learning, political engagement, and spirituality. This is not to say that private, excludable goods are not important, but if taken as ends unto themselves they become dangerous idols. Many goods essential to a healthy human life are excludable. It is an essential task for society to ensure that such goods are equitably distributed so that everyone has enough. When our basic needs are met and secured without the constant threat of being taken from us, only then can we reorient our lives to nobler pursuits.

Telos

Modern philosophy has gone out of its way to dispense with the notion of telos. Telos is the idea that reality is more than just a set of bare facts, but has a kind of directionality to it, an "oughtness" that is immanent within the "isness" of things. This can be readily understood in the tools that we make. We have these tools called knives, whose telos is cutting. We can tell a good knife from a bad one by how well it cuts. This telos is one that modern philosophy has no quarrel with, since it is a telos that we have assigned to knives—an extrinsic telos. Part of the disrepute of telos today is the notion that all telos is like this. If one posits a telos in nature, one is assumed to be making some sort of Intelligent Design argument in which an external creator is designing nature the way humans design a knife.

When Aristotle spoke of telos, he was not talking about

some Paleyan watchmaker God. He was speaking about how every organism has its own purpose. A plant seeks sunlight and nutrients. Animals seek food and mating opportunities. Life is intrinsically teleological, which is to say, purposive. The Scholastics certainly thought that God was a necessary part of telos, but not in the kind of direct way that Intelligent Design argues. From this perspective, God could effectively be bracketed from the discussion of the telos of living things, appearing only at a further point of inference.

The telos of all life is to flourish. There is a kind of telos in life's striving to prolong itself, both with the individual organism and its reproduction. Yet a species that becomes overpopulated to the extent that it threatens the ecological balance upon which it depends is not flourishing but suffocating itself. The flourishing of the individual organism, the flourishing of its species, and the flourishing of the web of life in which it finds itself are all dynamically interrelated. A predator may spell doom to an individual organism while being an asset to its species by keeping its population in check. The ecosystem in turn may survive the extinction of a species, as has happened repeatedly throughout Earth's history. Ecosystems themselves evolve over time and compete with one another. A forest may become grassland or vice-versa, with each supporting a different community of wildlife. No single organism, species, or ecosystem is of absolute importance, but each has its own dignity, its own telos, its own conditions for flourishing.

As humans, there is a certain *quiddity*, or essence, which we share in common with all other humans. A common telos to humanity comes from this common nature. At the same time, we also each have a *haecceity*, or "thisness," which constitutes our unique nature as individuals. From this, we have a unique telos to fulfill by being fully ourselves. Such telos cannot contradict our broader telos as humans. It is an articulation of that telos, just as we are each articulations of the species *Homo Sapiens Sapiens*. We fulfill our telos as humans by fulfilling our unique telos as individuals. The quiddity-haecceity distinction applies not only to humans, but to all of creation. All creatures are both members of some genus and unique individuals themselves. Every blade of grass is united with every other blade while also embodying its own unique singularity.

What does human flourishing look like? In answering this, we must avoid certain pitfalls. We must first avoid taking the values of industrial capitalism for granted. We must also avoid falling into the naturalistic fallacy of evolutionary psychology and sociobiology which project this capitalist ethos onto nature and into human nature. The conditions in which our Paleolithic ancestors lived may tell us something about the conditions in which our instincts evolved, but thriving is not simply a matter of following our instincts. There is no transhistorical or transcultural model of what a flourishing society looks like, but neither is such a thing arbitrarily constructed. One of the defining features of humanity is the ability to imagine things as they might be, rather than as they are. Our unique ability to recreate our world according to our imagination is a key feature of our telos. The plurality of cultures, of social systems, of technology and institutions is an expression of our intrinsically creative nature.

Innovations are not in themselves deviations from our nature. Rather, we must inquire into *how* institutions and innovations can contribute to human flourishing and in what ways they can stand in the way of it. Technology can be liberatory or authoritarian depending on whether it funnels people into the machine or enhances the creative powers of the person. Distributed networks exhibit greater resilience than centralized hierarchies. Repetitive tasks dull the mind, while liberating work engages our talent, creativity, and senses. Neither drudgery nor laziness, but meaningful, purposeful work constitutes the condition under which we thrive. That work may be intellectual, artistic, or it may involve varying degrees of physical exertion, but it is in the creative endeavor itself that we flourish. We flourish when work and play are continuous with one another. Work is made joyful when drudgery is lightened and our creative capacities are fully engaged.

Community

We flourish not alone but in community. In family, friendship, and romance, we find an invaluable form of support. These relationships can help us in material ways, providing sources of mutual aid. Yet it is the intangible forms of support they bring — that irreducible human element that feeds our need for connection, accompaniment, and mutual understanding — that they are most vital.

Relationships challenge us to be more responsive and responsible to one another. It is easy to care about people in the abstract. Yet in dealing with real people in all their complexity we are forced to confront our own flaws and shortcomings. Learning to forgive flaws in others helps us to forgive our own shortcomings, and vice-versa. We are all struggling to deal with imperfect upbringings, various degrees of trauma, neuroses, insecurities, and doubts. We are various degrees of wounded creatures, yet if we can learn to confront the prejudices and presumptions that block our ability to understand one another, we can begin the work of collective healing.

It is in community that we encounter one another as persons rather than abstractions. At the communal level, a fully democratic ethos means people are able to plan and make decisions on a deliberative basis. Deliberation becomes a pedagogical affair, in which answers are sought by pooling the collective wisdom of the group. People learn in the process of coming to a decision. This is what real democracy means, and any democratic institution should take this as its starting point. The direct communal encounter forms the foundation for larger communities that can send delegates to bring their concerns to the larger community. A community of communities begins to emerge, and a spirit of civic participation becomes the basis of politics.

In community we develop culture. Culture is the source of our self-understanding, our systems of meaning-making, our sense of identity and connection. Even those who don't identify strongly with their cultural heritage may be oblivious to the way it affects things like attachment styles, emotional expression, individuation, and familial relations. Culture is expressed in art, music, religion, ritual, food, and clothing. It also includes systems of ethics and codes of honor. We can never see past culture. It is our collective subjectivity, the lens through which we see the world. Because of this, we can never arrive at the true "natural law" — a rational moral order to the cosmos —

sought by the Scholastics. This does not mean that such natural law does not exist, but it does mean that it will always be filtered through a cultural lens. Different sets of virtues, systems of honor, and senses of identity will always have competing truth claims about this order.

This incommensurability does not preclude the possibility of a discourse that can communicate across these cultural understandings. A paradigm can pose problems that a competing paradigm must then evolve to address. There is then a kind of coevolution between different cultural systems of meaning, in which each can help improve the other through mutual encounter. Virtue grows not as a single standardized methodology, but as an ecosystem of value structures.

Culture is not static; it is continually reproduced through social interactions and mimesis. It is also a contentious ground which different parties are always seeking to influence. Cultural theorists Max Horkheimer and Theodor Adorno spoke of the "culture industry" that seeks to shape our tastes, values, and norms. All forms of mass media create narratives that tell us what we should want and limit our imaginations of what is possible or desirable. Yet as powerful as these forces are, their hegemony is never complete. In fact, this culture industry often finds itself on the defensive, seeking to co-opt and nullify popular expressions of resistance to the system they represent.

The reactionary media figure Andrew Breitbart quipped that politics lies downstream from culture. This was fitting for someone so committed to the Culture War. It would be more accurate, however, to say that culture and politics are dialectically intertwined. Political movements seek to influence the culture by promoting values and creating cultural narratives. The term "propaganda" is typically used pejoratively today, but it was once understood as simply propagating one's message. The dominant class uses propaganda to maintain its hegemony, but countervailing forces can also use propaganda to create counter-hegemony.

Such propaganda, however, extends far beyond slogans, fliers, and agitprop. Direct action itself conveys messages. When Food Not Bombs feeds the homeless, they are not merely doing charity work, but asserting a right to food and the dignity of the poor. As media theorist Marshall McLuhan put it, the medium is the message. Reclaiming public space and creating counter-institutions signals what sort of values we wish to promote and what sort of society we wish to create.

We must prefigure the world we wish to make. We create a new social order by building space for it here and now. We must build new institutions to counter ones that aren't working for the people. We must find ways to support people outside the normative confines of the system, helping people to whatever extent possible to overcome the traps of exploitation and exclusion set by the existing social hierarchy. We must build community power here and now to overcome the social atomization inflicted upon us by the capitalist megamachine.

We must develop democratic assemblies for managing the commons. The pedagogical role of these assemblies will train us in the art of governing our own affairs. We must learn from one another and combine our experience and wisdom to come to creative solutions together. Democracy is not about competing answers to pre-selected questions. It is about learning from one another to answer questions that arise in the process of action. It means living and thinking with one another in pursuit of the common good. It is a praxis that we learn together.

Ecology

Community extends to the natural world. Our excessive influence on the world around us means we have a special responsibility for the community of life on earth. Our own flourishing is tied to the flourishing of the biosphere. We first have a responsibility to the part of nature we have taken under our wing through domestication. Whatever the ethics of animal agriculture, the system of factory farming we have now is clearly both unsustainable and deeply inhumane.

A teleological perspective takes us beyond the question of what creatures are conscious or feel pain and focuses instead on their flourishing. We know the horrors of the slaughterhouse and the cramped conditions of feedlots. Regenerative agriculture with free-range grazing places these animals in a setting in which they can not only flourish, but contribute to the flourishing of other life, including a variety of crops and the mycorrhizal networks that connect them. Raising livestock means caring for an ecosystem that sustains them, and they in turn contribute to the ecosystem by contributing to the nutrient cycle.

Plants are considered to have no subjectivity, and thus are often valued only instrumentally, having no intrinsic value. Yet the teleological perspective does not require consciousness to see something as having dignity and deserving the conditions in which it can thrive. The environmental conditions that plants and animals alike need to flourish can be integrated into a system of agriculture that helps us flourish as well by building a more resilient food system.

The responsibility for the natural world extends to the wild as well. We must pursue the thriving of the Earth's ecosystems. This requires promoting biodiversity and resilience in the ecosystem. It means not only phasing out activities that harm the environment but taking a leading role in replenishing it. We must view the Earth's ecosystems not only in terms of their instrumental value for us, but their own intrinsic value. We can replenish habitats by ecological succession, preparing the soil and planting pioneer species, letting nature take over from there. The potential for habitat restoration is immense, but this restoration would not necessarily look like what came before. Nature is constantly innovating with novel combinations of species as it seeks complexity. Fixing broken ecosystems, therefore, involves creating novel ecosystems whose results one cannot predict ahead of time but whose health one can nonetheless measure through metrics of biodiversity and ecological balance.

Murray Bookchin described what we call "nature" as "first nature," while what we call "society" is "second nature." Second nature supervenes upon first nature, but we have built our social institutions in such a way that it has become self-destructive. Second nature is destroying first nature, and in the process destroying itself. The solution is not to collapse second nature into first nature as Deep Ecology would have us do, but to align with it. Second nature must flow organically from first nature, so that the ways of the latter are seamlessly interwoven with the former. This alignment creates a "third nature": the ecological society.

There is one universal telos flowing from a single Logos from which all things come and toward which all things are called. Yet this telos is articulated infinitely within all of creation. From the single Logos bursts forth an infinite fractal of distinct logoi. There is a single path that is also a constellation of all distinct paths. Their intersections, and their greater place in the fullness of time, are not for us to know in this mortal existence. Yet by holding to faith we do not abandon reason but instead place our trust in a greater reason that our minds cannot grasp.

Our telos as individuals must be in harmony with our telos as humans. So too must the human telos flow from the telos of the biosphere. Each level of individuation is an articulation of the Logos. Each haecceity is the quiddity of another haecceity. The cosmos is continually articulating new forms and singularities. The forces of domination, exploitation, and authoritarianism have corrupted the second nature of human society and set us dangerously off course from the Logos. This distortion of second nature has obscured our ability to realize our own individual telos. A society so deeply out of balance makes it nigh impossible for any of us to realize our full potential.

We must understand nature as family. The vision of Saint Francis in his famous Canticle should inspire us today to honor our relationships with one another and with all of creation. Those relationships have been horribly strained by the trauma of empire, conquest, capitalism, colonialism, and all manner of oppression, but they can be healed if we try. Life on this planet is important for its own sake and ours. We exist in a vast web of interdependence. The dignity of the person is tied to the dignity of the community and the family, which is tied to the dignity of humanity, which is tied to the dignity of life and of the natural world, and ultimately existence itself.

Spirit

Modernity has shaped our thinking toward what philosopher Charles Taylor calls the "immanent frame." This means that our desires, discourse, and modes of thought are all focused on matters of immediate material concern. Transcendent concerns of ascension or salvation or some higher purpose in life are certainly present, but are relegated to the private domain of religion. Such concerns are not to be raised in polite company.

In part this is simply a phenomenon of living in a pluralistic society, where no one creed can claim normativity over public discourse. Bringing up Christ, God, or heaven might offend the sensibilities of a Jew, Buddhist, or agnostic, and exclude them from the conversation. Moreover, we live in an age of scientific materialism, in which claims of transcendence are treated as at best unprovable and therefore outside the realm of discourse, and at worst as subject to ridicule and derision.

To the extent that spiritual matters are discussed, they must be framed in the language of aesthetics or self-help. Spirituality, in our modern era, is a *feeling*, not something with a claim on our beliefs or way of life. This is not to say that there is no emotional connection to spirituality. Indeed, the feeling of *wonder* is of central importance. It opens us up to the numinous dimension of reality — that which we grasp precisely as ineffable. Yet modern self-help spirituality often condenses this numinosity to a kind of self-congratulatory navel-gazing. Rather than humble us to some greater mystery, it ends up flattering the ego with delusions of grandeur.

There is a deeper reason for this neutering of spirituality. The public aspect of religion has been marginalized so that its devotions can only be directed to the nation-state and the idols of the market. The world has not become disenchanted, but *misenchanted*. It is capital that has come to claim enchantment for itself. The world of consumer goods is an enchanted wonderland seeking to catch our eye and promising some morsel of happiness and contentment. The grinding drudgery of wage labor becomes a kind of mortification of the self that will yield rewards through career advancement, money, and status. Yet where certain religious traditions advocate mortification of the flesh to increase spiritual awareness, we have instead a mortification of the soul to mold our spiritual desires into material ones. Wealth becomes a kind of charm attracting good luck to the wearer. Indeed, we see this in the double-meaning of the word "fortune."

Money is magic. Marx observed this when he noted that an ugly man with money could purchase for himself the most beautiful women, thereby negating his ugliness. Money gives us the power to attract possessions to us, much like the fabled Law of Attraction that has come to define modern New Age spirituality in its most perversely capitalist form. Money grants us the ability to summon whatever our heart desires. We can bind people to us and make them do our bidding.

Yet, like any black magic, money can take hold and enslave us. It is an idol that opens us up to demonic influence. When

Christ said one cannot serve both God and Mammon, he understood the demonic cult of Mammon worship for what it is. Past eras were no strangers to greed, but in capitalism greed has been mechanized and built into the system itself. It is largely inconsequential who the wealthy are. Any one of them is replaceable. What matters is their role in keeping the engine of capital moving. Should they abdicate this role, they will readily be replaced with someone else. The continuous flow of capital and the engine of growth that it feeds are the idols to be satiated. Upon their altars, countless lives and souls are sacrificed.

The wealthy have only fooled themselves into thinking they run the world. In fact, it is their wealth that runs them. They have been enchanted by the demon Mammon to build the machinery of global capital, by which this demon devours the resources of this planet and the souls of its inhabitants. This demonic body envelops the globe and in turn implicates us all. We are subject to it, but we are also culpable in it. We cannot escape its reach, and all that we wish to do must be done through the pathways it allows. This idol that we have raised will devour life on this planet if we let it.

Vladimir Lenin claimed that imperialism is the highest stage of capitalism. The reverse would be more accurate. The earliest empires laid the foundations for the exploitation of labor, the extraction of resources, and the mechanization of life that would come to characterize our modern era. Every incursion of state centralization, authoritarian technics, military expansion, and commodification has brought us closer to this system of self-destruction. Under Lenin's leadership, the worker councils known as soviets that had played such a vital part in the revolution were taken over by the centralized control of the party to advance the Soviet Union toward rapid industrialization and empire building.

This promethean impulse toward expansion, hegemony, and control is the idol of modernity, of which capitalism is one aspect. It is an egoic impulse to grasp, to manage, to seize for ourselves. Like any idol, it represents a distorted truth. We cannot simply do nothing and let all things manage themselves. We must be agents within the world, acting to better ourselves and our environment. Yet there is a point at which our need for control overtakes the demands of cooperation and humility, and we seek to impose ourselves upon others, on the environment, on our own nature. This is the forbidden fruit of the Garden: to impose our will upon creation and take from it in defiance for our own purposes.

The major world religions arose as a protest against this dehumanizing hegemony. The ancient Hebrews, a wandering pastoral tribe, followed a God with whom they personally had a covenant to keep them from falling into the corrupt ways of the empires and civilizations in their midst. Buddhism arose from a great prince who rejected the luxuries of his royal birth to seek the path of true liberation through the abandonment of attachment. Christianity arose in an oppressed corner of the Roman empire, and declared the true king was not Caesar, but a humble man from Galilee who also happened to be God. These religions became the belief systems of empires and kingdoms themselves, losing something of their liberating message, yet not completely. Even from the mouth of the master, the liberating message of the gospel was heard by the slave, who developed their own liberatory theologies.

Our collective liberation must be a spiritual as well as

material one. We must rediscover a spirituality that is liberating, not merely consoling. People today increasingly seek that spirituality outside the confines of organized religion, only to find another orthodoxy that is saturated with the values of the system. Mindfulness workshops are held in corporate offices. The Law of Attraction teaches people to extend their consumer mindset to the cosmic level. Alternative medicine becomes yet another money-making scheme, and fortune telling replaces any sense of real purpose to our existence.

The modern world has heralded the death of ritual and replaced it with mechanism. Both involve repetition, but where the repetition of ritual creates narrative and meaning, the mechanical repetition of the megamachine seeks only its own reproduction. The element of play is taken out of life, replaced with bare practicality. We lose the self-discipline of ritual only to be disciplined by capitalist regimentation of time and commodification of space.

The death of God has left us aimless and grasping at whatever idols avail themselves to us. We are no longer contained within the ordered medieval cosmos, ascending the Great Chain of Being from matter to soul to spirit up to the angelic realms and culminating in the divine itself. Yet this need not lead us to gross materialism or escapism. We must understand that the insular cosmos has burst open into a vast Web of Being. The divine interpenetrates all of existence and moves in and through us.

It is through action that we meet this incarnational presence. Philosopher Maurice Blondel saw human action as pointing us toward something beyond ourselves. There is something that we will in our action that is beyond that act, whose aim lies beyond what is known. Every action is co-action, something beyond us that acts in us and toward which our actions aim. Our actions are imbued with value that transcends them. We experience this, for example, with our conscience. Morality transcends our actions while leading to another level of transcendence which Blondel calls the superstitious, since it is unable to account for itself by a purely secular order of phenomena.

This is the realm of mythology. Even the secular order has a mythology, especially in its myth of having no mythology. Myth gives meaning to action that we are ultimately unable to account for. The insufficiency of our will to produce what it wills, as well is its ability to produce unforeseen consequences that it has not willed, leads us toward a transcendent source of will. This is the necessary one, the ground of Being we call divine. It is the divine life that lives in us.

We must discover a spirituality that is liberating, both individually and collectively. Organized religion has become calcified by clinging to a past that never was while New Age spirituality reduces spirituality to a commodity to be consumed. What is needed is a living faith that inspires us to seek the common good. We must find the Spirit in one another through the struggle for our common liberation. We must find the Logos within ourselves through spiritual practice and with one another by building community. We are called to be co-creators of the Kingdom.

Religion

Organized religion is a favorite target of modernity, and

often for understandable reasons. History shows no lack of atrocities committed by and in the name of religious authorities. They have long had a clever way of distorting messages of liberation into defenses of power. It would be all too convenient if we could easily disentangle religion from its ties to state power and the prejudices that have been propagated in its name. Those too are interwoven within the fabric of faith traditions. Patriarchy, heterosexism, casteism, colonialism: they all have deep roots in religious traditions. Yet there are numerous examples of movements within these traditions that have sought to interrogate these aspects of their faith and bring out the light within.

One must be careful about using the word "religion," as in the West we tend to mean first and foremost Christianity, in whose image we project other religions such as Judaism, Hinduism, or Islam. Yet each of these traditions understands themselves in ways that escape the bounds of Western theology. It is axiomatic of religion that it defines the very terms of its own self-understanding. It constructs a totality in which we understand our own existence. We find in religion our reason for being, the Logos of our existence. In its rituals and traditions, it structures our reality and gives it meaning.

Religion scholar William Cavanaugh speaks of the "myth of religious violence." By this, he does not mean that religion is innocent of violence, but rather that the demarcation of religion as a separate sphere with a particular tendency toward malicious and irrational violence that must be contained is a self-justifying myth of the modern nation-state. The violence of the nation-state is not to be questioned. The glorious martyrdom of dying for one's nation is held to be the highest honor. Religion is defined by those totalizing claims that compete with the totalizing claims of the state. Therefore, any dogma it teaches that makes a claim on the believer must be contained within the private sphere or done away with entirely.

Marxist analysis sees religion as arising from alienation. Trapped in the material conditions of class exploitation, people turn to religion as a source of transcendence. It projects their hopes for a better world outside of the material world and onto some higher realm, pacifying the people to accept their servility. It is because of this that Marx called it "the opium of the people" and the "heart of a heartless world." Marx was, in this criticism, reacting to the static atheism of the Young Hegelians. Their atheism, he thought, was still idealistic insofar as it saw religion as simply a kind of cognitive error that could be fixed through proper education. For Marx, however, the solution was to resolve the material contradictions that gave rise to religion. In a communist society, religion would wither away just as the state would.

Yet one can just as easily say that religion lights the fire of the radical imagination. The messianic hope of another world helps inspire the transformation of this world. Social movements from the Diggers and Levelers to the abolitionists to the civil rights movement to liberation theology have long been inspired by the radical message of the Gospel. Rather than place one's hope for liberation outside the world, the messianic promise of religion can help prepare the way for liberation by introducing to one's consciousness a liberation that is not yet attainable. It helps shape the mind by praxis and observance toward an understanding of the world not simply as it is but as it ought to be. The seed of hope is planted to germinate at the proper time.

Religion involves ritual as a means of attunement. The word "dogma," typically taken to be synonymous with unthinking belief, actually refers to mysteries that must be contemplated to reveal their truths to the believer. It is a revealed truth that grounds one's practice. It is within this structuring practice that one can discover new and deeper truths of the faith. It also helps structure one's experience of the social world. Such praxis may indeed cultivate a reactionary ethos, instilling in one a fear of outsiders and of social change, as is often found in religion today. Yet it can also cultivate a heart of compassion and zeal for justice. Such liberatory faith requires liberatory praxis, and it is this that must be developed.

Ancient religion was inexorably tied to the state. The power of the state itself was seen as divine in origin, with the arbitrary brutality of the sovereign seen as evidence of this. The high priests were servants of power, sanctifying their subjugation of the people. The Axial shift brought a rebellion against this form of religion, seeking a transcendent truth that was greater than any earthly power. Yet the temptation to serve power rather than faith remains with us and taints the hearts of many modern-day clerics and believers. The temptations of Caesarism run deep, and it is all too easy to seek the Kingdom of this world rather than the next. It is also easy to fall prey to the temptation of clericalism, treating a religious calling as a mark of superiority to be wielded over others. The call to servant leadership is distorted into despotism and corruption.

Sacred traditions should be interrogated, but they still have liberatory potential. They must change to create greater accountability to the people. It is those not at the center but the periphery of these faiths that have the most insight to offer. These ancient traditions have a way of calcifying the prejudices of the times in which they arose, which overshadows the liberatory elements that they introduced in the first place. Their essence must be grasped by rediscovering their liberatory roots and through a process of *ressourcement* bring about a renewal. They will have to change structurally to fully realize their liberatory potential. The teaching authority of the clergy must be brought into conversation and reciprocity with the tacit wisdom of the laity. The vertical authority of the lineage they hold must be reconciled with the horizontal authority of the Spirit's movement within history through the body of the faithful. Their teaching authority must anchor the faith, but not confine it. It must always be in conversation with the faithful, not simply dictating to them. It is through dialogue that the Logos can truly emerge.

Religion should be understood as a battlefield upon which liberatory movements must struggle with reactionary power structures. Considerable ground has been ceded to the reactionaries, placing the liberatory voices at the margins. This has long been the case. Prophets have been rejected and killed by authorities and religious hypocrites. Many a saint has been accused of heresy and blasphemy in their day. If religion does ultimately fall to reactionaries, there will be nothing of it worth salvaging. Yet the liberatory aspects of religion have always crept up from under the heel of authoritarian reactionaries to proclaim the truth of their traditions, for their truth comes not from the personalities of great figures but from their connection to the Logos.

Even in the darkest moments, there have always been

those willing to carry the light. It is through them that the sacred mysteries will survive and outlive the destructive authoritarian forces that dominate so many religious spaces. Perhaps religion will exhaust all meaning and die a well-deserved death as its cultured despisers have long predicted, or become totally subsumed under the megamachine, sanctifying its slaughter until ecological collapse kills us all. I believe, however, that the forces of reaction and oppression will not prevail, and the spark that has guided the saints will carry us toward a new age whose contours we can't yet imagine but whose image we hold in the depths of our hearts.

The Logos is not merely a passive principle, but the Light of the World that lives within us all. It is life itself, its pulse radiating throughout the cosmos in an infinitude of forms. It is the incarnation of truth revealed to us by reason, by revelation, by intuition and mystical seeking. The Logos unfolds in our lives not merely through an impersonal rational order but by the meaning we discover in living according to its call. The call of Spirit is not easy to discern, but if we are watchful and notice a directionality in our life, our intuitive sense of purpose, we begin to see a grander scheme beyond ourselves. It recedes from view, unable to reveal to us the secrets we would like to know, but it lives within us, beckoning us onward. We can then understand that same movement in history itself, guiding the paths of its subjects beyond their own intentions toward some new revelation.

All that is true in tradition emanates from the Logos. In the footsteps of these paths, we may approach the Logos and better integrate it into our own lives and into the world around us. These paths offer us a vision of the Logos as the perfect world, the utopia toward which our heart is called, the World to Come. The iterations of the Logos within each tradition offer different pathways of realization. These iterations involve conflicting truth claims and values, but these disagreements presuppose a common Logos. There are also real historical wounds between faith traditions, just as there are between cultures, and these wounds are not so easily healed, but by recognizing our common source in the universal Logos and trusting in its guidance, a path can be forged. Traditions may contradict one another on significant points of contention while still drawing from the deeper well of truth that lies beyond words. The Logos expresses itself in infinite forms, and our maps attempting to decode it always fall short. In dialogue with one another, we can gain a richer understanding of our own tradition through our understanding of the other.

That does not, however, mean that all spirituality necessarily springs from this well of truth. In cults, we find manipulation and abuse, where people are isolated and made afraid to question the leader's authority. These are the demonic manifestations of a distorted Logos. We must seek a pluralism that allows for diverse expressions of the Logos while also remaining vigilant against the darker spiritual forces of bigotry and oppression. The realm of the spirit includes demons as well as angels. Demons haunt every corner of our society today, from the rise in fascism to the nihilistic forces of capital accumulation, but they especially love the naïve spiritual seeker who can fall prey to their traps. It is a strength of long-standing spiritual traditions that they have developed time-tested practices for the discernment of spirits.

In our growing together in dialogue and discernment, we come to embody wisdom. Sophia, the personification of wisdom, is the soul of this world, the Logos in its particularity. If the Logos is eternal, Sophia is always changing. Logos is a primordial unity, but Sophia is the unfolding unity of all Being. Sophia is the integral cosmic actuality of divine humanity. We find in Sophia our highest expression. It is the "lure" that Alfred North Whitehead spoke of, Teilhard de Chardin's Omega Point. This unfolding world soul seeks ever after the Logos in its myriad expressions. A sense of growing together, or "concrescence" to use Whitehead's term, can allow the world's traditions to learn from one another and grow in dialogue, mutual respect, and self-reflection.

Religious traditions play a vital role in forming the imagination. They are the means through which we express truths that cannot otherwise be expressed. They point us toward the World to Come, in which this deep spiritual longing for a world we know in our hearts must be possible finds its expression. In seeking this World to Come, we learn to resist the power structures of this world mentally before we can resist them physically. This eschatological vision prefigures the hope for our own ideal world. We cannot immanentize the eschaton purely by our volition, but we are called to struggle toward that vision together as a multitude.

Liberation

The individual and the collective mutually construct one another. By building a pedagogical society, we train people to become co-creators of community. We gain a true sense of citizenship, in which we are active participants in the management of communal affairs. In this process, we become active participants in building community. The community must be pedagogical to form the person who in turn helps build community.

Hegemonic structures interrupt this process, tipping the scales so that those of a certain race, gender, or class extend their power over others. These structures recruit their beneficiaries to maintain them while pressuring the victims to submit to them. The privileged class takes this submission as assent, even agreement, and assumes there is no problem. This is simply the way things are, and anyone who disagrees is an unserious idealist with no grounding in the real world. The occasional uprisings, from slave and peasant revolts to riots or labor strikes, are feared not for the damage they cause in themselves but because they break the illusion of the social contract that the ruling class has imposed upon us all. This contract does not, it turns out, have everyone's signature, and the people are ready to tear it up.

Breaking these hegemonies means creating space for the voices of the oppressed, and people must participate in their own liberation. We can only acknowledge and amplify the voices of those who are already speaking out, not speak for them. We must organize our communities and build solidarity with other communities. An intercommunal ethos must be cultivated, building connections that cross borders and transcend social status. We must seek solidarity with all those fighting for liberation. In doing so, we will have partners in our own liberatory struggles.

These solidarity networks can form the basis of new global structures. Horizontal structures are not something that forms only when vertical structures are absent. Dominator hierarchies are parasitic upon horizontal bonds. They persist by intervening in their formation, creating arbitrary divisions, reshaping the social and physical environment to create barriers, enclosing the commons. To overcome this, we must recognize the communal relations that already exist and build upon them through radical social organization.

Organizing our communities means bringing their voices to the table by learning their concerns and advocating for them. In bringing together the different voices of the community, the community organizer helps facilitate popular democracy. Such organizing creates a forum in which people can collaborate in planning the affairs of their communities. Advocacy groups can then bring these agenda items into the political arena, and if they are organized enough, can galvanize the resources of the community to bring pressure on elected officials. By spreading these organizational models widely, such organized people's councils can break the hegemony of capital and its industries over city councils. With enough momentum, such a movement could run campaigns to subject municipal governments to popular control. Government institutions are a commons that can be liberated into a global commonwealth.

This is not an all-or-nothing affair. This is not something we wait to accomplish until "after the revolution." The revolution is the very process by which we interrupt hegemonies through solidarity. We can work on democratizing our cities into communes while also creating municipal autonomy from the state. We can support national struggles for liberation even as we seek to build a world beyond the nation-state.

Words like "radical" and "revolution" conjure up images of sudden, violent change. Yet revolution is a process of incremental change punctuated by a series of upheavals. What distinguishes it from reformism is which program is being incrementally built. The reformist seeks to incrementally improve the existing system, hoping to tweak it here and there to make it more equitable. The revolutionary seeks those incremental changes that will challenge existing power structures and create space for a new order. The changes that unfold are of a different logic than that of the system, even if they occur within the system. They seek to recode the social matrix according to the Logos.

By overcoming the systemic divisions placed upon us, by organizing to build collective power, we can overcome the hegemonic structures built on power and wealth. Capital is an organizing force brought to bear upon the people, so people must work hard to counter-organize against it. A global commonwealth must be built to overcome the Empire. We must learn to lift one another's voices. Only when we are invested in the liberation of our neighbor will our own liberation be secured.

13

Eschaton

In the World to Come, we see the fulfillment of our true nature. The telos of all things finds its completion in this world vision. Christ spoke of the "Kingdom of God," something both ever-present and just beyond the horizon. It is not only in things hoped for, but in the present as potential. This is because we are already more than the sum of matters of fact. Written within our nature is the kind of life we were born to live. The eschaton is the vision of that life, of the Good toward which we are all called.

The Axial traditions proclaim a vision of the World to Come. Tibetan Buddhism has Shambhala. Hinduism has the Satya Yuga. Christianity has the Kingdom of Heaven. The role that these promised utopias play in their respective religions varies, as does the understanding of time that underlies them, but the importance of such utopian visions remains. A great deal of interreligious dialogue is grounded in either a perennial tendency to downplay the differences or a postmodern tendency to relativize them. Such analyses tend to focus on the present, but a discourse about the future and each faith's vision of ultimate ends is necessary.

Faith plays a crucial role in forming the imagination, allowing us to resist social structures mentally before we can resist them materially. We must recover the prophetic imagination to orient ourselves to the World to Come. We live in an age when the end times are palpable: one needn't read the Revelation of St. John to sense that we are in a time of reckoning. Our current way of life is leading us on a path of certain destruction. No serious analysis could argue otherwise. We must radically reshape society and our way of life.

Our era is apocalyptic in the true sense of the word: it is an *unveiling*. The corrupt and broken systems that have held us captive are being exposed in all their emptiness. The exuberant promises of the Industrial Revolution have given way to the grim reality of climate change and ecological collapse. The cult of Mammon that promised a rising tide to lift all boats has found us shipwrecked on the shores of destitution. The prospect of our way of life continuing its current trajectory is unfathomable. Instead of waiting on economic growth to leave morsels for the rest of us, we must build a new society that works for all.

To be clear, I am not saying we are living through *the* apocalypse. We may well be, but the world has seen apocalyptic moments before. The Bronze Age collapse was an apocalyptic event. So was the fall of Rome, or the Black Plague, or the French Revolution. Scholars suggest that the Book of Revelation itself refers to the destruction of the Temple, which was certainly an apocalypse in its own right. But whatever happens in the coming years, the world will never be the same. Great horrors await us, but there is another world to be won. This is the World to Come, the one we know in our hearts is not only possible but necessary.

Throughout this book, I have described the fallen state of the world and ways that it can be realigned with the Logos. This realignment points us toward the eschatological hope of the World to Come. Such a world lies at the horizon of thought, beyond our comprehension, yet we can nurture sparks of it in the here and now. It is the intrusion of the eternal into the temporal, but we can prefigure it by aligning ourselves with the eternal. The Kingdom of God is spread out upon the Earth, yet men do not see it. We must manifest it by becoming visible signs of the Kingdom.

Utopia

Utopia gets a bad rap. To be called "utopian" is to be dismissed as someone whose head is in the clouds, full of unworkable ideas without any sense of practicality or realism. Yet utopias are manifestations of what makes us most human: imagination. The ability to imagine that things might be different than they are helps us *act* to make them different than they are. Karl Marx noted that the difference between a beehive and a building is that the architect first creates the building in their imagination before it is created in reality. Utopias help focus our energies on what is disordered in our society and guide us toward building a new kind of order. It is of course important that our utopian visions be grounded in social reality, taking account of the human condition and material limits, but even the most flawed utopias speak to some deep-seated human need that is not being met in the current era.

Utopias are a creative exercise, not only imagining a different world, but using these visions to shine light on what is wrong with our current one and envisioning how we might do things differently. Murray Bookchin was fond of saying he was not a futurist but a utopian. Futurism takes the world that exists today and projects it into the future. It envisions the modern world with advanced technology but essentially the same social structures. It appeals to the myth of progress to envision an inevitable trajectory for the future. Utopian thinking, on the other hand, seeks to change the present in order to achieve a different future.

Some of the earliest cities were utopian projects. Monastic orders have been founded on a utopian ideal of how we were meant to live. Christian monasticism developed at a time when the Roman empire had converted to the faith, and state power was seen as having corrupted and secularized it. Ascetics such as St. Anthony retreated into the desert to escape the sinful ways of the world and to confront his own demons. The life of holiness he led spurred others to follow him and form a community around this pursuit of holiness. Other orders developed their own practices. The ideal of monasticism was to embody the Kingdom of Heaven on Earth. Bringing the vision of the Kingdom to the people was the purpose of Mass, which seeks to manifest the Beloved Community. It is through this communion with the divine and with one another that we experience a taste of the World to Come.

Utopia is as old as humanity itself. We tend to think of social movements as something recent — things that sprung up in the modern industrial world in response to the rapid changes spurred by capitalism. But social movements have always been with us. When we think of the kinds of indigenous tribes studied by anthropologists, we imagine that they are "primitive" peoples whose lifestyle has persevered throughout centuries of modernization and urbanization. Yet "tribes" are not static, eternal things. They have formed and reformed countless times throughout all of human existence. They represent experiments in ways of living in community. Culture is not eternal — it is produced and reproduced by people developing new rituals, belief systems, communication styles, hierarchies, and modes of exchange. As long as people have been around, they have come together not just over blood but over ideas.

Ernst Bloch describes a "principle of hope" in which hope is not merely a subjective feeling but an objective assessment of the possibilities immanent within the present. The attitude of hope directs our attention toward the possibilities for change. It makes us aware of the not-yet-conscious, the tacit dimension from which these possibilities are actualized. Utopian thought helps train the mind toward this attitude of hope. It broadens our horizons so that we may direct our gaze toward the World to Come and realize it here and now.

Humanity's oldest technology is society itself. We have invented and reinvented ways of living together for as long as we have existed. *Homo sapiens sapiens* outlived their Neanderthal cousins in part because, while the latter were specialists well-adapted to one ecological niche, the former were generalists, adapting to new environments and new conditions as they expanded across the globe. The human imagination is what sets us apart from other animals. It allows us to conceive of a world as other than it is. The world is not just an external container for our lives. It is a product of our lives and choices. It is that which we co-create.

Consciousness

Modernity has seen a new eschatology which takes the myth of progress and applies it to consciousness, seeing an evolutionary ascent toward enlightenment. This idea stems from German idealism, especially from Hegel, who saw the course of history as Mind or Spirit unfolding upon itself through dialectical contradictions. Hegel posited a number of triads that Mind encounters in its unfolding. These have often been summarized as "thesis-antithesis-synthesis." However, the way he described it was "abstract-negative-concrete"; that is, there is first an idea that because of its abstractness invites contradiction, and through the interplay between these contradictions there emerges something concrete that incorporates the contradictions within a higher synthesis. In this way, Mind is continually transcending itself. For Hegel, the Mind here is not merely the individual human mind but some transcendent absolute Mind that is manifest within our own consciousness. In this scheme, human consciousness is universal consciousness coming to know itself.

This idealistic vision captured the imagination of Romantics. The sense of consciousness reaching toward some higher plane has motivated mystics throughout the ages. Yet the mystic goes through a self-emptying process, in which mind is cleared away so that pure presence may be found. The mystic seeks the always-already. The evolution of consciousness as seen in Hegelian idealism is not one of self-emptying but self-overcoming. Mind is constantly evolving to encompass more of the world within its understanding.

This idea was developed further over the course of the nineteenth and twentieth century. Pierre Teilhard de Chardin saw a pattern of history in what he called the Law of Complexity-Consciousness. The idea is that from the beginning the universe has been creating new and more complex arrangements of matter that manifest in new emerging levels of consciousness. Matter evolves from the simplest subatomic particles to form more complex arrangements, and ultimately sentient lifeforms like ourselves. Through the development of communications technology, he saw humans creating a new layer of consciousness called the noosphere. The noosphere is a kind of emerging collective mind that connects our individual minds together, developing our own consciousness in the process. For Chardin, this becomes the universal Mind that encompasses all. An ordained Jesuit, in his more religious works this universal Mind is understood as the Cosmic Christ. Humans, he thought, were on a path of taking on the mind of Christ through cosmic self-understanding.

The Swiss philosopher Jean Gebser attempted a kind of archaeology of human consciousness analyzing the different "mutations" it had undergone. Deep in humanity's history there was an archaic consciousness of a simple sensate nature like that of other animals. Later there develops a magical, animistic consciousness that sees energetic correlations between entities and seeks to master these connections ritualistically to gain some advantage over one's surroundings. From here emerges the mythic structure, in which there is not only correlation but a narrative tying these connections together. The cycles of life and of nature are ritualized and incorporated into stories that give a sense of meaning and belonging to life. Next comes the mental structure, in which these multiple narratives are interrogated in the search for a single rational structure. Here we see the beginnings of philosophy and science, but also monotheism and rational religion. The Trinity has a particular symbolic importance for this structure, which is three-dimensional, compared to the two-dimensional mythic structure, the one-dimensional magic structure, and the zero-dimensional archaic structure. Gebser sees an emerging fourth-dimensional structure he calls the integral-aperspectival structure. Under integral consciousness, the mind itself becomes an object of consciousness. The totalizing rational systems of the mental structure become relativized within a meta-perspective that integrates different perspectives within itself. A new experience of time emerges in which rather than rational categories of past, present, and future (or in addition to them), time is experienced as an intensity, with the past crystalized in the present in a trajectory toward the future in one continuous movement.

The term "Integral" was taken up by the Hindu mystic Sri Aurobindo, who blended the mystical consciousness of the Hindu tradition with the evolving consciousness of the Hegelian tradition into his system called "Integral Yoga." Followers of this school founded the California Institute of Integral Studies, which developed an interdisciplinary curriculum of philosophy, psychology, anthropology, integrative health, and several other disciplines with a vision of the spiritual development of the whole person.

The Integral mantle would later be claimed by Ken Wilber, a transpersonal psychologist and philosopher. Drawing from Teilhard de Chardin, Jean Gebser, Sri Aurobindo, Jean Piaget, and several others, he developed a four-quadrant model by which all phenomena have subjective and objective as well as individual and collective correlates. These four quadrants are always "tetra-arising." He synthesizes the evolutionary scheme of Gebser and Aurobindo with the Spiral Dynamics developmental theory of Don Beck and Chris Cowan.

This color-coded scheme sees Orange-rational consciousness reaching critical mass in Western society during the Enlightenment, but with Blue-mythic consciousness still playing a powerful role and Green-relative consciousness beginning to emerge around the mid-twentieth century with postmodern thought. His scheme goes on to suggest new Yellow and Turquoise levels of Integral consciousness standing above the Green-relative level, able to incorporate the relativization of perspectives into a still higher metaperspective. Naturally, he places his own ideas at this higher level. Each level is supposed to "transcend and include" its predecessors and therefore make an object of its previous level within a new perspective.

This schema conveniently recapitulates Western colonialist frameworks about cultural development while dressing it in a quasi-mystical language of ascension and enlightenment. Lewis Henry Morgan's map of "social evolution" becomes "conscious evolution" in which the Global North happens to be the most advanced spiritually as well as technologically. It incorporates the postmodern critique of modernity by assigning it its own level beyond modern rationality, while then negating this negation by positing levels beyond this level, in which these worldviews themselves can be objectified and ranked. The critique of hierarchy becomes a transitional phase toward more hierarchy.

For all his emphasis on "transcend and include," Wilber habitually chastises Green-relative consciousness and invokes it to project the laziest cultural stereotypes of postmodernism onto it. He uses his schema of development levels to respond to criticism by simple categorization. Those who disagree with him are necessarily Green or below because they must not be able to comprehend his perspective. Meanwhile, he assures his followers that by virtue of the fact that they are drawn to his work, they must necessarily be at an Integral level of consciousness.

This kind of elitism is a major pitfall of this "conscious evolution" perspective. It flatters the ego to think that it is on the cutting edge of evolution. One finds this conceit in the New Age concept of "Indigo Children," a concept with its origins in Theosophy.[23] A similar occult idea lay in the Nazi idea of the Aryan race, an idea also found in Theosophy. There is always an impulse in reactionary thought to see oneself as belonging to some sort of "natural aristocracy." It justifies one's place of leadership and power in the world one is seeking to make. Indeed, the sense of being at the cutting edge of cultural evolution had long been used by colonial powers to justify their own domination. In their minds they

---

[23] Theosophy recognizes seven "root races" appearing on the planet at different times. First there were the Polarians, then the Hyperboreans, then the Lemurians, and then the Aryan race. Helena Blavatsky predicted a coming sixth root race, which New Age spirituality identified with the Indigos. A seventh and final root race is supposed to emerge on a future continent in the Pacific.

were teaching civilization to the "primitives" under their rule.

Wilber's concept of "tetra-arising" fits well into the colonialist framework of social evolution. It suggests that as cultures become more socially complex and technologically advanced, they also realize higher stages of consciousness. Yet there are several instances of people abandoning such complex societies and choosing a different way of life. If we go by the four-quadrant model, we will have to say that these people are forsaking their level of consciousness and effectively choosing to become dumber. Yet these decisions are often based on a pointed critique of such a way of life. David Graeber and David Wengrow describe how the civilization around Cahokia, a hierarchical state society that practiced human sacrifices similar to the Maya and Aztecs, fell around 1350 CE, and whose descendants the Europeans encountered. The Jesuits kept diligent notes on their encounters with the Huron, who criticized the hierarchical and servile society of the Europeans. Graeber and Wengrow suggest that these views should not simply be seen as the innocent ideals of a primitive people, but the legacy of a history of resistance to such hierarchical societies. Their ancestors had experienced such unjust social conditions in Cahokia, and these people may have been expressing the ideology of those that rose against it.

Centering consciousness over material conditions often has reactionary implications. The solipsistic "Law of Attraction" of New Age discourse takes Just World Theory to the extreme, implying that any negative or positive events in one's life are a result of the thought patterns they put out into the universe. Such a perspective implies all victims of war, rape, and genocide were victims not of their oppressors but of their own thought patterns. It's no wonder this capitalistic quasi-religion has spread so widely in the world of multi-level marketing: it suggests people only need to believe in the certainty of their own success to achieve the wealth they desire, so long as they continue contributing to these modern-day capitalist cults. It is also no surprise that "mindfulness" has become a new buzzword in the modern workforce, emphasizing self-care as a palliative to the soul-crushing banality of the corporate world.

Karl Marx inverted Hegel's idealism into a historical materialism centered not on the development of consciousness but on the forces of production. He saw mind not as encountering itself but as arising from material conditions, which were subject to their own internal contradictions. The contradictions here are not between abstract ideas but between classes. Class struggle was for him the driving force of history, with each mode of production producing its own ruling class and exploited class, whose struggle for liberation would produce a new mode of production with its own class structure until eventually a classless society known as communism would emerge.

Consciousness emerges in one's relative relation to others, so raising people's consciousness requires addressing relationships. By building solidarity with one another in a common struggle for liberation, new relationships are forged that overcome the servile false consciousness induced by the machinery of capitalism. In this sense of comradery, people not only share their social lives with one another, but fight for each other so that all may benefit.

The liberation of consciousness cannot be separated from

liberation of material conditions. Mysticism must not be a matter of withdrawal from the world, but of deepening one's compassion and wisdom to better engage in its transformation, and in the process raising the consciousness of others. There is no hope in the evolution of consciousness without the transformation of the world. This is why we must take refuge in the World to Come. We must seek what the Zapatistas call a "world where many worlds fit." The drive to advance and achieve aperspectival consciousness is a positive one, but it means nothing if it is not applying itself to the fight for a better world for all.

A truly integral perspective requires that we include new spheres of concern in our awareness. We learn to make our own upbringing and cultural background an object of consciousness, and through this we can see that different cultural visions of the good life can have value without needing to impose one way of life on all. We become capable of holding our own perspectives in relation to multiple perspectives, in which multiple truth and value systems can coexist. This does not imply a vulgar relativism in which all perspectives are equal, but an ecosystem of perspectives that mutually inform and improve one another.

This process ultimately depends on the imagination. We expand our perspective by learning to imagine other perspectives. We learn to play make-believe and take on the role of another, and necessarily examine what limits the imagination. When we do that, we see that it is none other than the megamachine. The school system funnels children into a single institution where life is regimented, performance is quantified, and social norms and expectations are standardized. This quantified, standardized life then follows us into our work routine as adults. We are subjected to bureaucratic hierarchies that enforce obedience and undeviating adherence to procedure.

That anyone survives this process with their imagination intact is a testament to the miraculous tenacity of the human spirit. Imagination comes naturally to children but is swiftly shut down by our social institutions. We learn prejudices that inhibit our ability to imagine the perspective of others, and more importantly prevent us from seeking to learn from their perspectives. Imagination is just as much social as it is individual. How much of this social imagination is inhibited by an individualistic system that keeps us increasingly isolated from one another?

The inhibition of imagination is felt pointedly among those whose learning style and cognitive processing are different. Neurodiversity is often understood as a disability issue. Yet the social model of disability suggests that disabilities are simply mismatches between personal ability and social resources. Different neurotypes are not inherently disabling — they are simply maladapted to the conditions of the megamachine. In truth, no one is well-adjusted to the mechanization of life that plagues modernity, so neurotypicality and neurodivergence are relative terms. The liberation of consciousness means liberating the diversity of forms consciousness can take.

The vertical expansion of consciousness with which the Integral movement concerns itself pales in comparison to the horizontal diversity of consciousness. The development of consciousness can take a multitude of pathways. Liberating consciousness means creating space for all its different forms to flourish in their own way. The growth and expansion of consciousness is real, but any framework that reduces it to a single pathway closes off the vast diversity of forms consciousness can take. When we have an ecosystem of different modes of thought, we can create resilient systems that honor each person's gifts.

At the core of our humanity lies our capacity to imagine the world other than it is. Imagination, more than our status as "rational animals," may be the true quality that constitutes humanity's status as *Imago Dei*. Our ability to imagine is what gives us the ability to create, making us "like unto God." The liberation of consciousness means the liberation of the imagination. We must struggle against the megamachine and liberate our lives from its hold on our institutions. As the French radicals proclaimed in May of 1968, "All power to the imagination!"

Culture

A pedagogical society must develop the capacity for self-actualization. We must cultivate virtues conducive to civic participation and self-examination. Virtue is not a strict set of rules to be followed, but noble qualities to be cultivated. Proper formation requires community. We learn how to be contributing members of that community, and in so doing we cultivate the virtues of that community. But aren't a community's virtues subjective? Doesn't this get us into cultural relativism, the same "Green" mentality that Wilber so forcefully rages against?

On the contrary: this is simply a recognition that we can never look *behind* culture. Culture is the lens through which we see everything else. There is no culture-free world we can objectively perceive. We can learn about other cultures to enrich our understanding, but we will always be observing these cultures from the perspective of our own cultural background. When a scientist makes a measurement of some phenomenon, they are using a scientific language that has a specific history tied to cultural developments and cultural assumptions. This in no way means that they aren't describing objective phenomena; they are describing it through a culturally conditioned conceptual framework.

Thomas Kuhn suggested that science advances through paradigm shifts. A paradigm is an explanatory framework by which one can understand and examine phenomena. A paradigm is not just a set of theories and evidence, but a standard by which one judges what constitutes valid evidence, observations, and inferences. Kuhn saw the history of science unfolding not as continuous advancement but as a process of shifting and competing paradigms. Since each paradigm has its own standards of evidence and inference, there is no objective standard to which one can appeal to settle the dispute. However, paradigms can become messy when trying to explain anomalies. The epicycles of the planets presented anomalies for the Ptolemaic model that were more easily explained by the Copernican model. This did not disprove the Ptolemaic model. It did, however, give the Copernican model a competitive advantage as new anomalies emerged that were predictable from within that model, while the Ptolemaic model found itself increasingly on the defensive.

This competition forces each paradigm to evolve and better itself in order to face these challenges and present new ones to the competing paradigm. Paradigms may find ways to incorporate aspects of one another so that they begin to resemble each other in significant ways. This convergent evolution can apply to cross-cultural understanding. Genuine cultural exchange can occur when cultures are able to understand one another's perspectives and learn from them without appropriating them or imposing them on others. Even if one wishes to convert the other to a particular idea, one must first undergo a conversion of one's own to understand the perspective from which they approach it. In doing so, they will be able to understand the new idea from within their own framework.

Roy Bhaskar's critical realist approach emphasizes that there are three levels of reality: the empirical world that we experience directly through our senses; the actual world of observable phenomena studied by science; and the real world that cannot be observed but only inferred through scientific study. Critical realism suggests a causal relationship between these three levels. Competing paradigms might make differing claims about the nature of these causal relationships, but they all refer to the same underlying structures. Critical realism insists upon an ontology of the world that can be accessed by different epistemologies. We can apply this to different value systems by acknowledging that just as the empirical world is shaped by our senses, so too do different value systems arise from different social and historical contexts, attempting to analyze an actual world of moral phenomena based on what knowledge is available at the time, and seeking the real world of moral truth. A plurality of different value systems can help each to come closer to approaching the Good as such.

Moral revolutions occur when a cultural practice is seen from an outsider's perspective that is then incorporated into the cultural paradigm. The philosopher Kwame Anthony Appiah describes how this happened in the case of dueling, the slave trade, and Chinese foot binding. Dueling had been associated with the aristocracy, among whom it was seen as a matter of honor, yet it fell out of favor when it came to be seen as bringing dishonor upon the aristocracy itself. The slave trade was opposed by the English working class, not because they were particularly anti-racist, but because nothing so exemplified the indignity of labor as the forced labor practiced in the New World. Foot binding was a matter of honor marking a woman as belonging to a proper traditional family but came to be seen as bringing shame and dishonor to China in the eyes of the world. Appiah expresses his hope that a similar moral revolution might take place with the practice of honor killings. This did not mean adopting the value systems of outsiders. It meant seeing the other from within an ecology of perspectives and incorporating that perspective into their own value system.

We must also avoid considering any culture as monolithic and self-contained. Culture is porous and constantly evolving as it is reproduced in each generation. Subcultures can cross cultural boundaries, and different cultural groups can exist within a larger culture. Culture exists wherever norms exist, and norms only take a group of three to establish: the differences between two people are simply differences, and it takes a third party to establish a norm by which deviations can be judged. Any individual can participate in multiple cultures, and it is in this multiple participation that personal identity is formed.

Neither idealism nor materialism can fully capture the element of culture, where the ideal meets the material in the realm of habit, memory, and tacit knowledge. Culture is constituted by shared beliefs, values, epistemologies, rituals, shared understandings, practices, and history. It is the habits of thought and deed, as well as the stories and narratives passed down that tie those habits to this shared history. Whether we conceive of something as a commodity, a taboo object, a relic, or a sacrament is a cultural determination that affects how we interact with it. We do not have culture on one side and matter on the other, but a nexus of relations that are both cultural and material. Our relationship to objects is mediated by our relationship to one another, and our relationship to one another is mediated by our relationship to objects. Habits of thought and deed interpenetrate one another in an ongoing conversation.

Capitalism has colonized culture through endless commodification, the process by which we are alienated from the objects around us by their reduction to instrumental values. The value of an object has been reduced to its extrinsic exchange value. Use value and exchange value both conceal the dimension of intrinsic value. Transforming our broken world means not only overcoming the machinery of capitalism, but the culture of commodification upon which that machinery is built.

Creativity

Our ability to thrive is deeply rooted in our capacity for creative innovation. There is no single utopian blueprint that meets everyone's needs. We must recognize our innate creativity as an essential part of what it means for us to thrive. To fulfill the human telos requires that we not simply impose one person's creative vision upon everyone else but learn to work in harmony. We must work toward a society that can cultivate the creativity of its members in the most convivial way.

This creativity requires the freedom to pursue crafts and skills that interest us with as few social or economic barriers as possible. The paradigm of schooling we have now is built around funneling people through a predetermined curriculum by which they are all compared in terms of their fitness based on a prescribed style of learning, and then go on to earn credentials that solidify an existing class hierarchy. We call this "learning," but it is really a form of gatekeeping that continues the existence of an elite class. No amount of charter schools or vouchers can correct this fundamental fact. Schooling as we know it is fundamentally concerned with social control.

An educational system that truly honors the human drive to learn and improve ourselves would encompass society itself, rather than confining itself to some institution called "school." On some level, we already understand this. When we enter the workforce, regardless of what educational credentials we've earned, we learn most on the job. The educational requirements for most jobs have little to do with the knowledge necessary to perform the job, and everything to do with ensuring that only a certain class of people will be able to apply.

A flourishing society would be one in which work and education are intertwined. Skill-shares could help spread crafts far and wide, and allow people to discover their own creative muse. People could organize on the basis of shared disciplines, as the guilds of old once did. Yet where the guilds closely guarded their secrets to preserve their hierarchy, the free exchange of information could help everyone achieve their greatest creative potential.

Competition is often credited with spurring human creativity. Perhaps this is true when compared to monopoly power, in which one entity corners the market on some commodity. Yet the real contrast to competition is not monopoly, but cooperation, and it is here that we see creativity truly flourish. A great deal of market competition these days is simply trying to work around the patents of others, or selling something similar to the competition under a different brand name. This produces variety, but not innovation. Innovation happens when one person can build upon the ideas of another, and another is able to build on theirs, and so on. The collaboration of minds holds far greater creative potential than any mind of its own accord.

We already see the power of collaboration in the open-source movement. The innovations that people create in their spare time for free give us a mere taste of what would be possible if they had full access to patented technology and could pursue this passion without worrying about how to support themselves. People have an innate need to create, and the demand that they must sell their labor for a living is one of the greatest blocks to finding where their true creative abilities lie.

Creativity requires resilience. We must become resilient enough as a society to support resilience in others. Complexity theorist Stuart Kauffman describes a "razor's edge" between chaos and order where creativity thrives. An overly structured system becomes too rigid and can be toppled over by external shocks. An overly chaotic system is subject to positive feedback loops that cause cascading effects throughout the whole system. The razor's edge is an ordered system with low level chaos that produces negative feedback loops to maintain equilibrium.

This is achieved by distributed networks. The rigid boundaries of the nation-state give way to the rhizomatic structure of confederation, while the combination of decentralization and integration allows for a resilient system for social experiments. One community can learn from and adapt to changes in neighboring communities. Positive changes quickly ripple throughout the system while harmful ones are identified and isolated, forming a kind of immune system. Such a system would display a kind of collective intelligence and propensity for learning.

Resilient systems must find the right balance between autonomy and connection. This resilient design is one that works in our own bodies, that nature has used time and again, and that can be applied effectively to social organization. It means aligning oneself with the source of creativity that underlies this creative cosmos we inhabit.

Logos

Behind all complexity in the world, behind every pattern and phenomenon in nature, there is a supremely simple transcendent source. Behind every scientific law, every mathematical equation, every logical inference or moral truth, there is a singular source, a primordial unity from which all things flow and toward which all things strive.

This primordial unity is in one sense irresistible; it is the source of all things and therefore immune to deviation. And yet, in another sense, we have drifted away from it. This can be understood through the twofold movement that springs from this source. Insofar as the Logos is the source of all things, it is necessary for anything to exist at all. Yet as the telos toward which all things strive, this latter movement can be disrupted in any number of ways. That this divine Logos could produce that which goes against it is certainly a mystery, and one that can only be truly answered in the fullness of time. The beginnings of such an answer can be appreciated insofar as we imaginative beings are ourselves reflections of this Logos, capable of conceiving the world other than it is, even as we are also creatures of habit taking our cues from others around us.

We can, with some qualification, compare the Logos to the Chinese concept of Tao. From the Confucian point of view, Tao is understood as a proper social order, in which all aspects of political, family, and cultural life are oriented toward a harmonious balance. There was something conservative about it in this view: everything in society has its proper place, from which it should not deviate. Taoist thinkers like Laozi and Zhuangzi put an interesting spin on this. For them, Tao is understood as a natural order defined not by static categories but by spontaneity and flux. There is still an idea of social harmony and social order here, but it is at the same time a kind of anti-order achieved through freedom and simplicity.

With the Logos, we can see a similar kind of tension. One

can see it as a kind of eternal order into which all things fit, and various regimes have promoted some version of this to justify their social status and sovereignty. Yet in Christ we see a subversion of this. The "Kingdom of God" is not of this world, not in the sense of being supernatural, but in the sense that it is of a different kind of order from that on which the existing social order is founded. In this Kingdom, the last shall be first and the first shall be last. Those who exalt themselves shall be humbled, while those who humble themselves shall be exalted. Those who would lead must serve. Christ the King is draped in purple robes of mockery, wearing a crown of thorns with the cross as his throne. It is in this radical reversal of the ways of the world that we see the extent to which this world has fallen from the Logos.

The Tao is the Way of nature, but the Way, the Truth, and the Light must pass through the cross of history, from the Fall to the Eschaton. In *wei wu wei*, we empty ourselves of our resistance to the flow of the Way. In kenosis, we take up our cross in order to follow the Way. We conform to the Logos only through struggle with the Powers and Principalities of this world. By embracing the Logos, we find our anchor amidst the torrential storms of this fallen world. It centers us in that which is eternal even as it springs forth with endless creativity. It is that subtle center in which we live and move and have our Being, and by finding this stillness in our hearts we can move mountains, so long as they are moved according to the Logos.

Systems of power have created race, class, and gender hierarchies by which a privileged elite establish the criteria according to which others are permitted into their ranks. The calculating logic of the market has overtaken the spontaneity of organic social relationships. The process of capitalization has quantified everything in our world, and invaded our very consciousness with this objectified worldview. Cities have been subject to technocratic ambition while farming has been turned into a monopolistic competition with the forces of nature.

Behind all these deviations lies a cynical kind of hubris. The fall in the Garden of Eden was one such act of hubris: having everything we wanted, we gave into the temptation to go beyond, to know that which we were not meant to know. We sought to take control, to have the kind of mastery over our environment that was reserved for the creator alone. Rather than following the ways of the Logos, we sought ways to gain power over it, and in so doing produced false logoi. We worshiped our idols of power and control — the institutions by which one group enshrined their place over another — and mistook them for the true Logos. Patriarchy, aristocracy, white supremacy, and the market have all been presented at some point as manifestations of "Natural Law." Such systems constitute what critical theorist Jürgen Habermas describes as "steering media," diverting us from the communicative rationality in which the true Logos is found.

We cannot directly understand the Logos itself, yet we recognize it as we recognize the sun — by its light, we see everything. It is the simple way that underlies all complexity, and toward which all things strive. Each iteration of the Logos gives us new forms of complexity, yet the underlying unity persists. The Logos is the source of all, but it is also the telos of all things. To live in accordance with one's telos is to live well. There is one sense in which the telos of humanity is bound together in the Common Good, which each of us bears some responsibility for upholding. Yet the achievement of that Common Good is best realized when each of us can become fully actualized, creating space for all to thrive.

The Logos can be recognized by the sign of kenosis. Kenosis represents the strength that comes from humility and non-attachment. Throughout this book I have tried to explore the various ways that this principle manifests. I described the ways in which command bureaucracies could be dismantled into the free association of producers; that credit could be distributed into a horizontal system of mutual aid; that technology could be brought to human scale to support the advancement of creativity and self-actualization; that cities could develop organically through small-scale communal planning and vernacular construction; that farming could be done in harmony with natural processes. All these ideas are based on a critique of the authoritarian, bureaucratic, centralist forms of these institutions and underneath them exists a spontaneous order that can be organized toward liberation.

The Logos produces the order over which we seek to superimpose our own order. It is the order that was lost in that first act of disobedience in the Garden. We dig ourselves deeper and deeper into our fallen order because each attempt at control yields new problems that require new forms of control. To escape this cycle, we must take a step back and look at the ways in which our institutions create the very chaos they are meant to control. We must look beneath systems of control to find the spontaneous creative energies striving to be liberated. Once we apprehend these creative energies, we must learn to work with them. Rather than controlling them, we must gently guide them into harmony with one another. The Logos is not stuck at one point but persists across all time. It is both source and destination, the alpha and omega, the ever-present origin.

The Logos is emptiness. It is that void by which all things have their substance. It is that by which Being has its Being. Self, soul, substance, all exist by virtue of absence. It is by the closing of certain possibilities that a new range of possibilities become imminent via emergence. The "adjacent possible" described by Stuart Kauffman opens to the generative void of Logos. It is the nothingness by which all things come to be. It calls us to our source, the emptiness that is also a plenum. This emptiness is the play of possibilities actualizing themselves. It is both the field of possibilities and the closure of that field to generate higher-order fields of possibilities. Emergence arises from this play of emptiness.

The Logos is the Word; it is the immanent expression of the transcendent source that is beyond all understanding. Proceeding from this transcendent source and its immanent expression is the indwelling Spirit animating the cosmos. This Spirit is the life bursting forth from the primordial unity of the Big Bang. It is the flow of time by which the eternal is actualized. Together these form a triune singularity known as the Trinity. This reality — simultaneously three and one — reveals that the underlying unity of existence is already communal. This divine community, containing all that exists, is imprinted in all things. The world is trinities all the way down. We too are trinities. Each of us has our own inner depth unknown even to ourselves, our fundamental character and particularity, and our history of becoming.

The cosmos is organized as wholes containing other wholes, giving themselves over into ever-greater wholes. All things live and move and have their being within the community of this higher order unity. In the life of the Trinity, we are united with all of creation.

Frailty

Making any system work requires active participation. It is a matter of ingenuity and cooperative problem-solving, upon which human society has always depended. The problems that arise in such a system must be addressed by the stakeholders themselves. Cooperative decision-making is not so much the solution as it is a prerequisite for any authentic solution to emerge at all. There is no shortcut to a society that works for all without empowering the very people it is meant to serve.

This is where we are confronted with something unsettling. It turns out that people are fallen creatures who are driven by selfish, spiteful, prideful, short-sighted, and foolish motives. Changing social structures alone will not be sufficient to bring about this World to Come. There is a certain strain of leftist thought that sees such frailties as simply products of oppressive systems. There is some truth to this: economic inequality has strong correlations with violent crime, environmental stress, mental illness, abuse, and any number of societal ills. We must not be deceived into believing that we can solve these things simply by replacing one system with another.

An account demarcating before and after "the revolution"

is misleading. Political revolutions are frail things which easily revert to the oppressive systems they were meant to overthrow. A lasting revolution must be undertaken, which cannot be reduced to a single event. The course of such upheaval may indeed see multiple uprisings, social movements, insurrections, even wars, but these are convulsions within a period of chrysalis in which the new world begins to emerge. The revolution has in fact been underway for a long time. Each new moment of social uprising is a point of punctuation in this long process that brings us gradually closer to the ultimate goal of liberation.

The move to a more communal, democratic society will not alleviate many of the problems we face, but it will establish a foundation for addressing them. The oppressions visited upon humanity by empire, slavery, class society, and authoritarianism consist first and foremost of silencing those over whom they rule. One class of people is granted subjectivity, making decisions over the fate of others, while the others are objectified as tools for the ruling class to manipulate and direct as they see fit.

Correcting this situation does not mean that people will no longer be petty, hateful, selfish, or rude to one another, but it does mean that the systems that enabled one class to treat another class this way without consequence will no longer be there. People will have to wrestle with one another's shortcomings, face the difficulties of coming to amicable agreements, struggle with personality conflicts, and even deal with serious transgressions. And they will have to do this in a way that does not rely on the coercive authority of one class over another.

Fear of our own frailty leads to the psychology of domination. We flee from our humanity to arm ourselves against pain and loss in life. We come to despise weakness in others because it reminds us of our own weakness. We come to believe in some form of Just World Theory, the idea that the universe is organized in such a way that people get what they deserve — that people who suffer do so because they are bad and that people who succeed do so because they are good. This allows us to place some distance between ourselves and those who suffer and deny our own vulnerability. The poor, the homeless, the downtrodden, and the oppressed are blamed for their own plight. This allows us comfort in the belief that our own goodness will protect us from their fate.

These lies we tell ourselves prevent the empathic response needed to actually address the suffering in this world and lift ourselves up together. We build armor to protect ourselves from our own humanity when it is in our common humanity that we find our ultimate strength. Yet we all too often stop short of humanity as such, and instead create in-groups and out-groups. We exalt our own group as superior and more deserving. We use power to institutionalize our privilege, and if we belong to some out-group that is oppressed by another in-group wielding power over us, we direct our resentment toward another out-group in whose oppression we too can participate. There is a pecking order in which we locate ourselves between those above us and those below us.

But power ultimately holds power over us. White supremacy keeps white people united with their oppressors by a common racial designation while preventing them from developing solidarity with others based on common struggle. Men benefit from patriarchy at the cost of their own psychic mutilation through toxic masculinity. Even the wealthy capitalist is trapped in a mentality of endless accumulation with which they can never be satisfied. Religious traditions have long taught that wealth and power poison the soul. As Christ said, "For what shall it profit a man, if he shall gain the whole world, and lose his own soul?"[24]

We may never learn to be fully comfortable with our vulnerability, for there will always be times when we need to guard ourselves from being hurt. We can, however, learn to stop stigmatizing it. Repressed vulnerability can make monsters of us. We seek power to make ourselves invincible, but that same power devours our soul from within. True freedom requires that we recognize our vulnerability, tend to it with compassion and discernment, and view others through the same compassionate lens.

We cannot build a utopia that does not have space for failure. We must give people the space to make mistakes on the road to self-improvement while giving them the support needed to bounce back and find their path. Transformative justice is needed that can secure people from harm while giving space for those who have wronged others to grow and make restitution.

The criminal justice system is overwhelmingly based on retribution. Even attempts to reform offenders often fail to provide a meaningful way of living for them after serving their time. Caring for the basic needs of all requires extending that care not just to the innocent but to those we deem guilty as well. Victims of violence deserve safety, and any justice system must provide for that. But there is no safety in barring people from bettering themselves.

---

[24] Mark 8:36, KJV

We are a deeply traumatized civilization. We are not made for the daily stress and anxiety of life in the megamachine. Trauma and abuse may be understood as underlying the history of civilization itself. How do we make sense of human cruelty except by further human cruelty? The cycle goes back deep in time, to where only legend can reach: when Cain slew his brother Abel and was asked to account for it, he asked "Am I my brother's keeper?"[25] The course of history has thenceforth posed that question again and again. We have been isolated and turned against one another by power games of empire and capital. Our lives have been shaped by 5,000 years of patriarchy, conquest, slavery, exploitation, and commodification that have left a deep wound in our collective psyche. A true revolution requires not only the overthrow of the old society, but a way to heal these societal wounds. We must develop a culture of healing, in which we hold space for each other in our vulnerability so that we may heal together. Only in such a culture can we truly become self-realized.

This healing must be more than a sociopolitical transformation. It must touch the soul as well. If religion seeks to survive in a new era, it too must abandon the Dark Logos of patriarchal domination. In Christendom, there are two churches. I do not mean Catholic and Protestant, Eastern and Western. Each of these bodies contains this division within itself, between the Church of the Poor and the Church of Caesar. The Gates of Hell shall not prevail against one of them. The true church must realize her role as the Bride of Christ and embrace her femininity, forsaking her patriarchal

---

[25] Genesis 4:9

baggage. All paths that seek the Logos in whatever name should likewise abandon the fallen ways by which we grasp for power and control. We must allow the Logos to act through us, and in so doing respect the path that it paves for our neighbor. We must embrace the diversity by which it calls all of creation to delight in its creative wonder.

Kenosis

We live in a world ruled by power. The Great Power rivalry of Russia, China, and the US, as well as several regional powers, dominates and crushes the lives, hopes, and aspirations of all those caught in the middle of their power games. Capital interests compete for power over workers and the dispossessed. Patriarchy entails a struggle between men over their position in the pecking order. The power elite are not a united front. The marginalized people they exploit and oppress are not their enemy. They are mere pawns in their power games. The world is a sports competition between oppressors in which the oppressed are the ball. This game is known as differential accumulation, and it applies to political, economic, and social power alike.

In playing this game against one another, they use sabotage to maintain an exploited class of people who will serve their own struggle for power. They sabotage our daily lives to keep us isolated from one another, dependent on large hegemonic systems over which we are powerless, helpless over our own lives. We are tasked with servile, meaningless work, our daily routine regimented for us by a megamachine to whom we sacrifice our autonomy and sense of purpose.

We are kept busy with work assigned to us from on high rather than discovering what work truly has meaning for us. We learn to consume rather than create. Meaningful work is something we learn to do for ourselves. It may be in collaboration with others, but it is nonetheless chosen.

The powerful draw us into their games by making us choose between them rather than choosing our own power. If we are unhappy with our jobs, we simply have the option to look for another job. If we are unhappy with the government, we may vote for the other party next time. If we seek to stop the oppressive actions of one government or power, we must support another great power against them. This way of closing the horizon of possibilities is a truly diabolical form of sabotage, and one that fools us into thinking we are free.

The Kingdom lurks beneath the surface of this battlefield. As the great powers battle one another on the world stage, the path to liberation lies in the people identifying with one another rather than their rulers. The multitude of the oppressed, the marginalized, the exploited, the excluded, and the vulnerable crosses all borders and boundaries. We must forge connections with others across the artificial barriers used to divide us. The ruling class maintains its power by reproducing and leveraging the divisions between us. We must find solidarity with one another, embracing the struggle of others as our own. Only by reaching across these divisions can we find our own liberation.

In solidarity, we find kenosis. Kenosis does not impose one's order on others but seeks to free them to co-create another order together. Kenosis seeks free association, in which people collaborate and connect as equals, connected by mutual interest and unbounded by such barriers as property, race, class, or nation. Kenosis shows us both an end to be sought and a means toward that end. Through this kenotic path, we can build a new world in the shell of the old. We may for the time being remain trapped within the confines of existing systems of power, in which we must choose one power over another. Such choices may be necessary: we needn't succumb to the logic of the reformist to acknowledge that of two candidates running for office, one is indeed highly preferable, and the other may be genuinely dangerous. It is simply important that we not let these choices eclipse our horizons. We must build horizontal power that will eventually make these constrained choices irrelevant.

Where state power draws invisible lines over the earth to mark its borders, we must instead see an archipelago of cities and towns that cut right across them. Where capital splits our identity between that of worker and consumer, we must instead work toward a free association of producers in which we co-create the commons. Where capitalist modernity divides economic and social life, we see a communal life in which the exchange of goods is an extension of social relationships. Where scientific materialism separates the natural from the social, we find a world in which nature is itself intrinsically social.

We must overcome our atomization and find the rhizomatic terrain under our feet. The Kingdom is here among us, and we must awaken to it. It will be revealed through our cooperation and witness, but not by conquering force. We must seek the path of self-emptying, letting go of this grasping to power that has driven us to ruin, and seeking liberation in solidarity with our neighbor. We must orient ourselves kenotically toward the eschaton, seeking the World to Come and embodying it in our actions here and now. Only in our surrender to this mystery will we discover true freedom. We are all children of the Logos.

Movement

The system will not surrender its power voluntarily. It must be challenged and confronted, its weaknesses exposed and turned against it. Mass social movements employing a variety of strategies are necessary for building this new world. They can build institutions that seek to address social problems and lobby for resources within the system. They can take to the streets to demand change, building popular support and raising awareness. They can engage in direct action, acting without seeking the system's permission or approval, willing to break the law in the pursuit of some higher law to which the system itself must be held accountable. At the extreme, they may take up arms against the system, seeking to overthrow tyrants and their enforcers.

Liberals seek gradual change within the system through lobbying, legislation, and institution-building. This often leads to watered-down compromises at best, and regulatory capture at worst, in which institutions made to improve people's lives are taken over by forces with ulterior motives. They can become corrupted by the system they seek to change, copying the system's instrumental logic.

Systemic change happens when mass movements confront the system with popular demands and force concessions from institutions. More than anything, popular movements have a way of changing the discourse. Demands that appear radical at first can become mainstream by a persistence on being heard. Such movements change institutions by changing the culture. The justifications used before are no longer acceptable, and institutions must adapt to the new social reality.

Direct action must actively confront institutions. It relies on coordinated action to disrupt the flows of the system, making it impossible for institutions to go on operating as usual. Blocking pipelines and logging sites, sabotaging machinery, rent strikes, and engaging in strategic acts of property destruction can all disrupt the system and weaken it into a position where it has no choice but to compromise. They may find popular support as well, though this is not necessarily its purpose.

Finally, there are violent uprisings: armed revolution, civil war, assassinations, coups, terrorism. On the one hand, there is a great social taboo about such things, while on the other hand there are those militants who fetishize and glamorize political violence. Liberals who revere America's Founding Fathers and memorialize their revolution flinch at the idea of another such revolution happening now. In fact, their squeamishness about political militancy generally starts at a much lower threshold, including acts of vandalism such as graffiti and breaking windows. They will chastise radicals to act more peacefully like Gandhi or Martin Luther King, oblivious to the fact that their struggles were explicitly based around direct action that sought direct confrontation with the system.

At the same time, the guillotine has become a popular symbol in the left imagination, representing the swift justice with which they seek to dispose of the ruling class. Isolated from the daily reality of war, such enthusiasm rarely confronts the actual political cost of violent conflict as seen in places like Syria, where several factions fight each other with support from several different countries, leaving a desolate landscape of destruction in its wake. Armed political struggle may become necessary, but it should never be sought. If successful, it can lead to circular firing squads and unrestrained bloodlust. The Reign of Terror should not be repeated, and its signature form of execution should not be glorified. The Paris Commune was right to burn this instrument of brutality.

Armed struggle can become necessary as a matter of self-defense. Self-defense against a system that seeks to dominate and destroy is a radical act. Malcolm X was accused of being a violent extremist simply because he advocated black self-defense. Every slave uprising was an act of self-defense. Often popular movements that start with organizing and direct action are violently attacked by state forces and must take up arms to defend themselves. Such self-defense is a right, and once having secured one's position against the forces of the oppressor, it may be necessary to defend that position. Yet even against the worst of tyrannies, we must remember that the goal is to neutralize the threat, not to enact vengeance. When vengeance becomes the driving motivator, it leads to one tyranny replacing another.[26]

The atrocities of the prevailing social order cannot be

---

[26] One may recall here the Rwandan genocide against the Tutsis, who had been the ruling class under Dutch occupation, by the Hutus, who had previously overthrown them in a 1961 revolution.

answered by further atrocities. Healing is needed to secure a lasting peace. Any social movement must prepare itself for backlash: if their demands did not generate hostility, they would not be fighting against the system to begin with. Yet such hostility must not be met by becoming like one's oppressor. History is full of usurpers who overthrew a despot only to become a despot themselves. We must center ourselves in love for humanity, especially when in the name of such love it becomes necessary to defend the oppressed by force.

There is an anxiousness among radicals to bring about immediate change. Radicalism is, after all, born from a shocking realization of the utter depravity of the existing system and a deep conviction that it must be overturned. Change can be painfully slow, and in many cases it seems that it will come too late if at all. Such is the case with the current climate crisis, whose deadly outcomes we are already beginning to experience. We have a small window of time in which to act, and the slowness of the current system to enact the meaningful structural changes necessary could spell doom for our species.

In the face of such dire consequences, should we not resort to the most militant tactics possible? Is it not an act of self-defense to use any means necessary to fight the institutions that threaten the very survival of our species? These are pressing and valid questions, but we must be strategic. Militant action without the necessary resources and support can be a suicide mission. Movement building is necessary to achieve lasting outcomes. We must rise up together.

The uncomfortable fact is that we do not control such

moments. Uprisings will always have a spontaneous character to them, no matter how much organizing goes into them. Organizing alone cannot spark such moments. We must be attentive to the signs of the time. In moments of *kairos*, when history beckons, we must be ready to seize the day. Organized mobilization must work in concert with spontaneous upheavals to raise the stakes, taking advantage of moments of rupture to build alternatives to the system and support future uprisings.

To organize for a better world, we must orient ourselves toward the eschaton. This does not mean passively waiting for the World to Come, nor does it mean immanentizing the eschaton through forceful action. It means participating in our unique moment in history and leaving the rest up to providence. We are neither the authors of history nor its passive spectators: we are active participants in a future not of our own making.

We must cultivate the virtue of hope, which is not naïve optimism but the quiet resolve that drives us to act in the face of uncertainty. We must rise to the challenges of our time. The promise of a greater future calls to us in our hearts. We must answer the call of destiny and align our souls with our inner telos. The eschaton awaits us, and when it calls, we must answer. The future that awaits us must be a collaborative one. Not through dominator hierarchies and technocratic planning but through our cooperative action will we discover the World to Come. On the Last Day, we will finally re-enter the Gates of Eden, this time with open eyes to know it for the first time. In our journey from the Fall to the Eschaton, we must abide in the Spirit which guides our way home.

Bibliography

Alexander, Christopher. *The Nature of Order: An Essay on the Art of Building and the Nature of the Universe.* Center for Environmental Structure, 2004.

Alexander, Christopher. *The Timeless Way of Building.* Oxford University Press, 1980.

Anderson, Benedict R. *Imagined Communities: Reflections on the Origin and Spread of Nationalism*, Anvil Publishing, Mandaluyong City, Philippines, 2016.

Appiah, Kwame Anthony. *The Honor Code.* New York: WW Norton, 2011.

Arendt, Hannah. *The Origins of Totalitarianism.* Harcourt Brace, 1985.

Baranski, Marci. *The Globalization of Wheat: A Critical History of the Green Revolution.* University of Pittsburgh Press, 2022.

Bataille, Georges. *The Accursed Share: An Essay on General Economy.* Zone Books, 2007.

Bhaskar, Roy. *A Realist Theory of Science.* Routledge, Taylor

& Francis Group, 2015.

Bichler, Shimshon and Jonathan Nitzan (2020), 'Growing Through Sabotage. Energizing Hierarchical Power', *Review of Capital as Power*, Vol. 1, No. 5, pp. 1-78.

Bloch, Ernst. *The Principle of Hope*. Basil Blackwell, 1986.

Blondel, Maurice. *Action (1893): Essay on a Critique of Life and a Science of Practice*. University of Notre Dame Press, 2007.

Bohm, David. *Wholeness and the Implicate Order*. London: Routledge & Kegan Paul, 1981.

Bookchin, Murray. *The Ecology of Freedom: The Emergence and Dissolution of Hierarchy*. AK Press, 2005.

Bookchin, Murray. *Urbanization Without Cities: The Rise and Decline of Citizenship*. Black Rose Books, 1992.

Cavanaugh, William T. *The Myth of Religious Violence*. Oxford University Press, 2009.

Chardin, Pierre Teilhard De. *The Phenomenon of Man*. Trans. Julian Huxley and Bernard Wall. New York: Harper, 1959.

Daly, Herman E., John B. Cobb, and Clifford W. Cobb. *For the Common Good: Redirecting the Economy toward Community, the Environment, and a Sustainable Future*. Boston: Beacon, 1989.

Deacon, Terrence William. *Incomplete Nature: How Mind Emerged from Matter.* W.W. Norton, 2013.

Dreyfus, Hubert L. *Being-in-the-World: A Commentary on Heidegger's Being and Time, Division I.* MIT Press, 2009.

Freire, Paulo. *Pedagogy of the Oppressed.* Penguin Education, 1972.

Foucault, Michel. *The Birth of Biopolitics: Lectures at the College De France, 1978-1979.* Translated by Michel Senellart, Palgrave Macmillan, 2011.

Francis. *Praise Be to You - Laudato Si: On Care for Our Common Home.* Erlanger, KY: Dynamic Catholic Institute, 2015.

George, Henry. *Progress and Poverty.* Edited by Bob Drake, Robert Schalkenbach Foundation, 2006.

Gebser, Jean. *The Ever-present Origin.* Trans. Noel Barstad and Algis Mickunas. Athens, OH: Ohio UP, 1997.

Gibson, James J. *The Ecological Approach to Visual Perception.* Psychology Press, 2015.

Girard, René. *Violence and the Sacred.* Trans. Patrick Gregory. London: Continuum, 2005.

Graeber, David. *Bullshit Jobs: A Theory.* Penguin Books, 2019.

Graeber, David. *Debt: The First 5000 Years.* New York:

Melville, 2011.

Graeber, David. *Fragments of an Anarchist Anthropology.* The University of Chicago Press, 2004.

Graeber, David. *Toward an Anthropological Theory of Value: The False Coin of Our Own Dreams.* Palgrave, 2016.

Graeber, David, and David Wengrow. *Dawn of Everything: A New History of Humanity.* Picador, 2022.

Guénon, René. *The Reign of Quantity & the Signs of the times.* Ghent, NY: Sophia Perennis, 2001.

Habermas, Jürgen. *The Theory of Communicative Action.* London: Heinemann, 1984.

Hardt, Michael, and Antonio Negri. *Commonwealth.* Harvard University Press, 2011.

Hardt, Michael, and Antonio Negri. *Empire.* Harvard University Press, 2016.

Hardt, Michael, and Antonio Negri. *Multitude: War and Democracy in the Age of Empire.* Penguin Press, 2009.

Heidegger, Martin. *Being and Time.* Translated by John Macquarrie and Edward Robinson, HarperOne, 2008.

Illich, Ivan. *Tools for Conviviality.* Marion Boyars, 1973.

Jacobs, Jane. *Cities and the Wealth of Nations: Principles of Economic Life*. Random House, 1984.

Jacobs, Jane. *The Death and Life of Great American Cities*. Random House, 1961.

Jacobson, Mark Z. *100% Clean, Renewable Energy and Storage for Everything*. Cambridge University Press, 2021.

Kauffman, Stuart A. *At Home in the Universe: The Search for Laws of Self-organization and Complexity*. New York: Oxford UP, 1995.

Kropotkin, Peter. *Fields, Factories and Workshops*. Translated by Yaacov Oved, Routledge, 1993.

Kropotkin, Peter. *Mutual Aid: A Factor of Evolution*, translated by Peter Harry, Forgotten Books, London, 2015.

Kuhn, Thomas S. *The Structure of Scientific Revolutions*. Chicago: U of Chicago, 1970.

Lakoff, George, and Mark Johnson. *Metaphors We Live by*. Chicago: U of Chicago, 1980.

Latour, Bruno. *Reassembling the Social: An Introduction to Actor-network-theory*. Oxford: Oxford UP, 2005.

Latour, Bruno. *We Have Never Been Modern*. Cambridge, MA: Harvard UP, 2002.

Lefebvre, Henri. *The Urban Revolution*. University of Minnesota Press, 2011.

Lovejoy, Arthur. *The Great Chain of Being: A Study of the History of an Idea*. Routledge, 2017.

Lovins, Amory B. *Soft Energy Paths: Toward a Durable Peace*. Harper & Row, 1979.

MacIntyre, Alasdair C. *After Virtue: A Study in Moral Theory*. Bloomsbury, 2014.

McCarraher, Eugene. *The Enchantments of Mammon: How Capitalism Became the Religion of Modernity*. The Belknap Press of Harvard University Press, 2019.

Mills, C. Wright. *The Power Elite*. London: Oxford UP, 1977.

Mumford, Lewis. *The Culture of Cities*. Routledge, Thoemmes Press, 1997.

Mumford, Lewis. *The Myth of the Machine: Technics and Human Development*. Harcourt, Brace & World, 1967.

Nitzan, Jonathan, and Shimshon Bichler. *Capital as Power a Study of Order and Creorder*. London: Routledge, 2009.

Nussbaum, Martha C. *Upheavals of Thought the Intelligence of Emotions*. Cambridge University Press, 2009.

Öcalan, Abdullah. *Civilization: The Age of Masked Gods and*

Disguised Kings. New Compass Press, 2015.

Ostrom, Elinor. *Governing the Commons: The Evolution of Institutions for Collective Action*. Cambridge, UK: Cambridge UP, 1990.

Perkins, John. *Confessions of an Economic Hitman*, Berret-Koehler Publishers, San Francisco, CA, 2004.

Polanyi, Michael, and Harry Prosch. *Meaning*. The University of Chicago Press, 2012.

Rappaport, Roy A. *Ritual and Religion in the Making of Humanity*. Cambridge University Press, 2010.

Schumacher, E. F. *Small Is Beautiful; Economics as If People Mattered*. New York: Harper & Row, 1973.

Scott, James C. *Against the Grain: A Deep History of the Earliest States*. Yale Univ Press, 2018.

Tarnas, Richard. *The Passion of the Western Mind: Understanding the Ideas That Have Shaped Our World View*. Pimlico, 2010.

Taylor, Charles. *A Secular Age*. Belknap Press of Harvard University, 2007.

Veblen, Thorstein. *The Theory of Business Enterprise*. Augustus M. Kelley, 1965.

Whitehead, Alfred North. *Process and Reality: An Essay in*

Cosmology. Ed. David Ray Griffin and Donald W. Sherburne. New York: Free, 1978.

Wilber, Ken. *Sex, Ecology, Spirituality: The Spirit of Evolution*. Boston: Shambhala, 1995.

Index

Alexander, Christopher 113, 333, 336

alter-globalization 170, 359, 363, 416

anarchism 106

antisemitism 171-172, 183-184

Appiah, Kwame Anthony 131, 479, 502

appropriate technology 293-294, 296, 404

architecture 42, 61, 93, 113-114, 164, 274, 306, 317, 331-335, 337

Aquinas, Thomas 102

Arendt, Hannah 147, 502

credit 15, 59, 197, 211, 223, 227-228, 257, 260-262, 272, 297-298, 400, 487

Deacon, Terrence 108

debt 17, 22, 26, 30, 57-59, 136, 142-144, 198, 203, 207-209, 212, 214-215, 217-218, 228, 237, 242, 248, 251-252, 256-257, 322

deep ecology 405, 444

democracy 61, 147, 149-150, 176, 181, 187, 189, 191-196, 220, 262-264, 312-313, 320, 350, 360, 365-366, 374, 376-379, 409, 432, 440, 442, 460

Derrida, Jacques 63

Dharma 14, 33, 44, 79

Dugin, Aleksandr 352

empire 21, 27, 56, 62, 69-70, 86, 88, 91, 146-147, 151, 160-162, 164-167, 169-171, 196, 198, 202, 241, 244, 248, 253-254, 275-278, 294, 313, 334, 348-353, 357, 359-360, 362, 365, 367-372, 375, 388, 417, 445, 449, 461, 465, 490, 493

eschaton 35, 458, 462, 485, 496, 501

eudaimonia 84, 94, 419, 425

family 18, 20, 24, 64, 84, 121-125, 129-133, 166, 173, 182, 205, 210, 230, 274, 364, 384, 388, 391, 393, 407, 418, 425-428, 436, 439, 445, 479, 484

farming 19, 216, 242, 273, 298, 340, 342, 394-396, 398-399, 413-414, 443, 486-487

fascism 16, 181-189, 192, 362-363, 376-377, 457

favelas 323, 338

FIRE sector 251, 258-259, 266

Fordism 140

Foucault, Michel 349

Francis, Pope 406

Francis, Saint 407, 445

Friere, Paulo 379, 432

George, Henry 259, 322

Girard, René 62-63, 69, 434-435

Göbekli Tepe 49, 306

Graeber, David 25, 54, 57, 59, 127, 140, 203, 205-206, 236, 409, 472

Great Chain of Being 80, 82, 96, 98, 100, 103, 450

guilds 97, 199, 220-223, 232, 291, 432

haecceity 437-438, 445

Hardt, Michael and Negri, Antonio 348, 353, 372, 388

hegemony 58, 132, 151, 166, 185, 194, 203, 221, 232, 253-255, 265, 350, 352-353, 363, 368-369, 401, 415, 441-442, 449, 460

Heidegger, Martin 9, 120

Hinduism 14, 90, 164, 452, 462

honor 123, 129-133, 135-136, 276, 426, 434, 440-441, 445, 476, 479, 502

horizontalism 148, 358

IMF 136, 218

Illich, Ivan 294-295

Imago Dei 6, 336, 476

imperialism 201, 236, 242, 348, 389, 448

Industrial Revolution 114, 280-281, 288-289, 310, 394-395, 399, 463

intercommunalism 368, 370-371

Islam 44, 70, 91-92, 168, 452

Israelites 68-69, 77, 87, 209

Jacobs, Jane 178, 316, 340

Jesus 88, 91-92

jouissance 11, 418

Judaism 44, 87, 452

Jung, Carl 61, 63

Kauffman, Stuart 4, 111-112, 116, 303, 482, 488

kenosis 10, 36, 88, 115, 151-152, 485, 487, 494-495

Keynes, John Maynard 235, 239, 297

Kingdom of God 89, 152, 249, 462, 464, 485

Kropotkin, Peter 106, 390, 405

Kuhn, Thomas 74, 477

Lacan, Jacques 11, 418

Law of Attraction 249, 447, 450, 472

Lenin, Vladimir 347, 359, 368-369, 448

Logos 1, 6, 8, 10-12, 32-34, 43-44, 75, 80, 90, 94, 101, 107, 109, 112-115, 117, 126, 151-154, 189, 196, 229-231, 304, 333, 336, 397, 404, 417, 445, 451-452, 455-458, 461, 464, 483-488, 493

Lovins, Amory 286

magic 40, 46-48, 67-68, 447, 469

markets 16, 20, 22, 25, 59, 100, 105, 141-142, 192, 198-199, 202-203, 225, 227-231, 235-236, 243-244, 249, 254, 257, 288, 298, 342, 350, 356, 391, 423

Mammon 17, 57, 249, 448, 463

Mao Tse-Tung 378

megamachine 55-57, 62, 114-115, 117, 177, 189, 196, 269, 275, 278, 293, 296, 302, 307, 384, 401-402, 442, 450, 456, 474-476, 494

Marxism 171, 175-177, 182-183, 422

Marx, Karl 29, 174-177, 182, 204-206, 211, 234-235, 249-250, 264, 354, 357, 369, 385, 422-423, 447, 453, 464, 473

McLuhan, Marshall 442

monoculture 397

monotheism 68, 70, 469

Morgan, Lewis Henry 177, 470

multitude 220, 353-358, 360-363, 365-366, 368, 371, 374-375, 379, 458, 475, 495

Mumford, Lewis 55, 279-281

mutual aid 25, 58, 106, 128, 141, 148, 172, 197, 203, 225, 227-228, 308, 343, 360, 373, 375, 405, 425, 439, 487

mysticism 60, 78-80, 104, 107, 171

NAFTA 170-171, 388

nation-state 27, 134, 160, 168, 174, 180-181, 188, 194, 199, 201-203, 222, 291, 345-348, 365-368, 370, 375, 388, 412, 416, 447, 452, 460, 483

nationalism 168, 174, 188, 363, 412, 502

NATO 176, 350, 352, 372

Newton, Huey P. 355, 370

nuclear 282-284, 288, 426

occult 471

Occupy Wall Street 359

Ostrom, Elinor 219, 224, 375

paradigm 7, 33, 74, 91, 107, 223, 230, 257, 284, 290, 301, 348, 372, 400, 414, 428, 441, 477, 481

patriarchy 11, 62, 123-126, 151, 155-156, 302, 379, 452, 486, 491, 493-494

Perkins, John 248

permaculture 395, 397

Plato 15, 78, 80-81, 208, 312-313

police 160, 171, 178-182, 188-189, 236-237, 277-278, 325, 327-329, 341, 350, 352, 362, 370, 421

polis 312-313, 375, 429

population 55, 142, 150, 161, 166, 170, 195, 213, 224, 243, 262, 267, 279, 288-289, 297, 306, 310, 315, 322, 340-344, 347, 366, 386-391, 399, 409, 437

Porto Allegre 149, 196

property 18, 25, 83, 100, 122-124, 144, 209-212, 216, 218, 249, 254, 267, 291, 313, 316, 321, 323, 326, 331, 346-347, 349, 360, 372-376, 380, 384-385, 391-393, 410, 417, 426, 495, 498

Proudhon, Pierre-Joseph 227

Putin, Vladimir 352

quiddity 437-438, 445

Rappaport, Roy 44-45

rationalization 22, 68, 101, 104, 106

renewables 255, 286, 288, 385, 414-415

ressourcement 45, 455

ritual 19, 39-43, 46, 49, 64, 98, 128, 204-205, 269, 440, 450

Rojava 196, 327, 379

Roman grid 309, 313, 402

Russia 213, 352, 362, 368-369, 494

Scott, James C. 273

Soviet Union 176, 293, 347, 352, 368-369

Stalin, Joseph 230, 369

taboo 126-129, 225, 480, 498

Tao 33, 44, 79, 484-485

Tarnas, Richard 303

Taylorism 140

technics 231, 267-268, 293, 301, 307, 448

unfolding 10-11, 34-35, 50, 111, 113-117, 152, 168, 178, 196, 309, 317, 330, 339, 458, 467, 477 utopia 140, 312, 464-465, 492

Veblen, Thorstein 206, 234, 236, 259, 292, 385

wage labor 21, 233, 251-252, 299, 429, 447

Wallerstein, Immanuel 207

Weber, Max 138, 145

Westphalian sovereignty 146-147, 168, 345

Wilber, Ken 471, 476

World Bank 136, 218, 350

wu wei 36, 200, 229, 485

Zapatistas 196, 359, 474

About the Author

Jonathan Cobb is an activist and intellectual with a degree in Sociology and Anthropology from the University of Redlands. He has worked in social services for a decade and has been published in Metapsychosis Journal and the Journal and the Journal of Economics and Sociology. His grandfather is John B. Cobb, founder of process theology.

You can connect with me on:
- https://www.lettersfromtheeschaton.com
- https://twitter.com/Apocaloptimist5
- https://www.facebook.com/jonathan.cobb.39

Aristotle 81, 84, 91, 94, 110, 208, 313, 419, 436

Axial Age 58-59, 78, 104

Bhaskar, Roy 478, 502

Blondel, Maurice 45, 450-451

Bookchin, Murray 354, 444, 465

Buddhism 11, 14, 73, 86, 90, 109, 449, 462

bullshit jobs 236, 356

CIA 170, 370, 388

Campbell, Joseph 61, 63, 72

capitalism 13, 16-17, 21-23, 25, 27-30, 60, 68, 101, 140, 144, 160, 172, 175-176, 180, 182, 204, 206, 209, 211, 218, 221-222, 224-225, 229-231, 233, 235, 242-243, 249, 254-255, 257, 260, 265-266, 270, 280-281, 293, 298, 335, 341, 344, 348-349, 356, 370, 373-374, 386, 391, 399-401, 407, 419, 422-423, 425, 438, 445, 448-449, 473, 480

capitalization 18, 23, 29, 143, 146, 238-241, 250, 253, 257

Cavanaugh, William T. 452

China 123, 131, 169, 176, 200, 254, 293, 334, 351, 369, 479, 494

Christ 88-90, 165, 172-173, 435, 446, 462, 468, 485, 492-493

Christianity 14, 44, 53, 59, 70, 89-92, 98, 165, 168, 248, 363, 449, 452, 462

cities 5, 23, 52, 96, 139, 149, 157-160, 193, 199, 201-202, 207, 212, 222, 227, 274, 279, 296, 306-308, 310, 312, 314, 316-319, 333, 340-343, 346-347, 398, 410, 414, 427, 460, 465, 487, 496

colonialism 16, 146, 164, 177, 185, 213, 217, 241, 369-370, 401, 407, 410, 445, 452

commons 216-221, 229, 242, 259, 291, 298-299, 341-342, 349, 355, 357-358, 360, 363-364, 367, 372-375, 380, 384, 386, 393, 425, 430, 442, 460, 496

commonwealth 353, 372, 374-375, 380, 460-461

confederation 147, 151, 199, 347, 353, 365, 368, 483

conspiracy theories 172, 182, 184